Bedrohte Ordnungen

Edited by

Renate Dürr, Ewald Frie und Mischa Meier

17

Maike Hausen

Reviewing Britain's Presence East of Suez

Australian, Canadian and New Zealand Foreign Policy Considerations Surrounding Southeast Asia, 1956–1971

Mohr Siebeck

Maike Hausen, born in 1989; studies in History and Historical and Cultural Anthropology (BA) at the University of Tübingen and the University of Bologna; 2015 MA in Modern History (Tübingen); doctoral researcher at the Collaborative Research Centre 923 "Threatened Order – Societies under Stress" at the University of Tübingen; 2019 PhD; since 2021 editor at the 'Landeszentrale für politische Bildung Baden-Württemberg'.

Funded by the Deutsche Forschungsgemeinschaft (DFG, German Research Foundation) – Project-ID 170320015 – SFB 923

ISBN 978-3-16-161417-0 / eISBN 978-3-16-161418-7
DOI 10.1628/978-3-16-161418-7

ISSN 2197-5477 / eISSN 2568-4035 (Bedrohte Ordnungen)

The Deutsche Nationalbibliothek lists this publication in the Deutsche Nationalbibliographie; detailed bibliographic data are available at *http://dnb.dnb.de.*

The book was typeset by epline in Böblingen using Times typeface. It was printed on non-aging paper and bound by Beltz Grafische Betriebe GmbH in Bad Langensalza. The cover was designed by Uli Gleis in Tübingen. Image: Topographic Map of Southeast Asia, CCO.

Printed in Germany.

Introduction to the series *Threatened Order*

What happens to societies when the options for taking action become uncertain, behavioural expectations and routines are called into question, when actors have the feeling that they will probably not be able to rely on one another either now or in the near future, when threats are spoken of, and reasons for them are sought and mostly found? Time is a scarce commodity. Emotions come increasingly to the fore and change. The boundaries of social groups become questionable. Threatened orders have a high potential for rapid social change, though this does not always have to come into force.

Threatened orders can emerge from catastrophes, they can arise from sudden conflicts within society, can erupt from latent tensions, or be the result of competition between orders. Various research traditions therefore flow into studies that do not begin with classificatory terms such as turmoil, revolution, or natural catastrophe, but instead focus on dynamic social processes that are linked to the perception and assertion of threat and the recourse to order.

Threatened orders exist in all historical periods and all cultures of the world. Do similar mechanisms operate across time and space? Can different typologies be identified? The series *Threatened Order* invites historians, social scientists and cultural researchers to contribute to these questions. While it is linked to the Deutsche Forschungsgemeinschaft-funded Collaborative Research Centre 923 "Threatened Order. Societies under Stress", the series wishes to go beyond this in initiating and documenting research.

The Editors

Preface

The research, writing and publication of this study would not have been possible without the support of many people. Firstly, I am indebted to the resources and opportunities provided by the Collaborative Research Center 923 (CRC) "Threatened Order – Societies under Stress" at the Eberhard Karls University of Tuebingen. This study is based on research in the CRC-project "G04: End of Empire. Re-ordering in Australia, New Zealand and Canada, 1960–1980". With the generous financial support of the Deutsche Forschungsgesellschaft (DFG, German Research Foundation), the CRC provided the supportive framework to enable such an ambitious research project focussing on the comparative and transnational perspective of three countries. Additionally, I benefitted from the frequent contacts with other researchers and doctoral candidates, a helpful interdisciplinary exchange furthering my understanding of various sociological and cultural theories, which contributed to the theoretical underpinnings of this study. A special thanks goes to the CRC coordination staff of Andrea Kirstein, Cornelia Stoll and Heike Bäder.

I am most grateful for the support of my supervisor, Professor Ewald Frie, who not only offered me this exciting research topic, but also tremendously supported me in the intellectual elaboration and execution of this study. My gratitude also extends to the various researchers 'in the field' who improved the approach and outlook of this work, foremost Professor James Curran, who offered advice and support on various occasions, and whose own research contributed a great deal to the perspective of this study. Further essential contacts were Stuart Ward, Phillip Buckner, Ursula Lehmkuhl, and many more whose guidance and advice helped in giving this paper shape. Among contacts from the diplomatic field, I was fortunate to talk to Brian Lynch, Neil Walter, Terence O'Brien, John McCarthy and the late Blair Seaborn who graciously shared their recollections of their time in public service with me. I would also like to thank Graeme Davison for his hospitality during my research visit to Melbourne, and Paul Marsden for his kind guidance and support throughout my research stay in Ottawa. Thanks are also due to the staff of the many archives and libraries I visited in preparation of this study. Lastly, I am grateful for the numerous people I met during my research visits to the different countries under study who were willing to share their perspectives and thoughts on this topic.

During these years of research, I would have been lost in the academic jungle without my two colleagues and friends Clara Seltmann and Sebastian Koch. Our research group developed its own enthusiasm and drive for this topic, and I am happy and excited to see this publication come to fruition as part of a joint effort for a combined study of the End of Empire in Australia, Canada and New Zealand. I am indebted to them, not just for their support in my research and writing but also for their encouragement and endless support beyond academia.

Equally, this study would have not been possible without the support of my friends and family. I would like to thank my sister Nora for her tremendous help in sorting appendixes, corrections and amendments, and for her foresight and strength to bring such a large work to completion. I was also fortunate to have the support of Peter, who took it upon him to guide and improve my English skills from early drafts of the thesis up to the finished paper. To both of them I am indebted for their help, patience, and encouragement, especially on the last legs of this thesis. Further thanks go to Marie and Daniel for regularly checking on the progress of this project and offering support and help along the way.

This study is dedicated to my parents, who always supported and engaged on so many levels with my studies and research interests. The love and support I have received from them throughout the last years helped me tackle the usual frustrations of such a research project, and I am proud to finally share the results of my studies with them.

And finally, this study is dedicated to the memory of my brother Jonas.

Maike Hausen

Table of Contents

Introduction to the series *Threatened Order* V
Preface VII
Abbreviations XIII

Part 1: Introduction – The Former Dominions at the End of Empire 1

Part 2: Shifts in Foreign Policy Leading up to the East of Suez Debate 29

2.1 Setting up Policies for Southeast Asia after the Second World War 30
2.1.1 Diversifying their Security Networks – New Alliances in the Wake of the Second World War 30
2.1.2 Cold War Rationales in Southeast Asia – New Challenges 35

2.2 Ministers, Officers, Mandarins – The Expansion and Character of Dominion Policymaking 44
2.2.1 Channels of Diplomacy and Information throughout the Commonwealth 45
2.2.2 Institutions of Commonwealth Cooperation 49
2.2.3 A Community of Britons among the Policymakers 54

Part 3: Waiting for a Crisis? The Anticipation of a British Retreat from Southeast Asia, 1956–1965 61

3.1 The First Watershed Moment? The Suez Crisis as the Introduction of Uncertainty 68
3.2 Anticipating British Imperial Decline in the Aftermath of the Suez Crisis 74
3.2.1 Defence Reviews and Burden-Sharing 74
3.2.2 The British EEC Application as Indication and Catalyst of Changing Imperial Policy 82

3.3 Towards a Regional Postcolonial Order – Malaysia and Confrontation 86

3.3.1 The Creation of Malaya, Singapore and Greater Malaysia in Interdependence with Surrounding Conflicts, 1957–1963 87
3.3.2 Confrontation Enfolding – The Question of Anglo-American Coordination and Commonwealth Responsibility, 1962–1964 94
3.3.3 The Canadian Commitment to Malaysian Defence as a Commonwealth Effort, 1964–1965 97

3.4 Between British Exceptionalism and Self-Determination – Postcolonial Struggles in Southeast Asia 102
3.4.1 Facing Global Implications of Southeast-Asian Conflicts – The Question of Chinese Communism 103
3.4.2 Defending the Free World? Vietnam and Malaysia as Battlegrounds of the Cold War 106
3.4.3 Being the Better Briton? Relations with Newly Emerging Nations in Southeast Asia 111

3.5 Conclusion of Part 3 116

Part 4: A Watershed Moment – Reactions to the British Decision on Cutting Back East of Suez, 1965–1968 119

4.1 Experiencing Anger and Regret – The Potential Loss of a British Link 124
4.1.1 1965/1966 – Years of Conflicting Emotions? 125
4.1.2 1967 – "The Shock of a Family Separation" 135
4.1.3 1968 – The End of an Era 143

4.2 Experiencing Urgency and Uncertainty – The Dismantling of Regional Security 148
4.2.1 Undermining Forward Defence – Discussions on an Alternative Base in Australia 149
4.2.2 Questioning the Local Repercussions on the Strategic Framework of Southeast Asia 154
4.2.3 "And we are left out in the cold" – Disorientation and Uncertainty Following the British Decision 1967/68 159
4.2.4 Canada and East of Suez 163

4.3 Experiencing Doubt and Fear – Global Implications of Britain's Withdrawal 167
4.3.1 Dealing with a Continued Chinese Threat 169
4.3.2 "All the Way with LBJ" – Western Containment Strategy in Demise 177
4.3.3 At European Crossroads – Questioning White Presence in Southeast Asia 183

4.4 Conclusion of Part 4 194

Part 5: Consolations and New Beginnings –
Foreign Policy Re-Orientation Going into the 1970s 201

5.1 Towards a New Nationalism in Foreign Policy and Defence 205

5.1.1 Public and Departmental Discussions on a More Self-Reliant Foreign and Defence Policy, 1967–1968 206

5.1.2 Involvement or Isolationism after the British Withdrawal? 214

5.1.3 Where to Turn in the Anglosphere? Alternatives to a British or American Outlook 221

5.2 Towards a New Regional Framework of Security and Cooperation ... 226

5.2.1 "Sindausthailaysia!" – Establishing a Regional Strategic Framework after Britain's Departure, 1967/68 227

5.2.2 Australia and New Zealand on Ground Forces and ANZAC Cooperation, 1968/69 235

5.2.3 Australia, Canada and New Zealand as Asian-Pacific Nations 241

5.3 Groundworks for a New International Order 250

5.3.1 The End of a Chinese Threat in Security Discussions 251

5.3.2 New Regimes of Equality and Responsibility under Whitlam, Kirk and Trudeau 257

5.4 Conclusion of Part 5 269

Part 6: Conclusion – The End of the British Empire? 273

Bibliography 283

Primary Sources 283

Literature 296

Index 317

Abbreviations

ADC	Australian Defence Committee
ADEA	Australian Department of External Affairs
AEmb	Australian Embassy
AHC	Australian High Commission
AHoR	Australian House of Representatives
AIIA	Australian Institute for International Affairs
AJSS	Australian Joint Service Staff
ALP	Australian Labor Party
AMDA	Anglo-Malayan Defence Agreement
AMEA	Australian Minister for External Affairs
AMD	Australian Minister for Defence
ANU	Australian National University
ANZ	Archives New Zealand
ANZAAS	Australian and New Zealand Association for the Advancement of Science
ANZAC	Australian and New Zealand Army Corps
ANZAM	Defence arrangement formed by Australia, New Zealand and Malaya
ANZUK	Tripartite force formed by Australia, New Zealand and the United Kingdom
ANZUS	Australia, New Zealand, United States Security Treaty
APMD	Australian Prime Minister's Department
ASEA	Australian Secretary of the Department of External Affairs
ASEAN	Association of South East Asian Nations
ASPAC	Asian Pacific Council
AUD	Australian Dollar
BDCC (FE)	British Defence Coordination Committee (Far East)
BCDS	British Chief of the Defence Staff
BEmb	British Embassy
BLP	British Labour Party
BHC	British High Commission
BJSLS	British Joint Services Liaison Staff
CBS	Canadian Broadcasting Cooperation
CDEA	Canadian Department of External Affairs
CEmb	Canadian Embassy
CENTO	Central Treaty Organisation
CHC	Canadian High Commission
CHOGM	Commonwealth Heads of Government Meeting
CIIA	Canadian Institute for International Affairs
CINCFE	Commander in Chief Far East
CLARET	British Secret Operation in Borneo from about July 1964 until July 1966
CO	Commonwealth Office

COS	Chief of Staff
CRO	Commonwealth Relations Office
CSR	Commonwealth Strategic Reserve
CSSEA	Canadian Secretary of State for External Affairs
CUSSEA	Canadian Under-Secretary of State for External Affairs
DAFP	Documents on Australian Foreign Policy
DC	Defence Committee
DEA	Department of External Affairs
EA	External Affairs
EEC	European Economic Community
FADC	Foreign Affairs and Defence Committee
FO	Foreign Office
FPDA	Five Power Defence Arrangements
FPC	*Foreign Policy for Canadians*
ICCS	International Commission for Control and Supervision
ICSC	International Commission for Supervision and Control
LAC	Library and Archives Canada
LBJ	Lyndon B. Johnson
MP	Member of Parliament
NAA	National Archives Australia
NATO	North Atlantic Treaty Organisation
NCDS	New Zealand Chief of the Defence Staff
NDEA	New Zealand Department of External Affairs
NDLS	New Zealand Defence Liaison Staff
NEmb	New Zealand Embassy
NHC	New Zealand High Commission
NIIA	New Zealand Institute for International Affairs
NLA	National Library of Australia
NLNZ	National Library of New Zealand
NLP	New Zealand Labour Party
NMD	New Zealand Minister of Defence
NMEA	New Zealand Minister of External Affairs
NNP	New Zealand National Party
NORAD	North American Air Defence Agreement
NSEA	New Zealand Secretary of the Department of External Affairs
PKI	Partai Komunis Indonesia
PMD	Prime Minister's Department
PRC	People's Republic of China
RAAF	Royal Australian Air Force
SEA	Secretary of External Affairs
SEATO	Southeast Asia Treaty Organisation
SSEA	Secretary of State of External Affairs
TNA	National Archives Kew
UN	United Nations
UNEF	United Nations Emergency Force
US/USA	United States of America

Part 1

Introduction – The Former Dominions at the End of Empire

It must have been a truly unpleasant meeting. On the 21 April 1967, the British High Commissioner to Australia, Charles Johnston, met with a visibly upset Australian Prime Minister, Harold Holt, to discuss the latest British indications for a military withdrawal from its position 'East of Suez' in Southeast Asia. Holt had told him that the Australian government was shocked by the British plans to withdraw its military partially by 1971 and entirely by the mid-1970s. After the meeting, Johnston conveyed to his superiors that "for the first time in my experience of him, Mr. Holt looked badly shaken and grey in the face".[1] Holt had demanded him to convey his mood back to London; Australia was prepared for some reductions, but a complete withdrawal would undermine the Western security effort in the region.[2]

Almost a year later, the British military planning created another unpleasant gathering. This time, British Secretary for Commonwealth Affairs George Thomson was sent to Canberra to discuss the British plans of accelerating the entire withdrawal up to 1971. At the meeting, he was not only facing outraged Australian politicians, but also New Zealand representatives. Reporting back from his meeting, Thomson described the mood in New Zealand as one of great shock, and one that presented itself as regret over the end of a security partnership: "There was a sense of sadness rather than anger at what they clearly regarded as the ending of an era."[3] On the other side of the Pacific, in Canada, officials were observing the discussions closely. Even here, where British cooperation had played only a minor role in security concerns for Southeast Asia, officials considered the British decision as having "far reaching implications"[4] for all its allies and showed themselves sympathetic to the feelings in Australia and New Zealand.

As the reactions underline, the British presence 'East of Suez' had formed the cornerstone of a security relationship with all three countries that exceed-

[1] TNA FCO 46/54, BHC Canberra (Johnston) to CO 635, 21.4.1967, and BHC Canberra (Johnston) to CO 636, 21.4.1967.

[2] TNA FCO 46/54, BHC Canberra (Johnston) to CO 635, 21.4.1967; see also NAA A1838 TS691/1/1, Part 1, ADEA to AEmb. Washington 1246, 21.4.1967.

[3] TNA FCO 24/92, BHC Wellington 78, 12.1.1968.

[4] LAC RG25 A-3-c, Vol. 8903, 20-BRIT-1-3-E.Suez, BHC London, 22.1.1968.

ed the functional framework of strategic arrangements. The outrage and regret suggest that the British plans also undermined shared outlooks and cooperation originating from imperial times. However, as strong and charged as the Australasian reactions to the British decision were, they were dismissed only a few years later by statements of independent defence and national self-reliance in both Tasman countries. Realists could claim in the early 1970s that Britain's withdrawal from Southeast Asia was only a logical and necessary consequence to ease Britain's financial burdens and to respond to an altered strategic environment. In all three countries, voices would be heard that imperial defence had been already dismantled since the Second World War and that every following strategic concept had been solely determined by national interests and the American alliance. These contemporary assessments of the British strategic value are matched by current historical studies that suggest a Canadian disengagement from strategic interests shared with Britain since the late 1940s, followed by the Australian and New Zealand departure in the mid-1950s.[5]

While there is some ground to support the thesis of a predominant American alliance for all three countries after the Second World War, riddles about the British relationship remain. None of the assumptions of a strategic switch could explain why the British decision to leave Southeast Asia in the late 1960s was so strongly repudiated in Australia and New Zealand and was watched with mixed feelings in Canada. The contemporary rhetoric of crisis, anxiety and uncertainty seems to reveal a certain unease about the British course of action. The debate on the consequences of the withdrawal East of Suez was charged with emotions ranging from perplexity to anger and regret. Aside from expressed emotions, the narratives used during the debate show that officials felt forced to review their relationship with Britain as well as their self-perception. Not only were they fundamentally affected in their strategic framework, but it was also the conduct and context of Britain's decision that led to a highly charged atmosphere in Australia and New Zealand. While not being as affected in its security framework as the other two countries, Canada still worried about the long-term implications of the retreat. Britain's 'turn to Europe' challenged the relationship with their former 'mother country' as well as concepts of regional and international order in the age of Cold War and decolonisation.

To understand this impact of Britain's withdrawal on the former dominions' outlook, their special status within the British Empire has to be acknowledged. Here, all three countries represented a group of colonies that soon gained sub-

[5] *Jack L. Granatstein*, How Britain's Weakness Forced Canada Into the Arms of the United States, Toronto 1989; *Jack L. Granatstein*, From Mother Country to Far Away Relative: The Canadian-British Military Relationship From 1945, in: Canadian Military History 18/1, 2009, 55–60; *David McLean*, From British Colony to American Satellite? Australia and the USA During the Cold War, in: Australian Journal of Politics & History 52/1, 2006, 64–79; *Coral Bell*, Dependent Ally. A Study in Australian Foreign Policy, St. Leonards 1984.

stantial freedom and self-government, the so-called dominions.[6] Together with the fourth dominion, South Africa[7], they received special recognition within the Empire and felt attached to Britain by loyalty, shared values and common heritage rather than by colonial rule. Their origins as white settler colonies and the predominantly white Anglo-Saxon immigration throughout the nineteenth up to the mid-twentieth century established in all three countries a population that looked to Britain as a cultural, social and political model. Britain supported this positive relationship with a gradual concession of independence and self-government that culminated in the Balfour Report in 1926. This report, leading eventually to the constitutional act of the Statute of Westminster in 1931, defined the dominions as "autonomous communities within the British Empire, equal in status, in no way subordinate to one another in any aspect of their domestic or external affairs, though united by a common allegiance to the Crown, and freely associated as members of the British Commonwealth of Nations".[8]

With dominion status, independence of all three countries emerged in gradual steps and was "granted rather than wrested".[9] As a result, the transition from a colony to an independent nation is highly contested in all three countries. As New Zealand historian James Belich provokingly noted, "The histories of Australia, New Zealand, and Canada as independent nations share a curious characteristic: nobody knows when they began."[10] In contrast to processes of decolonisation elsewhere in the British Empire, the dominions did not engage in profound anticolonial conflicts to establish a cohesive and sovereign national state. Apart from the subjugation and repression of indigenous people within

[6] *John Darwin*, A Third British Empire? The Dominion Idea in Imperial Politics, in: Judith Brown/Wm R. Louis (Ed.), The Oxford History of the British Empire, Volume IV, Oxford 1999, 64–87. The following study takes some freedom of writing when it comes to the declaration of the three countries involved. In some cases, for the sake of a better reading, Australia, Canada and New Zealand are referred to as "dominions" or "nations" even though the status as either dominion or nation at the time under study can be argued. The term dominion was well used after the mid-decade, although all three countries did officially abolish the title after the Second World War. *Lorna Lloyd*, Us and Them? The Changing Nature of the Commonwealth Diplomacy, in: Journal of Commonwealth & Comparative Politics 39/3, 2001, 9–30, 13.

[7] The case of South Africa is not part of the presented study for a variety of reasons: Its composition as a settler colony with a white elite ruling over a marginalised black majority does not correspond with the political, ethnic and cultural issues Canada, Australia and New Zealand faced in the twentieth century. For a study of Commonwealth relations, South Africa also presented another case after its introduction of apartheid in 1948 and its departure from the Commonwealth in 1961; *Lorna Lloyd*, Diplomacy With a Difference. The Commonwealth Office of High Commissioner 1880–2006, Leiden/Boston 2010, 192.

[8] Quoted in: *Ronald Hyam*, Britain's Declining Empire. The Road to Decolonisation 1918–1968, Cambridge 2008, 70.

[9] As stated by *Malcolm McKinnon*, Independence and Foreign Policy. New Zealand in the World Since 1935, Auckland 1993, 149.

[10] *James Belich*, Replenishing the Earth. The Settler Revolution and the Rise of the Anglo-World 1783–1939, Oxford 2009, 461.

their territories[11], all three countries had no fundamental experience of claiming sovereignty in a violent struggle. Similarly, a radical departure from British institutions to profile indigenous or local elements did not take place. Since Britain was part of a preferential system of cooperation, including various areas of foreign policy, the close association of institutions and interests was not questioned.

Nevertheless, in the field of foreign policy and defence, all three countries consider themselves today as sovereign, self-reliant entities that perceive little of their imperial heritage as binding to a joint defence strategy. Most of this national self-confidence and assertion was created over discussions in the 1960s. Recent research related to this nation-building argues to consider this decade as a phase of disentanglement from the British 'mother country', and called to integrate it into a larger study on the 'End of Empire'. While earlier events or transformations have been proposed as decisive moments of transition from colony to nationhood, an analytical focus on the 1960s is likely to reveal a decade of departure from "imperial imagination".[12] During this decade, several events and developments seemed to underline the necessity for all three countries to divert their foreign policy from the former heavy focus on Britain. These events were interpreted under the impression of Britain's general decline. Following the Suez Crisis in 1956, the British applications to join the European Economic Community (EEC) and its plans to withdraw from Southeast Asia would cause further conflictual debates with the former dominions in the 1960s.

The intensity with which the dominions reacted to the British actions indicated that they were not only interested in keeping preferential foreign policy or trade links. Aside from the EEC and East of Suez debates, other steps enforcing the perception of a decline in Anglo-Dominion relations were unfolding in the spheres of the constitution, civic culture, and migration. During that time, Australia, Canada and New Zealand introduced steps of disentanglement themselves, e. g. by replacing national symbols such as flags, orders or an-

[11] The suppression and marginalisation of the indigenous people took place in a context that spans over the phase of the dominions' decolonisation and leaves deficits of equality even today. As Caroline Elkins and Susan Pedersen have pointed out, settler colonialism established an aggressive agenda towards indigenous people in either extinguishing them or assimilating them, *Caroline Elkins/Susan Pedersen*, Introduction: Settler Colonialism: A Concept and Its Uses, in: Caroline Elkins/Susan Pedersen (Ed.), Settler Colonialism in the Twentieth Century: Projects, Practices, Legacies, New York 2005, 1–20, 2 f. Within the period under study, it developed a dynamic that was important for the domestic issues at hand, but remained in the field of strategic and foreign policy mostly marginal and related to specific issues (e. g. the treatment of Pacific territories). While this is far from suggesting that the indigenous emancipation and civil right movements did not contribute in a crucial way to the question of national identity, it cannot be covered in this study in a way treating the complexities and the severity of the issue appropriately.

[12] Introduced as a concept by Christopher Waters for Australia, this is nevertheless applicable to all three dominions, *Christopher Waters*, Conflicts with Britain in the 1940s, in: David Lowe (Ed.), Australia and the End of Empires: The Impact of Decolonisation in Australia's Near North, 1945–65, Geelong 1996, 69–86, 73.

thems.[13] Yet, the character of their special relationship[14] with Britain only led them to reconsider parts of their national status, and these reconsiderations did not take place without considerable opposition from within the political establishment and public. Therefore, when Britain decided to withdraw its military from Southeast Asia in the late 1960s, especially for Australians and New Zealanders, but also for Canadians, the step was "yet another in the series of blows" that caused them to "look on Britain in an essentially demystified manner".[15]

Assessing the East of Suez discussions, Britain's withdrawal was linked to questions of continued imperial relationship, the role of Britain in Southeast Asia, and its position as a global power. Two sets of arguments came to the forefront of discussions: How would the British withdrawal impact its relationship with the dominions and its presence in the region? And how would all three countries (re-)locate themselves in relation to Britain, the region, and the ensuing international order? The East of Suez debate did not solely contribute to the disentanglement in those relations, but correlated to other events and processes undermining the imperial relationship. East of Suez became one moment of crisis in the process of declining British outlooks in the three countries that spanned from the post-war period up to the early 1970s when all three countries introduced new regimes of self-reliance and 'new nationalism'.

To study this crisis means to understand the intricate, sometimes paradox relationship the former dominions held with Britain after their formal independence. The strong emotions expressed during the East of Suez debate cannot be explained by merely focusing on strategic or political rationales held in all three countries. They have to be examined by taking a closer look at the constitution of all three countries as recently independent, yet strongly British-affiliated nations. Historians like John Darwin have emphasised the inconsistencies and contrary developments in British decolonisation up to the 1960s, pointing to underlying imperial interests that still saw Britain as a global influence and power.[16] In a similar vein, the developments of Australia, Canada and New Zea-

13 Canada adopted "Oh Canada" as national anthem in 1967. New Zealand used "God save New Zealand" for the first time as national anthem at the Munich Olympics 1972 and eventually made it the nation's second national anthem (besides "God Save the Queen") in 1977. Australia introduced its national anthem "Advance Australia Fair" under the Whitlam government, which had to be reintroduced in 1984 after it was abandoned in 1976; *Stuart Ward*, The New Nationalism in Australia, Canada and New Zealand: Civic Culture in the Wake of the British World, in: Joan Beaumont/Neville Meaney (Ed.), Australia and the World. A Festschrift for Neville Meaney, Sydney 2013, 191–214.

14 Not to be confused with the 'special relationship' between Britain and the USA which will be marked as such in the following.

15 *David Goldsworthy*, Losing the Blanket. Australia and the End of Britain's Empire, Carlton South 2002, 158.

16 *John Darwin*, British Decolonization Since 1945: A Pattern or a Puzzle?, in: The Journal of Imperial and Commonwealth History 12/2, 1984, 187–209.

land did not follow a compelling logic of inner decolonisation before or after their independence through the Statute of Westminster. Rather, their relationship with Britain remained close and was based on a common set of shared knowledge and culture, norms and values, assumptions and outlooks that could be explained as 'Britishness'. Britishness can be defined as "a commitment to certain institutions (most notably the monarchy and their parliamentary system) and a sense of values (including the rule of law, the freedom of the individual, the sanctity of private property, and some vague and rather ill-defined notions about duty and fair-play)".[17]

Britishness is understood here as an integral part of the national identity[18] of the dominions at the time under consideration. Ideas of shared history, myths[19] and traditions[20] sustain a collective identity and indicate how much such self-perceptions are shaped through subjective experiences and collective outlooks, emotional responses and factual markers. In the case of the dominions, a predominantly Anglo-Saxon population guaranteed adherence to Britishness as much as cultural and social practice. Civic symbols of all three countries were strongly embedded in a British orbit, with respective flags, constitutions, anthems and monarchy upholding bonds to the 'mother country'. As a result, Britishness lead to the perception of a shared family or community of British origin, and consequently allowed a close coherence among the dominions and Britain on international interests.[21]

Britishness itself related to the larger framework of the Empire. Since the nineteenth century, *Empire* developed into a "suggestive metaphor"[22], legitimising global rule with ideas of 'British exceptionalism' or a certain British

---

[17] *Phillip Buckner*, Introduction: Canada and the British Empire, in: Phillip Buckner (Ed.), Canada and the British Empire, Oxford 2010, 1–21, 6.

[18] As a concept of analysis, identity has always been contested, and critics such as Rogers Brubaker and Frederick Cooper called for replacing it with 'identification' or 'self-understanding', *Rogers Brubaker/Frederick Cooper*, Beyond "Identity" in: Theory and Society 29/1, 2000, 1–47. Yet, the term still offers the best vehicle to describe a deliberately elusive set of (self-)description and belonging. It is understood here, to follow Geoffrey Stokes, as "a dynamic, interactive, social process" where "an individual's personal identity is inextricably bound up with its relationship to a collectivity", *Geoffrey Stokes*, Introduction, in: Geoffrey Stokes (Ed.), The Politics of Identity in Australia, Cambridge 1997, 1–20.

[19] Myths are understood as narratives who gain their dynamic and significance largely from the alternation of history and current demands of sensemaking and identity formation. *Rebecca Collins*, Concealing the Poverty of Traditional Historiography: Myth as Mystification in Historical Discourse, in: Rethinking History 7/3, 2003, 341–365, 342.

[20] Eric Hobsbawm defined traditions as "a set of practices, normally governed by overtly or tacitly accepted rules and of a ritual or symbolic nature, which seek to inculcate certain values and norms of behaviour by repetition, which automatically implies continuity with the past", *Eric Hobsbawm*, Introduction: Inventing Traditions, in: Eric Hobsbawm/Terence Ranger (Ed.), The Invention of Tradition, Cambridge 1993, 1–14, 1.

[21] *Stephen Howe*, Empire and Ideology, in: Sarah Stockwell (Ed.), The British Empire: Themes and Perspectives. 2. publ, Malden 2010, 162 f.

[22] *Jörn Leonhard*, Introduction: The "Longue Durée of Empire": Toward a Comparative

mission in the world.[23] Within the dominions, this idea of exceptionalism was translated into concepts of cultural and ethnic superiority. In parts, this loyalty or allegiance to an imperial mission was created by the concept of 'Greater Britain' introduced in the early twentieth century.[24] By granting dominion status, Britain could include the white settler colonies into the legitimising framework of an Anglo-Saxon particularity that referred to notions of supremacy and the distribution and adaption of British institutions throughout the Empire.[25]

Still, other factors narrowed what concept of Britishness the dominion societies felt attached to. One defining element was social and ethnic distinction. For one, the process of 'Othering'[26] created symbolic boundaries between different groups in and outside the Empire. One of the boundaries was defined by racialised practices.[27] Outside the Empire, Non-Western groups were equally excluded as Non-British groups. Within the Empire frame, the dominions could refer to other colonies to distinguish their own, superior role vis-à-vis Britain.[28] Among themselves, all three dominions followed the idea of being 'better Britons', based on socio-economic measures they introduced at the turn of the twentieth century. Curiously, all three countries also followed in parts an egalitarian myth that set themselves apart from Britain's class-oriented society.

As a result, people of the dominions perceived themselves as a pinnacle of civilisation, both because they endured the local conditions as because of their British heritage.[29] Much of this perception of superiority relied on colonial dis-

---

Semantics of a Key Concept in Modern European History, in: Contributions to the History of Concepts 8/1, 2013, 1–25, 10.

[23] *Sarah Stockwell*, Britain and Decolonization in an Era of Global Change, in: Martin Thomas/Andrew S. Thompson (Ed.), The Oxford Handbook of the Ends of Empire, Oxford 2018, 65–101, 65.

[24] *Martin Thomas/Andrew Thompson*, Empire and Globalisation. From 'High Imperialism' to Decolonisation, in: The International History Review 36/1, 2013, 142–170, 144.

[25] *Leonhard*, Longue Durée of Empire, 19–22.

[26] *Edward Said*, Orientalism, London 1978, 54.

[27] In its historical meaning, the term 'race' referred to a certain identity determined by fixed biological factors such as blood or phenotype that defined an individual or collective identity. Today, this biological validity is repudiated and 'race' deconstructed as a social construction that is designed to justify the discrimination of other 'races'. In discussing the historical concept of 'race', this study does in no way give credibility to its content. Rather, it follows Srdjan Vucetic in referring to race as a marker of distinction and categorization, "a social kind that exists because people believe it exists. From this perspective, race is not real in the biological sense, but it is real in the sense that the social and political world is constituted by groups who have been, or were, treated as if they were races." *Srdjan Vucetic*, The Anglosphere. A Genealogy of a Racialized Identity in International Relations, Stanford 2011, 7. Moreover, as Paul Spickard points out, it is the act of essentialising the difference of the other in bodily attributes that defines racialising as a practice of power, *Paul R. Spickard*, Race and Nation, Identity and Power: Thinking Comparatively about Ethnic Systems, in: Paul R. Spickard (Ed.), Race and Nation: Ethnic Systems in the Modern World, New York 2004, 1–29, 13 f.

[28] *Leonhard*, Longue Durée of Empire, 11.

[29] *Belich*, Replenishing the Earth, 4–7; *Buckner*, Introduction, 6.

courses of 'race' and 'whiteness'[30] that were adopted throughout the Empire to create a hierarchy among different societies and people. All three dominions went to some length to safeguard their distinction within the Empire by introducing discriminatory immigration regimes.[31] The fact that transnational concepts of whiteness resulted in nationalist policies may seem like a paradox[32], just like the inclusion of Britishness in the dominions' identity seems contradictory to the idea of a dominion nationalism. Similar to the question of dominion independence, many scholars have tried to pinpoint the origins of a certain nationalism against the demise of the British connection. In this teleological interpretation, old British ties would necessarily and inevitably be replaced by a sense of 'true' nationhood, represented by own national myths and symbols. Consequently, they followed that a 'thwarted' nationalism must have existed in all three countries, which at some point replaced the British identity.[33]

However, being Canadian/Australian/New Zealand meant equally being British; both markers of identity were not exclusive or separate, but overlapped and were in many cases interdependent, such as when Australian historian W. D. Hancock described his fellow countrymen as 'Independent Australian Britons'[34] in the 1930s. Even after the end of colonial rule, all three countries considered themselves part of a larger British world community. The analogy of a British family of nations occurred in various forms throughout the time under study, mainly because it was an easy vehicle to describe how the former dominions perceived their relationship with Britain.[35] As within a family, this community set standards and rules of interaction that partly fused into the Commonwealth organisation and sustained it; with shared norms de-

[30] Similar to 'race', 'whiteness' refers here to the historical deterministic construction of a distinct white 'race'. However, even more than the analysis of other racialised practices, the study of 'whiteness' deconstructs the superior and privileged position as opposed to other, non-white 'races' or groups. Therefore, the study of 'whiteness' largely emerging from American research had been criticised by postcolonial studies as rewriting racism and continued discrimination and reintroducing privilege back into studies that should be freed of racialised markers of distinction. For a summary on this criticism and a proposal for postcolonial whiteness studies see *Alfred J. López*, Introduction: Whiteness after Empire, in: Alfred J. López (Ed.), Postcolonial Whiteness: A Critical Reader on Race and Empire, Albany 2005, 1–30.

[31] *Thomas/Thompson*, Empire and Globalisation, 151 f.

[32] *Marilyn Lake/Henry Reynolds*, Drawing the Global Colour Line. White Men's Countries and the International Challenge of Racial Equality, Cambridge 2008, 4.

[33] *Neville Meaney*, Britishness and Australian Identity. The Problem of Nationalism in Australian History and Historiography, in: Australian Historical Studies 32/116, 2001, 76–90; *McKinnon*, Independence and Foreign Policy, 180.

[34] *James Curran*, The Power of Speech. Australian Prime Ministers Defining the National Image, Carlton 2006, 8.

[35] *Stuart Ward*, Transcending the Nation: A Global Imperial History?, in: Antoinette M. Burton (Ed.), After the Imperial Turn: Thinking With and Through the Nation, Durham 2003, 44–56, 46.

fining the community's identity: "For the self-governing dominions, the organic, intangible bonds of the British Commonwealth were an independent community of values with a common rationality, to which responsibility was felt to be owed."[36]

Moreover, perceptions of an Anglo-Saxon community partly integrated the USA. As Winston Churchill described it in his 'Iron Curtain Speech' in 1946, Britain felt close to the USA because of a shared heritage resulting in "the great principles of freedom and the rights of man"[37] that fused equally into the Magna Carta and the American Declaration of Independence. What Churchill described as 'English-Speaking people' also included Australia, Canada and New Zealand.[38] Shared bonds constituted "a 'core' of a distinct international, transnational, civilizational and imperial entity within the global society, currently known as the 'Anglosphere'".[39] Definitions and identity of this Anglosphere also responded to changes of ideological outlook in and outside of the community: As they were initially shaped by ideas of an Anglo-Saxon race, these ideas were translated into moral particularity in the mid-twentieth century.

Based on this shared identity, Australians, Canadians and New Zealanders equally expected to share interests and rationales on a transnational and even global level. Despite the official abolition of imperial dependence, the perception of belonging to a British world community remained. Moreover, affiliation was transferred to the Commonwealth, which now represented two phenomena: On the one hand, it transformed the former Empire into a global organisation containing the former colonies as sovereign states. At the same time, the organisation was not limited to ideas of institutional cooperation, but also sustained ideas and values of a British world community. To describe these shared values, the Commonwealth also meant a rhetoric and symbolic form partly detached from the organisation, which referred more loosely to the former imperial space. When Britain decided to withdraw its forces, related discussions corresponded to other debates on decolonisation and British leadership in the Commonwealth.

[36] *Dan Halvorson*, From Commonwealth Responsibility to the National Interest. Australia and Post-War Decolonisation in South-East Asia, in: The International History Review 40/4, 2018, 870–892, 874; see also *Frank Bongiorno*, Comment: Australia, Nationalism and Transnationalism, in: History Australia 10/3, 2013, 77–84, 79.

[37] The Sinews of Peace ('Iron Curtain Speech'), Speech given by Right. Hon. Winston Churchill at Westminster College Fulton, Missouri, 5.3.1946. URL: https://winstonchurchill.org/resources/speeches/1946-1963-elder-statesman/the-sinews-of-peace/. Accessed August 22, 2019.

[38] *David Lowe*, Australia's Cold War: Britishness and English-Speaking Worlds Challenged Anew, in: Phillip Buckner/R. D. Francis (Ed.), Rediscovering the British World, Calgary 2005, 361–380, 369 f.

[39] *Vucetic*, Anglosphere, 2.

With a focus on security discussions, the following study will argue that the British decision represented a larger process of withdrawal from the Empire, which left the dominions without a sufficient interpretation for their (post-)imperial self. As such, this study supplements two existing bodies of research: For one, it complements studies on the British withdrawal East of Suez[40] with a profound transnational analysis of long-term considerations and narratives flowing back and forth between Britain and the dominions. As other studies focus on the British economic and political reasoning for withdrawal, most of them tend to disregard the discourses within the dominions. Although most studies acknowledge the dominions' protest, few have attempted to analyse underlying dispositions and outlooks. However, a closer look at negotiations filled with references to a lost or needed collective or national framework suggests that both British officials and their dominion counterparts perceived the period as one of crisis. Secondly, this study is pinned against a series of existing studies on the transformation within the former dominions at the 'End of Empire'. From the metropolitan perspective, publications of Carl Bridge, Kent Fedorowich[41] and Sarah Stockwell[42] have emphasised the important transnational link of Britishness that reflected back on Britain. In Australia, the first proposals were made by historian Neville Meaney who advocated to reintroduce the British connection into a historiography which previously saw the British connection solely as antagonistic to nationalist aspirations.[43] Meaney's approach paralleled the studies of Douglas Cole, who underlined the outspoken British character of dominion identities.[44] These arguments were further advanced through publications of Phillip Buckner, José Igartua and Charles Champion in Canada[45], Stuart Ward,

40 *Phillip Darby*, British Defence Policy East of Suez, 1947–1968, London 1973; *Jeffrey Pickering*, Britain's Withdrawal from East of Suez. The Politics of Retrenchment, Houndmills 1998; *Saki Dockrill*, Britain's Retreat from East of Suez. The Choice Between Europe and the World?, Houndmills/New York 2002.

41 *Carl Bridge/Kent Fedorowich*, Mapping the British World, in: Carl Bridge/Kent Fedorowich (Ed.), The British World: Diaspora, Culture, and Identity, London/Portland 2003, 1–15.

42 *Sarah Stockwell*, Ends of Empire, in: Sarah Stockwell (Ed.), The British Empire: Themes and Perspectives. 2. publ., Malden 2010, 269–293.

43 *Meaney*, Britishness and Australian Identity; *Neville Meaney*, Britishness and Australia: Some Reflections, in: Carl Bridge/Kent Fedorowich (Ed.), The British World: Diaspora, Culture, and Identity, London/Portland 2003, 121–135. For a review of Britishness within Australian historiography see also *Deborah Gare*, Britishness in Recent Australian Historiography, in: The Historical Journal 43/4, 2000, 1145–1155; for a larger discussion of all three countries' historiography see *Ward*, New Nationalism, 192–194.

44 *Douglas Cole*, The Problem of 'Nationalism' and 'Imperialism' in British Settlement Colonies, in: The Journal of British Studies 10/2, 1971, 160–182.

45 *Phillip Buckner/R. D. Francis* (Ed.), Rediscovering the British World, Calgary 2005; *Phillip Buckner* (Ed.), Canada and the End of Empire, Vancouver 2005; *Phillip Buckner* (Ed.), Canada and the British Empire, Oxford 2010; *José Eduardo Igartua*, The Other Quiet Revolution. National Identities in English Canada, 1945–71, Vancouver 2006; *C. P. Champion*, The Strange Demise of British Canada. The Liberals and Canadian Nationalism 1964–1968, Montreal/Ithaca 2010.

James Curran and Deryck Schreuder in Australia[46], and James Belich in New Zealand.[47]

This is not the first study to aim at a three-national analysis on the End of Empire[48], yet it is the first to look at security relations following imperial co-operation.[49] With the exception of the Canadian case, other studies have already addressed the East of Suez decision as part of a larger process at the End of Empire. In various degrees, Andrea Benvenuti[50], David Goldsworthy[51], and Stuart Ward[52] have all included the East of Suez debate into larger descriptions of demise in Anglo-Australian relations. Further studies have been produced

46 *Stuart Ward*, Australia and the British Embrace. The Demise of the Imperial Ideal, Carlton South 2001; *James Curran/Stuart Ward*, The Unknown Nation. Australia After Empire, Melbourne 2010; *Deryck M. Schreuder/Stuart Ward* (Ed.), Australia's Empire, Oxford 2008.

47 *James Belich*, Paradise Reforged. A History of the New Zealanders from the 1880s to the Year 2000, Honolulu 2001; *James Belich*, Making Peoples. A History of the New Zealanders from Polynesian Settlement to the End of the Nineteenth Century, Auckland 2001.

48 Aside from Stuart Ward, Jatinder Mann has presented a couple of publications comparing the concept of citizenship and multiculturalism; *Jatinder Mann* (Ed.), Citizenship in Transnational Perspective. Australia, Canada, and New Zealand, Cham 2017; *Jatinder Mann*, Redefining Citizenship in Australia, Canada, and Aotearoa New Zealand, New York 2019.

49 Exceptions for a three-national approach on defence and foreign policy are *Richard A. Preston/Ian Wards*, Military and Defence Developments in Canada, Australia and New Zealand: A Three Way Comparison, in: War & Society 5/1, 1987, 1–21; *Ramesh Thakur*, Defence Reviews in Australia, Canada, and New Zealand, in: International Journal: Canada's Journal of Global Policy Analysis 42/4, 1987, 890–897. The comparisons or nexus between two of the three countries in this period is more often represented by research. Noteworthy among those are *David McCraw*, Change and Continuity in Strategic Culture. The Cases of Australia and New Zealand, in: Australian Journal of International Affairs 65/2, 2011, 167–184; *Ian McGibbon*, Australian-New Zealand Relations and Commitments to Asian Conflicts 1950–1972, in: Journal of Military History 81/4, 2017, 1059–1074; *Robert Ayson*, When Cooperation Trumps Convergence. Emerging Trends in Australia-New Zealand Defence Relations, in: Security Challenges 2/3, 2006, 25–39; *John Charles Blaxland*, Strategic Cousins. Australian and Canadian Expeditionary Forces and the British and American Empires, Montreal 2006; *Greg Donaghy*, Parallel Paths. Canadian-Australian Relations Since the 1890s, Ottawa 1995; *Andrew F. Cooper*, Keeping in Touch: Patterns of Networking in the Canadian-Australian Diplomatic Relationship, in: Margaret MacMillan/Francine McKenzie (Ed.), Parties Long Estranged: Canada and Australia in the Twentieth Century, Vancouver 2003, 249–266.

50 *Andrea Benvenuti*, The British Military Withdrawal from Southeast Asia and its Impact on Australia's Cold War Strategic Interests, in: Cold War History 5/2, 2006, 189–210; *Andrea Benvenuti*, A Parting of the Ways. The British Military Withdrawal from Southeast Asia and its Critical Impact on Anglo-Australian Relations, 1965–68, in: Contemporary British History 20, 2006, 575–605; *Andrea Benvenuti*, Anglo-Australian Relations and the 'Turn to Europe', 1961–1972, London 2008; *Andrea Benvenuti*, Cold War and Decolonisation. Australia's Policy towards Britain's End of Empire in Southeast Asia, Singapore 2017.

51 *Goldsworthy*, Losing the Blanket.

52 *Ward*, British Embrace.

by Derek McDougall[53], Jeppe Kristensen[54] and Jack Doig[55], who contributed research on Australia and New Zealand. Given the exclusion of Canada from nearly all of these studies, no thorough attempt has been made to review all three dominions' foreign policy with a focus on security discussions on Britain's role in Southeast Asia at Empire's end.

The study of transnational security perceptions offers a multitude of perspectives on the dominions' outlook on national security and their relative position within regional and international orders in the 1960s. Here, this study benefits from a range of new impulses provided by the 'new' imperial history[56] and the academic fields of global history[57] and transnational history.[58] Latter replaced the classic concept of international history[59], which itself had emerged from the traditional diplomatic history reaching back to the nineteenth century.[60] All of these perspectives seek to overcome national perspectives by highlighting intrastate or supra-state phenomena and connections, flows and developments.

To study the manifold impact of Britain's retreat, an article by David Reynolds on different dimensions of Australian foreign policy[61] offers an analytical

[53] *Derek McDougall*, Australia and the British Military Withdrawal From East of Suez, in: Australian Journal of International Affairs 51/2, 1997, 183–194.

[54] *Jeppe Kristensen*, "In Essence Still a British Country". Britain's Withdrawal From East of Suez, in: Australian Journal of Politics & History 51/1, 2005, 40–52.

[55] *Jack Doig*, The Australian and New Zealand Governments' Responses to Britain's Decline in the 1960s. Identity, Geopolitics and the End of Empire, in: Journal of New Zealand & Pacific Studies 1/1, 2013, 41–54; *Jack Doig*, New Nationalism in Australia and New Zealand. The Construction of National Identities by Two Labo(u)r Governments in the Early 1970s, in: Australian Journal of Politics & History 59/4, 2013, 559–575.

[56] *Tony Ballantyne*, The Changing Shape of the Modern British Empire and its Historiography, in: The Historical Journal 53/2, 2010, 429–452; *Jane Burbank/Frederick Cooper*, Empires in World History. Power and the Politics of Difference, Princeton 2010; *John Darwin*, After Tamerlane. The Rise and Fall of Global Empires, 1400–2000, New York 2008; *Timothy H. Parsons*, The Rule of Empires. Those Who Built Them, Those Who Endured Them, and Why They Always Fall, Oxford/New York 2010; *Stephen Howe* (Ed.), The New Imperial Histories Reader, London 2010.

[57] For further introduction to the field of global history see *Dominic Sachsenmaier*, Global Perspectives on Global History. Theories and Approaches in a Connected World, Cambridge 2011; *Sebastian Conrad*, What Is Global History?, Princeton 2016. As examples for global history research see the cross-epochal and cross-imperial approach presented in *James Belich/John Darwin/Margret Frenz/Chris Wickham* (Ed.), The Prospect of Global History, Oxford/New York 2016.

[58] For an approach to the various fields of transnational history see *Akira Iriye/Pierre-Yves Saunier* (Ed.), The Palgrave Dictionary of Transnational History, Basingstoke 2009.

[59] International history focuses on the sum of all relations held between and among independent nations, *Akira Iriye*, Global and Transnational History. The Past, Present, and Future, Basingstoke 2013, 15 f.

[60] *Iriye*, Global and Transnational History, 5 f.

[61] *David Reynolds*, Empire, Region, World: The International Context of Australian Foreign Policy since 1939, in: Australian Journal of Politics & History 51/3, 2005, 346–358.

blueprint. During the East of Suez discussions, security and defence considerations revealed how the former dominions conceived security in interlocking spaces of (post-)imperial, regional, and world or 'global' order. This study argues that British resources were an important factor in retaining these specific concepts of order. British outlooks and attitudes served as a signpost on and within these orders as they resonated with the strong remnants of Britishness in the dominions. At the same time, Britain's role as a larger power or global player made the dominions rely on its resources and networks.

The focus on spatial orders allows a deeper understanding of the changing self-perception of all three former dominions in the wake of the British plans. The application of 'self' to different frameworks of foreign policy can be described as an act of localisation both in relation to others as well as in categories of time and space, following ideas that "identity is relationally constituted and always involves the construction of boundaries and thereby the delineation of space".[62]

Focusing briefly on the identity framework provided by spatial outlooks, the conceptions and experiences among all three dominions vary. In Australia, the tension between the national space as a scarcely populated yet vast island in an unsettling, potentially threatening neighbourhood created a specific agenda of survival in Australian foreign policy.[63] In comparison, Canada seemed appeased by the closeness to the USA and the implication that any threat to its national security would equally be a threat to its Southern neighbour. However, Canada also referred to its settler identity and adopted spatial perceptions – "an Atlantic nation, or a Pacific nation, or an Arctic nation"[64] – to counterbalance the dominance of the USA. It also resembled Australia in early narratives of an indefensibility of its large territory.[65] New Zealand lay somewhere between the spatial experiences of the other two dominions, being remote and isolated while still feeling exposed to certain conflicts in Southeast Asia.[66]

---

62 *Lene Hansen*, Security as Practice. Discourse Analysis and the Bosnian War, London 2006, 47.

63 See introductory remarks in the following studies: *Gareth J. Evans/Bruce Grant*, Australia's Foreign Relations in the World of the 1990s. 2. Ed., Carlton 1995; *Anthony Burke*, Fear of Security. Australia's Invasion Anxiety, Cambridge 2008; *Mathew Radcliffe*, Malaya Bound: Australia's Colonial Perceptions of Asia, 1955–1965, in: History Australia 12/3, 2015, 76–96; *Jeffrey Grey*, Coming of Age: Australian Defence and Strategic Policy in the Cold War, in: Ian McGibbon/John Crawford (Ed.), Seeing Red: New Zealand, the Commonwealth and the Cold War 1945–91, Wellington 2012, 127–134.

64 *Kim R. Nossal*, A European Nation? The Life and Times of Atlanticism in Canada, in: John English/Norman Hillmer (Ed.), Making a Difference? Canada's Foreign Policy in a Changing World Order, Toronto 1992, 79–102, 79.

65 *Roger Sarty*, The Interplay of Defence and Foreign Policy, in: Robert Bothwell (Ed.), Canada Among Nations, 2008: 100 Years of Canadian Foreign Policy, Montreal 2014, 111–141, 112; *Michael Tucker*, Canadian Foreign Policy. Contemporary Issues and Themes, Toronto 1980, 3.

66 *David Capie/Gerald McGhie*, Representing New Zealand: Identity, Diplomacy and the

Equally, the imperial connection strongly influenced the dominions' location. Empires essentially created 'space' as a framing category over issues such as distance to the metropole or the frontiers or borders within the colonial territory. The importance of space for imperial imagination is widely accepted; Hancock's "to be in love with two soils"[67] or Blainey's *Tyranny of Distance*[68] are only two examples of the variety of references to describe the settlers' relationship to both the land and the distant 'mother country'. In addition to a persistent Britishness, all three former dominions still contained a strong mental map[69] of a British world, a space created by imperial expansion and perpetuated after the end of colonial rule by transitory institutions such as the Commonwealth.

Their Anglocentric map was extended under the impression of the Cold War into a map divided along the ideological lines of the superpowers and their allies, the Western bloc and the Communist bloc.[70] These narratives were also created in institutions such as security alliances or the United Nations (UN). Here, these maps were equally challenged under the impact of decolonisation. Not only did new independent countries 'emerge' on the map that were previously unknown or of little interest, but the question of Cold War (non-)alignment also rearranged these countries' geopolitical position as part of specific blocs or formations that did not necessarily correspond to geographical realities. Instead, they were linked to ideological demarcation lines between 'North' and 'South'; 'developed', 'developing' or 'underdeveloped' countries; 'Have's' and 'Have-not's'. The powerful concept of a 'Third World'[71] underlines the influence of spatial Cold War categorisation.

Making of Foreign Policy, in: James H. Liu (Ed.), New Zealand Identities: Departures and Destinations, Wellington 2005, 230–241.

[67] W. K. Hancock: Australia. Melbourne 1961, 51; quoted in: *Ann Curthoys*, We've Just Started Making National Histories, and You Want us to Stop Already?, in: Antoinette M. Burton (Ed.), After the Imperial Turn: Thinking With and Through the Nation, Durham 2003, 70–90, 72.

[68] *Geoffrey Blainey*, The Tyranny of Distance. How Distance Shaped Australia's History, Melbourne 1966.

[69] According to historian Alan K. Henrikson, mental maps are "an ordered but continually adapting structure of the mind – alternatively conceivable as a process – by reference to which a person acquires, codes, stores, reorganises, and applies, in thought or in action, information about his or her large-scale geographical environment, in part or in its entirety. Still more briefly, such a map is the cognitive frame on the basis of which historians of international relations, like diplomats and others who think internationally, orient themselves in the world", *Alan K. Henrikson*, Mental Maps, in: Michael J. Hogan/Thomas G. Paterson (Ed.), Explaining the History of American Foreign Relations, Cambridge 1991, 177–193, 177.

[70] *Frank A. Ninkovich*, Modernity and Power. A History of the Domino Theory in the Twentieth Century, Chicago 1994.

[71] *Marcin Wojciech Solarz*, 'Third World'. The 60th Anniversary of a Concept That Changed History, in: Third World Quarterly 33/9, 2012, 1561–1573; *Tom Tomlinson*, What was the Third World?, in: Journal of Contemporary History 38, 2003, 307–321.

The discussions on a continued British presence in Southeast Asia can be reviewed from the perspective of these mental maps that resonate with the three intertwined spaces proposed by David Reynolds. For one, the British decision to review its position East of Suez was linked to its role as a former imperial power that provided a rationale for cooperation, but also for a British world community. As some perceived the withdrawal as a confirmation of Britain's determination to retreat from this role as a former imperial power, they feared the repercussions both in their bilateral relations with their former 'mother country' as within the Commonwealth. The question of British leadership was also related to the second framework, the question of regional order. Australia, Canada and New Zealand all perceived the British presence as an essential part of stabilising structures in the region.

On a third level, the British presence was related to perceptions of a desired world or 'global' order. While this order was hardly 'global' as it included little considerations for regions such as South America or Africa, nevertheless, it envisaged a set of universal parameters that should frame international politics.[72] The global Cold War[73] and decolonisation crucially influenced these parameters, dividing the world in the 'Free World' and the 'Communist World', or into the 'West', the 'East' and, later, the non-aligned states. Most of all, the Commonwealth came to represent the various challenges posed to a post-imperial organisation by the Cold War and decolonisation.[74] Policymakers tried to assess if their actions not only would have consequences for the (post-)imperial or regional framework, but could also develop a global impact. Such global impact was often linked to discussions in the UN as well as to regional security frameworks that nevertheless worked on supra-regional premises, such as the North Atlantic Treaty Organisation (NATO) or the Southeast Asia Treaty Organisation (SEATO).

Related to the argument of universal applicability was the question of how all three countries positioned themselves in a global sphere. Although this study focuses on three members of the Western world, their perception of decolonisation processes and their relations with countries of the non-aligned areas reveals more on the local dynamics of the Cold War. Focusing on the moment of crisis, the processes of framing and coping with conflicts might shed light on the variety of attitudes within the Western bloc. With Canada often taking a different attitude to regional and supra-regional conflicts, this comparison emphasises

72 *Glenda Sluga/Patricia M. Clavin*, Rethinking the History of Internationalism, in: Glenda Sluga/Patricia M. Clavin (Ed.), Internationalisms: A Twentieth-Century History, Cambridge 2017, 3–14.

73 *Odd Arne Westad*, The Global Cold War. Third World Interventions and the Making of Our Times. 3. Ed., Cambridge 2018; *Melvyn P. Leffler/Odd Arne Westad* (Ed.), The Cambridge History of the Cold War. Volume I: Beginnings, Cambridge 2010.

74 *Sue Onslow*, The Commonwealth and the Cold War, Neutralism, and Non-Alignment, in: The International History Review 37/5, 2015, 1059–1082.

the plurality of Western thinking on decolonisation and the Cold War. By focusing on transnational discussions, e. g. in SEATO, it also illustrates how the division of labour of Western security did not lead to a monolithic outlook on areas of responsibilities in the world, but rather complimentary networks that contributed to a larger reference framework for Western foreign and security policy. Again, the period of the 1960s offers a good focus on these questions as the multitude of different conflicts and theatres contributed to perceptions of a global Cold War.[75]

At the same time, security considerations were also embedded in spatial concepts of time. Within the British Empire, the idea of a historical mission and the 'successful' expansion of the Empire was a powerful metaphor for sustaining imperial control. To legitimise the imperial mission, but also developments of independence and decolonisation, foreign policy produced markers of temporal identity such as continuity, change, transformation, or progress. Such temporalities do not only relate to temporal self-perceptions, but can also refer to the diverging temporalities of 'others'.[76] The discussions of development and civilisation in the wake of 'Third World' discussions represent such phenomena of distinction by markers of temporality. A focus on temporal identity also reveals a remarkable awareness for history 'in the making' among people from the dominions in the period under study. Observers referred to a 'watershed moment' or the 'end of an era' when they described the developments of British retreat engulfing them. In general, policymakers found themselves in a 'threshold time' that gained further strength from the corresponding rapid domestic transformations under the Liberal and Labour governments in the early 1970s.

The focus on changing spatial orders allows some preliminary considerations for the East of Suez debate. With the global contractions of the Empire, all three countries experienced the time under consideration as one of external decolonisation and internal de-imperialisation. The first ascribes to the regional and global developments all three countries witnessed and participated in. De-imperialisation is understood here as referring more suitably to the internal developments in the dominions resulting from the British disentanglement. Decolonisation and de-imperialisation are interlinked concepts and might invite to be used simultaneously, yet the traditional focus of decolonisation studies on nationalist aspirations and anticolonial movements suggests that it has to be linked to the former dominions with some caution. Here, the new imperial his-

[75] For a review of 'external' issues in NATO see *Frode Liland*, Explaining NATO's Non-Policy on Out-of-Area Issues During the Cold War, in: Gustav Schmidt (Ed.), A History of NATO: The First Fifty Years, Houndmills 2001, 173–189; *Evanthis Hatzivassiliou*, Out-Of-Area. NATO Perceptions of the Third World, 1957–1967, in: Cold War History 13/1, 2012, 67–88.

[76] *Hansen*, Security as Practice, 49 f.

tory strongly benefits from the research of postcolonial studies[77] and subaltern studies.[78] Research of the British Empire and its aftermath has to be particularly aware of potential biases following from historiographic traditions and the 'making' of history of the Empire as postcolonial knowledge. Following the influential work of Edward Said[79] and others, postcolonial studies request a larger inclusion of colonised or indigenous perspectives in imperial history. They demand to 'provincialize'[80] European experiences as only one part of imperial history in order to include perspectives of local difference and to establish a counterpoint to traditional perceptions of Western universalism.[81]

The contestation of a classic description of the Empire as merely constituting and upholding its power over a large territorial space was also caused by the different strands of decolonisation studies.[82] In legal terms, decolonisation was largely understood as "the process whereby colonial powers transferred institutional and legal control over their territories and dependencies to indigenously based, formally sovereign, nation-states".[83] However, under the influence of recent research, decolonisation also characterises a fundamental global phenomenon that redefined power relations between the former European empires and the rest of the world and contributed to a change within the international normative framework correlating with conflicts of the Cold War.[84] As they assess the end of colonial rule stretching nominally from the emergence of American colonies to the transfer of power in Hong Kong in 1997, scholars questioned Britain's interests and expectations in retaining colonial control in some parts of the empire while shedding of responsibilities in other parts.[85] Moreover, to

---

77 For an introduction into the different perspectives proposed by the postcolonial studies see *Graham Huggan*, The Oxford Handbook of Postcolonial Studies, Oxford 2013.

78 *Partha Chatterjee*, A Brief History of Subaltern Studies, in: Gunilla Budde/Sebastian Conrad/Oliver Janz (Ed.), Transnationale Geschichte: Themen, Tendenzen und Theorien. 2. publ., Goettingen 2010, 94–104.

79 *Said*, Orientalism.

80 *Dipesh Chakrabarty*, Provincializing Europe. Postcolonial Thought and Historical Difference. Reissue, Princeton 2008.

81 *Darwin*, After Tamerlane, 13 f.

82 For an introduction see *Jan C. Jansen/Jürgen Osterhammel*, Decolonization. A Short History, Princeton/Oxford 2017.

83 *Prasenjit Duara*, Introduction: The Decolonization of Asia and Africa in the Twentieth Century, in: Prasenjit Duara (Ed.), Decolonization: Perspectives From Now and Then, London 2008, 1–18, 2.

84 *Jeremi Suri*, The Cold War, Decolonization, and Global Social Awakenings. Historical Intersections, in: Cold War History 6/3, 2006, 353–363.

85 *John Darwin*, Britain and Decolonisation. The Retreat from Empire in the Post-War World, Basingstoke 1988; *Hyam*, Britain's Declining Empire; *W. David McIntyre*, British Decolonization, 1946–1997: When, Why and How Did the British Empire Fall?, Basingstoke/New York 1998; *Martin Shipway*, Decolonization and its Impact. A Comparative Approach to the End of the Colonial Empires, Malden 2008. By comparing the British decolonisation with others, some scholars, especially from the subaltern studies, hope to regain a regional or local imperative that can be dispatched from colonial peculiarities and which can focus on indige-

transcend the narrow terms of the transition of legal and jurisdictive sovereignty from Britain to its former colonies, studies estimated the sphere of continued British influence through the research of 'informal empires'.[86]

Consequently, the new imperial history tries to overcome the paradigms of "nation, modernity, and Europe"[87] as primary trajectories for imperial studies and instead advocates a cross-epochal and cross-continental approach to the study of empires away from Eurocentrism. With their strong heritage of Britishness though, the former dominions are put in an awkward position when it comes to postcolonial studies. As Stuart Ward already argued for the Australian case in 2005, the term 'postcolonial' places Britain and the dominions at opposite ends, leading to assumptions of the latter being put into independence similar to other cases in the British Empire.[88] Traditionally, many historians have neglected to include the former white settler colonies in studies on decolonisation, based on the notion that the Australian, Canadian and New Zealand experiences did not relate to experiences postcolonial writer Frantz Fanon called the "cleansing force"[89] of violence as part of decolonisation. Another characterisation by Fanon, namely the "total, complete and absolute substitution"[90] of colonial rule, also does not fit with the gradual transitions in the dominions. The neglect of the dominions in postcolonial studies might therefore follow a political argument: Given their preferential treatment as white settler colonies, their inclusion might undermine the argument of injustice and oppression ascribed to colonial regimes.[91]

In order to avoid these difficulties, the term de-imperialisation can refer to the close identity of outlook and interest previously shared between Britain and the former dominions that came into crisis in the 1960s. New imperial histories demand a closer look at interactions within the empire without negating the power hierarchies between metropoles and peripheries. Rather, these studies ask how interdependent the different imperial spaces were and how much one needed the other as a referential framework of identity.[92] These perspectives

---

nous experiences, see *Remco Raben/Els Bogaerts* (Ed.), Beyond Empire and Nation. The Decolonization of African and Asian Societies, 1930s–1960s, Leiden 2012.

86 *Ulrike von Hirschhausen/Jörn Leonhard*, Zwischen Historisierung und Globalisierung. Titel, Themen und Trends der neueren Empire-Forschung, in: Neue Politische Literatur 56, 2011, 389–404, 390.

87 *Burbank/Cooper*, Empires in World History, 8.

88 *Stuart Ward*, "Post-Imperial" Australia. Introduction, in: Australian Journal of Politics & History 51/1, 2005, 1–5, 1.

89 *Frantz Fanon*, The Wretched of the Earth, New York 1968, quoted in: *Westad*, Global Cold War, 85; see also *Raymond F. Bretts*, Decolonisation: A Brief History of a Word, in: Remco Raben/Els Bogaerts (Ed.), Beyond Empire and Nation; The Decolonization of African and Asian Societies, 1930s–1960s, Leiden 2012, 23–38, 27.

90 Fanon, Wretched of the Earth, quoted in: *López*, Introduction, 13.

91 Ibid., 13 f.

92 *Ulrike von Hirschhausen*, A New Imperial History? Programm, Potenzial, Perspektiven, in: Geschichte und Gesellschaft 41, 2015, 718–757, 722.

highlight an empire 'in the making' by looking at processes and interaction between different imperial agents or stakeholders of the empire.[93] Moreover, it highlights the domestic issues that were not necessarily related to the British disentanglement, but which still bore elements of imperialism, such as the treatment of indigenous people or the colonial role Australia and New Zealand held with trust territories in the Asian-Pacific region. At the same time, unlike the term de-dominionisation[94], de-imperialisation allows a comparative element to other imperial orders of that time. In the last resort, de-imperialisation seems more apt to describe the continued links to Britain, which resulted in a (post-) imperial identity that contained elements of distinction and affiliation.

As recent studies have argued, most notably A. G. Hopkins[95], the former dominions prove to be an invaluable object of analysis for the liminal character of the British Empire as for the already mentioned question of nationhood. Given their strong British outlook, they equally came to question British imperial rule and influence both within their territories as within the Empire after the Second World War. Being witnesses to the decolonisation of the Empire, they transferred many of the related questions to their own position, asking if a proper departure from colonial status really took place. Furthermore, and this again contrasted with other experiences of decolonisation, they had more difficulties in departing from an identity defined by Britishness and struggled to find distinct national markers of identity. The former dominions therefore represent a special case at the End of Empire that highlights the scope and limits of decolonisation under the impression of shared institutions and outlooks. From the perspective of a study of decolonisation, they invaluably contribute to a broadening of decolonisation experiences, not least because of the perceived subtlety of disentanglement that contrasted with the rapid social change resulting from the British retreat. Moreover, their path to a nation-state challenges notions of path dependence, of ideas that postcolonial nations are born the moment colonies become independent.

To adopt this concept to the British Empire, large parts of the outlooks in the post-war dominions stemmed from colonial experiences. As the British Empire provided a strong narrative of historical cooperation and community, its demise

---

[93] *Antoinette M. Burton*, The Trouble with Empire. Challenges to Modern British Imperialism, Oxford et al. 2015.

[94] De-Dominionisation was proposed by Jim Davidson as characterising the unique experience in the dominions of reaching independence in accord with Britain. However, as Stuart Ward has noted, the proposal found little reception within the research on the End of Empire. *Jim Davidson*, The De-Dominionisation of Australia, in: Meanjin 38/2, 1979, 139–153; *Jim Davidson*, De-Dominionisation Revisited, in: Australian Journal of Politics & History 51/1, 2005, 108–113; *Ward*, Post-Imperial Australia. See also *Kosmas Tsokhas*, Dedominionization. The Anglo-Australian Experience, 1939–1945, in: The Historical Journal 37/4, 1994, 861–883.

[95] *A. G. Hopkins*, Rethinking Decolonization, in: Past & Present 200/1, 2008, 211–247.

in the 1960s caused officials to question not only their historical belonging, but also the future foundations of foreign and security policy in a framework of 'British' order. This study argues that the 1960s and 1970s were a crucial episode in need of new narratives and new orders that would allow policymakers to adapt to the demise of Britain. With the East of Suez discussion as the predominant object of study, these peaks are understood as highlights in an ongoing process of reflection and transition that spanned from the late 1950s to the early 1970s. Within those moments, actors increasingly looked back and ahead in attempts to give meaning to their current experiences. Moreover, these events were often characterised by a plurality of issues underlining a multitude of threats all three countries felt confronted with. Given that the British demise occurred simultaneously on various levels and in different fields, the synchronicity of threats increased the perception of urgency and pressure in discussions on a re-ordering of foreign policy.

This study argues that one characteristic of these moments of crisis was the multitude of conflict emotions. Despite the constant debate on the study of emotions[96], this book largely argues with the constitutive element of emotions in the construction of collective identity. Emotions always accompany the creation and definition of social groups, for example, by means of inclusion and exclusion, in the application of norms and sanctions and in the constitution of power and hegemony.[97] Certain emotional regimes[98] can determine how groups construct and define social behaviour and therewith shape responses to external challenges. Barbara Rosenwein has referred to emotional communities which share similar expressions and meanings of emotions, and often follow similar forms of emotion management by adhering to mutual emotional regimes.[99] Similarly, Benedict Anderson has underlined the role of emotions attached to the nation as equally constitutive as 'rational' explanations for shared action.[100]

---

[96] The most frequent criticism for a study of emotions relates to the consistent paradigm as seeing them as irrational factors opposed to rational means of policy and decision-making, *Barbara Rosenwein*, Worrying about Emotions in History, in: American Historical Review, 2002, 821–845.

[97] *Barbara Rosenwein*, Problems and Methods in the History of Emotions, in: Passions in Context 1, 2010, 1–32; *Joanna Bourke*, Fear and Anxiety. Writing about Emotion in Modern History, in: History Workshop Journal 55, 2003, 111–133.

[98] The idea of emotional regimes was first proposed by William Reddy, *William M. Reddy*, The Navigation of Feeling. A Framework for the History of Emotions, Cambridge 2006. Another concept is the term 'emotionology' introduced by Peter Stearns and Carol Stearns which describes the conventions, styles and practices attributed by a society to certain emotions, *Peter N. Stearns/Carol Z. Stearns*, Emotionology. Clarifying the History of Emotions and Emotional Standards, in: The American Historical Review 90/4, 1985, 813–836.

[99] *Rosenwein*, Problems and Methods.

[100] *Benedict Anderson*, Imagined Communities. Reflections on the Origin and Spread of Nationalism. Revised Ed., London 2006, 141 f.; *Nicole Eustace*, Emotion and Political Change, in: Susan Matt/Peter N. Stearns (Ed.), Doing Emotions History, Urbana 2014, 163–183, 174 f.

At the End of Empire, emotions played an important role as indicators of uncertainty, change and transformation. They reveal the fractures in social interaction and underline previous assumptions of cooperation undergoing a crisis. Moreover, conflicting emotions can point to the limits of a shared identity. Allegations over missed communications or appeals to a moral obligation were often accompanied by emotional statements that allow further study of the different attitudes and expectations held on foreign policy and security cooperation.

Relations between the former dominions and Britain were based on a shared set of principles and values that served as a basis for an emotional community. Here, constitutive norms can be understood as "collective, i. e., intersubjectively shared standards of appropriate behaviour".[101] Between Britain and the dominions, norms of trust and loyalty were institutionalised in concepts such as moral obligation and consultation. The adherence to such shared norms underlined the idea of a unique relationship within the Empire; at the same time, these norms served a substantive purpose in imperial cooperation, for example, with the reduction of contingency.[102] Furthermore, norms such as trust point to the crucial factor of personal relationships, which were often constituted by shared experiences and outlooks.[103]

Within Anglo-Dominion relations, trust helped to overcome the feeling of exposure of the vulnerable colonies at the beginning of settlerism and developed into a practice of foreign policy coordination by the time of the Statute of Westminster. By relying on their British partners, policymakers in the dominions could shed off some of the uncertainty regarding future scenarios and threats. Within the field of foreign policy, trust could also bridge gaps of knowledge not only about the future actions of the partner to trust, but also about larger international developments. Focusing on concepts such as trust as an amalgam of emotions and norms underlines how much these dispositions can be understood as a device of symbolical communication and a political resource in the debates on the End of Empire. Within the discussions on Britain's decision to withdraw from Southeast Asia, notions of shared values could increasingly be used as rhetorical strategies.

The norms defining the imperial relationship were constantly constructed by imperial agents, both within the dominions as within Britain. They were 'performed' on a daily basis by personal interaction among diplomats, pub-

---

[101] *Theresa Reinold*, Sovereignty and the Responsibility to Protect. The Power of Norms and the Norms of the Powerful, London/New York 2013, 19.

[102] To follow the work of sociologist Niklas Luhmann, the practice of trust can reduce social complexity and contingency by installing a set of principles which determine social behaviour, resembling a social contract. *Niklas Luhmann*, Trust, in: Christian Morgner/Michael King (Ed.), Trust and Power, Cambridge/Medford 2017, 1–114.

[103] *Ken Booth/Nicholas J. Wheeler*, The Security Dilemma. Fear, Cooperation and Trust in World Politics, Basingstoke 2008, 230.

lic servants and politicians throughout the Empire. At the same time, joint bodies, such as regular Commonwealth meetings, or narrations and images, for example in the idea of cooperative war efforts or a common threat, could stabilise these shared norms. The late 1960s saw an end to these norms on two levels, with a new generation of policymakers challenging the concept of imperial norms as well as the British turn to Europe putting the same norms into question. As new policymakers no longer shared the same transnational background, for example, through education or war experience, norms could no longer apply to the same mechanisms of social replication or coercion.

In all three countries, policymakers increasingly appreciated the nexus between (post-)imperial security, the regional environment of Southeast Asia and the changing international situation in the decades after World War II. Consequently, the study focuses on developments policymakers felt confronted with in the (post-)imperial, the regional and the global sphere. Similarly, security perceptions were processed by policymakers in different, often overlapping frameworks, ranging from a (post-)imperial to a regional and global framework. The overlap and multitude of these orders under consideration refer to the plurality of frameworks dominion policymakers located their nations in. This study employs the shorthand term of *frameworks* to describe a broader pattern of factors and perceptions shared by policymakers that predetermine actions and decisions. Frameworks allowed policymakers to locate and evaluate the British decision in a larger set of events and developments. The focus remains on the foreign policy of three ultimately national entities; their undertakings, exchanges and comparisons still unfold on the basis of conceptual nation-states in an international context.[104] This study argues that the countries' debates and reactions to Britain's retreat from East of Suez are essentially linked to the question of nationhood and national independence and ultimately contributed to different concepts of national identity.

To access these concepts of identity, this analysis focuses on the sphere of security. In this study, security is largely related to states' territorial integrity and can also be linked to metaphysical concepts of alliance security or collective security.[105] At the same time, security applies to a wide range of international

104 *Michael Mann*, Globalization, Macro-Regions and Nation-States, in: Gunilla Budde/Sebastian Conrad/Oliver Janz (Ed.), Transnationale Geschichte: Themen, Tendenzen und Theorien. 2. publ., Goettingen 2010, 21–31, 28.

105 Alliance security is understood here as the coordination of defence and security efforts among members of an association that is directed against potential aggression from outside the association. Examples are NATO or SEATO. Collective security is understood as the unilateral prevention of danger based on regulations and sanctions within an association whose membership is universal, meaning that the aggression is likely to stem from a member within the association. Primary example for collective security efforts is the United Nations. *Filippo Andreatta*, Collective Security: Theory and Practice of an Institution for Peace in the XXth Century, London 1996, PhD Thesis.

issues[106], as Australian historian Norman Harper already commented in 1965: "Security is something that extends far beyond the military sphere."[107] The already mentioned approach through emotions can serve as an angle in understanding the concepts of foreign policy[108], especially in the field of security and threat. Only recently, scholars have made the influence of emotions, such as fear in the Cold War era, the centre of their studies.[109] Moreover, different scholars have established certain emotions as constitutive elements of foreign policy in the three former dominions.[110]

After 1945, the dominions could still base their security frameworks on convictions and outlooks related to a shared British experience. During their time as colonies, all three dominions relied on British protection for their territorial safety. Moreover, imperial security was conducted in the same principles as outlined by scholars for other imperial relationships[111]: Security cooperation was underpinned by notions of Britishness, such as trust in British protection, loyalty, or obligation to burden-sharing in joint war efforts. Even at a time when colonial garrisons had been withdrawn for almost a century, Britain was still integrated into various, interlinked security frameworks that covered the countries' territories and position in the world. Applied to the East of Suez debate, Britain and its allies were convinced that the British presence in Southeast Asia was based as much on strategic necessities as on a moral obligation to defend its former colonies. This conviction was put into question by the British retreat; as a result, not only strategic frameworks had to be adjusted, but also outlooks that had been based on ideas of (post-)imperial cooperation.

By combining the study of strategic and foreign policies with special consideration for underlying cultural perceptions, this study highlights continued and changing characterisations of 'being British' in all three countries. From a methodological point of view, security frameworks serve as a starting point to look at ways policymakers 'framed' their relationship with Britain, their policy towards Southeast Asia and their perceptions of supra-regional developments. To look at certain frames means to assess current outlooks and attitudes on the

---

106 For a presentation of the scope of security concerns see *Mely C. Anthony* (Ed.), An Introduction to Non-Traditional Security Studies. A Transnational Approach, Los Angeles 2016.

107 *Norman Harper*, A Changing Commonwealth in A Chaotic World, in: Australian Outlook, April 1965, 20–34, 33.

108 For a valuable approach from the field of International Relations see *Maéva Clément/Eric Sangar* (Ed.), Researching Emotions in International Relations. Methodological Perspectives on the Emotional Turn, Cham 2018.

109 *Bernd Greiner/Claudia Weber/Dierk Walter/Christian T. Müller* (Ed.), Angst im Kalten Krieg, Hamburg 2009; see also *Patrick Bormann/Thomas Freiberger/Judith Michel* (Ed.), Angst in den Internationalen Beziehungen, Göttingen 2010.

110 *Burke*, Fear of Security; *Allan Gyngell*, Fear of Abandonment. Australia in the World Since 1942, Carlton 2017; *Richard Cavell* (Ed.), Love, Hate, and Fear in Canada's Cold War, Toronto/Buffalo 2004.

111 *Thomas/Thompson*, Empire and Globalisation, 146.

former dominion's position in regard to other variables on an imperial, regional and global level. Furthermore, it also assesses the envisaged position policymakers aimed at or wished for. When e. g. Canadian policymakers adopted the idea of a North Atlantic triangle, the metaphor did both reveal their current outlook on the relationship with Britain and the USA as well as desired outcomes of such a geopolitical format.[112]

In conclusion, the analysis of security discussions among and within the dominions highlights how much Britain's decision was linked to a demise of Anglocentric identity. The profoundness and plurality of transition should be revealed and assessed against markers of identity and difference. How did the three dominions process the British 'turn to Europe', how did the retreat affect their (post-)imperial, regional and global outlook, and how much did this process contribute to new concepts or ideas of an Australian, Canadian or New Zealand nation?

With a focus on ministerial and diplomatic correspondence, this study concentrates on policymakers within the dominions and in Britain. Here, policymaking is understood as the constant negotiation between different departments and agencies on the country's future political orientation regarding specific issues.[113] To access these frameworks which create and sustain identity, the textual focus is on foreign policy material, ranging foremost from departmental policy papers and records and diplomatic correspondence to newspaper articles and individual memoirs. These sources were produced by policymakers from the first and second fronts; members of government, diplomats, and public servants. Consequently, the sources used have stemmed mainly from official records of the respective agencies involved, such as the departments of external affairs[114] and the related diplomatic posts, the prime ministers' offices, and to a lesser extent, the defence and service departments. Before the establishment of diplomatic and departmental links, most of the dealing between Britain and

---

[112] *David G. Haglund*, The North Atlantic Triangle Revisited. (Geo)Political Metaphor and the Logic of Canadian Foreign Policy, in: American Review of Canadian Studies 29/2, 2009, 211–235, 211 f.

[113] *Allan Gyngell/Michael Wesley*, Making Australian Foreign Policy, New York 2003, 21–24.

[114] Australia's Department of External Affairs (ADEA) dates back to the Commonwealth foundation in 1901, Canada established its Department of External Affairs (CDEA) in 1909, and New Zealand's Department of External Affairs (NDEA) was established in 1943. *Russell B. Trood*, Australian Diplomatic Practice. Methods and Theory, in: Journal of Asian and African Studies 25/1, 1990, 88–113, 93; *Greg Donaghy/Michael K. Carroll*, Introduction, in: Greg Donaghy/Michael K. Carroll (Ed.), In the National Interest: Canadian Foreign Policy and the Department of Foreign Affairs and International Trade, 1909–2009, Calgary 2011, 1–9, 2; *Alister McIntosh*, The Origins of the Department of External Affairs and the Formulation of an Independent Foreign Policy, in: Alister McIntosh (Ed.), New Zealand in World Affairs: Vol. 1: 1945–1957, Wellington 1977, 9–36, 11.

the dominions (at their time of self-governing colonies) was on a direct government-to-government communication which brought the prime minister and his staff into a key position. Despite the following establishment of external affairs departments, this position of the prime minister was seen by many as an indication of the personal, unique dealing within the Commonwealth.[115] The role of the prime minister therefore remained central in the Commonwealth network. While the prime ministers in all three countries decided and executed policies rather than formulating them[116], they and their departments could often play an equally decisive role as the ministers for external affairs.[117]

In addition to external affairs and prime minister records, material from the respective departments for defence was used. Because of information restrictions that apply to security policies, this study is more concerned with the civil service and political sphere of discussions, and only assesses military-strategic inputs addressed to foreign policy circles. For similar reasons, the analysis rarely touches on the topics of nuclear and intelligence cooperation. Aside from departmental policymaking, the study incorporates the analysis of political communication within the public sphere, i. e., delivered speeches by governmental and political actors and press coverage concerning those activities and events. Without attempting a broad analysis of opinions and outlooks held by the greater public, cursory references to public discussions should broadly estimate the link or gap between official and public policymaking.

And not only public expectations could cause grievances among public servants: In all three countries, on a federal level, foreign policy was determined by a work division under the Westminster system, with bureaucrats within the departments aiming at an objective analysis of possible policies upon which elected government representatives should base their final decisions.[118] Despite

---

[115] *Lloyd*, Us and Them, 13 f.; *Garry Woodard*, Ministers and Mandarins: The Relationship between Ministers and Secretaries of External Affairs 1935–1970, in: Australian Journal of International Affairs 54/1, 2000, 79–95, 79 f.; *Frank Bongiorno*, The Price of Nostalgia: Menzies, the "Liberal" Tradition and Australian Foreign Policy, in: Australian Journal of Politics & History 51/3, 2005, 400–417, 401; *Peter Boehm*, Canada and the Modern Commonwealth. The Approaches of Lester Pearson and Pierre Trudeau, in: Bulletin of Canadian Studies 3/1, 1979, 23–39, 23; *Barry Gustafson*, Kiwi Keith. A Biography of Keith Holyoake, Chicago 2008, 166.

[116] See described for Australia *Trood*, Australian Diplomatic Practice, 98.

[117] Several of the Prime Ministers between 1945 and 1975 also temporarily held the portfolio of the Minister for External Affairs: In Australia Robert Menzies was also AMEA from 1960 to 1961; in New Zealand both Walter Nash (1957–1960) and Keith Holyoake (1960–1972) held the portfolio of Minister of External Affairs, with Holyoake remaining as Minister of External Affairs in the Cabinet of his successor John Marshall in 1972. In Canada, only John Diefenbaker was briefly Secrtary of State for External Affairs before the appointments of Sidney Smith and Howard Green.

[118] Gyngell and Wesley analyse this concept for the Australian case, nevertheless their analysis is applicable to Canada and New Zealand as well, *Gyngell/Wesley*, Australian Foreign Policy, 33 f.

this division of labour and power, disagreement could emerge between the political and the departmental level, leaving public servants often unsatisfied with the political decisions their governmental leaders chose to take.[119]

Among the civil servants, diplomats took a special position as it was expected that they would report on issues emerging at their location and would similarly mediate related national policies to their host country. A key group in this study are the high commissioners and their staff.[120] Established as a unique form of diplomatic representation between imperial and later Commonwealth countries, high commissioners enjoyed a special position among the diplomatic corps both in Britain and in former British colonies. They held direct access to the head of the government and often enjoyed close, informal relations with various local departments. In addition, their role held some prestige in public and ceremonial spheres, making them sometimes the personification of imperial culture by representing British kinship and familiarity.

In the decades under study, the high commissioner's office often included activities of political, economic, strategic and cultural nature and aimed at close cooperation in these fields with the hosting countries. Particularly in the case of Malaysia and Singapore, Australasian high commissioners were involved in strategic and command discussions of the British forces in place. As high commissioners both represented their own country's position and mediated the hosting country's position back to their home government, their records prove an important transnational source for this study. This study is further underpinned by a variety of published material related to the high commissioner's office. Besides Lorna Lloyd's work[121], there are also some publications on the history of Australian, Canadian and New Zealand high commissioners, ranging from biographies and memoirs[122] to works on the actual high commissions.[123] In a sec-

---

[119] See for the difficulties in distinguishing between policymakers and decisionmakers *Peter Edwards*, Sir Arthur Tange. Last of the Mandarins, St. Leonards 2006.

[120] On the following see the important study on Commonwealth diplomacy by Lorna Lloyd, *Lloyd*, Diplomacy With a Difference.

[121] Ibid.; see also *Lloyd*, Us and Them.

[122] See e. g. for Canada *Charles Ritchie*, Diplomatic Passport. More Undiplomatic Diaries 1946–1962, Toronto 1981; *Charles Ritchie*, Storm Signals. More Undiplomatic Diaries, 1962–1971, Toronto 1987; *Sheila Menzies/Arthur R. Menzies*, Australia & the South Pacific. Letters Home, 1965–1972, Manotick 2009; *Escott Reid*, Radical Mandarin. The Memoirs of Escott Reid, Toronto 1989. For Australia *Alan Renouf*, The Champagne Trail. Experiences of a Diplomat, Melbourne 1980; *Alan Watt*, Australian Diplomat, Sydney 1972; *Walter R. Crocker*, Australian Ambassador. International Relations at First Hand, Carlton 1971; *Keith Waller*, A Diplomatic Life. Some Memories, Nathan 1990. For New Zealand *Bryce Harland*, On Our Own. New Zealand Emerging in a Tripolar World, Wellington 1992.

[123] *Roy MacLaren*, Commissions High. Canada in London 1870–1971, Montreal 2010; *Carl Bridge/Frank Bongiorno/David Lee* (Ed.), The High Commissioners. Australia's Representatives in the United Kingdom, 1910–2010, Barton 2010. See also for the Canadian work of supervisory commissioners in Vietnam, Laos and Cambodia *Arthur E. Blanchette* (Ed.), Canadian Peacekeepers in Indochina, 1954–1973. Recollections, Ottawa 2002.

ond row, those publications were matched by accounts written by former diplomats and civil servants.[124]

The study follows a three-stepped structure resembling the stages of crisis attributed by some policymakers to the debate: Firstly, with the anticipation of the British plans; secondly, with the experience of negotiations; and lastly, with the review and coping with the British decision.

Before entering the analysis, an introductory section (Part 2) will present the historical background of the debate. It will give a particular focus on the respective policymakers involved, characterising them as a transnational imperial community sharing similar experiences and outlooks. The first analytical part of this study (Part 3) will present various stages of conflict that introduced an element of insecurity in Anglo-Dominion relations. The British dealings after the Second World War, mainly the events of the Suez Crisis and the first bid to enter the EEC, and ultimately its campaign for burden-sharing during the Indonesian Confrontation all contributed to perceptions that Britain was considering a break-away from the (post-)imperial preference system with the dominions, with early yet inconclusive considerations for alternative policies in all three countries.

Part 4 will deal with the negotiations and discussions once the British plans for withdrawal took shape in 1965. This part will largely end with the second British decision for accelerated withdrawal in January 1968. It deals with the strategies and arguments used during the negotiations and underlying perceptions and convictions held about the Commonwealth, Western security, and the ongoing Cold War and related conflicts of decolonisation. While most of the arguments presented by the former dominions were to no avail to British policymakers, one core argument of this part is the continued shared frame of Britishness that allowed references of moral obligation to resonate with both sides. At the same time, this shared framework resulted in a charged atmosphere of different emotions that would contribute to a distinct demise in Anglo-Dominion relations. Additionally, the charged climate would also result in a sense of disorientation and uncertainty following the East of Suez discussions in Australia and New Zealand. These anxieties resonated with parallel perceptions of a continued instability of the Southeast Asian region and insecurities about Chi-

---

[124] *John W. Holmes*, The Shaping of Peace: Canada and the Search for World Order, 1943–1957. Vol. 1, Toronto 1979; *John W. Holmes*, The Shaping of Peace: Canada and the Search for World Order, 1943–1957. Vol. 2, Toronto 1982; *Alan Watt*, The Evolution of Australian Foreign Policy 1938–1965, Cambridge 1967; *Arthur Andrew*, The Rise and Fall of a Middle Power. Canadian Diplomacy from King to Mulroney, Toronto 1993; *Brian D. Heeney*, The Things that Are Caesar's. The Memoirs of a Canadian Public Servant, Toronto 1972; *Brian J. Lynch* (Ed.), Celebrating New Zealand's Emergence. A Tribute to Sir George Laking and Frank Corner, Wellington 2005; *Malcolm Templeton* (Ed.), An Eye, an Ear and a Voice. 50 Years in New Zealand's External Relations 1943–1993, Wellington 1993.

na's role on an international level, resulting in emotions of fear and feelings of anxiety.

Lastly, Part 5 will assess the impact of Britain's decision on the changed course of foreign policy in all three countries. While Canada was largely motivated by domestic issues in questioning the relationship between foreign policy and its status as a nation, Australia and New Zealand felt compelled by the events of withdrawal to question the nexus of Britain's retreat to their nation's outlook. All three countries entered a period of self-questioning and review motivated by demands for an independent foreign policy representing their position as a nation. Britain's retreat from a larger world role correlated with a lessening of Cold War tensions and the end of mass decolonisation, leading the three dominions to assess what role they would undertake in this changing international environment. As a result, all three adopted new concepts of foreign policy. The part argues that in the early 1970s, the strong affiliation with Britain was in parts abandoned in favour of self-reliant, independent policies that should represent a nation which felt no longer represented in a dominant British framework.

After summarising the findings of the East of Suez discussion, the final part will reveal strands of continuity in discussions on the Australian, Canadian and New Zealand identity related to the period under review. The British connection developed in all three countries into a sort of unfinished business, with questions of belonging and identity still being fought about. While the 1970s might have seemed like a distinctive departure from a British framework, the following decades again saw a renewed identification with the British connection and a marked demise in independent ventures in foreign policy.

Part 2

Shifts in Foreign Policy Leading up to the East of Suez Debate

The East of Suez debate was preceded by a number of pivotal moments where British positions and actions caused sentiments of crises and anxiety among officials in Australia, Canada, and New Zealand. Most of these sentiments sprung from convictions and expectations of shared outlooks and interests. At the same time, policymakers sought to establish a foreign policy that could be more easily linked to their national interest of security. From a holistic view, a theme of ambivalence, between dependant loyalty and departure for a more self-reliant foreign and defence policy, is persistent throughout the twentieth century in the relationship between Britain and the former dominions.

In the immediate years following the Second World War, all three countries increased their international activities, which resulted in a pendulum swinging towards independent paths in foreign affairs. These activities were motivated not only by experiences of being ruled-over in traditional alliances, but also by the perception of changing power relations and dynamics: Firstly, the British Empire was left in a constant state of crisis symbolised by economic decline and ongoing decolonisation; secondly, the beginning of the Cold War led to changed views on security; and thirdly, it established new multilateral organisations, first and foremost the UN, enabling greater diplomatic access in international affairs.

For Canada, Australia and New Zealand, developments during and shortly after the Second World War were a pivotal time of international orientation. Given the global nature of the war, they developed an appreciation for new spaces of interaction and influence, but also of threat. With the demise of British military power, they had to consider how they would be affected in their security concerns. All three nations struggled with their new responsibilities in foreign policy and security as they departed for new alignments and independent positions following the war. However, their predominant outlook as former white settler colonies prevailed; with continued bonds of constitutional and political links to Great Britain strengthened during the war, all three remained in their self-perception as British or Anglo-Saxon countries. In particular, policymakers in political and departmental ranks continued identifying themselves with British counterparts and practice in a tight-knit community. As a result, foreign and security policymaking officials continued to heavily frame foreign policy issues, including those in Southeast Asia, with British perspectives.

2.1 Setting up Policies for Southeast Asia after the Second World War

Before analysing the attitudes among dominion policymakers prior to the East of Suez discussion, it is worth recalling the swift transformations taking place in Southeast Asia during and following the Second World War. Arguably, more than any other world region, Southeast Asia confronted Britain and the former dominions with geopolitical changes which would define global security discussions across forthcoming decades.

2.1.1 Diversifying their Security Networks – New Alliances in the Wake of the Second World War

From an imperial perspective, the unsettling commencement for these geopolitical shifts was the fall of Singapore in 1942. When Japanese troops overran the previously deemed impregnable British base, the assumptions of continued British protection were critically damaged. This was particularly true for Australia and New Zealand, where former strategies had massively relied on Singapore as a hub of regional security. In both countries, the Japanese victory reproduced strong fears of an Asian invasion which could be linked to earlier racial stereotypes of a 'Yellow Peril'.[1] In return, these fears exacerbated Tasman self-descriptions as European outposts in the Pacific, being either vast indefensible landmasses (Australia), or too small to defend themselves (New Zealand). Ultimately, the developments of the Pacific War inscribed a sense of vulnerability in their strategic outlooks, dominating defence planning for the following decades.[2] It also resulted in early requests for help with their sister dominion, Canada. The Canadians refused and pointed to restrained efforts in the Atlantic and European theatre, which would set a precedent for later points of friction over diverging security priorities when they would discuss strategies for the Southeast Asian region.[3]

The British defeat in Singapore made the former dominions question their concepts of imperial defence, both on a regional as well as a supra-regional level. Singapore also revealed flaws in the joint war effort – Australia and New Zealand had urged Britain to review its strategy before, but were ignored by British officials, introducing an element of mistrust in the close-knit com-

[1] *Stuart Ward*, Security: Defending Australia's Empire, in: Deryck M. Schreuder/Stuart Ward (Ed.), Australia's Empire, Oxford 2008, 232–258; *David Walker*, Survivalist Anxieties? Australian Responses to Asia, 1890s to the Present, in: Australian Historical Studies 120, 2002, 319–330.

[2] *McCraw*, Change and Continuity.

[3] *Donaghy*, Parallel Paths, 10–12.

munity of imperial cooperation. David Day and others have argued the defeat of the British not only led Australians and New Zealanders to come to terms with their own position and requirements for independent security policies, but that this 'Great Betrayal'[4] also alienated them from Britain in a way that marked the end of the prior and intimate imperial relationship. From an immediate perspective, the event yet only commenced a long-term assessment of the British connection, both in diplomatic and political realms.[5] Subsequently, Singapore came to represent larger discussions on new potential allies or enemies, which interfered with the traditional imperial framework of centre and periphery.

Following the lack of allied consultation and exposure experienced during the Pacific War, Australian and New Zealand policymakers entered the post-war era with an urge to prevent any new threat towards their region, and desired more resilient defence arrangements. Both nations expressed an interest in independent foreign policy and shared contingency planning, leading to the establishment of the ANZAC Pact in 1944.[6] Though the treaty itself did not immediately result in more frequent bilateral contacts, it underlined a general desire of both countries to cooperate on regional strategy.[7] How much the pact stands as a landmark for the growing regional conscience of both countries is inscribed in its definition of regional defence: It was not only defined by a geographical zone of defence that should stretch "through the arc of islands north and north-east of Australia to Western Samoa and New Zealand's possessions in the Cook Islands", but extended beyond geographic and military contexts with a plan "to advance the welfare of the native people and to promote their social and economic and political development".[8] This new regional conscience was also visible in the following Australian and New Zealand commitments – the participation in the allied forces in Japan and related discussions on the Japanese Peace Settlement, the regional transfer of European colonial au-

[4] *David Day*, The Great Betrayal. Britain Australia & the Onset of the Pacific War 1939–42, North Ryde 1988.

[5] *Ward*, Security, 248 f.

[6] The acronym ANZAC was given to the combined land forces of Australia and New Zealand in the First World War (Australian and New Zealand Army Corps). The term was accordingly applied to other military commitments both countries shared; *Jeffrey Grey*, War in the British World in the Twentieth Century, in: Phillip Buckner/R. D. Francis (Ed.), Rediscovering the British World, Calgary 2005, 233–250, 242.

[7] *Meg Gurry*, Identifying Australia's 'Region': From Evatt to Evans, in: Australian Journal of International Affairs 49/1, 1995, 17–31, 18 f.

[8] Evatt, Foreign Policy of Australia Speeches, 155 f., quoted in: *Daniel Oakman*, The Seed of Freedom. Regional Security and the Colombo Plan, in: Australian Journal of Politics & History 46/1, 2000, 67–85, 70.

thority through the South Pacific Commission[9] and various mandates and trusteeships.[10]

On the one hand, the Tasman nations assumed smaller roles of regional responsibility, but many of these were still linked to British cooperation. Conversely, arrangements such as the ANZAC Pact indicated a departure from the singular, British-centred approach towards foreign affairs. The Second World War also saw an expansion of diplomatic networks in all three former dominions beyond the traditional representation in London: Independent diplomatic offices for the three countries were established in Washington and Moscow, with frequent points of bilateral contacts introduced amongst themselves through respective High Commissions in Canberra, Ottawa and Wellington.[11] By 1946, Canada had 44 missions with 216 officers across the globe, compared to only six missions and a total of 16 officers in 1939[12], with Australia and New Zealand showing similar expansion. The establishment of diplomatic offices corresponded to the formation of individual departments of external affairs, which, for the first time, aimed at the professionalisation of respective staff and policy. While this rapid expansion put a considerable strain on government resources for each country, it substantially diversified and enhanced their individual positions on the international stage.

The most substantial diversification in foreign policy however, would come with the American alliance. Previous to the Second World War, all three countries had made ambivalent, isolated efforts to improve their security relations with the USA, while still prioritising their British relationship. Britain's exposure both in the Pacific as in the European war theatres enforced the need to pursue more substantial security alliances with the USA. While Canada signed the Ogdensburg Agreement and the establishment of the Permanent Joint Board

[9] The Governments of Australia, France, the Netherlands, New Zealand, the United Kingdom and the USA envisaged the South Pacific Commission to advance the welfare of the territories in the Pacific, see Agreement Establishing the South Pacific Commission, Canberra, 6.2.1947, URL: https://www.dfat.gov.au/about-us/publications/historical-documents/Pages/volume-12/551-agreement-establishing-the-south-pacific-commission. Accessed December 6, 2020.

[10] New Zealand previously established a Department of External Affairs in 1919 (renamed as Department of Island Territories in 1943) to serve the mandate over Western Samoa received through the League of Nations. It also took over the responsibility for the British colonies Niue, Tokelau and the Cook Islands, and shared a mandate with Australia over Nauru after the First World War. Australia most notably held a mandate over New Guinea.

[11] See a detailed list of all inter-dominion representation in *Lloyd*, Diplomacy With a Difference, 67.

[12] *Greg Donaghy*, Coming Off the Gold Standard: Re-Assessing the "Golden Age" of Canadian Diplomacy. Paper presented to the symposium A Very Modern Ministry: Foreign Affairs and International Trade Canada, University of Saskatchewan, 28 September 2009. URL: http://www.suezcrisis.ca/pdfs/Coming%20off%20the%20Gold%20Standard.pdf. Accessed May 25, 2021, 2f.

of Defence in 1940[13], Australia and New Zealand sought a permanent accommodation in America's security umbrella within the Pacific. Although it may not have become apparent at the time, the different efforts taken to establish security relations with the USA would inscribe distinct geopolitical priorities for a significant period following the war. Canadians translated their cooperation with the USA into one of a transatlantic community, or a North-Atlantic Triangle[14], which was soon integrated into the security alliance of NATO. NATO would not only develop into a cornerstone of Canadian Cold War policy, but Canadian officials also appreciated the organisation as an essential contribution to preventing a divide between American and British strategic interests.[15] Conversely, Australians and New Zealanders linked American cooperation to Pacific security. During the Second World War, Australia's Prime Minister John Curtin had already expressed a desire for American protection with a speech during Christmas of 1941: "Australia looks to America, free of any pangs as to our traditional links or kinship with the United Kingdom."[16] However, just as in Canada, Tasman officials conceived the American alliance as a relationship complementary to British cooperation. In fact, John Curtin and many other officials were quick to ascertain Australia's close ties to Britain on the following occasions.[17]

Nevertheless, the Second World War's aftermath left predominantly Australian and New Zealand policymakers with a precarious depiction of national security, namely with the impression that Britain was not able, and the USA not willing, to guarantee their protection. While Australian officials were unsuccessful in tying Americans down to a Pacific strategy in the immediate postwar years, the ensuing conflict in Korea in 1950/51 exposed policymakers of all three former dominions to the fundamental difficulties of establishing new security frameworks. The Korean War enforced the failure of internationalism, a brief period of world order and collective security, represented in the countries by Liberal and Labo(u)r governments embracing the UN's establishment.[18] In-

[13] See *Blaxland*, Strategic Cousins, 102; *Jack L. Granatstein*, When the Department of External Affairs Mattered: An When It Shouldn't Have, in: Greg Donaghy/Michael K. Carroll (Ed.), In the National Interest: Canadian Foreign Policy and the Department of Foreign Affairs and International Trade, 1909–2009, Calgary 2011, 69–79, 72f.

[14] This geopolitical concept was first presented by John Bartlet Brebner in 1945; *John Bartlet Brebner*, North Atlantic Triangle. The Interplay of Canada, the United States and Great Britain, New Haven 1945. See for an analysis of the different discussions on the North Atlantic Triangle *Hector Mackenzie*, Delineating the North Atlantic Triangle. The Second World War and Its Aftermath, in: The Round Table 95/383, 2006, 101–112; *Tony McCulloch*, The North Atlantic Triangle: A Canadian Myth?, in: International Journal 66/1, 2010/11, 197–207.

[15] *Andrew*, Middle Power, 26.

[16] Melbourne Herald 27.12.1941, quoted in: *Curran*, Power of Speech, 26.

[17] *David Day*, 27 December 1941: Prime Minister Curtin's New Year Message: Australia's Look to America, in: Martin Crotty/David A. Roberts (Ed.), Turning Points in Australian History, Sydney 2008, 129–142.

[18] *Thomas F. Keating*, Canada and World Order. The Multilateralist Tradition in Canadian Foreign Policy. 2. publ., Toronto 2002, 26f.; *David Lee*, The Curtin and Chifley Govern-

stead, it strengthened the bloc formations and issues of the Cold War, and partly replaced initial Commonwealth and UN rationalities with a dominance of the American alliance.

The American dominance during the war would set a precedent that would forecast issues all three dominions felt challenged by in their relationship with the USA. While Canadian officials attempted to constrain American aggression by quiet diplomacy[19], Australian and New Zealand officials struggled between mistrust of American policies and the desire to cover Southeast Asian defence in accordance with both Britain and the USA.[20] Nevertheless, the conflict rapidly enhanced their integration into the American security umbrella, as they could enter the so-called ANZUS Treaty over their acquiescence to a Japanese peace treaty. Even though the ANZUS treaty only consisted of a loose agreement for consultation, for officials like the Australian Minister for External Affairs Percy Spender, who had pursued American protection since the Second World War, the Treaty represented the desired security blanket for the Pacific.[21] And again, Australian and New Zealand officials appreciated the pact not in conflict, but as a supplement to their Commonwealth role: By stating the flexible application of ANZUS towards different theatres, they could honour their Commonwealth obligations even in theatres such as the Middle East. By linking various security frameworks, officials like Spender hoped to bridge the already emerging defragmentation of different spheres of defence responsibility visible with the establishment of NATO.[22]

In the aftermath of the Korean War, Australia and New Zealand continued to perceive cooperation with Britain in any future conflict as paramount. When the USA approached Australia in the wake of the Indochina crisis in early 1954, their political leaders refused to join a commitment without Britain:

> "This would be a terrible innovation for Australia to promote, for it would be the first cleavage in Commonwealth unity. [...] we can conceive nothing more destructive to Empire unity than for Australia to be neutral in a United Kingdom war or the United Kingdom to be neutral in an Australian war. It is thus clear that tremendous efforts must be made to keep United Kingdom and Australian policy in line."[23]

---

ments, Liberal Internationalism and World Organisation, in: David Lee/Christopher Waters (Ed.), Evatt to Evans: The Labor Tradition in Australian Foreign Policy, St. Leonards/Canberra 1997, 48–61.

[19] *Denis Stairs*, The Diplomacy of Constraint. Canada the Korean War and the United States, Toronto 1974; *Robert Prince*, The Limits of Constraint: Canadian-American Relations and the Korean War, 1950–51, in: Journal of Canadian Studies 27, 1992, 129–152.

[20] *W. David McIntyre*, Background to the Anzus Pact. Policy-Making Strategy and Diplomacy 1945–55, Basingstoke 1995.

[21] *David Lowe*, Percy Spender's Quest, in: Australian Journal of International Affairs 55/2, 2001, 194–197.

[22] *Neville Meaney*, Look Back in Fear. Percy Spender, the Japanese Peace Treaty and the ANZUS Pact, in: Japan Forum 15/3, 2003, 399–410.

[23] Menzies and Casey to Spender, 24.6.1954, quoted in: *David Lee*, Search for Security.

Aside from the strong desire for American protection, Australia and New Zealand continued to aim for British defence cooperation. In reality, the establishment of the ANZUS Treaty meant no retreat from the British alliance, despite Britain's exclusion from the treaty.[24] Similarly, ventures such as the ANZAC Pact were rather an indication of "loyal dissent"[25], a growing independence in accordance with British parameters. As a result, strategic planning in the former dominions continued on a long-established set of principles formed by arguments of a community of identity as well as a community of interest with Britain. The interdependence of different frameworks, which also included an American alliance, came to form what Vucetic termed the "Anglobalization of the Cold War".[26] Although all three countries adopted a similar take on security issues due to this 'Anglobalization', Australian and New Zealand officials were more interested than Canada in establishing an interdependent security framework within the Anglosphere, which would be particularly visible during the ensuing conflicts in Southeast Asia.

2.1.2 Cold War Rationales in Southeast Asia – New Challenges

Early Cold War polarisation increased restrictive tendencies, linking an anti-communist and conservative domestic policy to similar outlooks in foreign policy across all three former dominions.[27] Equally, global shifts of conflict forced them to focus on Southeast Asia, as nuclear deterrence and nationalist aspirations created new Cold War theatres in their periphery. Here, the Cold War could easily turn into a 'hot' war: proxy wars that were dominated by interests and forces of the superpowers, yet often channelled through indigenous conflicts.[28] The changing nature of threats, either in the form of nuclear extortion or minor 'cold' conflicts that could turn 'hot' and escalate into supra-regional wars, posed new demands for defence structures and planning.[29] Within a decade, traditional forms of contingency planning and military threat assessments were challenged by new conflicts of insurgencies and guerrilla warfare, requi-

---

Political Economy of Australia's Postwar Foreign and Defence Policy, St. Leonards 1995, 125.

24 *Ian McGibbon*, New Zealand and the Korean War. Vol. 1: Politics and Diplomacy. Reprint, Auckland 1996, 31.

25 *McKinnon*, Independence and Foreign Policy, 7.

26 *Vucetic*, Anglosphere, 68.

27 *Denis Stairs*, Realists at Work: Canadian Policy Makers and the Politics of Transition from Hot War to Cold War, in: Greg Donaghy (Ed.), Canada and the Early Cold War, 1943–1957: Canada au Début de la Guerre Froide, 1943–1957, Ottawa 1998, 91–116; *Peter Edwards*, The Origins of the Cold War, in: Carl Bridge (Ed.), Munich to Vietnam. Australia's Relations with Britain and the United States since the 1930's, Carlton 1991, 70–86.

28 *Albert Lau*, Introduction: Southeast Asia and the Cold War, in: Albert Lau (Ed.), Southeast Asia and the Cold War, London 2012, 1–12.

29 *Ian McGibbon*, Introduction, in: Ian McGibbon/John Crawford (Ed.), Seeing Red: New Zealand, the Commonwealth and the Cold War 1945–91, Wellington 2012, 13–21, 16.

ring different military tactics and defence structures.[30] This was also linked to another issue: The advent of the Cold War in the periphery coincided with and was determined by decolonisation, turning already ideological debates of postcolonial order into a battleground of worldviews, "a remarkable blurring of lines between colonizers and colonized, as well as West and East."[31] Issues such as neutrality, and notably the non-alignment movement following the Bandung Conference in 1955, substantially contributed to the complexities of the scene.[32] Ultimately, the Cold War was not only a series of violent conflicts but also an ongoing battle 'for the hearts and minds'[33], the attempt to counter the enemy's narrative and ideology by a nation's own narrative to not only win over local audiences, but also to legitimate own positions on a global level.

As a result, 'pure' security considerations had to be pinned against programmatic responses in other fields such as humanitarian aid or economic cooperation. As programs were checked against Cold War rationales and legitimate world views, initiatives such as the Colombo Plan (introduced in 1951 by the 'Old' Commonwealth as a scheme for economic relief to help the new members of the organisation) need to be understood as valued tools in the dominions' response to regional challenges of the Cold War.[34] These new challenges resonated heavily with prior difficulties faced by the three countries when integrating the region into their foreign policy frameworks. While only scarce contacts for all three countries had previously existed within Southeast Asia, the Pacific War and subsequent European recolonisation[35] particularly forced Australia and New Zealand to form policies on an area they had previously been unin-

[30] *Eric Andrews*, The Australian Centenary of Defence. Volume 5: The Department of Defence, Melbourne 2001, 140 f.

[31] *Suri*, Cold War, 359.

[32] *Roland Burke*, Decolonization and the Evolution of International Human Rights, Philadelphia 2010, 13–34.

[33] The origins of this term date back to the counter-insurgency campaign by British General Gerald Templer in the Malayan Emergency; *Simon Smith*, General Templer and Counter-Insurgency in Malaya. Hearts and Minds, Intelligence, and Propaganda, in: Intelligence and National Security 16/3, 2001, 60–78; *David H. Ucko*, The Malayan Emergency. The Legacy and Relevance of a Counter-Insurgency Success Story, in: Defence Studies 10/1–2, 2010, 13–39.

[34] See e. g. *Christopher Waters*, A Failure of Imagination: R. G. Casey and Australian Plans for Counter-Subversion in Asia, 1954–1956, in: Australian Journal of Politics & History 45/3, 1999, 347–363; *Peter Gifford*, The Cold War across Asia, in: David Goldsworthy/Peter Edwards (Ed.), Facing North: A Century of Australian Engagement with Asia, Melbourne 2001, 171–219, 174 f.; *David Lowe*, Australia, New Zealand and Cultural Diplomacy in the Cold War: An Unanticipated Consequence of the Colombo Plan for Aid to South and South-East Asia, in: Ian McGibbon/John Crawford (Ed.), Seeing Red: New Zealand, the Commonwealth and the Cold War 1945–91, Wellington 2012, 167–182.

[35] See on Britain's post-war policy in Southeast Asia *Nicholas Tarling*, Britain, Southeast Asia and the Onset of the Cold War, 1945–1950, Cambridge 1998; *Peter Lowe*, Contending with Nationalism and Communism. British Policy Towards Southeast Asia, 1945–65, Basingstoke 2009.

volved with. Following the Second World War, new and old local powers were no longer impaired along a line of indigenous forces opposing foreign powers, but rather an overlap of those two, presenting the area as a postcolonial battleground for conflicts of ideology, society, politics, culture, and 'race'. Above all, racialised prejudices also created hierarchies that deemed some countries as more opposed and inferior to European culture than others.[36] The highly ideologically charged overthrow of traditional power relations not only established the narrative of change, but the perception of political instability also matched traditional prejudices towards the region, leading Western observers to see the area as an uncontrollable threat to their interests.

Most Western fears were linked to the spread of communist ideology and the rise of communist China. When China's communist regime came to power in October 1949, Western allies had to consider how they would approach the new government.[37] The question of recognition was two-fold: Each country had to consider establishing bilateral relations; however, recognition meant also the consideration to admit the People's Republic of China (PRC) to the UN.[38] In both respects, the positions each dominion would eventually take were also determined by their appreciations for the Republic Government of China in Taiwan and the potential power the PRC could exert within Southeast Asia.[39]

Whereas the Soviet Union, the first communist superpower of the Cold War, was linked to Western efforts of resisting communism within Europe, Southeast Asia soon developed in Western eyes as the region where Chinese communism had to be contained.[40] In the following, Chinese influence and support of nationalist movements or insurgencies was perceived as one of the most likely scenarios of threat in the region, with departmental concerns focusing on Chinese minority groups in Southeast Asian countries which could support a subversive communist overthrow.[41] Additionally, these discussions could be linked to long-standing domestic discrimination of Chinese people dating back

36 One example is Papua New Guinea being considered substantially more archaic than its neighbouring Indonesia, *Brad Simpson*, Self-Determination and Decolonization, in: Martin Thomas/Andrew S. Thompson (Ed.), The Oxford Handbook of the Ends of Empire, Oxford 2018, 452–435, 425 f.

37 *Ritchie Ovendale*, The English-Speaking Alliance. Britain, the United States, the Dominions and the Cold War 1945–1951, London 1985, 185–200.

38 *Sandra K. Penrose*, Recognising the People's Republic of China: A Reappraisal of Australian Foreign Policy During the First Menzies Ministry 1950–51, in: Australian Journal of Politics & History 44/2, 1998, 209–224; *Stephen Beecroft*, Canadian Policy towards China, 1949–1957: The Recognition Problem, in: Paul M. Evans/Michael B. Frolic (Ed.), Reluctant Adversaries: Canada and the People's Republic of China 1949–1970, Toronto 1991, 43–72.

39 *Joel Atkinson*, Australian Support for an Independent Taiwan Prior to the Recognition of the People's Republic of China, in: Australian Journal of Politics & History 57/1, 2011, 68–85.

40 *Jim Rolfe*, New Zealand Defence Policy during the Cold War, in: Alexander Trapeznik/Aaron Fox (Ed.), Lenin's Legacy Down Under, Dunedin 2004, 35–56, 39; *Lachlan Strahan*, Australia's China. Changing Perceptions from the 1930s to the 1990s, Cambridge 1996.

41 *Reynolds*, Empire, Region, World, 353.

to the nineteenth century. Preconceptions of communism as ideology were now linked to prejudices of 'race', and thereby only enforced the sense of 'otherness' and enigma attributed to the region.[42] In all three countries, only a few policymakers challenged the strong Eurocentric views in perceptions applied to Asia. Even Canadians described the communist regime as "'the Yellow Peril under red lacquer'".[43]

As a consequence of this biased outlook, ideas of decolonisation and national sovereignty were perceived in an ambivalent perspective. Whilst the post-war governments made tentative approaches to assist new nations, prejudices towards Asia as being underdeveloped and simply different led many policymakers to see continued British colonial rule as desirable, even indispensable, as long as Southeast Asia proved unstable.[44] Equally, anti-colonialist and nationalist movements challenged their ideas of orderly decolonisation, and put especially Australia and New Zealand in an awkward position as being "both colonised and coloniser".[45] Therefore, some policymakers feared larger regional integration would only serve to underline fundamental differences, as New Zealand diplomat Frank Corner wrote in 1953: "We stand only to lose in South East Asia. The more we are known the more we shall be disliked – for our prosperity, for our racial exclusiveness [...], for being white."[46] Tasman officials continued to struggle with the proximity to the region. When the New Zealand Secretary of the Department of External Affairs (NSEA) Alister McIntosh met the Australian Minister for External Affairs (AMEA) Richard Casey and the Australian Secretary of the Department of External Affairs (ASEA) Alan Watt in 1952, both told McIntosh they felt "the breath of South East Asia on their neck".[47]

Linking Southeast Asia to perceptions of 'otherness' and threat, and contrasting this with positive affirmations of their own British-based identity, Australians and New Zealanders perpetuated feelings of racial and cultural superiority and homogeneity.[48] Both countries also continued a 'White' immigration policy to retain, preferably, an Anglo-Saxon community.[49] These restrictive immigration policies also corresponded to the idea of an overpopulating Asia that might

---

42 *Strahan*, Australia's China, 125–128.

43 *Evans*, Engaging China, 21.

44 *Goldsworthy*, Losing the Blanket, 31.

45 *Reynolds*, Empire, Region, World, 349.

46 Frank Corner to Alister McIntosh, 13.7.1953, quoted in: *Ian McGibbon* (Ed.), Unofficial Channels. Letters Between Alister McIntosh and Foss Shanahan, George Laking and Frank Corner; 1946–1966, Wellington 1999, 133–145, 145.

47 ANZ ACIE 8798 W2619 Box 218, 440/7/5, Part 1, Alister McIntosh to Minister of External Affairs Cliffton Webb, 5.5.1952.

48 *Wayne Hudson/Geoffrey Stokes*, Australia and Asia: Place, Determinism and National Identities, in: Geoffrey Stokes (Ed.), The Politics of Identity in Australia, Cambridge 1997, 145–157.

49 *John Ingleson/David Walker*, The Impact of Asia, in: Neville Meaney (Ed.), Under New Heavens: Cultural Transmission and the Making of Australia, Port Melbourne 1989, 287–324.

'swamp' the scarcely populated landmasses of Australia and New Zealand with their sheer surplus of people. For many years, the slogan "populate or perish"[50] successfully linked population and immigration policy to defence.

Some scholars have argued the communist threat helped Australia and New Zealand process the declining European power and the arrival of nationalism in the region, as it served as an antithetical framework to act upon in foreign policy.[51] The combination of racist and anti-communist perceptions was a conservatory power, aimed at the retention of Australian and New Zealand identity as predominantly white and European. The negative image of Asia served to refocus on ties with Britain: It allowed Australia and New Zealand, paradoxically, to cling to their European bonds of culture and history while they sharpened a dissociating view on Asian – especially Southeast Asian – developments. Such attitudes were amplified by the outbreak of the Korean War in June 1950. Despite being geographically outside of Southeast Asia, the conflict contributed to long-standing perceptions of Asian aggression, especially Chinese interference. It cemented attitudes towards Chinese recognition for the following decade and beyond: While all three states had considered Chinese recognition before the conflict, they postponed such a step indeterminately after the war commenced.

The Korean War had further ramifications for the idea of imperial defence among the former dominions. It would be the first and last conflict in the region where they were all militarily committed and united under a Commonwealth command. Although they supported the interdependence of security alliances, Canadian officials had already before opposed the strengthening elements of defence in the Commonwealth. Under Prime Minister William King, Canadian officials were advised to not engage in closer Commonwealth discussions on defence.[52] Early on, they dismissed a reintegration into imperial defence schemes, as Secretary to the Cabinet Arnold Heeney did in 1946: "Imperial Defence as such meant little or nothing to Canada […] Canada was not interested in ar-

[50] See e. g. the speech of Australian Minister of Immigration Arthur Calwell in 1945: "If Australians have learned one lesson from the Pacific War […], it is surely that we cannot continue to hold our island continent for ourselves and our descendants, unless we greatly increase our numbers.", Statement by the Right. Hon. Arthur Calwell in the AHoR, 2.8.1945, CPD, Vol. 31, 4911. In New Zealand, the future Minister of External Affairs Frederick Doidge stated in 1946: "We must be prepared to spend much more money on defence than we have in the past; we must populate for the purpose of strength; if we are to justify our occupation of this lovely land, we must be prepared to hold it against the cramped and hungry millions of the East.", NZPD 3.9.1946, quoted in: *Michael Stenson*, The Origins and Significance of 'Forward Defence' in Asia, in: Alister McIntosh (Ed.), New Zealand in World Affairs: Vol. 1: 1945–1957, Wellington 1977, 177–198, 183.

[51] *Judith Brett*, The Menzies Era, 1950–1966, in: Alison Bashford/Stuart McIntyre (Ed.), The Cambridge History of Australia: Vol. 2: The Commonwealth of Australia, Cambridge 2003, 112–134; *Neville Meaney*, The End of 'White Australia' and Australia's Changing Perceptions of Asia, 1945–1990, in: Australian Journal of International Affairs 49/2, 1995, 171–189, 180.

[52] *Keating*, Canada and World Order, 30; *MacLaren*, Commissions High, 417.

rangements for the defence of Burma and India however necessary they might be to the United Kingdom and to other members of the Commonwealth."[53] On Korea, Canadian officials first opposed participation, but obliged to a commitment after King's death and made subsequent arrangements to be part of a collective UN security effort. However, American pressure and the failure of an UN-based solution implanted doubts about any future military involvement in the area among Canadians that would persist in the following decades.[54]

Despite Canadian reservations, Britain, Australia and New Zealand toyed on several occasions with the inclusion of Canada in a Pacific pact[55], pointing to Canada's Pacific coastline as a marker of responsibility. While being sympathetic to information exchange and the provision of advice on the region, Canadian policymakers actively opposed such ideas, especially those of a security or defence commitment. They underlined that Southeast Asia was laying outside of their strategic framework, as Chief of General Staff Charles Foulkes pointed out in 1953: "Militarily we have no more interest in South East Asia than we would have in a case of communist aggression in Iran or Pakistan. It appears to me then the Canadian interest in the Pacific will really be directed more to the Northern Pacific than to the area around Southeast Asia."[56]

In contrast to Canada's limited security interests in the area, Australia and New Zealand left the Korean War with a strengthened sense of regional strategic interdependence. Adapting the American 'domino theory'[57], both nations framed the Southeast Asian region as vulnerable to communist attack, with policymakers from both countries fearing if one Southeast Asian country should become communist, its neighbours would soon follow, bringing communism sooner than later to their own shores.[58] A prominent example of these convictions was delivered by Australian Minister for Defence (AMD) Philip McBride in September 1954:

"It is a matter of vital importance to maintain the gap between Australia and the present high-water mark of the southward flow of communism. Should this gap narrow, the nature and scale of attack on Australia would become intensified as distance shortened. Finally, should the tide of communism lap on our shores, we would face an intolerable defence burden and a scale of attack which would be beyond our capacity to repel alone.

---

[53] Quoted in: *Francine McKenzie*, In the National Interest: Dominions' Support for Britain and the Commonwealth After the Second World War, in: The Journal of Imperial and Commonwealth History 34/4, 2006, 553–576, 568.

[54] *Norman Hillmer/Jack L. Granatstein*, Empire to Umpire. Canada and the World to the 1990s, Toronto 1994, 213–217.

[55] *McIntyre*, Background to the Anzus Pact, 260–267.

[56] Quoted in: *Robert Bothwell*, Eyes West: Canada and the Cold War in Asia, in: Greg Donaghy (Ed.), Canada and the Early Cold War, 1943–1957: Canada au Début de la Guerre Froide, 1943–1957, Ottawa 1998, 59–70, 67.

[57] For a genealogy of the concept in American thinking that largely related to Australian outlooks see *Ninkovich*, Modernity and Power.

[58] *Radcliffe*, Malaya Bound, 81; *Gifford*, Cold War across Asia, 197.

There is, therefore, every reason strategically and economically why Australia should co-operate to keep aggressive Communism within its present boundaries, and to stem its onward flow."[59]

The region surrounding the peninsula of Malaya was notably seen as vital for any defence strategy, and policymakers linked experiences of the Pacific War to future scenarios of Asian aggression, pointing to the crucial role geography played. In a parliamentary debate in 1954, New Zealand Minister of External Affairs (NMEA) T. C. Webb described Southeast Asia as "stepping stones leading down to Australia and New Zealand".[60] When further conflicts broke out in Malaya, Australian and New Zealand policymakers channelled their security concerns in a policy of forward defence[61] – the political and psychological construction of security by militarily meeting likely conflicts where they would first seem to emerge. Both countries contributed forces under the acronym ANZAM (Australia, New Zealand and Malaya), a joint body for contingency planning established for the region after the Second World War. In 1955, upon the announcement that Australian ground forces would serve under ANZAM in Malaya, Australian Prime Minister Robert Menzies justified this decision as a means to defend Australia "as far from our own soil as possible".[62] Given the limited resources of both countries, the best implementation of this defence conception could only be achieved in alliance with their 'great and powerful friends' Britain and the USA, as Menzies remarked on several occasions.[63] At the same time, officials like New Zealand Prime Minister Sidney Holland legitimised the commitment as essentially "a British thing to do".[64]

Aside from Malaya, Australians and New Zealanders would also align themselves with British and American objectives during the Indochina conflict. Following French decolonisation, the Geneva summit in 1954 was the first international attempt to settle this conflict. While North and South Vietnam were divided along the Seventeenth Parallel, the chance of reunification through elections was planned for 1956. The summit also established the International Commission for Supervision and Control (ICSC), consisting of India, Poland and

---

59 Statement by Philip McBride in AHoR 28.9.1954, quoted in: *Thomas B. Millar*, Australia in Peace and War. External Relations Since 1788, Canberra 1991, 200.

60 Speech by T. C. Webb in the House of Representatives, 6.7.1954, quoted in: *New Zealand Ministry of Foreign Affairs* (Ed.), Statements and Documents, 1943–1957, Wellington 1972, 344–354, 350.

61 *Ian McGibbon*, Forward Defence: The Southeast Asian Commitment, in: Malcolm McKinnon (Ed.), New Zealand in World Affairs: Vol. 2: 1957–1972, Wellington 1991, 9–39.

62 CNIA 26/4 (1955), 279, quoted in: *Gurry*, Identifying Australia's 'Region', 22.

63 See e. g. Robert Menzies in the AHoR, 26.3.1962: "It will be a poor day for Australia if [...] we abandon our [...] great and powerful friends", quoted in: *Derek McDougall*, The Malayan Emergency and Confrontation, in: Carl Bridge (Ed.), Munich to Vietnam. Australia's Relations with Britain and the United States since the 1930's, Carlton 1991, 130–139.

64 Quoted in: *Ian McGibbon*, The Defence of New Zealand 1945–1957, in: Alister McIntosh (Ed.), New Zealand in World Affairs: Vol. 1: 1945–1957, Wellington 1977, 143–176, 169.

Canada, to control the agreed ceasefire in Vietnam, Laos and Cambodia. Incidentally, the Canadian delegation had left the Geneva Conference before the decision for the ICSC was taken, a step that once again symbolised the lack of interest in Southeast Asian affairs.[65] CSSEA Lester Pearson wrote Prime Minister Louis St. Laurent upon departure from Geneva that the Canadian delegation had made its position clear "that we have not, and do not expect to have, any special obligation in respect to Indochina or any special claim or desire to be included in the formal Indochinese Conference".[66] However, other participants at the conference saw Canada as suitable for the role of Western representation, given its lack of colonial past and its limited yet friendly connections to Asia.[67]

As Canadian officials reluctantly accepted the task in the Indochina conflict as one of peacekeeping, Australian and New Zealand counterparts applied a different security concept provided by their cooperation with Britain and the USA. Before and during the Geneva Conference, British and American officials showed interest in conferring with other concerned states on the desirability of security arrangements for Southeast Asia.[68] Australia and New Zealand welcomed this initiative which would ultimately lead to the establishment of SEATO.[69] Canada had watched the establishment of SEATO closely, but dismissed any integration on the ground of its stretched resources in commitments to both NATO and the UN[70], as well as its membership in the ICSC being incompatible with such an alliance.

SEATO bridged, for a moment, the dilemma Australia and New Zealand faced regarding the reconciliation of diverging British and American interests in Southeast Asia. With Thailand, Pakistan and the Philippines, the alliance also

---

65 *James Eayrs*, In Defence of Canada. Vol. 5: Indochina – Roots of Complicity, Toronto 1983, 39–42.

66 LAC RG25 A-3-b, 50273-40, Part 3, quoted in: *Robert Bothwell*, The Further Shore. Canada and Vietnam, in: International Journal of Canadian Studies 51/1, 2000/2001, 89–114, 91.

67 *John W. Holmes*, Canada and the Vietnam War, in: Jack L. Granatstein (Ed.), Canadian Foreign Policy: Historical Readings, Toronto 1986, 198–208, 201.

68 For a closer examination of Anglo-American dealings on Geneva and Indochina see *Philip Hughes*, Division and Discord: British Policy, Indochina, and the Origins of the Vietnam War, 1954–1956, in: Kent Fedorowich/Martin Thomas (Ed.), International Diplomacy and Colonial Retreat, London 2001, 94–112.

69 The Southeast Asia Treaty Organisation (SEATO) followed the signing of the Southeast Asian Collective Defence Treaty in Manila on 8 September 1954. Members of the organisation were the United Kingdom, the United States, France, Australia, New Zealand, Thailand, the Philippines and Pakistan. In addition, Laos, Cambodia and South Vietnam were associated by a protocol as the Geneva Accords did not permit their inclusion into any alliance. *Damien Fenton*, To Cage the Red Dragon. SEATO and the Defence of Southeast Asia, 1955–1965, Singapore 2012.

70 LAC RG25 A-3-b, Vol. 6022, 50273-40, Part 7, "SEADO", Far Eastern Div. Memorandum, 21.10.1954.

included three Asian countries who could discard any recriminations from other Asian states that SEATO was a 'white man's club'. However, the organisation could never shed off allegations of being determined by Western and not regional objectives. Many Southeast Asian states would object to inclusion or even cooperation with the alliance because of its outspoken anti-communist outlook.

SEATO would be the last stone in a chain of Western security alliances stretching from East Asia to Europe in an attempt to contain communism. ANZUS, ANZAM, SEATO, and in a second row NATO and CENTO[71]: The 1950s established regional yet interwoven security frameworks to tackle the aggression of communism and serve the notion of global stability. The pacts contributed to a multilateral approach to, and appreciation of, security concerns in Southeast Asia. In addition, information and intelligence sharing within these alliances adapted to the region in a way that proved not only crucial in the defence context, but for the broader area of foreign policy and global order concepts.[72] In a way, alliance cooperation helped shape and demystify Southeast Asia as a region being largely unknown to the West. However, this mental mapping chiefly took shape through a lens of security interests and threat perceptions.

The strategic and institutional overlaps between the various pacts were in constant debate, yet, except for information sharing, no genuine attempts were made to coordinate strategic interests. In late 1957, British High Commissioner George Mallaby complained about the relative isolation of the pacts: "ANZAM does not talk to the Americans, ANZUS does not talk to the United Kingdom and it is difficult to talk realistically in SEATO."[73] This lack of coordination was deplorable for Australia and New Zealand and, to a lesser degree, Canada, as those alliances served as access to British and American strategic thinking, as well as a security blanket against a communist threat. At the same time, Mallaby's complaints point to the crucial impact of policymakers who moved between the various alliances in a community of like-minded officials. Their relationships, rather than documents and treaties, would underpin the shared framework of security cooperation among the former imperial community in the 1950s and 1960s.

---

71 The Central Treaty Organisation (CENTO) emerged from the Baghdad Pact of 1955 and was an anti-communist Middle Eastern alliance composed of Turkey, Iraq, Iran and Pakistan and backed by Britain; *Michael L. Dockrill*, British Defence Since 1945, Oxford/New York 1989, 54 f.

72 This became even visible in the formerly Eurocentric information framework of NATO where officials began in the late 1950s to consider potential impacts of a 'global Cold War' on the alliance by dealing with extra-European theatres in specific committees and reports, see *Hatzivassiliou*, Out-of-Area.

73 TNA FO 1091/89, BHC Wellington to CRO, 20.12.1957.

2.2 Ministers, Officers, Mandarins – The Expansion and Character of Dominion Policymaking

In his retrospective on Canadian foreign policy published in the late 1990s, former Canadian diplomat Arthur Andrew observed how Canada abolished British ties in the civic culture in the 1950s and 1960s: "[…] oddly enough, it was led by people who had close personal links with the United Kingdom in the form of a British university education – Oxford, Cambridge and the London School of Economics preferred."[74] In retrospect, it seems inconceivable that a group of Canadian officials closely affiliated with Britain could be promoters of nationalist policies. On the other side of the Pacific, a call for closer links with Britain on an institutional level was voiced around the same time. In 1954, Australian public servant Walter Crocker could still propose to make a British person the head of the Australian Department of Extern Affairs (ADEA).[75] Even if this proposal was deemed a bold choice for an independent nation, British involvement or guidance in foreign affairs was not understood as incompatible with Australia's national interests.[76]

For all three countries, the 1950s and 1960s were characterised by institutional indecision between continued British traditions and links within the policymaking sphere, or their diminution or abolition. Most of the issues on British relations which emerged in the external departments stemmed from sustained individual and collective entanglement of policymakers with Britain. Given the density and amplitude of personal affiliations and Anglo-Saxon backgrounds, it makes sense to consider policymakers in the former dominions as a community socialised within the same British orbit. The shared educational and cultural background and joint war experience helped bridge geographical distances between the former colonies and Britain with perceptions of personal closeness, and in some cases resulted in ideas of a transnational emotional community.

As the examples from Canadian and Australian external affairs indicate, it appears this generation of policymakers was on the brink of moving from one frame of mind to another. Therefore, it is worth analysing the different factors influencing the particular framework of diplomatic and political overlaps and connections which characterised the policymaker community discussing British demise during the 1960s. To understand the transition from a British-oriented to a more self-reliant, independent framework of foreign policy, actors and structures are presented which were heavily influenced by elements of British-

---

74 *Andrew*, Middle Power, 27.

75 *Walter Russell Crocker*, Travelling Back. The Memoirs of Sir Walter Crocker, South Melbourne 1981, 192; Sir Walter Crocker (1902–2002), born in South Australia, served in the British Colonial Service and the British Army in the Second World War before entering the Australian diplomatic service.

76 *Gyngell/Wesley*, Australian Foreign Policy, 71 f.

ness in dominion foreign policy. As the previous section illustrated, there were several developments, both in the national as well as the international context, which fused into a specific Australian, Canadian and New Zealand perception of Southeast Asia and surrounding challenges after the Second World War. How did those developments serve, in interaction with a certain collective conscience and departmental structure, to establish an 'official mind'[77] among policymakers on the question of continued allegiance with Britain?

2.2.1 Channels of Diplomacy and Information throughout the Commonwealth

As Australian diplomat William Pritchett recollected, the immediate post-war years symbolised a departure in Australian foreign policy, which was embodied by its policymakers:

> "We were a new generation coming through […] in a rather incoherent way at that time but we didn't have to formulate it. But we had a feeling if not yet a coherent vision of an independent Australia […] making its own mark, establishing a position with the new countries, the nation states of South East Asia and so forth."[78]

Aside from its 'incoherent' formulation, foreign service in the three countries only started to become more independent with their own means of diplomacy and foreign policy. It would also largely remain a field for experts in the 1950s: Little awareness within the public was matched by relatively little political interest – all former dominions held parliamentary debates on foreign policy only once a year.[79] Over the ensuing conflicts in Southeast Asia, they were nevertheless forced to consider their appreciations towards essential geostrategic areas previously uncovered by external affairs. If they had diplomatic links established with the region, they were at most rudimentary, with Britain remaining crucial for the knowledge of and interaction with the area.

This reliance on information and diplomatic representation by Britain prevailed throughout the 1950s. Even if new frameworks such as the Colombo Plan or SEATO demanded their own proper representation in the area, Southeast Asia remained, for large parts, uncovered by Australian, Canadian and New Zealand diplomacy. This was not only a consequence of strained resources, but

[77] An "official mind" encompasses shared ideas, experiences and outlooks among civil servants or other groups of policymakers and therewith creates a certain administrative culture that determines examinations and policy-making, in this case in departments concerned with foreign affairs. For further elaboration on this concept see *Poppy Cullen*, Kenya and Britain After Independence. Beyond Neo-Colonialism, Cham 2017, 11.

[78] NLA TRC 4903, Transcript of Interview with William Pritchett by Garry Woodard, 28.10.2002/4.2.2003, 49.

[79] *Andrew*, Middle Power, 35; *Malcolm Templeton*, Ties of Blood and Empire. New Zealand's Involvement in Middle East Defence and the Suez Crisis, 1947–57, Auckland 1994, 182.

also due to limited political interest or indifference towards departmental calls for independent representation. Former ASEA Arthur Tange recollected the heavy Eurocentric focus he was confronted with during his time as Secretary:

"I'm afraid that the regulatory authorities in government administration were a pretty good mirror of the worst prejudices and the grip of the past that prevailed in Australia in those days. They were men who had been brought up to believe that if you said 'Singapore' you thought of the Union Jack, if you said 'Manila' you thought of the American flag, if you said 'Indo-China' you'd think of a French flag; to them, the centres of Australia's prime interests outside Australia were the great centres of administration or finance – London, Washington, to a lesser extent like-minded people like Canadians, and sometimes New Zealanders."[80]

For him, this outlook clearly stemmed from the British influence:

"It had its impact on our foreign policy, inside the Cabinet Room and right down to the way we conducted our diplomacy and effectiveness, in the Department of External Affairs in Canberra, and in missions abroad. It had its effect on the attitudes and responses of the Defence machine, Chiefs of Staff and their advisers, and many other places."[81]

This was experienced not only by Tange, but also by his British colleague Saville Garner, who recollected how strong the admiration for British material was in the Commonwealth, in both its content and its form.[82] The continued reliance on Britain was justified with the strong confidence and trust regarding British assessments of international affairs and with the difference in resources in the early 1950s as Britain foreign services and posts already employed thousands of personnel.

The daily work with British material and close cooperation perpetuated a strong British outlook in the External Departments.[83] While officials like Tange were aware this close relationship could lead to a bias in opinion, Britain remained the first address to turn to on information and representation. Especially in Southeast Asia, dominion officials continued to praise the work of the British Commissioner-General and his office in Singapore, which served as a linchpin between the diplomatic and military side of the British presence.[84] The strong reliance on British information was primarily evident in Canadian departments. Here, officials received most of the information on the region from London's overseas departments, depicting Asian affairs in a known British set of cultural customs and practices.[85] When the Foreign Office (FO) ceased to draft monthly

80 NLA TRC 1023: Oral History Section. Interview with Arthur Tange by J. D. B. Miller, April 1981, 90 f.

81 Ibid., 109.

82 *Joe Garner*, The Commonwealth Office, 1925–1968, London 1978, 300.

83 Corner in *Templeton*, An Eye, 78 f.

84 For Australian attitudes towards this British institution see e. g. the praises by Australian High Commissioner to Malaya Alan Watt in talks with Canadian official Benjamin Rogers, 5.3.1955, LAC RG25 A-3-b, Vol. 3008, 3534-40.

85 *Bothwell*, Eyes West, 61.

reports that were also shared with Canadians in early 1955, a memo by the Canadian Far Eastern Division deplored the considerable loss of information that could not be covered by other sources from Australia or New Zealand. The note suggested that Canadian information on regions such as Burma, Thailand and Malaya would be inadequate without British guidance.[86]

With a strong reliance on British resources, each country opening their own post therefore meant, in the broadest sense, extending the mental maps officials had of the Southeast Asian area. The expansion of missions in the region during the 1950s resulted from new geopolitical agendas, the desire to become acquainted with formerly unimportant areas, which now mattered from a perspective of long-term policymaking on Southeast Asia. As a potential new theatre of Cold War conflict, the region gained considerable importance inside and in parts outside of the departments. Their individual representation increased regular coverage and conduct of foreign policy within the departments for these countries, as communications between capitals and posts were no longer confined to singular issues such as current political conflicts. Consequently, those diplomatic links served considerably to extend the diplomatic horizon to matters outside the confinement of politics, such as economic growth, culture, social issues, and humanitarian development.

In general, Canada lagged behind in this development compared to Australian and New Zealand diplomacy. This was not only apparent in the limited information on Burma and Thailand they had previously received from London. Little geopolitical interest matched with sparse regional commitments, occasionally leading to the creation of whole (mental) maps on the spot: Upon commitment to the Indochina discussions in 1954, Canadian officials had to purchase a map of the region prior to the conference in Geneva, as they had no previous knowledge of the area.[87] Thanks to the diplomatic expansion of its allies in Southeast Asia throughout the 1950s, Canada could, for some areas, rely on material received from the British High Commission in Ottawa as well as through their channels to Australia and New Zealand.[88] In particular, Canada and New Zealand developed a close relationship on security information, with New Zealand providing Canada with extensive access to material on Southeast Asian security relations. Already in 1958, New Zealand praised Canada "to whom we have passed considerable information on SEATO activities and whose reactions [...] have often weighed heavily in the determination of our attitude".[89] Cana-

[86] LAC RG25 A-3-b, Vol. 4731, 50062-40, Part 3, Memorandum Far Eastern Div. (Menzies), 30.1.1956.

[87] *Adam Chapnick*, Canada's Voice. The Public Life of John Wendell Holmes, Vancouver 2009, 83.

[88] LAC RG25 A-3-b, Vol. 6136, 50397-40, Memorandum Far Eastern Div. (Menzies) to Commonwealth Div., 30.9.1957.

[89] ANZ ABFK W5767 19754 Box 95, 45/1/1, Part 1, NDEA to Posts, 2.10.1958.

dian officials described the relations with the New Zealand DEAs as "so close that it seemed all one had to do was to ask for information and it was forthcoming".[90] At the same time, Canadian officials were overly cautious that gaining information would not imply further commitments, with Ottawa regularly recommending its posts to refrain from anything more than non-committal talks.

For New Zealand, Canada functioned as a traditional ally outside of its other alliances, trustworthy due to their shared history in the empire that was reinforced by Canada's remoteness to issues concerning New Zealand's foreign service. Additionally, they bonded over feelings of being dominated by a dominant neighbour.[91] For Canada, New Zealand was a fellow member of the 'Old' Commonwealth worthy to receive advice because of its minor status. This thought continued into the 1960s when Canadian officials saw potential in a closer relationship with New Zealand. Reporting back to Ottawa in October 1965, Ray Robinson at the Canadian High Commission in Wellington praised the high level of intimacy found between the High Commission and the New Zealand Department of External Affairs (NDEA). At the same time, he urged his superiors to allow a greater flow of information to New Zealand to balance the strong Australian influence, as he saw his post in an "unconscious struggle with the Australians over New Zealand's future foreign policy orientation".[92] To Robinson, New Zealand foreign policy had become inflexible on international affairs and tended to follow a small yet influential pro-Australian group in the NDEA, especially within the Asian Division. Robinson received a fairly flat denial in response to his letter promoting better relations. Canadian officials in Ottawa replied they saw little scope to save New Zealand from "'the Big Bobism'"[93] of Robert Menzies in the long run. Canada's interest in profoundly influencing New Zealand in the period under review was clearly limited; apart from specific personal appreciations and joint approaches under the Commonwealth, both countries did not pursue coordination of foreign policies. One aspect in this limited interest was policy on Southeast Asia, a field where Canadians wanted to stay informed and welcomed discussions, but where closer coordination of policies could have suggested to New Zealanders a deeper interest in an area Canada was not willing to get involved in.

In a similar vein, Canada tried to conduct close information sharing with Australia. Especially AMEA Richard Casey and Canadian Prime Minister Lester Pearson established personal links enabling information-sharing for the purpose of a like-minded policy towards Britain, the USA and international

---

[90] LAC RG25 A-3-b, Vol. 5074, 4533-40, Part 4, Memorandum for File, 29.11.1961.

[91] Frank Corner in *Templeton*, An Eye, 88.

[92] LAC RG25 A-3-c, Vol.10055, 20-1-2-NZ, Ray Robinson (CHC Wellington) to Commonwealth Div., 11.10.1965.

[93] LAC RG25 A-3-c, Vol.10055, 20-1-2-NZ, NDEA to Ray Robinson (CHC Wellington), 23.12.1965.

frameworks such as the UN.[94] However, differences in foreign policy seemed harder to reconcile with Australia than with New Zealand. Particularly when it came to Indochina, Canada, because of its ICSC membership, could not establish close consultation links with Australia.[95] Indeed, relations between both middle powers continued to be rocky, and former Canadian High Commissioner to Australia E. W. T. Gill resumed in 1965 that both geography and "a feeling among Australians that Australia was somehow in competition with Canada"[96] were responsible for the limited interest and contacts between both countries.

Across the Tasman, Australia and New Zealand had already established closer links through their Canberra agreement in 1944. However, Australian officials complained about the disparity in the information exchanged: Whereas Australia could provide New Zealand officials with up to 250 valuable telegrams per week, New Zealanders only made 10–15 telegrams available.[97] At the same time, even the close Tasman cooperation could demonstrate how much inter-dominion relations still lagged behind the predominant reliance on the British connection. When, for example, Richard Casey offered during a meeting with Alister McIntosh to put a New Zealand officer in one of their posts in Southeast Asia, McIntosh was grateful for ASEA Alan Watt to back New Zealand's doubts: "[…] he pointed out that if we stationed an officer with the Australians this might affect our relations with the United Kingdom upon whom we, in common with all British Commonwealth countries, tend to rely in various parts of the world where we had no separate representation of our own."[98] New Zealanders, akin to Australians, still gave priority to their British connection. On occasion, respective media would pick up the idea of shared representation[99], but departments never followed this proposal. Diplomatic representation by Commonwealth partners was still not considered the same as a representation by the British.

2.2.2 Institutions of Commonwealth Cooperation

Arthur Tange, who tried to establish a different, less British focused course for his department during his time as ASEA, made political attitudes responsible for the long hold of a British-oriented foreign policy: "[…] our politicians had

94 See the records of personal correspondence kept in Lester Pearson's Papers, LAC MG26 N1, Vol. 2.

95 See e. g. LAC RG25 A-3-b, Vol. 6023, 50273-40, Part 12, F. Ballachey (Far Eastern Div.) to Don Cornett (CHC Canberra), 21.5.1957.

96 LAC RG25 A-3-c, Vol. 10041, 20-1-2-AUSTL, Commonwealth Div. for File, 1.3.1965.

97 NAA A1838 370/1/19, Part 4, Draft on "Australian-New Zealand Relations", n. d. (1965).

98 ANZ ACIE 8798 W2619, Box 218, 440/7/5, Part 1, Alister McIntosh to NMEA Clifton Webb, 5.5.1952.

99 See e. g. "NZ Diplomatic Services Abroad", Auckland Star, 2.1.1963.

grown up, like all Australians, immersed in British history and concepts of loyalty to the crown and some confusion of mind […] whether loyalty to the Crown was identical with loyalty to the interests of the United Kingdom, and things of that kind."[100] Within the conduct of foreign affairs, the relationship with Britain was still considered the dominions' most valuable asset, and the posts conducting foreign policy with Britain were ranked as the most prestigious.

This was partly caused by the traditional conduct of imperial or Commonwealth affairs established in a set of symbolic practices. High commissioners held the right to direct access to the hosting prime minister, which could result in the circumvention of responsible departments. Commonwealth prime ministers upheld, amongst themselves, contacts in an atmosphere of candidness, intimacy and frankness. This exclusive and symbolically charged access created a framework of its own that was largely sustained by personal relationships, conversely causing frustrations among civil servants and diplomats. In Canada, Prime Minister John Diefenbaker did not share letters from British Prime Minister Harold Macmillan with the Canadian Department of External Affairs (CDEA) because he believed them to be genuinely private. Faced with similar attitudes among some political appointees to the High Commission in London, civil servants within the CDEA felt that they could not develop a full perspective on relations with Britain.[101] With these complications, similarly experienced in Australia and New Zealand policymaking, the prime minister remained in a pivotal position to deal with Britain. Aside from his exclusive access, it was also due to strong anglophile preferences in the political elite in all three countries as well as the continuous influence of the prime minister in the decision-making, which sustained a British-oriented foreign policy.

The symbolical dimension of 'British' foreign affairs found its peak in the annual Commonwealth prime ministers' meetings. Usually held in London, Commonwealth leaders would engage in discussions of world affairs and used the meetings to foster bilateral relations. Most prime ministers emphasised the cordiality, frankness and informality of these and other Commonwealth gatherings, setting them aside from other international conferences.[102] As Saville Garner had described it for the early 1950s, the Commonwealth prime ministers' meetings were held in the office of Downing Street No. 10, restricted in

100 NLA TRC 1023: Oral History Section. Interview with Arthur Tange by J. D. B. Miller, April 1981, 110.

101 Diefenbaker as well as some High Commissioners such as George Drew shared a mistrust for the civil servant staff in foreign policy, therewith complicating working relationships, *George Ignatieff*, The Making of a Peacemonger. The Memoirs of George Ignatieff, Toronto 1985, 173; *Henry B. Robinson*, Diefenbaker's World. A Populist in World Affairs, Toronto 1989, 34–38; *John F. Hilliker/Donald Barry*, Canada's Department of External Affairs. Vol. 2: Coming of Age, 1946–1968, Montreal 1995, 158.

102 *McKenzie*, In the National Interest, 558 f.

size (not more than 30 people) and without a fixed agenda.[103] Both space and practice of the meetings therefore symbolically condensed the exclusiveness, informality and intimacy among Commonwealth leaders.

Various examples can be found among Commonwealth prime ministers that returned from such meetings as ardent supporters of the organisation. Having no previous deeper affiliations with Britain, John Diefenbaker experienced his first trip to London to attend the Commonwealth Prime Ministers Meeting as a "pilgrimage"[104], and many perceived his pro-British course endorsed back in Canada as a direct consequence of the trip. There is an argument to assume that the rituals and practices involved in the Commonwealth meetings could develop a high symbolical value as a representation of what the Commonwealth and the British relationship was. Attending a Commonwealth meeting could be a rite de passage, a moment of conversion even for later critics such as Pierre Trudeau and Gough Whitlam, who returned as promoters of Commonwealth ideas and values from such meetings.

While not all of them engaged in foreign affairs with the same enthusiasm[105], most of the prime ministers in the decades after the war perceived the British relationship as a personal matter and secured themselves a strong influence on these prestigious affairs. Although they represented their own country in the world, the close affiliation with Britain led prime ministers in all three countries to frame their role and identity within a British framework. In this regard, the most prominent example is Robert Menzies, who described himself as "British to the bootheels".[106] Menzies' ardent support of Britain and his Anglophilia has been the object of many studies which have analysed his behaviour as imperial nostalgia, outdated and contradictory for a time where Australia had to look after its own interests.[107] However, recent studies have shown Menzies' foreign policy was not a blind following of the British, but rather an assessment of benefits and necessities of the alliance with Britain.[108] These benefits were not only confined to strategies of foreign affairs and defence, but also resonated with a psychological need for shared outlooks and identities.[109] At the same time, Menzies' state of mind corresponded to that of his Canadian and New

---

[103] *Garner*, Commonwealth Office, 296 f.

[104] *Robinson*, Diefenbaker's World, 60.

[105] One example is New Zealand Prime Minister Sidney Holland who asked the NDEA, while still being leader of opposition, to make a "'survey of the entire world scene' on not more than a page", *McIntyre*, Background to the Anzus Pact, 7.

[106] *Bell*, Dependent Ally, 62.

[107] *Gregory Pemberton*, An Imperial Imagination: Explaining the Post-1945 Foreign Policy of Robert Gordon Menzies, in: Frank Cain (Ed.), Menzies in War and Peace, St. Leonards 1997, 154–175.

[108] *Bongiorno*, Price of Nostalgia.

[109] See for a thorough analysis of Menzies' adjustment to and mediation of international transformations *Stephanie Brookes*, Politics, Media and Campaign Language. Australia's Identity Anxiety, London/New York 2017, 47–52.

Zealand counterparts. As new Prime Minister in Canada, John Diefenbaker engaged in a revival episode of Canadian-British relations[110]; and New Zealand Prime Minister Sidney Holland perceived foreign policy as "what the British Government said it was".[111]

Another contemporary of Robert Menzies, Canadian Prime Minister Lester B. Pearson, appeared to stand at the other end of the political spectrum. Being a former diplomat himself, his state of mind corresponded more to departmental traditions of internationalism and liberalism, and it is not a surprise that his term as Prime Minister was seen as a relief by the CDEA staff. At the same time, Pearson and his generation can be seen as border-crossers within a transformative period linked to their Anglo-Saxon identity. In the words of Canadian historian C. P. Champion, Pearson represented a generation of like-minded officials whose "psyche incorporated pro- and anti-British elements, enthusiasm for the best in the English liberal inheritance alongside a scepticism towards elements of the British legacy that they deemed to be backward".[112] The doubt towards outdated British institutions explains why this generation might have engaged in the abolition of British ties – most prominently depicted in the Canadian abolition of the Red Ensign in 1964/65[113] –, despite their close personal relationship, as stated at the beginning of this section. Yet Pearson's support for a sustained close connection to Britain becomes apparent in a 1957 reply to a Canadian citizen, Kathleen White, who criticised Canada's link to the Crown and Canadians being described as British subjects.[114] Pearson replied that allegiance to the Queen "does not detract in any way from our Canadianism […] In short, to be true Canadian and proud of our own country, I do not think it is necessary or desirable to deny our historic links with the United Kingdom".[115] Ultimately, Pearson belonged to the same generation as Robert Menzies, who was brought up in the Empire and 'Old' Commonwealth and who did not perceive Canadian/Australian and British markers of identity as incompatible.

The conduct of intimate Commonwealth relations was not confined to the level of prime ministers, as other policymakers also endorsed the practices of frankness, trust, and close consultation. In 1960, Canadian diplomat John Hadwen described the advantages of the Commonwealth forum: "[…] that the political leaders and the officials of Commonwealth countries are almost invariably able to establish close, friendly and useful relationships with their Common-

110 *Stuart Ward*, Worlds Apart: Three "British" Prime Ministers at Empire's End, in: Phillip Buckner/R. D. Francis (Ed.), Rediscovering the British World, Calgary 2005, 399–420, 402.

111 George Laking in *Templeton*, An Eye, 52.

112 *Champion*, Strange Demise, 94.

113 On the Canadian flag debate see *Igartua*, Other Quiet Revolution, 171–192.

114 LAC RG25 A-3-b, Vol. 6613, 11142-40, Letter to Lester Pearson by Kathleen White (Victoria, BC), 1.1.1957.

115 LAC RG25 A-3-b, Vol. 6613, 11142-40, Lester Pearson to Kathleen White, 9.1.1957.

wealth colleagues wherever and whenever they meet."[116] Here, the Commonwealth was perceived as a community of like-minded states, with policymakers looking at fellow Commonwealth nations for support on specific initiatives. This idea of like-mindedness did not necessarily stem from similar approaches to specific issues but from the idea that both a shared set of principles and an adherence to shared values within the Commonwealth would allow a particular closeness. One Canadian memo drafted for Diefenbaker's 'Commonwealth Tour' in 1958, ranked those shared norms as a common interest in a) "acceptance of a general political philosophy," b) "desire for peace," c) "renunciation of aggression," d) "opposition to aggression from other sources" and e) "settlement of international disputes by negotiation and legal procedure". It concluded: "[…] those who are not concerned in its practice do not realise how close Commonwealth governments can be to each other by these various means and how valuable this contact is."[117] In New Zealand, Prime Minister Walter Nash highlighted what can be understood as the core argument for Britishness in foreign affairs. While presenting on the Commonwealth, Nash underlined the "*naturalness* of the Commonwealth link"[118] as the vital element of the organisation. Like him, Menzies and other leaders constantly stressed the organic, informal character of the community.[119]

On many occasions, this characterisation was used to create a sense of identity that distinguished the Commonwealth from other organisations. It could also create a Commonwealth identity within other organisations such as the UN, where the Commonwealth even held a joint non-permanent seat in the Security Council until 1965. Here, regular meetings were held under the principle of consultation; officials exchanged information and ideas but did not object to national variances in foreign policy.[120] To the former dominions, these spaces of cooperation helped develop their own perspectives on foreign policy. When it came to conflicts of international impact, all three countries were part of the Western bloc whose implications were strengthened by the special relationship of the Anglosphere.

In this realm, in contrast to limited contacts in other fields, Australia and Canada could establish a working relationship based on their middle power status. Despite earlier differences, officials like John Holmes or Paul Hasluck remembered "a certain Canadian-Australian community of feeling"[121] in the

[116] John Hadwen: "The Commonwealth in 1960", quoted in: *Lloyd*, Diplomacy With a Difference, 183.

[117] LAC RG25 A-3-b, Vol. 7824, 12687-A-40, Draft for Diefenbaker's Commonwealth Tour, n. d. (Nov 1958).

[118] *Walter Nash*, A New Zealand View, in: The English-Speaking World XLII/4, July 1960, 23–25, 24 (emphasis in original).

[119] *Goldsworthy*, Losing the Blanket, 22 f.; *Ward*, Worlds Apart, 401.

[120] *Lloyd*, Diplomacy With a Difference, 185 f.

[121] Paul Hasluck quoted in: *Cooper*, Keeping in Touch, 255.

cooperation that would benefit from strands of internationalism in both foreign services. Joint internationalism produced even stronger ideas of shared outlooks between Canada and New Zealand, fusing into a myth-producing narrative of international idealism.[122] The idea of being a 'good citizen of the world'[123] drew both countries, Canada arguably more than New Zealand, into initiatives of peacekeeping. In the 1960s, topics including disarmament, self-determination and humanitarian relief would begin to contribute further to this moral strand in foreign policy.

2.2.3 A Community of Britons among the Policymakers

The continued and close conduct of affairs with Britain was based not only on a set of customs but also on convictions officials had developed from collective experiences: through foreign policy structures of all three nations and through relationships forged by the Second World War. Many of the dominion policymakers had personal links to the military and strategic institutions of the World Wars, either by serving in the armed forces, or on allied councils that focused on the planning of the war effort.[124] Those experiences could serve as a stabilising factor in the following conduct of foreign affairs: Given the changed settings after the war, experiences of imperial war cooperation were often used as a contrasting lens to the uncertainties posed by the Cold War. Consequently, many security or defence issues in relations with Britain and the Commonwealth were checked against this experience, pointing either to the narrative of a joint strenuous war effort, or the allegiance shown by the old colonies to its former 'mother country'.

In addition, given the relatively young history of settlement and the predominant British migration to all three countries, most policymakers were linked by their British background. The selective mechanisms of professional and political advancement, restricting the diplomatic service and spheres of policy to a predominantly white, male, Anglo-Saxon group, had a similar peer group effect.[125] Many of these actors also came from similar educational backgrounds

[122] Frank Corner in *Templeton*, An Eye, 87 f.; *Adam Chapnick*, The Canadian Middle Power Myth, in: International Journal 55, 2000, 188–206.

[123] *Robert Bothwell*, Canada's Moment: Lester Pearson, Canada and the World, in: Norman Hillmer (Ed.), Pearson, the Unlikely Gladiator, Montreal 1999, 19–29, 19.

[124] As described by David Lowe for the Australian Parliament, *David Lowe*, Menzies and the 'Great World Struggle'. Australia's Cold War, 1948–1954, Sydney 1999, 368.

[125] Regarding indigenous officers, only one prominent figure, the New Zealand High Commissioner to Malaya Charles Bennett, stands out in this analysis as an exemption of individual indigenous success. His integration into the foreign service was accompanied by a lot of prejudices and criticism, visible in communications between Alister McIntosh and Bennett; McIntosh papers in NLNZ MS-Papers-6759-224. An equal issue arose over the integration of French officers in Canada. In the CDEA, the bicultural background of Canadian so-

and had spent some time in Britain, during military service and/or during their education.[126]

As Canadian historian Robert Bothwell has pointed out, "it was both an internationalizing (perhaps the term should be 'de-provincializing') and nationalizing experience"[127] to go to Britain. To dominion officials, this experience often made them aware of their distinct, yet British-linked, national identity for the first time.[128] As former diplomat Arnold Heeney remembered in the early 1970s, his studies in Oxford in the interwar years served to underline both his Canadian background as well as his affiliation with Britain: "Although we remained loyal to the crown and attached to the old country, we were determined to be free of the vestiges of colonialism."[129] Lester Pearson made a similar assessment in 1940: "I have more than once been struck by the fact that some of our more ardent nationalists are Oxford graduates who find it quite easy to reconcile their Canadian nationalism with a devotion to Oxford."[130]

Again, a sense of nationalism did not conflict with a sense of Britishness. Being brought up in both structures, back home and in Britain, could mean a sense of community and equality that allowed a more balanced approach to the former 'mother country', as Richard Casey's biography demonstrates. Casey was educated in Cambridge and served as the first liaison officer for Australia in London during the 1920s and the Second World War.[131] In contrast to many of his Cabinet colleagues, Casey's sense of belonging to Britain did not result in a blind devotion based on a sense of inferiority.[132] To British colleagues, Casey "embodied a certain paradox [...] in his outward appearance and to some degree in tastes, associates and instincts he was more European, more British than most Australians in politics at that time. [...] He was, nevertheless, a great

ciety was not resembled in the staff structure, 1953 saw only 13.4 percent French Canadians in top positions in the public service; *Jack L. Granatstein*, The Ottawa Men. The Civil Service Mandarins 1935–1957, Toronto 1998, 5. Equally, restrictions prevented female officers to establish themselves. In the all three countries, female public servants had been allowed to serve since the 1940s, but had to give up their position upon marriage. *Peter Edwards*, Prime Ministers and Diplomats. The Making of Australian Foreign Policy; 1901–1949, Melbourne 1983, 105.

[126] For a collective biography on Canadian mandarins up to 1957 see *Granatstein*, Ottawa Men; on Australia see *Edwards*, Prime Ministers and Diplomats.

[127] *Bothwell*, Canada's Moment, 20.

[128] See for an illustration *Champion*, Strange Demise, 60–68.

[129] *Heeney*, Things that Are Caesar's, 14.

[130] Quoted in *Champion*, Strange Demise, 118.

[131] *Laurence McIntyre*, Reflections on Australian Diplomacy, in: Peter J. Boyce/J. R. Angel (Ed.), Independence and Alliance: Australia in World Affairs 1976–80, Sydney 1983, 311–319, 311.

[132] *W. J. Hudson*, The Suez Crisis of 1956, in: Carl Bridge (Ed.), Munich to Vietnam. Australia's Relations with Britain and the United States since the 1930's, Carlton 1991, 114–129, 120 f.; *Thomas B. Millar/Richard Gardiner Casey* (Ed.), Australian Foreign Minister. The Diaries of R. G. Casey, 1951–60, London 1972, 10.

and independent Australian patriot."[133] Casey's biography resembled in some ways many of those of his generation. Another example is the Canadian Arnold Smith, the later Commonwealth Secretary-General, who served in the British public service during the Second World War.[134]

Professionals from the three countries could enter British institutions and ranks just as the British could still represent Australian, Canadian and New Zealand interests in certain forums. For one, this was made possible by a shared institutional upbringing. With little own academic structures, officials attained their higher university degrees mostly still from Oxford and Cambridge. Some public servants also took leave to spend time at the Imperial Defence College in London.[135] In 1950, 27 percent of the Canadian Foreign Service officers had been educated in Britain.[136] On occasion, this personal background even occurred among fellow diplomats or politicians from the larger Anglosphere; for example, Dean Acheson, who was of Canadian descent, or Dean Rusk, who was Oxford-educated and a Rhodes Scholar.[137]

There were British who worked in the dominion services and ministries and vice-versa, Canadians, Australians or New Zealanders worked in the British counterparts. Well into the 1960s, one could find, especially in the military services, officials of British origin in dominion departments. A prominent example of this continued practice was the New Zealand Chief of Naval Staff position held by a British national until the late 1950s.[138] This state of affairs was seldom questioned, although it caused confusion sometimes. In 1957, the Canadian High Commission in Wellington reported about New Zealand frustrations that their representative, Rear-Admiral J. E. H. McBeath, had misrepresented their position and merely followed the British position. However, he was not suspected of deliberately having done so: "Probably he had simply failed to appreciate its different emphasis. He was British and therefore might be expected to give more weight to United Kingdom views than a New Zealander."[139]

Even as all three countries lessened the immigration regulations after the war to accept new immigrant groups, the ethnic background of British descent was simply replaced by a more value-based understanding of being British, pointing to "a set of universal political and legal values such as responsible government, liberty, property, and jury trial in the British-Atlantic world – the 'rights

---

133 *Peter Alexander Rupert Carrington*, Reflect on Things Past. The Memoirs of Lord Carrington. 2. publ., London 1988, 117.

134 *David McIntyre*, Canada and the Creation of the Commonwealth Secretariat, 1965, in: International Journal 53/4, 1998, 753–777, 774 f.

135 E. g. George Ignatieff from the Canadian Staff in the early 1950s, *Ignatieff*, Making of a Peacemonger, 120.

136 *Andrew*, Middle Power, 57.

137 *Bothwell*, Canada's Moment, 25 f.; *McIntyre*, Background to the Anzus Pact, 46 f.

138 Frank Corner in *Templeton*, An Eye, 119.

139 LAC RG25 A-3-b, Vol. 4768, 50073-A-40, CHC Wellington, 17.9.1957.

and liberties of Englishmen'".[140] If officials did not attend studies in Britain, they were, nevertheless, brought up in Australian, Canadian and New Zealand institutions, which often based their structures and premises on British models. The external affairs departments could draw on a specific ethos of objectivity and principle because of their British background rooting in the Westminster system.[141] To take this argument further, officials like Walter Crocker could claim that a British official would fit as Head of Department because of the adaptability of similar structures.

Given the overall constant British influence on the institutional and informational framework in all three countries, it made sense to describe the policymakers as "more a nation of engineers than architects"[142], being more adoptive of British ideas and institutions than aiming at a distinct national foreign policy administration made from scratch. In the last resort, this adaption of British foreign policy style was supported by policymaking networks of other institutions established during imperial times. Lead examples are the respective Institutes of International Affairs which dealt with a professional, non-governmental examination of foreign policy. They cooperated closely with the departments and in the flow of information and professionals.[143]

The structure and outlook of the various institutions resulted in different degrees of closeness to the British counterparts, not only among the former dominions, but also on a national level. While the external departments slowly evolved a more self-reliant outlook, defence departments and armed services held a stronger rapport with British military institutions.[144] On the one hand, this can be explained by the strong influence on shared outlooks by war experiences; on the other, one can think of the impact of military traditions on shared identities. After 1945, peacetime cooperation upheld the feeling of community within military circles. The establishment of liaison offices within the Commonwealth allowed close contact on military planning. Moreover, the staff cooperation in alliances such as NATO, ANZAM and SEATO established a network of regular contacts. Ultimately, the various commitments to Asia were often served by the same group of service members, with Australian, British and New Zealand officers serving together in the allied forces in Japan and Korea collaborating again in Malaysia and Singapore. "The training, doctrine, organisation, and outlook of the three national groups had so much in common that service together and under one another's command raised no significant problems."[145]

---

140 *Champion*, Strange Demise, 58.

141 *Woodard*, Ministers and Mandarins, 79.

142 *Trood*, Australian Diplomatic Practice, 101.

143 *Priscilla Roberts*, Tweaking the Lion's Tail: Edgar J. Tarr, the Canadian Institute of International Affairs, and the British Empire, 1931–1950, in: Diplomacy & Statecraft 23, 2012, 636–659; *James Cotton*, The Australian School of International Relations, New York 2013, 7–11.

144 *Preston/Wards*, Military and Defence Developments, 13.

145 *Thomas B. Millar*, Anglo-Australian Partnership in Defence of the Malaysian Area, in:

The rapid expansion and professionalisation of external affairs departments in all three countries after the Second World War gave way to traditional scholarly praise for the work of diplomats and civil servants. The three countries' post-war governments are celebrated for establishing an independent foreign service and inducing a certain esprit de corps.[146] Combined with the international success and relative influence enjoyed particularly in the period of establishment of the UN, the early decades of dominion foreign service are often presented as a founding myth. Specifically in Canada, later generations of diplomats and historians perceived this era as one of golden diplomacy motivated by idealistic and independent internationalism, symbolised in achievements such as Pearson's Nobel Peace Prize.[147] The foreign policy established and undertaken in the late 1940s up to the early 1950s seemed to define a picture of how the respective national foreign policy and diplomacy should be presented.

However, such a perception turns a blind eye to the shortcomings officials were still struggling with, since they only just commenced establishing a foreign policy for themselves while adjusting to a declining British or imperial frame of reference. These difficulties are visible among these policymakers on the brink, like Richard Casey. Casey, "an indefatigable champion for better understanding of Asian views and problems"[148], was known within and outside the Commonwealth for promoting better relations with Southeast Asia.[149] However, in 1956, Canadian High Commissioner to Australia Arthur Irwin reported on confusing talks with Richard Casey, who had shared with him his concerns that the current British government would clinch to an empire gone by, making it impossible to foot its presence and relations within Asia on a fresh, positive approach. Given that Casey also struggled with the bad state of relations Australia upheld with some countries, most notably India, Irwin believed Casey was "a considerably frustrated man", torn between an imperial and post-imperial outlook:

> "My reading is that one part of him knows that the current Australian approach to Asia is inadequate and would like to do something concrete about putting it on a more effective basis. Another part of him, however, is still emotionally, and to some extent intellectually, nostalgically involved in the colonial era. This makes it difficult for him to really face up to the implications of the passing of that era."[150]

A. F. Madden/W. H. Morris-Jones/Kenneth Wheare (Ed.), Australia and Britain: Studies in a Changing Relationship, Sydney 1980, 71–89, 78.

[146] See for New Zealand the recollections by George Laking and Frank Corner in *Templeton*, An Eye; for Canada *Granatstein*, Ottawa Men.

[147] *Cooper*, Keeping in Touch, 250 f.; *Greg Donaghy*, Introduction, in: Greg Donaghy (Ed.), Canada and the Early Cold War, 1943–1957: Canada au Début de la Guerre Froide, 1943–1957, Ottawa 1998, 14–29, 20 f.

[148] LAC RG25 A-3-b, Vol. 6865, 4533-40, CHC Canberra 31, 14.1.1960.

[149] *Craig Mclean*, R. G. Casey and Australian Foreign Policy. Engaging with China and Southeast Asia, 1951–1960, Melbourne 2008, PhD Thesis.

[150] LAC RG25 A-3-b, Vol. 4731, 50062-40, Part 3, Irwin (CHC Canberra) to Pearson, 28.3.1956.

According to Irwin, Casey was capable, because of his exceptional knowledge of Asian affairs, to estimate the inadequacy of politics applied to the region. However, his roots within an imperial, colonial mindset prevented him from grasping the chances of a more independent, less British-oriented foreign policy. Irwin's impression was matched by Canadian reports on a visit Casey made to Wellington a few years later, where he gave the impression to be very pessimistic about relations with Asian countries, confessing "that he felt like rolling up the map of Asia and putting it behind the cupboard".[151]

In his reply to Irwin in 1956, Pearson described Casey's difficulties in coming to terms with a transformation of the British world as universal since he saw many Commonwealth officials struggle with the implications of a demise of British rule in Asia. To Pearson, Canadians were simply lucky in their geographical distance to an emerging Asia: "[…] we never feel in our bones the fears and anxieties which Australians must have when they look towards their Near North."[152]

As this correspondence indicates, officials from both sides could be aware of the mental maps framing their perceptions, both of the former British Empire and the Southeast Asian region. From Pearson's perspective, Casey was stuck in his perceptions of Asia as a former imperial space, both as results of his British outlook and the challenging proximity of Asia. However, the adjustment to the changes both in the British world and in Southeast Asia could not be easily transferred into new mental maps, as those rested both on geopolitical and cultural codes that were formed by upbringing, personal experience and – in the case of policymakers – professional culture. Most of the changes in the individual and collective outlook influencing the ensuing discussions on the British retreat from the region resulted from the administrative opening to the region in the 1960s. In all three countries, diplomats with a background of serving in Southeast Asia started to challenge the traditional British lens on foreign policy, contesting perceptions on the region as prefabricated by ignorance or lack of knowledge. They were supported by policymakers who were similarly willing to challenge the preconceived idea of a British worldview on other foreign policy areas, including their relationship with Britain itself.

Concurrently, discussions of a British retreat permitted these changes in mental maps as well. As the following analysis will show, the debates on Britain's withdrawal East of Suez influenced and corresponded to the changing perceptions among policymakers of a (former) British connection and developments in Southeast Asia.

---

151 LAC RG25 A-3-b, Vol. 6136, 50397-40, CHC Wellington (Heasman), 5.9.1958.

152 LAC RG25 A-3-b, Vol. 4731, 50062-40, Part 3, Pearson to Irwin (CHC Canberra), 25.4.1956.

Part 3

Waiting for a Crisis? The Anticipation of a British Retreat from Southeast Asia, 1956–1965

"[...] for in those days we thought, still, in terms of a British orbit."[1]

Both their departures for alternative security frameworks and altered professional outlooks were only tentative attempts of policymakers among the former dominions to adjust to the pressing changes after the Second World War, particularly to the British demise as a world power. Having left the war heavily damaged in economic and financial terms, Britain now relied on the help of its allies.[2] While it struggled with a notorious balance of payment deficit and an economy damaged by the war effort, British policymakers were also faced with complex issues over its colonial territories. Whether it was the hasty retreat from India in 1947 or the reintroduction of colonial rule in Southeast Asia, the immediate post-war years only presaged the difficulties of finding appropriate ways of transition or continued colonial rule experienced in the following decades.

Nevertheless, British officials and politicians continued to support the idea of Britain as a world power.[3] As Churchill had described it in 1948, Britain perceived its role in the post-war era as one situated in three interlocking circles, linking the European, Atlantic and Commonwealth alliance.[4] With its extraordinary capacities of the different foreign offices in London, Britain remained the best informed global actor across numerous fields, and thus exceptional at mediating issues between various institutions and organisations. Despite its continuous economic difficulties, many officials – not only in London but also in the dominions – could still look at Britain's place in the world as a metropolis representing and interlocking different communities of interest.[5]

---

1 Former British High Commissioner to Australia Lord Carrington referring to trips he made to Malaya during his time in Canberra; *Carrington*, Reflect on Things Past, 140.

2 *McKenzie*, In the National Interest, 554.

3 *George C. Peden*, Recognising and Responding to Relative Decline. The Case of Post-War Britain, in: Diplomacy & Statecraft 24/1, 2013, 59–76.

4 *McIntyre*, Background to the Anzus Pact, 35.

5 *Michael Kandiah/Gillian Staerck*, 'At the Top Table': British Elites' Perceptions of the UK's International Position, 1950–91, in: J. Young/E. Pedaliu/M. Kandiah (Ed.), Britain in Global Politics Volume 2: From Churchill to Blair. 2. publ., London 2014, 179–197, 182 f.

Such a British intermediary role was also advocated for Southeast Asia, not only by British officials, but also by its allies, not least because the Cold War established new rationalities for a continued British presence in the area. Here, Britain continued to exert colonial power, on the one hand, because it feared a communist overturn of many countries after their independence, and on the other hand because it believed that many of them were too weak to become independent.[6] This attitude was also translated into a new belief that the Commonwealth could serve Britain as a tool to mediate its power globally, to assist decolonisation and to offer a third perspective to the dual superpower structure of the Cold War. Now, the British civilising mission was transferred into the idea of 'gradual transition', which should leave enough time to establish a stable, meaning British-oriented, postcolonial order.[7]

Despite all this support for a revival of its imperial role, due to the impact of the Second World War, Britain could only stay in the region with American backing.[8] Although American and British policies on Southeast Asia showed some frictions early on, American officials valued the British as much for their information as for their shared outlooks defined by a common set of values and standards.[9] In the ideologically charged atmosphere of the Cold War, the Anglo-American 'special relationship' meant strong support for the 'Free World' in opposition to the communist bloc.

Similarly, the former dominions welcomed Britain's altered yet essentially continued role as a world power. Given their status as former settler colonies, naturally, they followed the British post-war recovery closely. At the same time, they continued on the path of more substantial independence taken up before the war. Between 1946 and 1948, all three countries adopted national citizenship acts, making their citizens Canadians, Australians and New Zealanders before being declared British subjects.[10] But while all three had introduced the citizenship acts as their own decisions, it was less of a desire to distinguish their citizens from Britain than the new demands of the Commonwealth that brought the acts into being. Similar motives and measures backed the abolition of the dominion title and other colonial references in the late 1940s and early

---

6 *John Darwin*, Britain's Withdrawal East of Suez, in: Carl Bridge (Ed.), Munich to Vietnam. Australia's Relations with Britain and the United States since the 1930's, Carlton 1991, 140–158, 142 f.; *Hyam*, Britain's Declining Empire, 95.

7 *Darwin*, British Decolonization, 188 f.

8 *Christopher Alan Bayly/Timothy N. Harper*, Forgotten Wars. The End of Britain's Asian Empire, London 2007, 519 f.

9 *Ursula Lehmkuhl*, Pax Anglo-Americana. Machtstrukturelle Grundlagen anglo-amerikanischer Asien- und Fernostpolitik in den 1950er Jahren, München 1999, 14.

10 *Lorna Lloyd*, Britain and the Transformation from Empire to Commonwealth. The Significance of the Immediate Post-War Years, in: The Round Table 86/343, 1997, 333–360, 339; *John Chesterman*, Natural-Born Subjects? Race and British Subjecthood in Australia, in: Australian Journal of Politics & History 51/1, 2005, 30–39, 34.

1950s.[11] The dominions also accepted the change of Commonwealth membership terms to include members such as India.[12]

At the same time, these steps fell in line with what New Zealand historian James Belich described as the "recolonisation" of the first half of the twentieth century when New Zealand aimed at the "tightening of relations between 'metropolis' and periphery after an era of mass settlement".[13] Rather than abolishing British ties after their independence, the dominions perceived the transformations within and outside the former Empire as warranting continued cooperation with Britain. The scope and extent of this recolonisation is more negotiable in the case of Australia and Canada than in New Zealand. But without a doubt, all three countries committed to the Commonwealth as a means of continuing close collaboration and maintaining links with Britain. After all, the continued cooperation was not only warranted by economic and strategic interests, but also by a solid British outlook of all three settler societies. Post-war polls in Australia indicated that the majority of the population perceived itself as British and supported the continued alliance with the former 'mother country'.[14] Canada competed with the other two dominions for British migrants after the war[15], and in New Zealand, many still referred to Britain as 'home', and to their country as "little Britain of the South Seas".[16]

As it essentially reinstated colonial rule with American backing after the Second World War, Britain continued to struggle over demands of economic recovery and global decolonisation, which increasingly affected its military position in Southeast Asia. From the aftermath of the Suez Crisis in 1956 until the secession of Singapore from Malaysia in August 1965, British officials expressed their concerns over the future of their presence in Southeast Asia in three sets of arguments: First, they claimed that the British overstretch in resources made

---

[11] *Jenny Carlyon/Diana Morrow*, Changing Times. New Zealand since 1945, Auckland 2013, 48 f.; *Meaney*, Britishness and Australia, 129 f.

[12] Both Britain and the dominions invested in the continued membership of India in the Commonwealth because of its political importance, above all because officials believed in a mediating Indian role in the ideological struggle of the Cold War. The concessions made to India were not granted in concurrent discussions on Burmese membership after the country had become a republic. As a result, Burma left the Commonwealth in 1948. Lorna *Lloyd*, Diplomacy With a Difference, 129 f.

[13] *Belich*, Paradise Reforged, 11.

[14] *Mark McKenna*, The Captive Republic. A History of Republicanism in Australia, 1788–1996, Cambridge 1996, 217; *Trevor Matthews/John Ravenhill*, Adrift in an Alien Sea? Australian Perspectives on the World, in: Richard W. Baker (Ed.), Australia, New Zealand, and the United States. Internal Change and Alliance Relations in the ANZUS States, New York 1991, 159–182, 166.

[15] *Phillip Buckner*, The Long Goodbye. English Canadians and the British World, in: Phillip Buckner/R. D. Francis (Ed.), Rediscovering the British World, Calgary 2005, 181–208, 199 f.; *Igartua*, Other Quiet Revolution, 54 f.

[16] *Carlyon/Morrow*, Changing Times, 49.

the massive defence spending related to their East of Suez position hard to justify. While being induced by economic necessities, the withdrawal argument gained a strong political impetus from the implications of a diminished British power status that would affect its world role and position in alliances such as the Commonwealth. Second, they pointed to the general instability of the Southeast Asian area and claimed that continued presence could draw them into regional conflicts, or could even cause them. In detail, this argument related to "the dangers of staying too long and [...] withdrawing too fast"[17] and focused on the local political acceptance to tenure in Singapore. Third, they underlined growing international resistance of foreign bases, indicating that Western, European, or simply White powers were not accepted anymore on a permanent basis on Asian soil. The discussions on a continued presence in Southeast Asia coincided with regional and supra-regional, or global, developments that reinforced perceptions of Britain being in a precarious position, leaving the former dominions to assess how they perceived the region themselves and how they valued the British presence.

The ensuing discussions focused on the British military presence East of Suez[18], symbolically represented in the large naval base in Singapore.[19] The term 'East of Suez' itself evoked images of imperial times: "No other part of the imperial experience produced any equivalent of Conrad and Kipling and Maugham and the many others who celebrated it in poetry and stories and plays."[20] Singapore was conceived as a crucial geopolitical hub and represented an entire imperial strategy, but the Pacific War and Indian independence had strongly undermined this concept and made the strategic purpose of Singapore questionable.[21] Moreover, under the impression of global decolonisation, foreign bases became more and more a vestige of colonialism to indigenous forces who demanded independence and sovereignty over their own land. However, the advent of the

[17] British Foreign Secretary Gordon Walker in 1964, quoted in: *Hyam*, Britain's Declining Empire, 390.

[18] The term East of Suez was a description for Britain's colonial position stretching from the Middle East along the Persian Gulf to Southeast Asia, *David M. McCourt*, What Was Britain's "East of Suez Role"? Reassessing the Withdrawal, 1964–1968, in: Diplomacy & Statecraft 20/3, 2009, 453–472, 454 f. The British military presence in the Persian Gulf caused different issues of sovereignty and security in the 1960s which cannot be covered in this study. For this issue see *W. R. Louis*, Withdrawal from the Gulf, in: W. R. Louis (Ed.), Ends of British Imperialism: The Scramble for Empire, Suez, and Decolonization, London et al. 2006, 877–906.

[19] Singapore was the discursive representation of several British military posts in the region. The following analysis, like the historical discussion, focuses on the naval base in Singapore and on further British bases in Malaya, namely the Butterworth air base and the Terendak army base, constructed since 1959, which housed the 28th Commonwealth Brigade. Further sites used during this period were: Minden/Penang (Malaysia), Changi (Singapore) and Tengah (Singapore).

[20] *Bell*, Dependent Ally, 80.

[21] *Darby*, British Defence Policy, 10.

Cold War provided Britain, like other imperial powers, with an imperative to sustain its military positions.[22] In the following, Britain continued to use Singapore as a centre of communication in the region as well as a strategic point in its defence of the Malayan area. Aside from strategic considerations, Malaya also served as a key area for British political and economic influence in Southeast Asia, and gained vital importance in containment strategies against Chinese communism.[23]

Consecutive conflicts revived the strategic interest in the region shortly after the Second World War. In Malaya, communist insurgencies started soon after the war in reaction to the British implementation of the Federation of Malaya in 1948. The so-called Malayan Emergency lingered on as a destabilising conflict until the mid-1950s; its official end came in 1960.[24] With the Emergency unfolding, but also in the wake of allied regional strategic planning under SEATO and ANZAM, British officials proposed the formation of a Commonwealth Strategic Reserve Far East (CSR) that should be stationed in Malaya. In 1955, both Australia and New Zealand announced that they would send a contribution to the CSR.[25] The core element was the 28th Brigade, a formation consisting of different Commonwealth infantries dating back to the Korean War. The Australian and New Zealand contributions were integrated into the existing British logistic structure, whereas command rotated among all three nations.[26]

Aside from strategic considerations, the Malayan Emergency also heightened British desires to find a solution for challenging national aspirations and its growing defence expenditure. As a result, plans for an independent Malaya were carefully examined and accelerated in 1955, when, with the political leader Tunku Abdul Rahman, a Malayan government won the British trust and Malayan independence was reached in 1957.[27] Singapore followed suit two years later with the right of self-government, although it proved a more delicate case

22 *Joshua-John Tian Ser Seah*, Imperial Outposts and the War Beyond. Singapore, Hong Kong and the British Empire's Land Force Contribution to the Korean War, in: The Journal of Imperial and Commonwealth History 45/4, 2017, 672–696.

23 *A. J. Stockwell*, British Imperial Policy and Decolonisation in Malaya, 1942–1952, in: The Journal of Imperial and Commonwealth History 13/1, 1984, 68–87.

24 *Karl Hack*, Defence and Decolonisation in Southeast Asia. Britain, Malaya and Singapore 1941–1968, Richmond 2001, 113–21.

25 Australia proposed a contribution of one battalion, two fighter and one bomber-squadron, with two frigate/destroyers and a potential air carrier in the Malayan waters. New Zealand intended to send a frigate, an SAS squadron and one squadron each for fighting aircraft and transport aircraft, *McIntyre*, Background to the Anzus Pact, 390 f.

26 See for a description on the composition and military operations of the CSR *H. B. Eaton*, Something Extra. 28 Commonwealth Brigade 1951 to 1974, Edinburgh 1993; see for a detailed command description *David M. Horner*, Strategic Command. General Sir John Wilton and Australia's Asian Wars, South Melbourne 2005.

27 *Joseph M. Fernando*, The Cold War, Malayan Decolonization and the Making of the Federation of Malaysia, in: Albert Lau (Ed.), Southeast Asia and the Cold War, London 2012, 67–85, 72 f.

for British policymakers. With a large Chinese population and the growing popularity of left-wing parties, officials were afraid that Singapore could become a point of entry for communism in the region.[28] Therefore, self-government did not mean complete independence for both countries: Britain reserved its right to intervene and control issues of defence, in Malaya with the Anglo-Malayan Defence Agreement (AMDA) established in 1957, in Singapore with constitutional exceptions.

This retention of British control seemed necessary in the light of the region's rapid decolonisation, which would not allow for a self-sufficient defence structure to be established in time. Australia and New Zealand closely followed the political talks between Britain and its former colonies. While both wanted to be included in strategic planning and thinking, they were reluctant to consider an association with the regional British defence framework, as they feared any entanglement with the internal security issue of Malaya or Singapore. In 1959, both associated themselves with the AMDA, but put restrictions on the use of their forces.[29]

Soon after gaining self-government, Malaya and Singapore became part of a larger British plot for further decolonisation in the area. Even before their independence, British officials considered the benefit of a merger of both countries into a federation that should also cover the Borneo territories of Brunei, Sabah and Sarawak. The background to this 'Grand Design' was the British plan to release all its territories into relative independence without enabling ethnic tensions or a rise of communism in one of them. Finally, economic and financial interests also played a significant role in British considerations about the region's future. With the Grand Design of 'Greater Malaysia', they hoped to relieve financial burdens and eventually defence obligations.[30]

When the British plans were made public, the Philippines objected to the inclusion of the Borneo territories. Similarly, Indonesia repudiated the scheme as a neo-colonialist attempt for a continued, more informal, British dominance of the region.[31] Various diplomatic efforts to mediate the ensuing conflict failed, and under its president Sukarno, Indonesia declared a policy of Confrontation

[28] *Albert Lau*, Decolonization and the Cold War in Singapore, 1955–9, in: Albert Lau (Ed.), Southeast Asia and the Cold War, London 2012, 43–66; *Andrea Benvenuti*, Australia, the 'Marshall Experiment' and the Decolonisation of Singapore, 1955–56, in: Journal of Southeast Asian Studies 43/2, 2012, 257–279.

[29] *Mark G. Rolls*, Growing Apart: New Zealand and Malaysia, in: Anthony L. Smith (Ed.), Southeast Asia and New Zealand. A History of Regional and Bilateral Relations, Singapore/Wellington 2005, 209–262, 215; *Peter Dennis/Jeffrey Grey/Peter Geoffrey Edwards*, Emergency and Confrontation. Australian Military Operations in Malaya & Borneo, 1950–1966, St. Leonards 1996, 173 f.

[30] *A. J. Stockwell*, Malaysia: The Making of a Grand Design, in: Asian Affairs 34/3, 2003, 227–242.

[31] *John Subritzky*, Britain, Konfrontasi and the End of Empire in Southeast Asia, 1961–1965, in: The Journal of Imperial and Commonwealth History 28, 2000, 209–227, 213.

or *Konfrontasi* in January 1963. Although never a war in the open, the "low intensity conflict"[32] of *Konfrontasi* put a heavy strain on British resources by stressing its military, political and diplomatic capacities.[33] Instead of implementing defence cuts that had been discussed since the late 1950s, Britain now had to extend its defence posture for the time of Confrontation. In the following years, the conflict would put a strain on Britain's relations with Australia and New Zealand under ANZAM, and the USA.[34] At the end of Confrontation, around 50 000 British servicemen would be stationed in the area.[35]

Confrontation refocused Britain's strategic interests back to Southeast Asia after a series of considerations that could be interpreted as a desire to turn to Europe. For large parts of the conflict, Indonesia represented a minor threat to Malaysia's territorial existence, and therewith to the British military presence. But Indonesia's flirtations with the communist bloc[36], Western apprehensions about non-alignment and colonial connotations surrounding the conflict all served to increase the perceptions of instability and danger, and expanded *Konfrontasi* from a regional low-scale conflict to a supra-regional issue. Moreover, the struggle of Malaysia was exacerbated by further conflicts in its proximity, most notably in Vietnam.

The sum of these conflicts kept Britain heavily engaged in the region, despite initiatives to shed off some of its international responsibilities were rolled out since the late 1950s. A catalyst and starting point for these initiatives was the Suez Crisis in 1956, which fundamentally shook British convictions in both its

---

32 *Dennis/Grey/Edwards*, Emergency and Confrontation, 172.

33 See for a detailed description of diplomatic and military developments during Confrontation *John Subritzky*, Confronting Sukarno. British, American, Australian and New Zealand Diplomacy in the Malaysian-Indonesian Confrontation, 1961–5, New York 2000; *David Easter*, Britain and the Confrontation with Indonesia, 1960–1966, London 2004; *Peter Edwards/Gregory Pemberton*, Crises and Commitments. The Politics and Diplomacy of Australia's Involvement in Southeast Asian Conflicts, 1948–1965, Sydney 1992; *Dennis/Grey/Edwards*, Emergency and Confrontation; *Moreen Dee*, The Regional Significance of the Indonesian-Malaysian Confrontation 1963–1966, And The Lessons Australia, New Zealand And Great Britain Drew From It, in: Melbourne Historical Journal 27/27, 1999, 84–99.

34 See for the Anglo-American history of the conflict *Matthew Jones*, Conflict and Confrontation in South East Asia, 1961–1965. Britain the United States and the Creation of Malaysia, Cambridge 2002; *Wm Roger Louis*, The Dissolution of the British Empire and the Era of Vietnam, in: American Historical Review 107/1, 2002, 1–25.

35 The exact numbers of British servicemen vary in the literature, as some estimations also include the local dependants and civilians being linked to the bases. Derek McDougall estimates 90 000 people at the end of Confrontation, with 55 000 uniformed personnel, *Derek McDougall*, The Wilson Government and the British Defence Commitment in Malaysia-Singapore, in: Journal of Southeast Asian Studies 4/2, 1973, 229–240, 229. See also *Hugh Hanning*, East of Suez – Facts and Figures, in: International Affairs 42/2, 1966, 253–260.

36 Indonesia received assistance from the Soviet Union and upheld friendly ties with the People's Republic of China which unsettled Western counterparts. However, those relations with the communist bloc never lead to a serious communist conversion of the Indonesian government; *Jones*, Conflict and Confrontation, 273.

role as a world power and as a leader in the Commonwealth community. Similarly, the episode initiated discussions on the British role with the former dominions.

3.1 The First Watershed Moment? The Suez Crisis as the Introduction of Uncertainty

The Suez Crisis served as a first significant disruption in Anglo-Dominion relations that also affected the Commonwealth and the American relationship. When Britain and France backed the Israeli invasion into the Sinai in late October 1956 and eventually used military force, the former dominions reacted with shock. Misgivings pointed in two directions: Not only were officials upset because Britain had not consulted them before, a routine to which they felt entitled as close Commonwealth allies. They also feared the implications for the Anglo-American relationship, given America's open hostility to the British action.[37] Moreover, the dominions expected a negative impact on the ongoing UN explorations to solve the conflict. Britain's intervention felt like "a return to gunboat diplomacy of the Victorian Age"[38], at a time when aspiring nationalism and growing Cold War bias demanded a more sensitive approach to international conflicts.

However, while all three deplored the British actions, the dominions took different courses of action after the British-French ultimatum. The Australian government, under the dominant lead of Prime Minister Robert Menzies, wholeheartedly supported Britain's position, while officials from the ADEA unsuccessfully demanded caution from its government.[39] In his letter to Eden after the British invasion, Menzies underlined the loyalty to Britain: "You must never entertain any doubts about the British quality of this country."[40] Similarly, in New Zealand, the government and public expressed loyalty while some officials developed considerable doubts and distance to Britain throughout the crisis. In marked contrast to the other two countries, the Canadian government openly

---

[37] *Marc J. O'Reilly*, Following Ike? Explaining Canadian-Us Co-Operation During the 1956 Suez Crisis, in: Journal of Commonwealth & Comparative Politics 35/3, 1997, 75–107, 82–86.

[38] *Robert W. Reford*, Peacekeeping at Suez, 1956, in: Don Munton/John J. Kirton (Ed.), Canadian Foreign Policy: Selected Cases, Scarborough 1992, 58–77, 60. Canadian diplomat Georg Ignatieff characterised the British action similarly, *Ignatieff*, Making of a Peacemonger, 122.

[39] See for a review of Australian policy during the Suez Crisis *Hudson*, Suez Crisis of 1956; *J. D. B. Miller*, Australia and the Crisis, in: William R. Louis/Roger Owen (Ed.), Suez 1956: The Crisis and Its Consequences, Oxford/New York 1989, 275–283.

[40] Canberra to AHC London, 1.11.1956, TNA DO 35/6334, quoted in: *Templeton*, Ties of Blood and Empire, 100.

condemned the British invasion and was subsequently faced with an agitated domestic public debate. Like New Zealand counterparts, Canadian officials also regretted that Britain had not sought consultations with their allies beforehand.[41] With Canadian activism at the forefront, all three dominions engaged in similar approaches to mitigate the crisis: While they expressed their recriminations to Britain in private, officials tried to seek a solution for the conflict which was ultimately found with the proposal of a peacekeeping force under UN auspices, the United Nations Emergency Force (UNEF). Canadians agreed to act as mediator among Commonwealth countries and nations within the UN to search for a speedy solution, and hoped to save some of Britain's international prestige.[42] As Canadian commitment to a solution was later rewarded with the Nobel Peace Prize for Lester Pearson, it institutionalised within and outside Canada the belief in a role as a 'helpful fixer'. Serving on UNEF would establish in many ways the perception and culture of Canada's peacekeeping tradition.[43]

While the conflict could be stalled with UN measures, the impact of the Suez Crisis on Britain's position in the world was indeed profound. It demonstrated that Britain would not be able to exert any international interventionist role without the consent of the USA anymore.[44] It also proved a humiliating episode for a nation that still perceived itself as an imperial power. As Eden was forced by international pressure and American economic and financial sanctions to withdraw from the canal, many inside and outside the Commonwealth perceived this as the ultimate defeat.[45] At the same time, some arguments point to patterns of continuity in British imperial politics. Britain itself perceived the crisis as a lesson that any transfer of colonial power should be taken carefully and with gradual steps.[46] Some even argued that the Suez Crisis led to a renewal of imperial self-perception and atmosphere within Britain and the Commonwealth.[47] A comment among New Zealand policymakers indicates such a position: While not all New Zealanders would be supportive of the British actions,

---

41 *John Hilliker/Greg Donaghy*, Canadian Relations with the United Kingdom at the End of Empire, 1956–1973, in: Phillip Buckner (Ed.), Canada and the End of Empire, Vancouver 2005, 25–46, 27; *MacLaren*, Commissions High, 465 f.

42 *O'Reilly*, Following Ike.

43 *Reford*, Peacekeeping at Suez, 75.

44 *Lehmkuhl*, Pax Anglo-Americana, 234; *A. J. Stockwell*, Suez 1956 and the Moral Disarmament of the British Empire, in: Simon C. Smith (Ed.), Reassessing Suez 1956: New Perspectives on the Crisis and its Aftermath, Aldershot 2008, 227–238, 232.

45 *Peter Stursberg*, Lester Pearson and the American Dilemma, Toronto, Ontario 1980, 136.

46 *George C. Peden*, Suez and Britain's Decline as a World Power, in: The Historical Journal 55/4, 2012, 1073–1096.

47 See for this discussion *Stockwell*, Suez 1956; *Peter Lyon*, The Commonwealth and the Suez Crisis, in: William R. Louis/Roger Owen (Ed.), Suez 1956: The Crisis and Its Consequences, Oxford/New York 1989, 257–273, 271–273.

some would be "delighted to think that the old lion still had a throaty roar and a sharp claw which, on occasions, he was still prepared to use".[48]

As the degree of demise in Britain's world position and its self-perception as a global player during the crisis remains negotiable, the episode certainly proved a watershed moment in the Anglo-Dominion relations. The crisis affected the core of the dominions' Anglocentric outlook in foreign policy and questioned their identification with British values. Before, all three countries had in similar ways supported Britain and its politics in the world. Previous disagreements were short-lived or issue-related and did not question the fundamentals of each country's close relations with Britain. Especially within the Commonwealth and on decolonisation, Canada, Australia, and New Zealand still tended to support the British position. They saw the British power in the world as the best influence and expected British officials to be experienced enough to take the right decisions in foreign affairs.[49] Such debates confirmed established positions on 'good' imperialism and the benefit of Commonwealth solidarity. Moreover, the British link also served as a strong backbone to all three countries' self-assertion as British nations. The shared history and common customs and values were the foundation of the Commonwealth, as they were the proud heritage of Canada, Australia and New Zealand.

Since the British action in Egypt put those norms and values – such as prior consultation, respect for the law, and national integrity – into question, all three countries experienced this episode as unsettling and demanding, both for their appreciation of Britain as for their own position.[50] Canada's St. Laurent specifically objected to the use of military force against Nasser and "repeated twice empathically that this is something we in Canada cannot support".[51] In a similar vein, New Zealand's loudest critic of the British action, Ambassador to Washington, Carl Berendsen, saw Eden's course of action as diametric to "British traditions of peace and order, defence and fair dealing among nations".[52] But for the self-perception as part of a Commonwealth family, the missed consultation and British dismissal of allied critique proved the most challenging issue to reconcile. As Robert Reford had pointed out, it was the "mockery of the principle of consultation so important during times of crisis"[53] that led to the most severe recrimination from officials in all three countries. When Canadian High

48 Comment by Alister McIntosh to Herbert Norman on New Zealand Labour Party's acquiescence to the British actions, 20.12.1956, quoted in: *Templeton*, Ties of Blood and Empire, 182.

49 *Igartua*, Other Quiet Revolution, 115; *Hudson*, Suez Crisis of 1956, 127.

50 *Hillmer/Granatstein*, Empire to Umpire, 226.

51 TNA DO 35/5008, Report by British High Commissioner Saville Garner on Talks with Louis St. Laurent, BHC Ottawa 1065, 5.11.1956.

52 Comment by Berendsen in Evening Post, 13.12.1956, quoted in: *Templeton*, Ties of Blood and Empire, 184.

53 *Reford*, Peacekeeping at Suez, 62.

Commissioner, Norman Robertson, assessed the Anglo-Canadian relations in the following summer, he noted a "loss of confidence in the British judgment and good sense, which derives from the whole handling of the Suez problem".[54] Equally, missed consultation could also harm the Commonwealth as a whole, as Australian Leader of Opposition Herbert Evatt expressed in parliamentary discussions following the crisis. He urged the government to promote a reestablishment of the practice: "If that does not happen very quickly to meet this emergency, the British Commonwealth will not be a Commonwealth at all."[55] Consequently, the crisis was experienced by most officials as the introduction of uncertainty, both on Britain's future course in international affairs as on its attitude towards future cooperation with the dominions.

The lack of consultation had unsettled a system of cooperation built on shared outlooks and values, but also mutual trust. As a result, the whole episode was discussed in an emotionally charged atmosphere, both among policymakers as within the public. During this episode, emotions of regret and perplexity collided with sympathy and loyalty to Britain. As historian Peter Lyon describes the general atmosphere among Commonwealth members, feelings matched those expressed by Norman Robertson:

"Complaints in different tones of regret and irritation, slightly querulous enquiries, or plain requests for more information, recur throughout the official British files and confidential dispatches of the day. Requests that an emergency meeting of Commonwealth Prime Ministers should be convened, threats that some members would leave the Commonwealth, or the belief that the whole association was on the verge of dissolution – these were some of the emotional currents, hitherto unprecedented in their intensity in Commonwealth history, which surfaced during the crisis."[56]

The difficulty of reconciling the inconsistent emotions of these days is documented in the diaries of Canadian diplomat, Charles Ritchie. During the Suez Crisis, Ritchie was put on the spot both by British officials and friends in London for Canada's criticism, and his diaries reveal his difficulties mediating his Canadian identity and British affiliation:

"I hate being in London when so much is at stake for the English and when I do not feel at one with them. I am haunted by memories of 1940 when I felt such a complete identity with the Londoners. It seems like a desertion on my part and no doubt many of my friends here think that it is a desertion of them on the part of Canada."[57]

He went on describing how sickened he felt after reading British newspapers "to which British prestige has been brought, and divide between my certainty

---

[54] Quoted in: *Jack L. Granatstein*, A Man of Influence. Norman A. Robertson and Canadian Statecraft, 1929–1968, Ottawa 1981, 308.

[55] Speech by Herbert Evatt, AHoR, 8.11.1956, quoted in: *James Eayrs* (Ed.), The Commonwealth and Suez. A Documentary Survey, London 1964, 240.

[56] *Lyon*, Commonwealth and the Suez Crisis, 264 f.

[57] *Ritchie*, Diplomatic Passport, 120.

that their government's policy has been a colossal, disastrous blunder and my emotional sympathy for the English, particularly when isolated and when so many are turning against them".[58] Ritchie's recollections are shared by other diplomats serving in London at that time who described the demanding atmosphere in the metropolis during these days.[59]

There is no doubt that policymakers experienced a conflict of loyalties, comparable to previous experiences of wartime cooperation, and that they were aware of the pitfalls of any indication of disloyalty towards Britain. The message Louis St. Laurent sent to Anthony Eden on 1 November 1956 can be seen as one example: It had been drafted in different versions to console the Canadian Cabinet that the government would not send a message indicating Canadian disloyalty to Britain.[60] As the Canadian historian José Igartua described it for Canada, the Suez crisis became "a litmus test"[61] for the international outlook, national values and unity of the country. The impact was the most disturbing in Canada, but had similar unsettling effects in New Zealand and Australia. Within Canada, the debate gained strong political impetus, leading conservatives to point to the government's lack of loyalty to Britain while liberals welcomed the Canadian initiative as a sign of growing independence in foreign policy.[62] While some research underlines the electoral defeat of the Liberal government one year later as a consequence of the Suez debate[63], others doubt the impact of the crisis on the election.[64] In any case, support for detachment from Britain was controversial enough that the successive government under Diefenbaker could gain support for a policy of British re-orientation. Given Canada's constitution as a bicultural country, the debate also stirred ethnic discrimination, e. g. against St. Laurent as being disloyal because of his French Canadian background.[65]

Despite the momentary rift in Anglo-Dominion relations that exceeded beyond traditional arenas of foreign policy into a broader media discourse in all three countries, the immediate continuation of a British oriented foreign poli-

[58] Ibid., 121.

[59] The Canadian High Commissioner in London, Norman Robertson, described the days of the Suez Crisis simply as "bad three months", quoted in: *MacLaren*, Commissions High, 467.

[60] *Hilliker/Barry*, Canada's Department of External Affairs Vol. 2, 125; *Hillmer/Granatstein*, Empire to Umpire, 226.

[61] *José E. Igartua*, 'Ready, Aye, Ready' No More? Canada, Britain and the Suez Crisis in the Canadian Press, in: Phillip Buckner (Ed.), Canada and the End of Empire, Vancouver 2005, 47–65, 48.

[62] *Vucetic*, Anglosphere, 81; *Igartua*, Other Quiet Revolution, 124–129.

[63] *Phillip Buckner*, Canada and the End of Empire, 1939–1982, in: Phillip Buckner (Ed.), Canada and the British Empire, Oxford 2010, 107–126, 119.

[64] *Reford*, Peacekeeping at Suez, 75; *Andrea Benvenuti/Stuart Ward*, Britain, Europe, and the 'Other Quiet Revolution' in Canada, in: Phillip Buckner (Ed.), Canada and the End of Empire, Vancouver 2005, 165–182, 168.

[65] *Igartua*, Ready, Aye, Ready, 58.

cy should not be underestimated. Lester Pearson himself expressed, on several occasions, his continued allegiance to Britain. Similarly, officials showed a continued interest in Commonwealth cooperation. During the Commonwealth Prime Ministers' Meeting in 1957, the rift over Suez was characterised as a 'family conflict', with statements such as the one made by Pearson describing the episode as "the kind of relationship that makes the Commonwealth worthwhile".[66] Even Canadian officials could still argue that the crisis was so intensively and fervently debated because of "an emotionalism which would be absent if relations were less intimate, and if there were not special ties of history and sentiment between us".[67] The Suez Crisis did not mean an immediate change in patterns of cooperation or outlook among the former dominions, but was fought in a framework of British identity.[68]

Canadian diplomat John Holmes argued ten years after the crisis that Suez "was mitigated by the fact that differences on the subject among the people of the Commonwealth were not strictly along national lines".[69] To follow Holmes' argument, there are reasons to believe Suez proved as divisive as it could bring new qualities to the Commonwealth. Canada used its good relations with India to persuade Nasser while Australia convinced Pakistan not to leave the Commonwealth over the affair. These diplomatic ventures allowed them to adopt a new distinct position. The same goes for intra-dominion relations: During his visit to Canada at the height of the crisis, Richard Casey learned that Egypt broke off their diplomatic relations with Australia. Subsequently, he asked his Canadian hosts if they would represent Australia diplomatically for the time of the crisis.[70] Hence the crisis forestalled some of the conflicts, but also some of the Commonwealth approaches in the decade to come.

For the foreign policy framework of all three former dominions, the Suez Crisis had served as a profoundly unsettling moment in their relationship with Britain, and led them to question Britain's role and power. Suez had been unsettling in two respects that reflected on strategical policy: On one hand, it made officials question the basis of their foreign policy perceptions and outlooks that were strongly influenced by the British connection. British handling of Suez

[66] "Where Canada Stands in the World Crisis", Lester Pearson in Maclean's Magazine, 6.7.1957, quoted in: *Eayrs*, Commonwealth and Suez, 427–435, 434. The fresh start was also symbolised by the first participation of a new Commonwealth member (Ghana) at a Commonwealth prime ministers' meeting in almost a decade; *Lyon*, Commonwealth and the Suez Crisis, 271.

[67] LAC RG25 A-3-b, Vol. 6614, 11142-40, "Canada-United Kingdom Relations", Memorandum by Commonwealth Div., n. d. (October 1959).

[68] *Igartua*, Other Quiet Revolution, 129.

[69] *John W. Holmes*, The Commonwealth and the United Nations, in: William Baskerville Hamilton (Ed.), A Decade of the Commonwealth: 1955–1964, Durham 1966, 349–365, 353.

[70] Casey Diary Entry, 7.11.1956, in: *Millar/Casey*, Australian Foreign Minister, 252.

had damaged its reputation as a moderate imperial power and made officials aware of possible dividing lines based on region, ideology and race that could run through international organisations including the Commonwealth. Furthermore, policymakers wondered if they still shared with Britain similar perceptions of foreign policy and security issues.

On the other hand, the conduct of affairs during the Suez Crisis revealed a shift in practices. The apparent failure of Britain to consult added to the difficulties of reconciling national with British interests on the levels of politics and administration. The concept of traditional cooperation based on principles of mutual understanding and trust came under scrutiny when officials complained about the British lack of concern for its Commonwealth allies. Both aspects, a changing foreign policy previously based on a British outlook and a changing world of (post-)imperial practices concerned officials in the aftermath of Suez and set the tone for the following decade, including the discussions on a British retreat from Southeast Asia.

3.2 Anticipating British Imperial Decline in the Aftermath of the Suez Crisis

3.2.1 Defence Reviews and Burden-Sharing

Following the Suez Crisis, British Prime Minister Harold Macmillan had entered office with a clear determination to review Britain's liabilities and commitments across the world. The resulting White Paper, published in April 1957, indicated a shift in British defence thinking. While conventional forces should be substantially cut, Britain intended to rely on nuclear weapons in the future, meaning that British officials did not envisage committing to large anti-insurgency campaigns as in imperial times.[71] At the same time, the review emphasised that global commitments should be retained to maintain Britain's global role.[72]

When Duncan Sandys visited Australia to discuss the British plans in August 1957, it became clear Australian and New Zealand officials feared grave consequences for their position in Southeast Asia over the new direction in British thinking. After the talks, Richard Casey noted in his diaries that Sandys had indicated a shut-down of the Singapore base.[73] According to Canadian sources,

[71] *Simon J. Ball*, Harold Macmillan and the Politics of Defence: The Market for Strategic Ideas during the 'Sandys Era' Revisited, in: Twentieth Century British History 6, 1995, 78–100, 83 f.; *Dockrill*, British Defence, 65 f.; *R. F. Holland*, The Imperial Factor in British Strategies From Attlee to Macmillan, 1945–63, in: The Journal of Imperial and Commonwealth History 12/2, 1984, 165–186, 179.

[72] *Dockrill*, Britain's Retreat, 24.

[73] Casey Diary Entry, 26.8.1957, quoted in: *Millar/Casey*, Australian Foreign Minister, 268 f.

particularly AMD Philip McBride showed his anger about the British plans during discussions: "Mr. McBride [...] is regarded as being particularly difficult towards the British; it is said he has never got over the events of 1942 in Singapore."[74] Other Australian officials also linked the British plans to earlier experiences. A month after Sandys' visit to Australia, the British Embassy in Saigon reported on difficulties they experienced with the Australian Minister F. J. Blakeney. During a social gathering, Blakeney told the British representative Terence Garvin "that the days of Britain's material power had gone, but that the British generally failed to recognise this".[75] Garvin continued to describe how distorted Britain's position was according to Blakeney:

> "Britain was, whatever anyone said, paring away her defence commitments in the Far East. No one would seriously mind, though they might regret it emotionally, if we had the honesty to say that we could not stand the financial strain. Instead we engaged in much double-talk about our modernisation of the armed forces and our increased fire-power, in a desperate attempt to maintain face and sustain our imperial position. No one was in the last deceived and it did us great harm."[76]

However, Blakeney urged Garvin that Britain should continue to contribute with "Britain's accumulated experience, wisdom and expertise"[77] to the progress of the region. Thus, while he realised Britain's resources were stretched, he nevertheless wished for its continued presence in the area. An attached letter by Ambassador Roderick Parkes explained Blakeney's outlook further: "For practical purposes [...], Blakeney's main fixations are the 1942 debacle and what I might call the 'mother hen' complex. So far as he is concerned, Australia is a growing bird; and whilst completely loyal to the Crown, his allegiance is exclusive to Her Majesty the Queen of Australia."[78] In Parkes' eyes, Blakeney's position represented the dilemma many Australians faced: They tried to express Australia's independence in conversations which represented, in themselves, the continuous struggle with the former 'mother country'.

At the same time, Australasian feelings of grief and anger expressed during the talks with British officials referred to a robust informal bond that linked a British responsibility to the region. This responsibility corresponded to ideas of British moral obligation for the defence of Australia and New Zealand. The concept of moral obligation floated on multiple levels within the Commonwealth and was not defined in any clear range of potential threats and responses.[79] A New Zealand paper described it in the mid-1950s as follows: "There is an unwritten obligation on members of the Commonwealth which is, by its nature,

[74] LAC RG25 A-3-b, Vol. 3338, 1894–40, CHC Canberra 497, 21.8.1957.
[75] TNA FO 371/129758, Report by BEmb. Saigon (Garvin), 28.9.1957.
[76] Ibid.
[77] Ibid.
[78] TNA FO 371/129758, BEmb. Saigon (Parkes) to FO (Morland), 14.10.1957.
[79] See references already made under Macmillan in *Dockrill*, Britain's Retreat, 33.

difficult to define but which may be broadly described as an obligation to come to the assistance of other members who are the victims of aggression."[80]

The essence of Britain's obligation for Australia and New Zealand stemmed from two sources: on the one hand, it was firmly embedded in a narrative of joint imperial war effort frequently expressed by references to Australia's and New Zealand's support for Britain in the World Wars.[81] On the other hand, customs within the Commonwealth nurtured the feeling of family values that did not need a written agreement. In 1957, British officials explained to Canadians that no fixed arrangements had been made for ANZAM procedures, as "written agreements on such matters of mutual interest were less usual among Commonwealth countries".[82]

During his visit, Sandys could discern some of the fears he met as he explicitly underlined Britain's continued interest in its commitments overseas.[83] However, as the attitudes of some officials had revealed, Australians and New Zealanders expected, or suspected, Britain's acknowledgement of its economic difficulties as it planned to reduce forces and to cut defence costs overseas in spite of Commonwealth arrangements. In contrast to former imperial cooperation, Sandys' visit in 1957 symbolised a new period of precarious presence in Southeast Asia. Given the changes in regional and global power structures, British officials were now more able to present their case as a crucial one by framing their presence as a liability rather than an asset. The resulting nervousness among Australian and New Zealand counterparts about Britain's long-term plans was also known to British officials. In 1961, the British Liaison Staff reported from Canberra: "[…] any plans to re-deploy some of the United Kingdom forces […] will be viewed with some measure of suspicion, any outright or drastic reduction of our military strength in the South East Asian theatre would inevitably place a considerable strain on United Kingdom/Australian relations […]."[84]

In the following, aside from internal defence reviews that failed due to ministerial resistance or lack of resources[85], Australia and New Zealand therefore considered diversifying their security links, e. g. through equipment standardisation.[86] For this purpose, both dominions consulted Canadian counterparts. Al-

---

80 ANZ ABHS 5242 950, Box 68, 87/32/1, "New Zealand's Defence Commitments", NDEA Memorandum, 1.6.1959.

81 *Benvenuti*, Anglo-Australian Relations, 23.

82 LAC RG25 A-3-b, Vol. 4768, 50073-A-40, CHC London, 26.8.1957.

83 LAC RG25 A-3-b, Vol. 4768, 50073-40, Part 12/13, CHC Canberra 539, 30.8.1957.

84 TNA DO 164/39, "Review of Australian Defence Planning", British Joint Services Liaison Staff (BJSLS) Canberra 1549, 27.1.1961.

85 *Paul Dibb*, The Self-Reliant Defence of Australia: The History of an Idea, in: Ronald Huisken/Meredith Thatcher (Ed.), History as Policy: Framing the Debate on the Future of Australia's Defence Policy, Canberra 2007, 11–26, 13; *Rolfe*, New Zealand Defence Policy, 54.

86 For a general description of the equipment used see the respective articles in *Peter Den-*

ready in 1955, Australian officials had expressed a desire to obtain Canadian advice on changing from British to American equipment: "They hope that within the family we will give them the benefit of our experience in resolving this problem and will also advise them on how to approach Washington."[87] Canadian officials could claim to have reached substantial defence integration with the USA through the North American Air Defence Agreement (NORAD) in 1957, which focused on cooperation in air defence and envisaged planning in case of a Soviet attack. In reality, however, collaboration with the United States was far from easy. Under the Diefenbaker government, several incidents caused frictions, such as Canada's failure to provide adequate support for the Kennedy administration during the Cuba Crisis and the subsequent Bomarc affair.[88] Despite constant elements of dissonance in their relationship with the USA, Canada could still claim a longer cooperation tradition than Australians and New Zealanders.

In contrast, the latter had to consider the consequences of a closer US alliance for their British relationship. As the 1957 Australian White Paper advised a switch to American equipment, Menzies emphasised in a statement in parliament that the transfer should not be understood as treason, even for "a wholeheartedly British nation"[89] like Australia. During Sandys visit, Casey felt the need to explain the Australian plans for standardisation with the USA as a pragmatic step: "For survival Australia had to rely on the United States. […] Australia is just as warmly attached as ever to the United Kingdom, but these are the facts of life."[90]

New Zealand plans for shifting equipment equally unsettled British officials.[91] Similar to Australia, New Zealand considerations were also motivated by fears of Britain's declining ability to provide for its forces. Moreover, the question of continued British logistic support turned into another bone of contention. New Zealand strongly relied on the British provision of transport and facilities since its forces were too small to act independently. When British officials indicated in 1961 that their economic restraints would not allow continued

nis, The Oxford Companion to Australian Military History. 2. Ed., Oxford 2008; *Ian McGibbon* (Ed.), The Oxford Companion to New Zealand Military History, Auckland 2000.

87 LAC RG25 A-3-b, Vol. 6022, 50273-40, Part 8, CHC Canberra (Irwin), 13.1.1955.

88 *Hilliker/Barry*, Canada's Department of External Affairs Vol. 2, 249 f.; *Gordon T. Stewart*, An Objective of US Foreign Policy since the Founding of the Republic: The United States and the End of Empire in Canada, in: Phillip Buckner (Ed.), Canada and the End of Empire, Vancouver 2005, 94–116, 108.

89 Robert Menzies in HoR, 4.4.1957, quoted in: *Edwards/Pemberton*, Crises and Commitments, 205.

90 Minutes of a Meeting with Duncan Sandys, 26.8.1957, quoted in: *Andrea Benvenuti*, Australian Reactions to Britain's Declining Presence in Southeast Asia, 1955–63, in: The Journal of Imperial and Commonwealth History 34/3, 2006, 407–429, 411.

91 ANZ ACIE 8798 EA1 103, 156/10/2, Part 2, George Mallaby (BHC Wellington) to Walter Nash, 16.6.1959.

logistic support of New Zealand in the future, Keith Holyoake alarmingly wrote to Macmillan, emphasising Southeast Asia as "the theatre, perhaps the only one in which we shall be directly involved in any future war".[92] If Britain ceased to give logistic support, New Zealand would have to turn to the USA or Australia and "may be faced with the need for painful decisions, with sentiment pulling one way and material considerations another".[93]

In the end, a complete shift to American equipment did not take place in both countries, not least because the USA (and in New Zealand's case, Australia) was unwilling to support the step.[94] However, just as the British White Paper and its implications for the British presence in Southeast Asia scared the Tasman nations, the Australian and New Zealand plans to standardise with American equipment disturbed the British.[95] As equipment and logistic debates indicated, all three ANZAM members relied to a certain extent on established routines and practices of cooperation. While declining resources or new strategic considerations demanded a review of that traditional cooperation, sentiment pulled the other way, just as Holyoake said. Especially on the political level, recommendations from service officials had to be mediated through a rhetoric of continued allegiance to Britain.

A lack of alternative partners also caused unease. The Tasman relationship introduced by the Canberra Pact only grew slowly. When Australian public servant Patrick Shaw[96] visited New Zealand in 1963, a series of briefs and reports underlined both countries' ambivalent relationship. In a brief for Shaw, one ADEA official elaborated on the need for greater cooperation between both countries:

> "The New Zealanders still look to the United Kingdom for political guidance, defence support and trade. There is a growing awareness that times are changing and it is a matter for us to encourage this new awareness in directions which are in accord with Australia's national policies and objectives."[97]

Interdependence of Australian and New Zealand defence as a consequence of geopolitical transformations seemed logical in this perception. However, not all

[92] ANZ ABHS W4628 7148, Box 123, LONB 106/7/1, Part 1, Holyoake to Macmillan, 13.12.1961.
[93] Ibid.
[94] *Andrews*, Department of Defence, 162; *McGibbon*, Forward Defence, 19–21.
[95] *David Lee*, Australia and Allied Strategy in the Far East, 1952–1957, in: Journal of Strategic Studies 16/4, 1993, 511–538, 533.
[96] Patrick Shaw (1913–1975) served at the AHC Wellington from 1943 to 1945 where he established good contacts with his New Zealand counterparts; *David Lee*, 'Shaw, Sir Patrick (1913–1975)'. URL: http://adb.anu.edu.au/biography/shaw-sir-patrick-11667/text20845. Accessed August 18, 2019; see also the recollections of New Zealand's Frank Corner on the impact Shaw had on Australian-New Zealand relations, Corner in *Templeton*, An Eye, 86.
[97] NAA A1838 370/1/19, Part 3, Notes for Visit of Patrick Shaw to New Zealand, April 1963.

Australian officials agreed with the responsibilities implied, as a handwritten comment indicates:

"I'm not convinced of this. We will provide the first line of defence for NZ – ergo NZ should seek to be close to us, to influence our thinking and other ways to strengthen us and support our policies. In trade and civil aviation she wants and needs things from us, and concessions by us at some disadvantage to us. It is for her to make the gestures to us to encourage us to make such concessions."[98]

The Australian awareness for potential Australian-New Zealand defence cooperation resembled, in some ways, the perceptions on the other side of the Tasman. New Zealand diplomats, service officials and parts of the public urged to improve defence cooperation in the face of Southeast Asian instability.[99] However, first approaches for consultation did not result in broader ties.[100] One reason was the low political appreciation for one another, caused by New Zealand suspicions and Australian dominance. Patrick Shaw reported after his visit that Australians had come to be regarded "as a rather rough and uncouth Big Brother who over the years has done down more gullible and less pushing New Zealanders".[101] Although officials would be willing to cooperate with Australia, the problem seemed to be public opinion: "The problem is that the Government is so sensitive to public opinion that it is not able to give a clear lead on those lines and is in danger of becoming bound by its own public opinion in a way which we have seen occur in the United States and Canada."[102] The degree of closeness and the roles both countries would play in the defence of Southeast Asia had yet to be determined.[103] Still, both sides seemed to agree that a relationship similar to the Canadian-US relationship was not desirable. The arguments indicate the Canadian-American relationship was perceived as disparate and unsuitable to serve as a model.

While Australia and New Zealand felt forced by British plans to review their strategic links, Canada was only partly affected by commencing discussions on the British presence East of Suez. However, the developments of the Suez Crisis had renewed a Canadian interest in the Commonwealth that spread to previously unknown parts of the former Empire. In that sense, 1958 marked a turning point in Canadian awareness for the Southeast Asian region as part of

98 NAA A1838 370/1/19, Part 3, Handwritten Comment on Notes for Visit of Patrick Shaw to New Zealand, April 1963.

99 ANZ ACIE 8798 W2619 434/8/1, Part 6, New Zealand Commissioner to Southeast Asia, 1.8.1957; "NZ Must Expand her Defences Along with Australia", Evening Post, 15.6.1963.

100 See documents in ANZ AAFD W3738 811 Box 1321, CAB 223/13/1, Part 1.

101 NAA A1838 370/2/9, Part 1, Report by Patrick Shaw (First Ass. Division II), 1.5.1963.

102 Ibid.

103 See also *Carlyon/Morrow*, Changing Times, 68 f.

the Commonwealth orbit. Not only did new Prime Minister John Diefenbaker embark on a tour that should only visit Commonwealth countries in the Asian-Pacific area, meaning newly independent Malaya besides Australia, New Zealand, India and Pakistan. 1958 also saw the establishment of a Canadian High Commission in Kuala Lumpur.

The attention brought to Malaya under the Diefenbaker government stood in contrast to previous governments. When Louis St. Laurent went on a world tour in 1954, he only visited India, Korea and Japan as Asian countries. Afterwards, Canadian officials fend off requests made by Commonwealth partners for more extensive regional representation. On one instance, Canadian official Benjamin Rogers opposed offers for a joint approach to the area made by the Australian High Commissioner to Malaya, Alan Watt:

"I agreed that it might be difficult for us to avoid participation if a war were to break out in this part of the world: after all, we had felt it was necessary to participate in Korea. There was a difference, however, between participation and the undertaking of defence commitments in some kind of regional collective security arrangement."[104]

Canadian officials clearly felt a presence in the region could drag them into unwanted commitments. Therefore, the approach to diplomatic representation was tentative and, until the late 1950s, mostly non-committal. Between their High Commission in New Delhi and their Embassy in Djakarta (opened in 1953), Canadians were only present in Southeast Asia by their ICSC commission in Saigon.[105]

By 1958, the setting had changed. Growing geopolitical interest in the region was matched by a governmental interest in using the Commonwealth for a regional approach. On his tour to Malaya, Diefenbaker vividly contrasted the country's location in a destabilised area with Commonwealth traditions like parliamentary democracy sustaining a strong independent country.[106] At the same time, the Canadian government also considered ways of permanent links to Malaya. Even before his visit, Diefenbaker had pushed Kuala Lumpur as a new mission and dropped Rangoon and Saigon as new posts proposed by the CDEA. Diefenbaker relied on British comments on the issue: The Commonwealth Relations Office (CRO) had objected to the other posts and also dismissed the previously floated idea of a dual accreditation of the Ambassador to Indonesia to Malaya. British officials urged the Canadian government to consider a mission in Malaya since Canada, "as a senior member of the Common-

---

[104] LAC RG25 A-3-b, Vol. 3008, 3534-40, Record of Benjamin Rogers on Talks with AHC Alan Watt, 3.3.1955.

[105] Apart from these missions, there were Canadian trade commissioners in Hong Kong and Singapore and a Consul General in Manila, but these posts did little political reporting, see Roger's description in his talks with Alan Watt, LAC RG25 A-3-b, Vol. 3008, 3534-40.

[106] *David Webster*, Fire and the Full Moon. Canada and Indonesia in a Decolonizing World, Vancouver 2009, 74 f.

wealth and a multi racial country"[107], would be a good adviser to the young nation. The importance given to the post was further emphasised through its first head, Arthur Menzies, a capable diplomat acquainted with Southeast Asian affairs as previous Head of the Far Eastern Division.[108]

For one thing, Cold War and decolonisation issues dragged the region into Canadian professional conscience, but their first point of entry remained the Commonwealth. At the same time, officials were anxious not to be drawn into larger responsibilities. In April 1958, after talks with the Tunku in which the Malayan leader wished for help from "other free countries in the free world who share our conception of the importance of the conflict in which we are engaged", Menzies was quick to assure his superiors: "I am sure, however, that remark will not be the prelude to a request for Canadian troops!"[109]

Equally, the Commonwealth connection had to be approached with caution, as the changes within the institution evoked criticism and anxiety among the former dominions since the late 1950s. With the admission of newly independent members, but most of all with the loss of the 'sister dominion' South Africa in 1961, many officials lamented the difficulties of integrating issues of self-determination, non-alignment and equality in the organisation.[110] Moreover, South Africa's departure challenged the foundation of Britishness just as much as new customs and procedures did. Before, the Commonwealth had been cherished for its ambiguity and vagueness. Rather than reaching a consensus among its members, the different national outlooks of its members should be integrated under the principle of frank discussions and declarations in a unanimous fashion.[111] Now, new members challenged these principles while the expanded size of the organisation hampered ideas of intimate discussions.[112]

All three countries reacted to the changing character of the Commonwealth with anxiety. However, their position varied: While Australia opposed many transitions under Robert Menzies[113], Canada tried to enable changes by mir-

---

[107] LAC RG25 A-3-b, Vol. 4245, 8250-C-40, Part 1, Draft Memorandum (Commonwealth Division) for CSSEA, 21.11.1957.

[108] Arthur Menzies (1916–2010) was born in China as son of Christian missionaries and spent some time of his education in Japan. Shortly after entering the CDEA he became an expert for affairs with Asia, holding the desk for China since 1944 and heading the Far Eastern Commission to Japan from 1950–1953; *Menzies/Menzies*, Letters Home.

[109] LAC RG25 A-3-b, Vol. 4728, 50058-40, CHC Kuala Lumpur 15, 3.4.1958.

[110] *W. David McIntyre*, The Significance of the Commonwealth, 1965–90, Basingstoke 1991, 17 f.

[111] *Philip Murphy*, Book Review: The Queen's Other Realms. The Crown and Its Legacy in Australia, Canada and New Zealand, in: The Journal of Imperial and Commonwealth History 37/4, 2009, 629–636, 631.

[112] *Lloyd*, Diplomacy With a Difference, 169 f.

[113] *Nikola Pijovic*, The Commonwealth: Australia's Traditional 'Window' Into Africa, in: The Round Table 103/4, 2014, 383–397, 386.

roring domestic debates of equality into the Commonwealth.[114] For all three, the future identity of the organisation became crucially apparent with the issue of apartheid. After South Africa's departure, Keith Holyoake commented: "Although the Commonwealth lost one of its most powerful and oldest members, I believe it gained in moral stature by coming to a decision based on a question in principle. If it had failed to do so, its disintegration as a Commonwealth based on multiracial association would have been much more likely."[115]

South Africa's departure challenged convictions of Commonwealth values and the shape of the organisation. Further signals from the metropole increased dominion perceptions that the British world community was changing. In 1962, Harold Macmillan caused a minor outrage at the Commonwealth Prime Ministers' Conference when he described the Commonwealth as a body of "friends and relations" and not as a bond of family or relatives as done before.[116] Further ruptures came with the British plans to merge the CRO and the Commonwealth Office (CO), forcing Canadian High Commissioner George Drew to complain back to Ottawa about the prospect to deal with Colonial officers in the future: "If the clock has not been set back nearly one hundred years, it has been set back at least forty years."[117] But nothing prepared both sides for the conflict enfolding over Britain's plans to enter the EEC. While Commonwealth politics surrounding the decolonisation of the former Empire had brought concerns over adequate administrative practices and shared values to the forefront, the debate on Britain's entry into the EEC would shake the assumption of a continued close Commonwealth cooperation to the core.

3.2.2 The British EEC Application as Indication and Catalyst of Changing Imperial Policy

In 1963, the Australian DEA decided to establish a policy planning division, relying mainly on the work of one officer, Garry Woodard. His first assigned task was the question of continued British interests and commitments in Southeast Asia. In retrospective, Woodard recollected that the task sprung from a growing unease about Britain's long-term strategy, although many still believed that the British presence should be left untouched and unquestioned.[118] The resulting paper, published in August 1963, looked critically at recent British decisions for a gradual military reduction in Southeast Asia and the general trend revealed

---

114 *Asa McKercher*, Sound and Fury. Diefenbaker, Human Rights, and Canadian Foreign Policy, in: Canadian Historical Review 97/2, 2016, 165–194.

115 NLNZ MS-Papers-6759-135, Notes for Reports to Cabinet by Prime Minister Keith Holyoake, 4.4.1961.

116 *Ward*, British Embrace, 205.

117 LAC MG26 N3, Vol. 319, 810 Secr., George Drew (CHC London) to Lester Pearson, 28.10.1963.

118 NLA MS10135, Box 5, File 23, Garry Woodard, Draft for publication on Arthur Tange.

by the British application to join the EEC. To Woodard, current British developments indicated that "British strategy in the Far East [...] is essentially one with a limited application which is likely to contract".[119] He noted that Britain's application to the EEC had shown a shift in international priorities that would continue for the coming decade. Although the Malayan peninsula seemed to be spared from Britain's declining interest in Southeast Asia, Australians could expect a greater demand for burden-sharing: "[...] we are seeing only a temporary levelling off in the gradual downward curve of British influence and activity in Asia, and no modification of the principles that Britain must rely on combining with friends and allies and beware of spreading her resources too widely."[120]

For Woodard, as for others, the British decision to apply for entry into the EEC added to perceptions of shifting priorities in British foreign policy. In all three former dominions, uncertainty and anxiety developed after the British announcement. The British decision was especially antithetical to ideas under John Diefenbaker to enhance Anglo-Canadian trade relations, such as his passionate proposal to divert 15 percent of Canadian imports from American to British imports.[121]

After Britain announced its decision to apply for entry into the EEC in July 1961, all three countries engaged in different initiatives and activities to make Britain reconsider its plans. For many officials, the British plan was a sign of shifting from preference for the Commonwealth to favouritism of European partners. Britain's interest in joining the EEC was perceived both as a symptom of and a catalyst for its steady decline. Although they could understand the British motives, they deplored its acceptance of defeat as a world power.[122]

The vigorous and emotional reactions exposed during the discussions revealed the continued assumptions of a shared identity with Britain, both in outlook and interest, in the former dominions.[123] With the economic disadvantages in the background, many mourned the British decision on the premise of his-

---

119 NAA A1838 625/2, "An examination of the nature and extent of current British economic interests and military and political commitments in South and South East Asia, their likely course over the next ten years, and the implications for Australia", Circular by Policy Planning Officer Garry Woodard, 30.8.1963, (found in NLA MS10135, Box 5, File 23).

120 Ibid.

121 On the controversy of Diefenbaker's announcement see *McLaren*, Commissions High, 477 f. See also the amusing recollections of George Drew's Deputy in London, George Ignatieff, who remembered how Drew made the 15 percent diversion his personal goal, "determined as any Soviet commissar", and even tried to sell Canadian rye whisky to Scottish representatives. According to Ignatieff, Drew was like Diefenbaker deeply immersed in ideas of Britishness. *Ignatieff*, Making of a Peacemonger, 176 f., quote on 177.

122 *Benvenuti*, Australian Reactions, 421.

123 For a much more detailed analysis of this argument I am happy to refer to the work of my colleague *Clara Seltmann*, Butter, Wut und Tränen. Australien, Kanada und Neuseeland während Großbritanniens Verhandlungen mit der Europäischen Wirtschaftsgemeinschaft, 1958–1973, Tübingen 2020.

tory and attachment. Following the traditional rhetoric of Commonwealth co-operation, officials and the public understood the British decision as a betrayal of a shared background that would demand a similar outlook and relied in parts on an imperial imagination and sentiment.[124] These perceptions were matched by feelings of distrust and British disingenuity as British officials again, similar to the Suez Crisis, kept plans about the EEC entry deliberately vague or secret. Moreover, the former dominions argued with a British duty for preferential treatment of the Commonwealth.

By putting the British plans into a general pattern of British reorientation, the EEC discussions only heightened fears in Australia and New Zealand that the British could finish their commitments to Southeast Asia to prioritise Europe. The simultaneous discussions on Britain's military presence East of Suez enforced this perception. Following talks with the British Chief of the Defence Staff (BCDS) Earl Mountbatten in 1961, New Zealand officials were left with the impression that "the British, at present, 'couldn't care less' about Southeast Asia".[125] In the current climate, officials feared that any talks on Britain's defence position could accelerate a British retreat altogether.[126]

Ultimately, both Australia and New Zealand adopted an attitude of reluctant acceptance over the British EEC plans as they feared for their defence position.[127] Officials also accepted British reassurances that European integrity would strengthen Britain's global position. Yet they considered preparatory measures to deal with a potential British retreat: "Above all we need to know if [the] UK has decided to make a switch. We would prefer stronger UK support – if they can't support us the sooner we know the better. Comforting assurances, without firm backing are worse than help."[128] This attitude was in a remarkable variance to statements demanding a continued British presence. Yet it was also supplemented by public comments, for example in the Australian *Financial Review* in September 1962:

"It will also mean that if we really do want to have our voice heard on matters that affect our business, we may have to take a much more serious interest in measuring up to our responsibilities in areas where we don't particularly care to move – in areas such as defence and foreign aid [...] we may have to stop thinking about Britain as 'Home' and

[124] See for an analysis of this discussion *Ward*, British Embrace; *Benvenuti*, Anglo-Australian Relations, 55–57.

[125] LAC RG25 A-3-b, Vol. 3811, 8449-40, CHC Wellington 159, 13.4.1961.

[126] NAA A1838 370/1/19, Part 3, Report by Defence Liaison Officer Keith Brennan, 22.10.1961.

[127] *Stuart Ward*, A Matter of Preference: The EEC and the Erosion of the Old Commonwealth Relationship, in: Alex May (Ed.), Britain, the Commonwealth and Europe: The Commonwealth and Britain's Applications to Join the European Communities, Basingstoke 2001, 156–180, 169 f.

[128] NAA A1838 67/1/3, Part 2, "Relations with the United Kingdom", Memorandum, 14.3.1961.

start thinking urgently about getting to know very much more of our Asian neighbours' needs."[129]

In the end, the veto by French President Charles de Gaulle in January 1963 prevented the need for a profound readjustment. Nevertheless, the EEC debate introduced an element of uncertainty regarding the future of British and Commonwealth cooperation. An ongoing atmosphere of rumours and tip-toeing resulted not only from an appreciation on both sides that a reevaluation of the British defence position was necessary but also from the perception that consultation, conducted traditionally close, did no longer include the dominions. Moreover, the discussions on a British EEC entry were similarly concerned with questions of sentimental and historical attachment to the former 'mother country'.[130] As a result, some officials like Woodard demanded a more self-reliant assessment of economic and defence interests. However, with anglophile political leaders like Robert Menzies and a society sustained by Britishness, the group of policymakers within the departments which demanded a change remained relatively small.

The EEC debate also confirmed that most Commonwealth relations were increasingly perceived as bilateral relationships between each dominion and Britain. This attitude resulted in isolated national approaches rather than teaming up to influence Britain, a fact deplored by some officials in retrospect. The question of Commonwealth cooperation to change British minds would infuse future moments of Anglo-Dominion frictions as much as the now indicated dichotomy between Britain and Commonwealth interests.[131] This dichotomy remained in the following discussions and amplified the perceptions among dominion officials that Britain was considering a turn away from its role in the Commonwealth and a British world community.

Indeed, metropolitan attitudes sustained these perceptions. In Britain, the allegations officials had faced from the Commonwealth during the EEC discussions produced some criticism towards the periphery.[132] As they were simultaneously facing criticism over decolonisation in Africa, British officials felt the Commonwealth as increasingly inhibiting[133], leading into a public debate in 1964 when the *Times* printed a series of articles written by an anonymous conservative, calling the Commonwealth a "gigantic farce".[134]

---

129 Australian Financial Review, 25.09.1962, quoted in: *Ward*, British Embrace, 217.

130 *Ward*, British Embrace, 78.

131 *Alex May*, Commonwealth or Europe? Macmillan's Dilemma, 1961–63, in: Alex May (Ed.), Britain, the Commonwealth and Europe: The Commonwealth and Britain's Applications to Join the European Communities, Basingstoke 2001, 82–110, 95.

132 *Margaret Doxey*, Canada and the Modern Commonwealth, in: Behind the Headlines 40/2, 1982, 1–17, 8.

133 *Lawrence J. Butler/Sarah Stockwell*, Introduction, in: Lawrence J. Butler/Sarah Stockwell (Ed.), The Wind of Change: Harold Macmillan and British Decolonization, Houndmills/ Basingstoke 2013, 1–19.

134 One of the believed authors was British conservative Enoch Powell who had declined

Naturally, the British debate reflected back to the dominions. New Zealand officials commented on the British discussion in preparation for the following Commonwealth Prime Ministers' Meeting with a brief called *The Future of the Commonwealth.* The brief denounced the "selfish" attitude both British parties took in regards to the Commonwealth and mainly blamed Britain for what officials perceived as the three current deficiencies of the organisation: lack of loyalty and solidarity; lack of consultation; and missing advantages to give the Commonwealth a unique standing in contrast to other regional groupings.[135] Above all, they expected this situation to become worse if Britain would apply to the EEC again.[136]

All three discussions – the defence review in 1957, the EEC debate, and the discussion surrounding the Commonwealth – bore resemblances in narratives and arguments. Most of all, policymakers from the former dominions felt they witnessed Britain's demise as a world power and leader of a (post-)imperial community that would require adherence to certain principles and responsibilities. Similar arguments would also be visible in discussions on Southeast Asia.

3.3 Towards a Regional Postcolonial Order – Malaysia and Confrontation

It was not only the discussion on Britain's defence reviews or its attempt for a changing course within Europe and the Commonwealth that generated discussions of its role and presence in Southeast Asia. Since the late 1950s, the situation on the subcontinent itself had dramatically changed under the impression of local conflicts and the related Cold War security considerations. At the beginning of the 1960s, the West looked at the region as further destabilised by the communist threat, despite the alliance efforts introduced in the previous decade.

For British officials, it was especially Indonesia's *Konfrontasi* commencing in 1963 which made them realise that the instability of the region reversed their plan to withdraw from colonial responsibilities. As a "formidable liability"[137], the uncertain future of Malaysia and its conflict with Indonesia meant an additional burden for the already strained British defence East of Suez. Observing Britain's struggle with its Southeast Asian presence, the dominions also

to serve under the cabinet of new British Prime Minister Sir Alec Douglas-Home since he criticised Britain's continued imperial ambitions; *Philip Murphy*, Britain and the Commonwealth. Confronting the Past – Imagining the Future, in: The Round Table 100/414, 2011, 267–283, 280.

[135] ANZ ABHS W5503 7148, 142, LONB 65/1, "The Future of the Commonwealth", Brief for Commonwealth Prime Ministers' Meeting, July 1964.

[136] Ibid.

[137] Macmillan to Home, 3.4.1963, TNA PREM 11/4347, quoted in: *Jones*, Conflict and Confrontation, 223.

assessed the implications of a British retreat in the context of regional developments. Already in 1957, New Zealand's Commissioner to Southeast Asia, Foss Shanahan, advised on a "major rethinking of the defence position in this part of the world".[138] Others, such as New Zealand's Ambassador to Thailand, Brian Landrum, criticised that so far, New Zealand's policy had only been "a series of reflex actions to which continuity has been given only by the underlying community of attitudes and aspirations among New Zealanders".[139]

It seemed that a critical lens had been adopted within the policymaking process after the Suez Crisis and the following defence reviews. Similar to considerations in Australia, New Zealand officials had to pin their regional interests and practices against a precarious British presence. Less often were such considerations matched by Canadian concerns. With their peacekeeping presence in the ICSC, they stood at variance to Australia's and New Zealand's forward defence commitment. Being confronted with British deliberations of retreat, Canadians nevertheless assessed possible outcomes for the Southeast Asian region. The ongoing British defence reviews and the constant rhetoric of decline in British dealings contributed to a certain insecurity and unease in all three countries.

The overall deteriorating situation in the region itself, aside from Malaysia also prominently represented by the conflicts in Indochina, created the perception of continued local, all-encompassing instability. Being confronted with these various factors of uncertainty and risk, policymakers in Britain and the dominions perceived the future of their military presence as endangered, and therefore embarked on a series of early policy reviews.

3.3.1 The Creation of Malaya, Singapore and Greater Malaysia in Interdependence with Surrounding Conflicts, 1957–1963

In 1957, the establishment of Malaya opened up further difficulties for British and dominion military planning that would only increase over the next decade. The dual purpose of Commonwealth forces stationed in Malaya, serving the defence during Emergency under the AMDA while being also earmarked for SEATO contingency planning, was far from being uncontroversial.[140] After independence, the Tunku assured the British in private that he saw SEATO as a beneficial deterrent against communism. At the same time, he publicly expressed concerns about SEATO's implications for a successful integration of the region.[141] In consequence, a careful, discreet agreement between British and Malayans had to be found to safeguard the SEATO role of the Commonwealth

[138] ANZ ACIE 8798 W2619 434/8/1, Part 6, New Zealand Commissioner to Southeast Asia to NMEA, 2.1.1957.

[139] ANZ ACIE 8798 W2619 434/8/1, Part 6, NEmb. Bangkok, 17.4.1957.

[140] *Rolls*, Growing Apart, 213.

[141] *Hack*, Defence and Decolonisation, 228 f.; *Jones*, Conflict and Confrontation, 9.

forces. These arrangements relied on the leadership of the Tunku, meaning that the delicate balance between private assurances and public opinion created a precarious state for the British presence that was at risk to be subject to local sensitivities at any given time.

In 1958, British Undersecretary for War Julian Armery caused a minor uproar when he insisted that his visit to Malaya was not addressing any potential reductions. Canadian officials questioned the need for any public disturbance of that kind: "[…] we thought that Mr. Armery's statement […] was rather unwise since it could easily be misinterpreted by the public to be the first large stride toward total withdrawal of British troops from the Federation."[142] While dominion officials, especially those present in the region, anticipated a likely change in British defence thinking on Southeast Asia[143], they objected at the same time any public statement that could be an indication of Britain's unwillingness to provide for regional stability. This concern was also shared by British officials in the region who insisted that any public considerations for reduction could undermine local stability: "[…] confidence begets confidence; any visible signs that political uncertainties are causing us drastically to cut our defence investment might result in a more general loss of confidence in the future stability of the country […]."[144]

The pressure on the present arrangements only grew when a merger between Malaya and Singapore was discussed from 1961 on. With a more fervent political composition, Singapore posed the threat of falling under anti-Western governments that could object to the further stationing of Western troops.[145] Moreover, the Tunku had indicated at the beginning of discussions that he would not allow a further quarantine use of the bases for SEATO purposes after the merger.[146] A British brief from November 1960 summarised the problematic scenario:

> "In fact time is not on our side. If discouragement from the Federation continues, the pressure towards an independent Singapore will be strengthened and Mr. Lee Kuan Yew will either have to give way or be overthrown. The result to be feared would be the emergence of a more Left-Wing Government and probably an outbreak of violence. Faced with a 'Cyprus situation' the United Kingdom Government would have difficult decisions to make on whether it should hold to the base by repression or leave the island. This sort of situation would help the Malayans least of all."[147]

---

142 LAC RG25 A-3-b, Vol. 6023, 50273-40, Part 12, CHC Kuala Lumpur (Menzies) 394, 6.11.1958.

143 See e. g. LAC RG25 A-3-b, Vol. 6136, 50397-40, Part 3, CHC Kuala Lumpur 296, 19.9.1958.

144 LAC RG25 A-3-b, Vol. 8205, 8250-H-40, BHC Kuala Lumpur (Geoffrey Tory) to CRO, 104/132/1, Dispatch No. 1, 2.1.1959.

145 NAA A4940, C3389, Submission 1304, Menzies to Cabinet, 11.8.1961, quoted in: *Moreen Dee*, Australia and the Formation of Malaysia. 1961–1966, Barton 2005, 1–9.

146 *Benvenuti*, Cold War and Decolonisation, 193.

147 TNA FO 371/1552145, Brief for Commonwealth Secr. 14.11.1960; quoted in: *Jones*, Conflict and Confrontation, 18.

In the end, the Tunku and Lee Kuan Yew accepted the continued stationing of forces, including those serving SEATO purposes but refused to join SEATO.[148] The role both leaders played in the discussions on the Malaysian Federation only underlined the dependence of the British bases on local receptions. The need to pay closer attention to regional developments and personal relationships was not only lost on Britain and its ANZAM partners, but was also noticed by Canadians. Regarding the British reliance on the Tunku, one Canadian memo underlined the need to establish closer contacts with Malayan services through a service attaché.[149] This proposal followed earlier appreciations in the CDEA for service contacts that could enhance local appreciations for the Western effort.[150] Nevertheless, the proposal recommended that the envisaged military personnel should keep a distance from being involved in SEATO military planning.[151] This cautious approach was not shared by the Far Eastern Division, which emphasised the value of establishing links with Malayan forces and ANZAM planning bodies. An attaché could closely monitor regional developments to discuss security issues, including the issue of Britain's bases in relations to SEATO: "The state of these Commonwealth forces and the terms under which they might be utilized in support of SEATO activities will be of continuing political interest to Canada."[152]

In the end, the Canadian government did not follow the recommendations but felt sufficiently informed by its information arrangements with London, Canberra and Wellington. On SEATO, Canada received enough material from Australia and New Zealand to witness their frustrations within the organisation over the conflicts in Indochina. Here, Britain's reluctance to fully commit to the alliance added to Australian and New Zealand fears of a premature withdrawal from Malaya and Singapore. Various British statements in the early 1960s indicated to Tasman officials that the British were reviewing their SEATO commitment. Australians felt compelled to consider Britain soon "as a brake"[153] in the organisation, unwilling and unable to support the alliance effort. Most of all, concerns for British actions in SEATO were related to the ANZUS relation-

148 In fact, AMDA was extended to Singapore and the Borneo territories and allowed Britain to use the facilities "for the purpose of assisting the defence of Malaysia, and for Commonwealth defence and for the preservation of peace in Southeast Asia"; TNA CAB 129/107, C (61) 190, 22.11.1961, quoted in: *Benvenuti*, Cold War and Decolonisation, 212.

149 LAC RG25 A-3-b, Vol. 4245, 8250-C-40, Memorandum by D. L. (2) Division to F. R. Miller, 23.3.1962.

150 See e. g. the proposal by Far Eastern Division to offer military training in Canada to foreigners, Far Eastern Div. to Defence Liaison (1) Division, 23.11.1959, LAC RG25 A-3-b, Vol. 6379, 4457-B-40.

151 LAC RG25 A-3-b, Vol. 4245, 8250-C-40, Memorandum by Defence Liaison (2) Division, 23.3.1962.

152 LAC RG25 A-3-b, Vol. 4245, 8250-C-40, Memorandum by Far Eastern Div., 3.4.1962.

153 NAA A1838/2, 67/1/3, Part 2, Harry to Tange, 12.3.1962, quoted in: *Benvenuti*, British Military Withdrawal, 192.

ship. To secure American backing, both New Zealand and Australia supported American security efforts in Thailand from 1962 on, with Australia being committed to South Vietnam commencing the same year.[154] Supporting the American position in SEATO, Australians soon appeared frustrated about the growing British reluctance to commit to the alliance. During the SEATO Council Meeting in 1961, British officials were disturbed by Australian representative Malcolm Booker's hostile attitude. In the debriefing of the meeting, officials considered Booker's position as strongly influenced by American thinking, favouring "the Western powers and SEATO holding Laos down militarily by a series of jungle forts, indefinitely if need be, rather like the North West Frontier of the old days".[155] Similar to the case of F. J. Blakeney, British officials found explanations for Booker's aggressive tone in the complicated relationship he held with Britain. Given that Booker was born in Britain, "as a result of this he is always particularly anxious to eliminate any 'European' thoughts from his mind and to show himself a stalwart and enthusiastic 'convert' to the interests of Australia".[156] British and Australian interest in SEATO seemed to be drifting apart, a development that was obviously hurtful to individuals such as Booker, who were brought up in an orbit of Britishness, but who felt obliged to advocate national interests.

As they criticised British tendencies of withdrawal from the alliance, Australians and New Zealanders struggled with the implications of any diminishing of the alliance. While they privately acknowledged that SEATO would never establish a similar security framework such as NATO, they did not want to abolish it.[157] Further ambivalence over SEATO stemmed from doubts about the Malaysian Federation. According to AMEA Garfield Barwick, it was not "a perfect solution, but at least it was the best available for the de-colonisation of the remaining British territories in the area and for the maintenance of Western influence in Singapore and perhaps indeed in Malaysia itself".[158] However, some feared the creation of Greater Malaysia would be the first step to British disentanglement from its defence responsibilities in the region.[159] In 1961, Robert Menzies asked Harold Macmillan for clarification considering rumours that indicated an

[154] *Blaxland*, Strategic Cousins, 144; *McGibbon*, Defence Dimension, 20 f.

[155] TNA DO 169/198, Lord Selkirk (Commissioner-General to Southeast Asia) to Frederick H. Millar (FO), 3.6.1961.

[156] TNA DO 169/198, D. MacDermot (BEmb. Bangkok) to Lord Home, 6.7.1961.

[157] See discussions between Alister McIntosh and Patrick Shaw in April 1963, NAA A1838 370/2/9, Part 1, Report by Patrick Shaw (First Ass. Division II), 1.5.1963.

[158] Garfield Barwick during the ANZUS Council Meeting in June 1963, ANZ ABHS W5400 20358, Box 85, KL 101/1/2, Part 1, Report of ANZUS Meeting (5./6.6.1963), 11.6.1963. A year after foundation, the Canadian High Commissioner came to a similar conclusion but criticised the inherent ethnic division and Britain's continued dominance on politics in the Federation; LAC RG25 A-3-c, Vol. 8917, 20-INDON-1-3-MLSIA, CHC Kuala Lumpur 394, 23.9.1964.

[159] *Benvenuti*, Australian Reactions, 418.

imminent British withdrawal.[160] Among British policymakers, proposals had indeed been put forward to consider the envisaged Federation as a landmark to withdraw British forces. Confronted with Australasian protests, which underlined the lack of any alternative to the sites in Malaya/Singapore, Macmillan instructed policymakers to pause further considerations for the time being.[161]

British plans alarmed Australians and New Zealanders, and in the following they tried to find a balance of independent representation in ANZAM. Already in May 1958, Foss Shanahan had complained about the automatic equation of British and New Zealand forces:

> "There was a tendency at first, at least in certain quarters, to regard New Zealand forces as virtually United Kingdom forces and to feel that, except where specific reservations had been made, they could be used with complete discretion and without necessarily informing the authorities concerned in New Zealand or in this mission."[162]

Further complaints were made when Britain planned to abolish ANZAM's operational support, the British Defence Coordination Committee (Far East) [BDCC (FE)], in 1959. With a new strategic body in Singapore, Australasian officials feared that their views would be less considered than in the previous committee: "While from military viewpoint present arrangements may seem cumbersome, we consider it essential if Australia and New Zealand are to share responsibility for defence of the area that we should at least have a finger on the pulse of United Kingdom thinking at the formative stage of policy making for the area."[163] Officials insisted that any change in the regional framework should be processed to retain the equal status of ANZAM members, yet British plans continued without considering these objections and therewith created suspicions among the dominions.[164] Further recriminations developed over Britain's decision to abolish a key point of information, the post of the Commissioner-General.[165]

For Australia and New Zealand, the dismantling of these structures undermined long-standing principles ingrained in these institutions: trust in and reliance on shared cooperation and consultation. They committed to the ANZAM defence scheme not only because of their interest in allied protection, but also because they knew from traditional partnership how to take the British. At the

160 ANZ ABFK W5767 19764, Box 95, 46/2/1, Part 1, 46/2/1, Part 1, Robert Menzies to Harold Macmillan 3.2.1961.

161 ANZ ABFK W5767 19754, Box 119, 156/1/1, Part 1, Wellington to NHC London 2082, 19.10.1961, with message of Keith Holyoake to Harold Macmillan.

162 ANZ ABHS W4628 6958, Box 51, NYP 3/22/4, New Zealand Commissioner to Southeast Asia, 24.5.1958.

163 ANZ ABHS W4627 950, Box 4508, 434/8/8, Part 1, NDEA to NHC London 1382, 17.12.1959.

164 ANZ ABHS W4627 950, Box 4508, 434/8/8, Part 1, Handwritten Statement by Alister McIntosh, 30.6.1960.

165 ANZ ABHS W4627 950, Box 4508, 434/8/8, Part 1, NDEA to NHC London 1382, 17.12.1959, New Zealand Commissioner to Southeast Asia, 8.5.1959.

same time, they expected a full inclusion into any future planning body both because of their close relations with Britain and their increased activities in the area: "Our contribution to the defence of the area entitles us to no less a degree of participation than we enjoy at the present."[166]

Allegations that Britain was ignoring allied interests also emerged over Britain's political course over the establishment of Malaysia. When it came to the introduction of the Federation, Australasian policymakers were dismayed by Britain's neglect of local sensitivities regarding SEATO.[167] To some Tasman officials, Britain had also not done enough to discern Philippine and Indonesian fears in the wake of the Federation.[168] Especially Australia expressed on several occasions the desire to retain a free hand on its relations with Indonesia[169], not only because of the proximity between both countries, but also because of the ongoing frictions caused by Australia's mandate over Papua and New Guinea. Australians and New Zealanders also doubted British claims that Indonesia was on a course of expansionism under Sukarno. When British officials drafted a circular for their allies with strong recriminations against Sukarno in January 1963, ADEA officials were confused by what they perceived as a complete reverse of perception in contrast to the British position during the West New Guinea dispute a year earlier.[170]

Vocal criticism came especially from Australian Ambassador to Indonesia, Keith Shann, who saw Britain's hostile attitude as based on "a series of assertions for which no evidence is advanced".[171] Shann himself believed that a change in Australian foreign policy was adamant given the rapid changes in the region in recent years:

> "Australia is a large and empty continent, populated by Europeans, in a heavily populated area of the world seeing eye to eye with us in very few streams of foreign policy, and almost entirely non-European in background and outlook. We must over the next decade face up to our true position in the world, a position which is a complex of the decline in British power, the rise of Asian nationalism, and the fact that we can no longer deal with our Asian neighbours by the comfortable process of dealing through European Foreign Offices whose language and systems of thought we are able to understand."[172]

---

[166] ANZ ABHS W4627 950, Box 4508, 434/8/8 Part 1, 434/8/8, Part 1, Brief for Prime Minister Keith Holyoake on his Visit to London, 1.4.1960.

[167] NAA A9735 201/7/2, Part 4, Arthur Tange in Talks with Smith (CRO), 23.5.1960.

[168] ANZ ABFK W5767 19754, Box 119, 156/1/1, Part 1, Wellington to NHC Canberra 68, 4.2.1963.

[169] NAA A1838 370/2/9, Part 1, Report by Patrick Shaw (First Ass. Division II), 1.5.1963.

[170] *Benvenuti*, Cold War and Decolonisation, 220 f.

[171] Keith Shann to ADEA, 2.2.1963, NAA A1838/280, 3034/7/1/1, Part 1, quoted in: *David Lee*, The Origins of the Menzies Government's Policy on Indonesia's Confrontation of Malaysia, in: Frank Cain (Ed.), Menzies in War and Peace, St. Leonards 1997, 72–98, 79.

[172] NAA M4324, Box 2, "Australian Foreign Relations in the Next Decade", Paper by Keith Shann, 4.9.1962.

This was far from the traditional Eurocentric approach in foreign policy Australia had adopted so far, yet it indicates the concerns among professionals regarding the recent direction of British policy. Moreover, while he gave tentative support to Australian troops in the region, Shann saw their presence in a precarious state of existence, given that the planned Malaysian Federation may turn neutralist or hostile to Western interests within a couple of years:

"If this is so, the presence of our base presents us with a problem of delicate balance in the policy which we should follow, and it may well be that our real long-term interest will lie in its withdrawal in our good time with the benefits that will flow therefrom in our relations not only with the Malayans, but with others, rather than that it should be withdrawn under pressure and in circumstances which will damage those relations."[173]

At a time when forward defence constituted one of the pillars of Australian defence thinking, Shann's presentation on alternatives to traditional alliances and his sensitivity for local acceptance was an unusual position. His proposal for an independent policy was ultimately rejected in favour of Australia's traditional partnerships. When he questioned officials on the need to push the Federation through, asking if Australia would see Malaysia as 'sacred', his colleague Keith Waller replied:

"I suppose the question should really be 'Is our forward position in South East Asia sacred?' […] The problem is that we cannot look only at Malaysia; our strategic reserve and in fact our whole defence policy is involved. All our strategy, as you know, is based on our forward position in South East Asia and we would be cutting our own throats if we were to pull out of Malaya."[174]

As Waller's reply indicates, like New Zealand officials, Australians eventually gave support to the new Federation to sustain their forward defence position. Therefore, despite doubts and misgivings about the British handling in establishing the Federation, the Australian and New Zealand governments gave verbal support to the new state after Malaysia came into being in September 1963. Both governments underlined their support with notions of Commonwealth solidarity and the long-standing entanglement with British defence politics. They now linked their commitment to a moral obligation to assist Britain in its conflicts in Southeast Asia, as Robert Menzies stated in Australian Parliament: "[…] we each apply in a spirit of mutual confidence a golden rule of mutual obligation […] our vital engagements with the United Kingdom are not written or in any way formalised. Yet we know and she knows that in this part of the world we look to her, and she looks to us."[175] Nevertheless, the complexity of

173 Ibid.

174 ADEA (Waller) to Shann, 21.2.1963, NAA 3006/4/7, Part 5, CRS A1838/333, quoted in: *Lee*, Menzies Government's Policy, 81.

175 Ministerial Statement by Robert Menzies in AHoR, CPD 39/1963, 25.9.1963, 1338 f., 1339.

a Commonwealth obligation to Malaysia should become even more difficult in the course of *Konfrontasi*.

3.3.2 Confrontation Enfolding – The Question of Anglo-American Coordination and Commonwealth Responsibility, 1962–1964

Apart from the vocal support they gave Malaysia as an independent nation in the face of Indonesian aggression, Australian and New Zealand officials were divided if and how they would support Britain militarily. The request for an independent say in military planning expressed in the years before continued in the discussions on a contribution to support Britain during Confrontation. In reverse, Britain, being militarily committed since the beginning of the conflict, exerted pressure on the Antipodes to contribute forces.

For Australia and New Zealand, appreciations for local sensitivities demanded a crucial consideration for every military commitment. Yet most of all, a military contribution was rejected based on the profound concern that it could free Britain to withdraw its forces. The reluctance to enable a British withdrawal therefore also showed in the field of contingency planning. In the light of the precarious local acceptance of the bases and the continuous financial difficulties of Britain, other options such as an alternative military basis in Western Australia were discussed.[176] British liaison staff in Canberra had already recommended in January 1961 to look into an alternative site as soon as possible to allay Australian fears that Britain could withdraw entirely from the region over local resistance.[177] In August 1962, Australian Cabinet Secretary John Bunting recommended starting joint planning with Britain and New Zealand for possible facilities.[178]

However, this and other initiatives soon run dry among Australian policy-maker circles; again, fears of a precondition for British withdrawal appeared. Both Australian and New Zealand officials needed the military bases as a contextualisation of the British defence position in the Western effort against communism. The dual accreditation of the CSR to both Malayan defence and SEATO helped bridge the gap between British and American regional interests of defence.[179] As a result, Australian and New Zealand officials were against an alternative site off the Southeast main area.

Reversely, with America's growing involvement in Indochina, Australians were critically aware of the position the USA would take on any security ap-

---

[176] *Dennis/Grey/Edwards*, Emergency and Confrontation, 174; ANZ ABHS W4627 950, Box 4022, 253/3/5/1, Part 6, NHC London (R. L. Jermyn), 30.4.1963.

[177] TNA DO 164/39, "Review of Australian Defence Planning", Paper in BJSLS 1549, 27.1.1961.

[178] NAA A1209 1962/790, John Bunting to Robert Menzies, 29.8.1962.

[179] *Lee*, Menzies Government's Policy, 76.

preciation for Malaysia. Both Australians and New Zealanders hoped to cover strategies for Southeast Asia by a quadripartite approach. While American officials appreciated informal links between ANZAM, SEATO and ANZUS that could represent the joint Western effort against communism, their unwillingness to fully commit themselves to the whole of Southeast Asia had shown already during the ANZUS discussions in the 1950s.[180] Applied to the Southeast Asian region, they preferred a spatial system of defence responsibilities which they communicated on various occasions to their allies. While Indochina should be covered by SEATO arrangements and ultimately American efforts, Malaysia should be a Commonwealth or ANZAM responsibility.[181]

Nevertheless, Australian and New Zealand officials were strongly influenced by the aim to establish Malaysia as part of the Western strategy:

"[…] our whole military strategy is based on the necessity for a forward position in South East Asia. In other words, we are committed to the idea of the Strategic Reserve in Malaya. To withdraw from this position would deal a heavy blow to the whole Western position in South East Asia, not only with the aligned countries but with the non-aligned countries who, while publicly deploring our presence privately derive some comfort from a Western (and Australian) military presence in the area."[182]

Although officially denying any link to Malaysian defence, also US officials gave discreet support to the Australian effort. In early 1963, American official Avery Harriman confined to Tasman officials that the US administration would perceive a commitment under ANZUS to Malaysia as a 'grey area' that would be in a second tier to the Commonwealth commitment.[183] However, US guarantees were never explicit, and American officials were quick to renounce their support for such a guarantee under public pressure on more than one occasion.

Without a compelling US security umbrella, Australasians were anxious to be drawn entirely into British defence plans. While British officials increasingly perceived the region as "a primary area of Australia/New Zealand strategic interest"[184], Australasian officials doubted British threat assessments concerning Indonesia.[185] Again, the issue of burden-sharing caused mutual suspicions that the other side was deliberately covering ulterior motives. After talks with

---

[180] *Matthew Jones*, The Radford Bombshell. Anglo-Australia-US Relations, Nuclear Weapons and the Defence of South East Asia, 1954–1957, in: Journal of Strategic Studies 27/4, 2004, 636–662.

[181] *Nicholas Tarling*, Britain, Malaysia and Southeast Asia: Past, Present and Future, in: International Journal of Asia Pacific Studies 6/1, 2010, 77–93, 86.

[182] NAA A5619 C470, Part 1, Cabinet Submiss. 576 by Garfield Barwick, 26.2.1963.

[183] ANZ ABFK W5767 19754, Box 119, 156/1/1, Part 1, NEmb. Washington 84, 12.2.1963 and NEmb. Washington 85, 13.2.1963.

[184] ANZ ABFK W5767 19754, Box 93, 43/3/1, Part 1, Extract of COS Meeting (COS (62) 15), 5.4.1962.

[185] See e.g. NHC Canberra 351, 24.4.1964 and NHC Singapore 224, 2.7.1964, both in ANZ ABHS W4628 7148, Box 115, LONB 106/2/7, Part 2.

British officials in December 1963, Canadian representatives in Wellington assessed British threats to leave the region as a current theme of bargaining:

"[…] the UK no longer had interests to protect in this area, if Australia and NZ refuse to accept proper share of their own self defence they might find UK washing its hand of situation altogether. (UK is of course unlikely either to do this or even to threaten to do it, but possibility is one that N[ew]Z[ealand]ers and Australians may nevertheless weigh in balance in making up their minds.)"[186]

In turn, Tasman officials revealed to their Canadian colleagues that they were concerned that Britain would try to cast off the primary responsibility for Malayan defence. Moreover, they lamented the "failure of the network of direct personal relationships on which we pride ourselves as a substitute for too many dotted I's and crossed t's"[187] and felt forced to adapt to changes in a system previously based on trust and traditional cooperation.

As a result of the difficulties experienced with the British, considerations for a closer Tasman cooperation reemerged. In 1963, Garfield Barwick held a speech at Victoria University in which he urged his New Zealand audience to come to terms with its proximity to Asia. He finished with a plea for defence support to Australia: "If Chinese expansion should occur – and we would be foolish to plan our lives on the assumption that it never will – if it should occur, then I am sure that it will be essential for New Zealand that the umbrella which some regard the mainland of Australia to be is in good shape and that none of its ribs are broken."[188] A week later, the *Auckland Star* self-critically responded: "Perhaps one day it will occur to us that we do have an obligation to help to hold the umbrella up – to strengthen the ribs according to our means if we are not to be merely the residual legatee of fortuitous geography."[189] Calls for closer cooperation seem to be sanctioned by proximity, but also by a shared imperial background in British history. This became nowhere more apparent than in a New Zealand broadcast which proposed to give the dignified traditional slogan of the Second World War a new meaning by changing it into "'Where Australia stands, we stand; where Australia goes, we go'."[190]

Yet further considerations, some even suggesting a political merger between both countries[191], were overthrown by the continuous differences in foreign policy, especially in dealings with the USA. Diverging attitudes resulted in different priorities given to the ANZUS relationship: While Australia considered the

186 LAC RG25 A-3-c, Vol. 10285, 27-1-2-MLSIA, CHC Wellington, 23.12.1963.

187 ANZ ABFK W5767 19754, Box 123, 156/2/9, Part 2, NHC Kuala Lumpur 482, 2.11.1964.

188 "Australia and her Neighbours", Address given by Garfield Barwick at Victoria University, 29.5.1963, ANZ ABHS W5422 950, Box 34, 111/3/3/15, Part 5.

189 "Ribs for an Umbrella", Auckland Star, 5.6.1963.

190 "Result of ANZUS Conference", Lookout Broadcast, 8.6.1963, quoted in: ANZ ABHS W4628 7148, Box 118, LONB 106/4/2, NHC Canberra, 28.2.1963.

191 See Reports by AHC Wellington, 25.6.1962, NAA A1838 370/1/19, Part 3.

alliance with the USA as a crucial factor of any future commitment to Southeast Asia[192], New Zealand refrained from a close reliance on the American framework and preferred the British cooperation. However, in the last resort, even Australians continued to struggle with American unwillingness to become involved in Malaysian defence.

As their doubts about British motives continued, it was only after Indonesian infiltrations into the Malayan peninsula in August and September 1964 that both countries agreed to dispatch some of their forces to Borneo. In the last resort, the Commonwealth frame of reference served as a strong motivator to consider support for a fellow member in need. Moreover, as both governments feared that a commitment could forestall a British reduction or retreat and had stated on several occasions that any Australian contribution would be a support of, not a replacement for British troops[193], the Commonwealth reference could deter notions of replacement. In talks with George Thomson in London in November 1964, AMEA Paul Hasluck stressed again that Australia was committed to the region because of its Commonwealth commitment and not because it was a British responsibility.[194]

The narrative of Commonwealth support can also be traced in the justifications for Canada's participation in Malaysia's defence that came to fruition in 1964/1965.

3.3.3 The Canadian Commitment to Malaysian Defence as a Commonwealth Effort, 1964–1965

Although it had opened a mission in Kuala Lumpur on the advent of Malayan independence, Canada tried to uphold an observant yet non-committal policy when it came to the unfolding conflicts of decolonisation in the region, including Emergency and *Konfrontasi*. Officials followed the discussions on regional security closely but ensured Canada did not pose as a potential candidate for collective defence cooperation, including such proposals as the global coordination of the respective regional security alliances.[195] Even though Diefenbaker had acknowledged after his visit in 1958 that Malaya's struggle against communism "will affect the lives of Canadians for many years to come"[196], alle-

---

[192] See e. g. NAA A1838 TS682/4, Part 5, Patrick Shaw to Gordon Jockel, 19.8.1964.

[193] *Dee*, Regional Significance, 92.

[194] NAA A1838 67/1/3, Part 3, AHC London 7621, 9.11.1964.

[195] Richard Casey, in talks with Canadian High Commissioner Terence McDermot in April 1958, floated the idea of regular meetings of the three Secretary-Generals of NATO, SEATO and CENTO to keep each other informed "of the degree of menace" in the world, NAA A1838 229/9/5, Note for File on Talks between Casey and CHC McDermot, 30.4.1958.

[196] John Diefenbaker in Television Broadcast, 21.12.1958, in: External Affairs Vol. X, No. 12 (Dec 1958), 304–309, 307.

giance to the Commonwealth and Western framework was not translated into a more active relationship with the country.

In discussions, it became Canadian policy to use the country's commitment to the ICSC to fend off proposals for defence cooperation. In early 1964, one Canadian memo described the commissions as ineffective; however, "the Commissions save us from demands to take part in military efforts in Indochina and Malaysia. In other words, the Commissions go a long way to save us from doing the sort of thing we did in Korea in 1950–1953."[197] Although Canadians could reject military commitment based on their experience in Korea, the ICSC still served to strengthen a Western outlook on the conflicts in Southeast Asia. The commissions had enabled more foreign service officials than ever before to see the complexities of Southeast Asian security through first-hand experience, and many of them returned to Canada with a more decisive anti-communist attitude than before.[198]

Canada's role in the ICSC also brought a new level of cooperation to their American relationship: With access to officials in Hanoi, Canadian officials offered on various occasions to use the Canadian commission for approaches to North Vietnam. Most prominently, the diplomatic missions of Blair Seaborn (1964) and Chester Ronning (1966) could be interpreted as siding with the USA.[199] Yet Seaborn himself and others have described the ambivalent, sometimes contradicting American attitude to the Canadian initiatives.[200] While the degree of Canadian collaboration or dissociation in the face of American actions in Vietnam remains debatable, the missions exemplify a strengthened Canadian interest to cooperate with Western allies in the region, both for access to allied thinking and influence on the development of the conflict from a broader perspective of peacekeeping and international mediation.

Especially in the Commonwealth framework, Canadian considerations also looked at opportunities to strengthen local structures. With military assistance seen as an apt tool of decolonisation, Canadians hoped to influence the transfer from colonial protection and security to a self-reliant indigenous force.[201] In

[197] LAC RG25 A-3-c, Vol. 8599, 20-1-1-12, Briefing points by R. L. Rogers (Far Eastern Div.) for Arnold Smith, 21.1.1964.

[198] *Holmes*, Canada and the Vietnam War, 201 f.; see also the recollections assembled in *Blanchette*, Canadian Peacekeepers.

[199] Most historians acknowledge the Canadian desire to influence American policy with these missions; *Greg Donaghy*, Minding the Minister: Pearson, Martin, and the American Policy in Asia, 1963–1967, in: Norman Hillmer (Ed.), Pearson, the Unlikely Gladiator, Montreal 1999, 131–149; *Andrew Preston*, Balancing War and Peace. Canadian Foreign Policy and the Vietnam War, 1961–1965, in: Diplomatic History 27/1, 2003, 73–111.

[200] *Blair Seaborn*, Mission to Hanoi: The Canadian Channel, May 1964–November 1965, in: Arthur E. Blanchette (Ed.), Canadian Peacekeepers in Indochina, 1954–1973: Recollections, Ottawa 2002, 85–111.

[201] *Greg Donaghy*, The Rise and Fall of Canadian Military Assistance in the Developing World, 1952–1971, in: Canadian Military History 4/1, 1995, 75–84.

1964, officials reviewed options to grant Malaysia military assistance following the escalation of *Konfrontasi*. Canadian considerations for a Commonwealth scheme took further shape after other ideas such as a UN peacekeeping force or diplomatic mediation had failed.[202] Especially Canadian Secretary of State for External Affairs (CSSEA) Paul Martin showed concerns that the Canadian public would expect the government to do more for a Commonwealth ally.[203] The expectations for a Commonwealth scheme only increased when Malaysian Prime Minister Tunku Abdul Rahman visited Canada in the summer of 1964. Within days of his arrival, the Canadian government announced to expand its help to Malaysia by military and financial assistance.[204]

In the following, further pressure from Commonwealth allies led to concessions by individual officials that seemed surprising in the light of Canada's traditional non-committal attitude. At a meeting of the Commonwealth Finance Ministers in Tokyo in August 1964, the other Commonwealth representatives were able to impress on Canadian Minister of Finance Walter Gordon the urgency for a concerted Commonwealth action on Confrontation.[205] Gordon promised to impress on his government the need for Canadian action. Also, he accepted to participate in a joint Commonwealth approach to the US representative C. Douglas Dillon: "I thought that Dillon might be impressed if he knew that all four of our countries, Britain, Australia, N[ew] Z[ealand] and C[ana] DA, would be providing additional assistance and especially that C[ana]DA would be participating."[206]

Gordon's enthusiasm for a Commonwealth effort had been backed by some reports in Canadian media which insisted that "Canada, as a member of the Commonwealth, has a moral stake in the fate of her Malaysian partner".[207] However, back home, his assurances caught officials off guard as there had been no considerations for a more substantial contribution to the conflict.[208] The fact that Gordon quietly dropped his initiative in the face of official resistance showed the limits of Canada's appreciation for a joint Commonwealth approach. Canadian officials feared any connotation of imperial defence that came

[202] LAC RG25 A-3-c, Vol. 8917, 20-INDON-1-3-MLSIA, Memorandum (Robertson) to SSEA, 12.3.1964.

[203] LAC RG25 A-3-c, Vol. 8917, 20-INDON-1-3-MLSIA, Report on Interdepartmental Meeting, 25.3.1964.

[204] LAC RG24-B-1, Vol. 21493, CSC 2137:12, Memorandum by CSSEA for Cabinet Committee, 13.8.1964; *Peter J. Boyce/R. K. Davis*, Malaysia tests the Commonwealth, in: Australian Quarterly 37/3, 1965, 59–68, 62.

[205] ANZ ABHS W4628 7148, Box 116, LONB 106/2/7, Part 3, NEmb. Tokyo 225, 11.9.1964; ANZ ABHS W4628 7148, Box 116, LONB 106/2/7, Part 3, Record by Malaysian Treasury on Meeting of Finance Ministers in Tokyo held on 11.9.1964, 15.10.1964.

[206] LAC RG24-B-1, Vol. 21493, CSC 2137:12, CEmb. Tokyo, 11.9.1964.

[207] "Help for our Malaysian partner", Toronto Daily Star, 25.6.1964.

[208] ANZ ABHS W4628 7148, Box 116, LONB 106/2/7, Part 3, NHC Ottawa 409, 25.9.1964.

with the closer Commonwealth framework: "We could not consider helping our Malaysian brethren resist aggression from Sukarno because it was not a UN operation. The blunt fact, of course, was that anything that could, however distortedly, be called a defence of empire would raise all kinds of local hornets."[209]

Reservations about the need for support of Malaysia remained: Officials would be sympathetic to a request for assistance "while continuing to believe that the primary responsibility for the defence of Malaysia should be borne by countries having a direct national interest in the security of the area".[210] Nevertheless, in January 1965, the Canadian government increased its military aid to Malaysia.[211] Canadian officials could immediately see the benefit of their commitment: only weeks later, in February, the Canadian High Commission in Kuala Lumpur reported that Canadian officials were invited for the first time into the "inner circle"[212] of a meeting with the Tunku and the ANZAM partners. To him, this invitation directly resulted from the Canadian offer of military assistance.

Whereas Canada's military assistance could be drafted as an extraordinary effort for the Commonwealth, Australia and New Zealand were expected to do more. Following the Indonesian landings on the Malayan peninsula in 1964, the British increased its defence force, including a range of cross-border persecutions under CLARET.[213] It also increased the pressure on its ANZAM partners to finally commit troops to Borneo. Up to early 1965, Australia and New Zealand had supported the British effort in different ways, e. g. by making its troops available for border service in Malaya[214], but had resisted the use of their forces in Borneo for political reasons.

---

[209] *John W. Holmes*, Canada and the Pax Americana, in: Harvey L. Dyck/Hans P. Krosby (Ed.), Empire and Nations: Essays in Honour of Frederic H. Soward, Toronto 1969, 73–90, 87.

[210] LAC RG24-B-1, Vol. 21493, CSC 2137:12, Memorandum by CSSEA for Cabinet Committee, 13.8.1964.

[211] In the end, Canada offered four Caribou planes, 250 police motorcycles and training assistance to Malaysia. It also cancelled an aircraft sale to Indonesia; LAC MG26 N3, Vol. 135, 313.45 London Jan 65 Conf.

[212] LAC RG25 A-3-c, Vol. 8917, 20-INDON-1-3-MLSIA, CHC Kuala Lumpur 100, 23.2.1965.

[213] CLARET was a secret operation in Borneo that emerged from British considerations for retaliatory actions since 1964. Initially, the operation envisaged cross-border raids and pursuits of up to 3 000 yards into Indonesian territory; this envisaged frame was extended in August 1964 to 10 000 yards. British officials were aware of the political risks of such operations that could be used in advantage of Indonesia's international case if made public. As a strategy in case of exposure of those operations, they advised to mask them as mistakes over an "ill-defined" border situation. *Jones*, Conflict and Confrontation, 235 f.; *Christopher Pugsley*, From Emergency to Confrontation. The New Zealand Armed Forces in Malaya and Borneo 1949–1966, Melbourne 2003, 255 f.

[214] ANZ ABHS W4628 7148, Box 115, LONB 106/2/7, Part 2, Brief for Commonwealth Prime Minister's Meeting and ANZUS Council, 1.7.1964; *Benvenuti*, Cold War and Decolonisation, 245 f.

Meanwhile, with the parallel deterioration in Vietnam, Australia and New Zealand were also forced to consider further contributions there. What had started as token forces to indicate support for the US alliance and its presence in the region developed into a more substantial commitment that had to be assessed against their effort in Malaysia. In both countries, the decision to send combat forces to Malaysia and Vietnam came in early 1965.[215] Notions of interdependence between both conflicts supported simultaneous commitments. Upon the Australian decision, John McEwen wrote to Harold Wilson that his country perceived Vietnam and Malaysia as "part of a common pattern and common threat".[216]

Aside from being both framed through a policy of forward defence, both commitments had important differences that would prove crucial in the following discussions. For one, a commitment to Vietnam bore considerable obstacles in legitimisation as it was a potential breach of the Geneva accords. Despite tacit Canadian and British support[217], Vietnam also fell out of previous schemes of imperial cooperation as it was the first Australasian commitment without Britain. Ten years earlier, such an arrangement might have been unthinkable for Australasian policymakers.[218] Now, it was explained by an increased awareness for Southeast Asian tensions and the reliance on the USA.

A contribution without Britain might also explain why New Zealanders struggled more with a commitment to Vietnam. New Zealanders were more afraid than Australians to lose preferential, familiar ways of cooperation within the old Empire framework, even more so as they relied on British logistics and equipment.[219] Moreover, New Zealand officials both mistrusted Australian and American assessments of the level of threat stemming from North Vietnam. Ultimately however, especially NDEA officials perceived the commitment to Vietnam as a price to pay for American protection, even if they were sceptical about the outcome of the war early on.[220] In the end, New Zealand policymakers presented their Vietnam commitment like Australians in a Commonwealth frame of reference: They declared to see Vietnam now as the crucial struggle

---

[215] New Zealand decided to send a SAS unit and an infantry battalion to Borneo in January 1965, ANZ AAFD W3738 811 Box 1316, CAB 222/3/1, Part 2, Note for Cabinet, 26.1.1965. Australia had decided to send a battalion to Borneo in February 1965; *Thomas B. Millar*, Australian Defence, 1945–1965, in: Gordon Greenwood/Norman Harper (Ed.), Australia in World Affairs. 1961–1965, London 1968, 251–312, 288.

[216] ANZ ABHS W4628 7148, Box 116, LONB 106/2/7, Part 4, NHC Canberra 44, 20.1.1965.

[217] LAC RG25 A-3-c, Vol. 8842, 20-AUSTL-1-3, Part 3, Memorandum to CSSEA, 29.4.1965 and CDEA to ICC Saigon 352, 30.4.1965.

[218] *Ward*, British Embrace, 249.

[219] ANZ ABFK W5767 19754, Box 10, 1/4/4, "Deployment of ANZUK Forces under SEATO Plans", COS Paper (COS (64) 76), 13.8.1964.

[220] McIntosh to Corner, 5.5.1965, quoted in: *McGibbon*, Unofficial Channels, 329.

for Southeast Asia, on which ultimately the future of Malaysia and the British presence would depend.[221]

3.4 Between British Exceptionalism and Self-Determination – Postcolonial Struggles in Southeast Asia

Throughout the 1960s, discussions on Malaysia and Vietnam spurred more fundamental debates on the effect of strategic alliances or concepts such as forward defence and their implications for an overall Western effort against communism. As a result, the military bases in the region gained a considerable political dimension in the context of the Cold War and decolonisation. Global movements of nationalism and self-determination challenged concepts of imperialism and white supremacy on a regional level. With UN discussions turning to the righteousness of colonialism, the bases also had to be assessed against legal implications that could follow from a stronger international emphasis on racial equality and sovereignty.[222] Not only was their purpose for SEATO debated, different voices on a local and global level also pointed to the larger question if a Western presence on foreign, Non-Western soil was still acceptable. These international discussions increased British concerns for the tenure of their bases. They feared their presence could be used in relation to allegations of neo-colonialism, not only by the communist world, but also by nonaligned countries like Indonesia. As a result, the international image of the forces involved became more important than the question of local distortions and reasons underlying the conflicts.[223]

Within this fluctuating global climate, Australia, Canada, and New Zealand had to determine how to frame their role concerning local security. Assessing the need and legitimacy of the Western presence in the region, the former dominions were furthermore confronted with alternatives to create regional security such as neutralisation or simply local self-determination. Those alternatives stood in opposition to concepts of postcolonial rule that supported a continued Western control or influence. Not only did they challenge the legitimacy of British presence, ultimately, these alternative orders also touched on the countries' engagement with the region as Western white Anglo-Saxon countries. These orders also offered a different path in the Western response to communism that could potentially affect the global direction of the Cold War. With growing concerns for Chinese intervention since the Korean War, all three countries had to

[221] ANZ ABHS W4628 7148, Box 119, LONB 106/5, Part 1, Wellington to London 1215, 30.4.1965.

[222] *Jan Eckel*, Utopie der Moral, Kalkül der Macht. Menschenrechte in der globalen Politik nach 1945, in: Archiv für Sozialgeschichte 49, 2009, 437–484, 455.

[223] *Subritzky*, End of Empire, 218.

consider how they would deal with China as a subversive or at least influential force in Southeast Asia. In the following, they had to position themselves on containment of or engagement with China. Moreover, the concerns for Chinese subversion also stimulated debates on the likelihood of open conflict, and the need to consider measures of containment outside the military framework, such as development assistance.

Even if Canada had mainly remained uninvolved in the conflicts in Southeast Asia, the implications of a British retreat for the regional security framework were, by all three former dominions, more or less assessed in a similar manner. It was in the sphere of global Cold War considerations framing the regional instability as part of global security structures where they differed the most in their national outlook. Australia and New Zealand increasingly promoted the inclusion of Southeast Asian struggles into global Cold War considerations and supported a military involvement by pointing to a threat in their 'Near North' that could turn into a global war. In contrast, Canada approached the region the other way around, namely by applying global Cold War considerations on the regional level. Following this position, it could promote alternative concepts of stabilisation such as neutralisation based on its appreciations for a global balance of power while Australia and New Zealand often rejected such considerations out of fear for local implications.

3.4.1 *Facing Global Implications of Southeast-Asian Conflicts – The Question of Chinese Communism*

When Australia and New Zealand committed troops to Malaysia and Vietnam in early 1965, the differences in outlook with Canada became apparent. During an address to an Ottawa audience, Australian High Commissioner Kenneth Bailey contrasted the history and British background shared by both countries with their differing assessments of a threat stemming from Southeast Asia. By reiterating previous narratives of geographical proximity, Bailey insisted that Australia had to militarily commit itself to the conflicts in the region because, "in a real and painful sense, the defence of the rimlands of Asia is the defence of Australia's own frontiers".[224]

Bailey's remarks exemplified the growing Australian unease that Canada was not backing the Western effort in Southeast Asia. Similar discomfort had been voiced by ASEA Arthur Tange a year earlier: "It is by no means apparent that the potential threat of Chinese communism is seen in the same way in Ottawa as it is in Canberra, nor that the significance of SEATO and ANZUS and

224 LAC RG25 A-3-c, Vol. 8842, 20-AUSTL-1-3, Part 2, "Through Australian Windows", Address by AHC Kenneth Bailey to Ottawa Canadian Men's Club, 11.3.1965.

of what we are trying to do in support of Malaysia is as completely understood as we would like it to be."[225]

Canada's military assistance to Malaysia was clearly not enough for Australian officials like Tange. Yet it was Canada's stance on Communist China that caused more substantial frictions among the former dominions, especially surrounding the recent Canadian considerations for recognition. A recognition of the PRC, both bilaterally and in the UN, had been discussed among the West since the communist regime had come into being in October 1949. Although Britain had recognised the PRC early on, the former dominions had not followed this lead due to experiences in the Korean War and strong American objections.[226] Nevertheless, denying political recognition resulted in an ongoing issue for international dealings, especially within the UN. As a result, especially Canada continuously engaged in considerations for recognition, both to mediate Cold War polarisation and to explore opportunities in bilateral cooperation. In contrast, while some Tasman officials urged recognition to reach a *modus vivendi* and were opposed to the hysteria attached to Chinese communism, most policymakers here still objected to this step based on regional security considerations.[227]

Equally, they tried to convince Canadians of the need to revise their interest in recognition. Appealing to Canadian appreciations for multilateral cooperation in the Commonwealth, Bailey's predecessor, D. O. Day, gave a speech on the "Commonwealth and the Challenge of Communism"[228] in early 1964. To Day, regional cooperation under a Commonwealth scheme could resist communism by promoting values that

> "are inherently Commonwealth in character: governments responsive to the will of the people democratically revealed, respect for the law, independence of the judiciary which administers the law, respect for minorities whether political or racial, freedom of the mind particularly in universities, economic growth without totalitarian controls".[229]

He proposed to Canadians another reason to reconsider recognition: By pointing to the values of the Commonwealth, Day urged Canadians to assess the impact of recognition on the regional structures and to compare the justice of communist countries with that of Commonwealth countries.

For Australians and New Zealanders, Chinese recognition would also undermine the confidence Southeast Asian states would have in Western protection,

---

[225] NAA A1838 229/9/1, Part 2, Arthur Tange to L. G. Sellars (Acting AHC Ottawa), 5.6.1964.

[226] *Penrose*, Recognising China; *Beecroft*, Recognition Problem.

[227] *Dane Kennedy*, Australian Policy Towards China, in: Gordon Greenwood/Norman Harper (Ed.), Australia in World Affairs. 1961–1965, London 1968, 397–415.

[228] LAC RG25 A-3-c, Vol. 8842, 20-AUSTL-1-3, "The Commonwealth and the Challenge of Communism – An Australian Viewpoint", Address by Australian High Commissioner D. O. Day, to University of Manitoba Conference on Commonwealth Affairs, 20.1.1964.

[229] Ibid.

confidence that had been partially created by alliances such as SEATO. Consequently, Australasians were critically aware of any move that could underline the psychological value of their defence framework, which included the British bases as a physical representation of said alliances. Aside from Canadian interest in recognition, also British considerations for a reduction of conventional forces worried them. As British briefs started to question the concept of SEATO from the late 1950s on, Australasians became increasingly alarmed by notions of alternative regional order such as neutralisation.[230] When British Commissioner-General Lord Selkirk encouraged Prime Minister Harold Macmillan in 1961 to reconsider British policy in the region by focusing more on the strengthening of local nationalism and self-reliance[231], Macmillan reminded Selkirk that any policy change had to be adapted gradually because of Australasian sensitivities: "[…] we must not give them any cause to blame us for leaving them precipitately in the lurch."[232]

As they suspected a British change of heart, it made sense for Tasman policymakers to object to every weakening of their presence in Southeast Asia, and to insist on the bases as a valuable psychological deterrent. This task became even more difficult when growing differences within the Western alliance showed in their entirety over France's move to recognise the PRC in 1964. For Australia and New Zealand, French recognition opened up dangerous debates among Western allies on security objectives in Southeast Asia that could be considered academic by outside powers but crucial to those engaged in regional conflicts. When Charles de Gaulle proposed a neutralisation of Southeast Asia, AMEA Garfield Barwick reacted with a statement of refusal:

> "While it is handsome for someone to talk about Asia having its future determined by Asians, it must be remembered we have an interest, as well as other Western countries, in this area, and our interest in maintaining peace and stability will not be served by the withdrawal of military forces, nor those of other countries by the loss of bases at Singapore and in the Philippines."[233]

As Barwick's remarks indicate, many Australians, and to some extent New Zealanders, felt a certain unease about proposals to limit Western influence in Southeast Asia. Not only did neutralisation contest their policy of forward defence, but it also challenged the basis of their interaction with the region as nations of European or Western origin.

---

230 *Lowe*, Contending with Nationalism, 90 f.

231 Lord Selkirk to Harold Macmillan, 14.8.1961, TNA PREM 11/3737, quoted in: *Jones*, Conflict and Confrontation, 26.

232 Harold Macmillan to Lord Selkirk, 17.10.1961, TNA PREM 11/3737, quoted in: *Jones*, Conflict and Confrontation, 27.

233 LAC RG25 A-3-c, Vol. 8842, 20-AUSTL-1-3, Part 1, CHC Canberra 48, 6.2.1964; see also *Christopher Waters*, The Menzies Government and de Gaulle's Proposal for the Neutralisation of Southeast Asia: 1963–1965, in: Frank Cain (Ed.), Menzies in War and Peace, St. Leonards 1997, 138–153.

In contrast, Canadian officials perceived the French approach as an opportunity for the West to approach Peking further[234], therewith alarming the Australian government. In talks on France's proposal for neutralisation, Australians confided to their Canadian colleagues they felt the French initiative did not recognise how much Australians invested in the region's stability by backing the US effort in Vietnam.[235] When Paul Hasluck met with Paul Martin in November 1964, he cautioned the Canadian government to await any recognition amidst the current deterioration in Indochina and Malaysia. Moreover, he indicated that any Australian government considering a vote favouring UN admission of the PRC would be defeated in the next federal election.[236] On the other side of the table, Paul Martin also argued with domestic opinion when he said that Canadians supported recognition as an acceptance of reality. Amongst the Canadian public and officials, unease had grown about the exclusion of the PRC from world affairs. Moreover, the continuous commercial relationship with China seemed to demand acceptance for broader ties. Again, Canada and Australia shared the same concerns but came to different results: Australia had also established a silent wheat trade with China, but resisted pressures from industry and parts of the public to consider closer ties with the PRC.[237]

For the time being, Canada refrained from recognition, not least because of American objections. As Australian interventions had shown, it was also the pressure within the Commonwealth that shaped outlooks on the question of communism. For Canada, these outlooks also dominated discussions on Malaysia and Vietnam.

3.4.2 Defending the Free World? Vietnam and Malaysia as Battlegrounds of the Cold War

Canada's balancing act between being a member of the Commonwealth and Western alliance and wanting to sustain a non-committal position to the conflicts in Southeast Asia soon exposed fractures within the country. In January 1965, during Canadian considerations for Malaysian assistance, a reader of the *To-*

---

234 *Don Page*, The Representation of China in the United Nations: Canadian Perspectives and Initiatives, 1949–1971, in: Paul M. Evans/Michael B. Frolic (Ed.), Reluctant Adversaries: Canada and the People's Republic of China 1949–1970, Toronto 1991, 73–105, 89 f.

235 LAC RG25 A-3-c, Vol. 8599, 20-1-1-12, Part 1, CHC Canberra 92, 20.2.1964 and CHC Canberra 112, 4.3.1964.

236 LAC RG25-A-3-c, Volume 12617, 20-AUSTL-1-3-MLSIA, Record of Meeting between Martin and Hasluck on 27.11.1964.

237 Both countries left the trade arrangements to their wheat boards and therewith could counter every argument of governmental involvement. See for a contemporary Australian analysis of this ambivalent policy *John Reynolds*, Recognition by Trade. The Controversial Wheat Sales to China, in: Australian Outlook 18/2, 1964, 117–126; *J. Wilczynski*, The Economics and Politics of Wheat Exports to China, in: The Australian Quarterly 37/2, 1965, 44–55.

ronto Star expressed his anger about Canada's apparent neglect for the underlying issues of Confrontation: "If Malaysia succumbs to the onward advances of Communism, then our Commonwealth neighbours, Australia and New Zealand, will be in danger."[238] Some Canadians moved even closer to a Western containment strategy. In a following *Toronto Star* comment, the author called Canada lucky in staying out of Vietnam; "But we can hardly stay aloof from the struggle for Asia, although our actions must be limited by our resources and other commitments."[239] His call was supported by a reader's letter that called the American objection to assist Malaysia ironic, given it was committed to Vietnam. In contrast, Britain should be praised for its help to Malaysia,

> "Certainly, I see the importance of holding South Viet Nam against aggressors: but why wait for Malaysia to be at its knees before coming to its aid? At the same time, if Canada has money for Royal visits and other imperialistic trivia, it certainly has the means to help defend an outpost of democracy."[240]

Although most of these opinion pieces were isolated in Canadian media, which primarily focused on North America and Europe, they nevertheless indicate a growing awareness for the global context of Malaysia. Moreover, as the last letter illustrates, some perceived it as Canada's duty to become involved as part of its historical partnership with Britain that should not be confined to symbolic expressions such as royal visits.

Over the deterioration of both conflicts, Cold War attitudes increasingly dominated discussions, both in Canada as in Australia and New Zealand. In Australia, the tightening of positions was marked by new AMEA Paul Hasluck, who repeatedly underlined the potential dangers of Southeast Asian deterioration: "We in Australia live on the edge of perhaps the most dangerous area of the world as regards the major power contest and the most troubled and fear-ridden region in the subsidiary aggression. We cannot stand apart from this reality."[241] While policymakers increasingly used regional instability and communist threat as links between the conflicts in Malaysia and Vietnam, these notions of interdependence failed to cover the differences between both disputes. Soon the commitment to Malaysia developed a more positive reputation than Vietnam, not least because of its connection to the Commonwealth. Continuous diplomatic links to Indonesia, such as the outstanding work of Australian diplomat Keith Shann, underlined ideas that the Commonwealth framework would provide better opportunities for local contacts, including those with lead-

[238] *James H. Gallagher* (Toronto, Ontario), "If Malaysia Falls", Letter to Editor, Toronto Star, 16.1.1965.

[239] "The Battleground is Asia", Toronto Daily Star, 19.1.1965.

[240] *Bernard Feldspar* (Trenton, Ontario), "Help Malaysia", Letter to Editor, Toronto Daily Star, 21.1.1965.

[241] Speech by AMEA Paul Hasluck at the American Australian Association, New York 8.12.1964, found in LAC RG25 A-3-c, Vol. 8842, 20-AUSTL-1-3, Part 2.

ers from Malaysia and Singapore.[242] Additionally, assistance to Malaysia could be drafted as resistance against unjust aggression since the majority of the Malaysian population supported the Tunku.

In comparison, officials could never fully endorse South Vietnamese leaders and struggled to give cultural meaning to their alliance with Saigon.[243] Moreover, difficulties with American command loomed large in policymaking. The American dominance on the operational level caused several frustrations in Australian and New Zealand circles. In contrast, ANZAM cooperation in Malaysia dated back to the early 1950s and was sustained by traditional schemes of cooperation in the departments involved.

Consequently, Australasian commitments to the Malaysian conflict translated into familiarity and opportunity, and policymakers were able to present their efforts as being motivated by solidarity and responsibility within the Commonwealth. Both in Australia and New Zealand, the commitment to Vietnam lacked the benevolence the Malaysian contribution received.[244] Early doubts about a successful outcome further complicated any political support for intervention in Vietnam. Concerns over the US policy and the local setting of the Vietnam War corresponded to inherent anti-Americanist tendencies in the public that picked up the war in their criticism of American imperialism.[245] On Vietnam, public opinion was therefore divided, arguably more in New Zealand than in Australia.[246] The New Zealand public was more outspoken in criticising a potential Vietnam commitment than the Australian public, a fact that was illustrated by the formation of different initiatives against the Vietnam War already in the early 1960s.[247] Here, the commitment to Malaysia developed into a political instrument for both supporters and protesters of the Vietnam War. While protesters could oppose a Vietnam commitment because they feared a withdrawal of resources from Malaysia, supporters could parallel the causes for commitment in Malaysia and Vietnam. Through this political debate, the Malaysian conflict was drafted as more justified than the Vietnam War by pointing to the help Malaysia deserved as a Commonwealth country.

242 *Dennis/Grey/Edwards*, Emergency and Confrontation, 320.

243 *Peter Edwards*, Some Reflections on the Australian Government's Commitment to the Vietnam War, in: Jeffrey Grey/Jeff Doyle (Ed.), Vietnam: War, Myth and Memory: Comparative Perspectives on Australia's War in Vietnam, Crows Nest 1992, 1–13, 12.

244 See comments made by New Zealand official Ralph Mullins during the Four Power Information Conference 1965, ANZ ABHS W5400 20358, Box 88, KL 101/5/1, Record of Four Power Information Conference, 3.11.1965.

245 *Peter Edwards*, A Nation at War. Australian Politics, Society and Diplomacy During the Vietnam War, 1965–1975, St. Leonards 1997, 99.

246 *David Lee/Moreen Dee*, Southeast Asian Conflicts, in: David Goldsworthy/Peter Edwards (Ed.), Facing North: A Century of Australian Engagement with Asia, Melbourne 2001, 262–309, 294.

247 *Robert Rabel*, The Vietnam Antiwar Movement in New Zealand, in: Peace & Change 17/1, 1992, 3–33.

Yet, in Australia, the strong emphasis on Commonwealth values caused some concern. Officials feared for New Zealand's allegiance to ANZUS, with officials like Arthur Tange recommending lecturing New Zealanders on their Vietnam obligations.[248] However, both Australian and New Zealand audiences agreed that there was a crucial argument in retaining a distinct British force in the region. Public discussions in both countries showed that Britain's image and role seemed to be less controversial in comparison to the American presence. For some officials, British exceptionalism as represented in distinct practices and values deserved some positive consideration. For all three former dominions, Britain could still have a mission of 'civilisation' and 'progress' based on its Anglo-Saxon background. However, Britain's approach to the creation of Malaysia and its insistence on Indonesian aggression contributed to growing international criticism of its colonial record. Moreover, UN resolutions in support of self-determination and racial equality increased the pressure on colonial powers still exerting suppressive or discriminatory rule.[249]

Especially Canada, with its record of UN activism, faced a dilemma over the support of British values. While Canadians objected to calls for swift decolonisation and Afro-Asian allegations against colonialist white countries[250], they were critically aware of the political pitfalls of a continued British presence in Southeast Asia. When British officials considered adopting resettlement schemes during Confrontation, Canadian officials in Kuala Lumpur were doubtful about the scheme and warned of potential international recrimination if Canada became associated with the British plans: "According to the Treasury paper there will be barbed wire fencing around resettlement areas in Sarawak. They won't be very pretty whatever the criterion used and […] our association with them if effected, would not be very politic either."[251] Similar concerns had been voiced earlier when Canadians learned about British CLARET plans. In contrast to the moral criticism caused by the resettlement schemes, CLARET let them fear for Malaysia's political case in international organisations, above all in the UN. From Canada's perspective, Malaysia's standing in the Afro-Asian bloc in and outside the Commonwealth had already been low; any publication of border raids could further distort its image as a victim of Indonesian aggression.[252]

---

248 NAA A1838 370/9/3, Arthur Tange to AHC Wellington (Cameron), 4.6.1964.

249 *Samuel Moyn*, Imperialism, Self-Determination, and the Rise of Human Rights, in: Akira Iriye/Petra Goede/William I. Hitchcock (Ed.), The Human Rights Revolution: An International History, Oxford 2012, 159–178; *Burke*, Decolonization, 35–55.

250 *McKercher*, Sound and Fury.

251 LAC RG25 A-3-c, Vol. 8917, 20-INDON-1-3-MLSIA, Part 6, CHC Kuala Lumpur, 14.7.1964.

252 See discussions in Commonwealth Div. to Economic Div., 23.4.1964 and Brief for NATO Minister Meeting (May 64), 27.4.1964, LAC RG25 A-3-c, Vol. 8917, 20-INDON-1-3-MLSIA.

Australian and New Zealand officials shared some of these concerns. Besides arguing for Malaysia's international standing, both governments were also afraid that CLARET border raids could escalate Confrontation. New Zealand representatives in Kuala Lumpur saw Britain's vague notions of an 'ill-defined' border as an easy target for "valid charges of falsehood".[253] Based on these doubts about British practice, both governments delayed their participation in the cross-border operations repeatedly and only agreed after Indonesia's withdrawal from the UN in early 1965.[254]

Heightened awareness for international repercussions was also caused by decolonisation conflicts in other parts of the former Empire. At a time when African decolonisation became an explosive issue of supra-regional dimension, white forces could become a similar issue as the presence of forces labelled as 'West'. On the height of Confrontation, Britain's High Commission in Kuala Lumpur therefore advised to review the ANZAM presence in the light of potential recriminations from the 'Third World':

"[…] it is extremely unlikely that white, foreign, Western bases will continue to be acceptable in South-East Asia for an indefinite time. All our experience since the war argues against this […] in the councils of the Afro-Asian countries the presence of a Western base on an independence country's territory is the supreme badge of the stooge."[255]

The fears over a continued presence corresponded to doubts regarding the course of the Commonwealth during and after decolonisation. In 1963, Lester Pearson confided in talks with Americans his convictions that

"the British Empire and Commonwealth, as it had previously existed, was in rapid dissolution by the emergence of colonial entities into independent states and that the advent of African Commonwealth States doomed the Commonwealth system. He [Lester Pearson] expressed the hope, but by no means confidently, that some special relationship would continue to be maintained between Canada, New Zealand, Australia and the United Kingdom and perhaps India."[256]

Similar to Pearson's concerns, New Zealand representatives feared that with the advent of new members to forums such as the UN, issues would be increasingly decided "along a line of colour".[257] They could argue even more so when the Commonwealth meetings over the next years discussed Southeast Asian con-

[253] ANZ ABHS W4628 7148, Box 115, LONB 106/2/7, Part 2, NHC Kuala Lumpur 201, 9.5.1964.

[254] ANZ ABHS W4628 7148, Box 116, LONB 106/2/7, Part 4, Record of Meeting between Robert Menzies, Keith Holyoake and Denis Healey in London, 1.2.1965.

[255] TNA FO 371/175067, BHC Kuala Lumpur to CRO 3, 14.4.1964, quoted in: *Matthew Jones*, A Decision Delayed. Britain's Withdrawal from South East Asia Reconsidered, 1961–68, in: The English Historical Review 117/472, 2002, 569–595, 595.

[256] Lester B. Pearson in talks with American officials, 23.4.1963, quoted in: *Stewart*, Objective of US Foreign Policy, 96.

[257] ANZ ABHS W5400 20358, Box 88, KL 101/5/1, Paper by New Zealand Delegation to Four Power Information Conference, 24.3.1964.

flicts along the lines of alignment. In 1965, the annual meeting could neither find a definite position on Vietnam nor on Malaysia, and policymakers from the former dominions faced strong criticism, particularly from African members.[258] Following the meeting, Keith Holyoake shared his frustrations:

> "My immediate mood after the meeting with its quarrels, unreasonableness and brow-beating, was to wonder whether the Commonwealth Prime Minister's meeting was worth repeating and whether it might not be better to tell our people that they would need to revise their ideas of this new and ever-expanding Commonwealth, in which those of British stock are now in such a conspicuous minority."[259]

Britain and the former dominions alike were concerned with the strength of Afro-Asian recriminations, both in and outside the Commonwealth. As a result, officials voiced their concerns that the bases East of Suez could become a potential issue with racialised connotations. Upon British request for support in Borneo, Australians were only willing to commit forces after American assurances as they were afraid that they could end up as "the only 'white faces' fighting the Indonesians".[260] When Australian officials were informed about British plans for CLARET, the Australian Defence Committee recommended using non-European forces to soften the blow of potential Indonesian allegations of Malaysia as being a neo-colonialist stooge.[261] In a similar vein, New Zealand officials objected to the Borneo commitment and particularly CLARET operations since they could be used by Indonesian propaganda to blame "White imperialists".[262] Unsuccessfully, they even hoped to commit African members to some form of military aid to Malaysia as it would delegitimise Indonesian claims of white dominance.[263]

3.4.3 Being the Better Briton? Relations with Newly Emerging Nations in Southeast Asia

The longer *Konfrontasi* dragged on, the more the conflict put Malaysia and Britain's position in the spotlight of international debates on decolonisation and national sovereignty. To enhance Malaysia's chances for international support during Confrontation, Britain and the dominions increasingly reviewed options to legitimise Malaysia's cause and their own military presence. Despite the con-

---

258 ANZ ABHS W4627 950, Box 1409, 56/2/3, Part 2, Minutes of EA Committee, 4.8.1965.

259 ANZ ABHS W5400 20358, Box 85, KL 101/1/2, Part 1, Report by Keith Holyoake to Cabinet, 20.7.1965.

260 Australian officials in talks with New Zealand officials in Wellington on 4.5.1964, AHC Wellington 273, 5.5.1964, quoted in: *Dee*, Regional Significance, 94.

261 *Horner*, Strategic Command, 214.

262 Keith Holyoake in ANZAM Talks in London, Record of Meeting, 1.2.1965, ANZ ABHS W4628 7148, Box 116, LONB 106/2/7, Part 4.

263 ANZ ABHS W4628 7148, Box 116, LONB 106/2/7, Part 4, NHC Kuala Lumpur, Guidance Survey 22/65, 28.6.1965.

troversial state of British decolonisation, an emphasis on Commonwealth links seemed increasingly beneficial compared to the reference frame of the 'Free World' that would put Malaysia aside other anti-communist efforts in Korea and Vietnam. As the comparison between the commitments to Vietnam and Malaysia had shown, the British background and the Commonwealth frame could serve as a more favourable framework to pursue relations with the region, at least in comparison to the American alliance and SEATO. Despite its imperial background, the Commonwealth seemed to offer a value-based structure that was perceived as less Cold War biased and Eurocentric than other frameworks.[264]

Throughout the 1950s and 1960s, Commonwealth cooperation helped in all three former dominions to establish the idea of being a bridge between white and non-white countries.[265] Their own colonial history and recent independence now became the asset to frame a role close but distinct to Britain. Moreover, geographical proximity or a middle size in power or territory should enable better rapports with Asian countries. When the Tunku stated publicly in April 1965 that he would welcome the replacement of Commonwealth troops by non-white troops, New Zealand High Commissioner Hunter Wade objected to this proposal in talks with Malaysian Secretary of Foreign Affairs Tun Razak: "I pointed out particularly that the Australians and ourselves do not consider we are outsiders in relation to events in Southeast-Asia."[266] He got reassured by Razak that Malaysian statements had underlined the wish to replace big powers from outside the region, "he [Razak] was differentiating between Britain on the one hand and Australia and New Zealand on the other".[267]

Similarly, all three countries felt compelled to draw a distinction to the USA. Already in 1956, Paul Martin had critically reported on the US economic assistance to the region:

> "Nevertheless, the fact is that their motives are suspect and because of this there seems to be an important role for the smaller countries with long and influential associations – like Canada and Australia – to act as a sort of balance, interpreting the United States viewpoint while at the same time recognizing and maintaining the Commonwealth relationship, a relationship + a community that must not be weakened."[268]

Martin's comment outlined the envisioned Canadian role benefitting both from a North American identity shared with the USA as from the Commonwealth link, but also from its middle power status. Most of all, a distance to the USA

[264] *Onslow*, Commonwealth and the Cold War, 1060.

[265] *David Webster*, Canadian-Indonesian Relations 1945–1963. International Relations and Public Diplomacy, University of British Columbia 2005, PhD Thesis, 11 f.

[266] ANZ ABHS W4628 7148, Box 116, LONB 106/2/7, Part 4, Hunter Wade (NHC Kuala Lumpur) to NSEA, 23.4.1965.

[267] Ibid.

[268] LAC MG32 B12 (Paul Martin Fonds), Vol. 23, Paul Martin to Collard (Montreal Gazette), 1.12.1956.

would enable a position less easily to exploit in the ideological context of the Cold War. As one brief stated in 1964, officials hoped to establish "a network of 'special' contacts with the newly-emerging nations in Asia and Africa at a time when the crude East-West conflict centred in Europe is being transformed into a contest with international communism for the ideological allegiance of these new nations".[269]

In regards to Malaysia, it was not only the middle power status, but also Canada's geographical distance that made it a primary mediator. Its remoteness allowed an approach to the region that was not met with recriminations as voiced towards Australia and New Zealand. As Canadians reported in September 1964, Australia saw Canada as better suited to represent Malaysia because of "our reputation for objectivity and independence", which would allow Canada to "play a constructive role".[270] However embryonic it might seem for officials from the 'Old' Commonwealth, Canada's interest for the region was praised by local leaders, as they assumed a Canadian effort to be even greater and more exceptional, given the geographical distance.

Like Canadians, New Zealand officials expected to receive better reception among Southeast Asian nations because their country would have "no axe to grind, no imperialist past and is not suspected of having any territorial or other ambitions in Asia".[271] In drawing credibility from initiatives such as the independence of Western Samoa in 1962[272], they hoped to avoid allegations of imperialism. When New Zealand's High Commission in Kuala Lumpur recommended a contribution to Borneo, it did so believing in the strength of New Zealand's international image: "We are both in a position where, if we are to pursue our policy of supporting the Malaysians against confrontation, we have to run certain risks that some people will try to pin a neo-colonialist tag on to us. I think our record is good enough for it not to stick."[273]

Equally, New Zealand officials expected a lesser identification with colonial power and legacy because of their small territorial size. Moreover, they hoped to establish a reputation for being sensitive about race relations because of their Maori population. Prime Minister Walter Nash stated on several occasions that New Zealand would not have a problem of racialism as both Pakeha and Maori

---

[269] LAC MG26 N3, Vol. 319, 812.3-1964 Minutes Secret., Brief for Prime Minister for the Commonwealth Prime Ministers' Conference, 17.6.1964.

[270] LAC RG25 A-3-c, Vol. 8917, 20-INDON-1-3-MLSIA, CHC Canberra 397, 11.9.1964.

[271] ANZ ABHS W4628 7148, Box 36, LONB 62/1, Airmail Bulletin 1959/29, 13.8.1959.

[272] Following the support for the UN Resolution 1514 in abolition of colonial rule passed in December 1960, New Zealand invited a UN supervisory mission to observe the first elections following independence in Western Samoa in 1965. While most of its closer allies were irritated by the New Zealand decision, others hailed the indication of Western sensitivity towards that issue, see *Gustafson*, Kiwi Keith, 189 f.

[273] ANZ ABFK W5807 7281, Box 166, 226/7/3, Part 5, NHC Kuala Lumpur (Arawa), 22.3.1966.

peoples were treated as equal.[274] In some ways, New Zealand officials felt superior to Australians on this issue, despite the continuous discrimination of Maoris, in the context of foreign affairs prominently depicted in the institutional isolation of Maori-descent Charles Bennett.[275]

Being increasingly involved in the affairs of Southeast Asia and closest to it, Australians struggled the most in giving meaning to their regional ties. Yet the constant discussion of Asian ties produced a growing interest in the underlying factors inhibiting regional stability. In some documents, a certain sense of responsibility for guiding the newly emerging countries is visible.[276] Especially the Commonwealth framework provided policymakers with a sense of familiarity and shared values that facilitated local partnerships.[277] Closer attention for the region also permitted first attempts of identification. In his already mentioned address to Victoria University, Garfield Barwick underlined the growing appreciation in Australia for its geographical setting: "We are a nation of European origin and there is no call for us to pretend we are something else.[...] What I have stressed, however, is that we are geographically a part of the Asian region viewed broadly and that we are seeking to adjust our thinking and our actions accordingly."[278]

Geography rather than history should define relations with the region, as political analyst Usha Mahajani asked in the programmatic article *Is Australia Part of Asia?*.[279] According to Mahajani, Australians had to live up to their geographic environment by engaging with their Asian neighbours:

"A confused terminology has underlain the ambivalence of Australian attitude towards Asia. Australians have regarded their European background as a historical fact and the location of their continent as a geographical accident. This terminology should be reversed. The European content of Australia's population is a historical accident; its position on the map, an unalterable geographical fact."[280]

Tasman officials increasingly underlined the need to improve diplomatic relations, notably as both Australia and New Zealand continued to have ambiguous

274 ANZ ACIE 8798, Box 227, 59/2/176/1, Part 1, Notes of Discussion of Walter Nash with David Marshall (Singapore), 4.3.1958.

275 Charles Bennett would establish one of the closest diplomatic relations with Malaysian leaders during his time as High Commissioner in Kuala Lumpur. For Bennett's position within the NDEA see the correspondence between Alister McIntosh and Hunter Wade in NLNZ MS-Papers-6759-362.

276 See as an example "Factors for Unity and Disunity in Southeast Asia", Brief for the ANZUS Council Meeting 1965, n. d. (April 1965), ANZ ABHS W5400 20358, Box 85, KL 101/1/2, Part 1.

277 *Dan Halvorson*, Commonwealth Responsibility and Cold War Solidarity. Australia in Asia, 1944–1974, Acton 2019, 85 f.

278 ANZ ABHS W5422 950, Box 34, 111/3/3/15, Part 5, "Australia and her Neighbours", Address by Garfield Barwick to Victoria University, 29.5.1963.

279 *Usha Mahajani*, Is Australia Part of Asia?, in: Australian Quarterly 36/2, 1964, 25–34.

280 Ibid., 34.

relations with Asia. Aside from their colonial background, the discussions on SEATO had shown that their forward defence policy troubled some officials when it came to those alliances inhibiting closer relations with local powers.[281] As a way of overcoming this perception of unease both abroad and back home, Tasman posts within the region urged their governments to consider alternative roles, arguably close to the Canadian profile. In 1965, the Australian Embassy in Phnom Penh advised establishing a more independent role "as a sort of amicus curiae by offering the sort of general guidance and material help".[282] To them, contingency planning should be balanced by economic and humanitarian assistance.

As they expected recriminations over their wealth that contrasted local conditions, Australians and New Zealanders felt challenged by geographical proximity, and struggled to find a position vis-à-vis local aspirations for independence and self-determination. Already in 1957, recalling Afro-Asian recriminations over Suez, the New Zealand Embassy in Bangkok urged for a major rethinking on New Zealand's position: "Whether we like it or not – and it is of course true that most New Zealanders do not – we must face the fact that we do have relations with a number of Asian countries and that our actions in almost any sphere are likely to affect and be affected by them."[283] In a similar vein, Arthur Tange had already called in 1955 for an activist Australian policy towards the region. This policy should abolish ties to SEATO and ANZUS and should also refrain from an overemphasis of the Colombo Plan that could be taken as patronising by Southeast Asian countries: "Australia's great opportunity in Asia lies in our own historical break *away* from colonialism."[284]

The neglect of Asian affairs was also discussed in public media. Here, publicists criticised a continued suspicion towards the neighbourhood that would apply to the entire Australian society. In his widely claimed snapshot *The Lucky Country,* Australian author Donald Horne could still lament that "most Australians have not gained a real 'feel' for the part of the world they live in, even if many of them now talk about it [...] Australians talk of Asia as if they were still living in Europe".[285] To him, the political initiatives in the previous decade had not enabled a broader understanding of or cooperation with the Asian continent. The unfolding conflicts in Indochina and Malaysia only added to the feeling of otherness and threat.

---

281 *Christopher Waters*, After Decolonization: Australia and the Emergence of the Non-aligned Movement in Asia, 1954–55, in: Diplomacy & Statecraft 12/2, 2001, 153–174.

282 NAA A1838 3004/11/14, Part 2, AEmb. Phnom Penh to Arthur Tange, 22.3.1961.

283 ANZ ACIE 8798 W2619 434/8/1, Part 6, NEmb. Bangkok, 17.4.1957.

284 NAA A1838 625/2, Arthur Tange to MEA, 22.6.1955 (found in NLA MS10135, Box 5, File 23), emphasis in original.

285 *Donald Horne*, The Lucky Country. The Classic Study of Australia in the Sixties, Ringwood 1964, 93.

Proximity also proved challenging in New Zealand: "We have been inclined to think of them as 'the far east' when, geographically, they are just over the horizon."[286] Here, broad public disinterest and ignorance for the region were nursed by feelings of remoteness. Quoting Keith Sinclair's line on New Zealand being "banned by tides from the sorrows of continents", Keith Buchanan commented in 1964: "This physical remoteness attenuates our awareness of the wider world and this attenuation persists, even in an age of jet travel, as a kind of historical hangover."[287] Despite the calls for regional approaches, most policymakers in all three dominions showed themselves still convinced of the truisms represented by contemporary governmental foreign policy. The suggestions made by officials like Tange or public commentators such as Buchanan would have required an assessment of values and principles shaped by Britishness against growing international norms in support of anti-racialism and anti-colonialism. Given the apprehensions towards a challenging and threatening neighbourhood, an identification with opportunities in the region through liberal policies was however delayed, similar to any changes on immigration policies.[288] All three former dominions remained in an Anglocentric outlook in foreign policy, focused on issues of security and stability, with Australia and New Zealand firmly attached to the concept of forward defence.

3.5 Conclusion of Part 3

A variance of British considerations following the Suez Crisis led the former dominions to anticipate a potential British withdrawal from Southeast Asia. This anticipation was not only created by various negotiations on organisational structures, equipment and burden-sharing, but also rested on perceptions that British thinking on strategy was gradually departing from a Western framework of containment and forward defence. Over discussions on the EEC and decolonisation within the former Empire, Britain's East of Suez position was increasingly questioned. It was further undermined by regional conflicts and instabilities, which were embedded in a global Cold War context of alignment and national self-determination. As a result, the issue of British forces in Southeast Asia was discussed more frequently among the allies and soon gained connotations of a precarious arrangement.

---

286 "Our 'Near North' neighbours", Dominion, 6.10.1961, found in NAA A1838 370/1/1, Part 4.

287 *Keith Buchanan*, Banned by Tides: New Zealand in the Asian Century, in: Chris Elder (Ed.), New Zealand's China Experience: Its Genesis, Triumphs, and Occasional Moments of Less Than Complete Success, [Eastern Horizon vol. 3/no. 9 (1964)], Wellington 2012, 176–179, 176.

288 *Gurry*, Identifying Australia's 'Region', 23.

In consequence, officials in the former dominions anticipated British adjustments of its defence position East of Suez. While Australia and New Zealand both considered potential alternatives, these considerations were often dropped because of their strong allegiance to the British relationship and political opposition to a retreat from their traditional foreign policy framework. Moreover, the only other viable option, namely a strong alliance with the USA, was inhibited by suspicions for American practices and American unwillingness to have the ANZUS partners take a larger share in policymaking regarding Southeast Asia.

In contrast to the other two countries, Canada approached the question of regional security as a distant bystander, interested in solution-finding by means of peacekeeping but opposed to an interventionist role. As the issue of Malaysia had shown, Canadian officials could legitimise a more significant involvement by referring to the Commonwealth relationship and experiences in the field of peacekeeping. However, the analysis already showed the dominant pattern of alliance partners approaching Canada for help rather than intrinsic considerations leading to Canadian action.

Despite indications of a British policy shift, the former dominions continued to place their policies on British cornerstones. Confrontation strengthened the references of Commonwealth solidarity and responsibility rather than leading to a fundamental review of premises on regional cooperation. Here as with other issues of Asian decolonisation in the Commonwealth framework[289], the former dominions perceived their role as one of responsibility for the Southeast Asian countries while they equally sustained a belief in Britain as a key player in this normative framework. Similarly, the discussions and experiences with American counterparts only strengthened perceptions that Britain was needed, both because of its place in a spatial system of security responsibilities as for regular practices of trust that sustained cooperation. In spite of various, yet isolated departmental calls for fundamental foreign and strategic reviews to establish a more self-reliant position, this advice was not followed up. Instead, due to various reasons such as traditional political cooperation or the lack of resources, all three dominions continued to rely on Britain's role as a regional and global power. In the end, discussions on a moral obligation or a preferential treatment within the Commonwealth indicate the fundamental emotional dimension of Anglo-Dominion relations that affected most of the strategic considerations. It was the deep identification with British structures and relationships as opposed to unknown interactions with Asian surroundings and actors that made officials continue to rely on Britain.

289 See on this argument also *Halvorson*, Australia in Asia.

Part 4

A Watershed Moment – Reactions to the British Decision on Cutting Back East of Suez, 1965–1968

In October 1964, for the first time in thirteen years, the British Labour Party gained back the majority to form a government. Under the leadership of Prime Minister Harold Wilson, Britain would decide in 1967/68 to abandon its role East of Suez, including its presence in Southeast Asia, by the end of the decade. However, the path up to this decision was not as straightforward as the continued British economic and financial decline, following Wilson's election, might have suggested. While a cut in British overseas commitments might have been an easy solution to exempt the British household, a departure from the underlying defence obligations proved more difficult. As presented before, these obligations were linked to resilient perceptions of Britain as a world power that stemmed from its imperial role and which still resonated with large parts of politics and public, both in Britain as in the former dominions. As a result, Labour's decision to withdraw in 1967/68 might not have been as foreseeable at the beginning of Wilson's term as it is perceived as logical and rational in retrospect.[1]

Immediately after entering office, Wilson had to acknowledge the unsolved financial issues: Upon election, the general British deficit on the balance of payments had amounted to 800 million British Pounds.[2] Meanwhile, defence efforts for the Singapore base alone were set around 300 million British Pounds per year. In the following, the stationing of 28 000 British troops in the Malaysian region in 1964 would further increase up to around 50 000 servicemen in early 1966, with 18 battalions in total and ten battalions operating in Borneo

[1] For the relevant British sources on the discussion on East of Suez see *S. R. Ashton/W. Roger Louis* (Ed.), British Documents on the End of Empire. Series A, Vol 5: East of Suez and the Commonwealth 1964–1971. Vol. 1: East of Suez, London 2004. For the wide research on the British decisionmaking see *Dockrill*, Britain's Retreat; *Phuong L. Pham*, Ending "East of Suez". The British Decision to Withdraw From Malaysia and Singapore, 1964–1968, Oxford 2010; *Jones*, Decision Delayed; *McCourt*, Britain's "East of Suez Role"; *Pickering*, Britain's Withdrawal; *Edward Longinotti*, Britain's Withdrawal from East of Suez. From Economic Determinism to Political Choice, in: Contemporary British History 29/3, 2014, 318–340.

[2] *S. R. Ashton/Wm R. Louis*, Introduction, in: S. R. Ashton/W. R. Louis (Ed.), British Documents on the End of Empire. Series A, Vol. 5: East of Suez and the Commonwealth 1964–1971: Vol. 1: East of Suez, London 2004, XXIX–CXXXV, XXXIII.

alone.[3] With Confrontation enfolding, British governmental studies already indicated in 1964 that Britain would not be able to uphold its various military commitments, including obligations to NATO and SEATO.[4] The considerations under Wilson for potential reductions were not lost on dominion officials in London. Canadian Deputy High Commissioner Geoffrey Murray had already predicted significant changes in British foreign policy after the Labour victory.[5] Following British cabinet meetings in late 1964, he reported that Britain might consider shedding its "Great power status in the interest of a more practical and less costly approach to international affairs".[6] Australian officials became aware of renewed British interests in defence reductions when they were approached again on the issue of burden-sharing.[7]

At the same time, political rhetoric presented views contradictory to the commenced planning of defence cuts. In best imperial tradition, Wilson himself spoke of the reach of Britain's Empire, with its frontiers extending so far as the Himalaya.[8] Considerable attitudes inside and outside of the British government in favour of a continued global role seem to overrule any cuts in the East of Suez position; "the very visibility and traditional feel of the East of Suez policy had become almost synonymous with the nation's determination to maintain its prestige in the world generally".[9] Although opponents of the British presence overseas could point to recent anti-colonialist recriminations, supporters of this position could relate the British presence in Southeast Asia as promoting British values abroad. The historic role Britain had played was still considered a valuable resource of influence, and lay bare the emotional ties to the former Empire many people in the 'Old' Commonwealth still held.[10]

Aside from imperial attitudes, Wilson's room for political manoeuvre was also limited by a firm belief in the Anglo-American alliance. He could not ignore the implications a British withdrawal would have for the American position in Southeast Asia, especially in Vietnam. Focusing on this conflict, Americans would be the loudest voice for the retention of British forces in the following years, aside from Australian and New Zealand objections.

---

3 The figures for early 1966 also cover the Hongkong garrison which usually consisted of four battalions, *Hanning*, East of Suez, 257 f.

4 *William D. James*, Global Britain's Strategic Problem East of Suez, in: European Journal of International Security 6/2, 2021, 171–189, 174.

5 LAC MG31 E83 (Basil Robinson Papers), Box 13, Geoffrey Murray (CHC London) to Basil Robinson, 14.10.1964.

6 LAC MG31 E83, Box 13, Geoffrey Murray (CHC London) to Basil Robinson, 20.11.1964.

7 NAA A1838 67/1/3, Part 2, Talks between ASEA James Plimsoll and Henry Hardman (British Undersecretary at the Ministry of Defence), 29.7.1964.

8 *Curran*, Power of Speech, 49 f.

9 *R. F. Holland*, The Pursuit of Greatness. Britain and the World Role, 1900–1970, London 1991, 330.

10 *Darwin*, Britain and Decolonisation, 290 f.

Due to these two factors, strong residues of a traditional world role and allied resistance, as well as the ongoing conflict with Indonesia, British officials refrained from any definite planning on defence cuts. In November 1964, Wilson underlined his government's willingness to uphold its position East of Suez: "We cannot afford to relinquish our world role, our role which, for shorthand purposes, is sometimes called our 'east of Suez' role."[11] However, the antagonism between Britain's limited ability to provide for such a role and the symbolic connotations attached to it were growing under the Wilson government.

Half a year later, Britain's allies noticed again signs of British planning on defence cuts. Now, the stage for new British considerations had been set by two recent regional developments. For one, the secession of Singapore from the Malaysian Federation in August 1965 brought British plans back into allied discussions. From the beginning of Confrontation, there had been differences between Malaysia and Singapore leaders that were supported by communal tensions. Although Britain and Australia could both temporarily dissolve the differences by diplomatic pressure, secret separation talks between the Tunku and Lee ensued in July 1965, which resulted in Singapore's separation from the Federation on 9 August 1965.[12] Aside from the secrecy surrounding the separation plans it was the potential severe implications for both the Federation and the Southeast Asian region that troubled policymakers and dominated ensuing discussions on separation. In addition, given the precarious state of agreements for the dispatch of their forces under AMDA, officials wondered if local powers could grow more hostile towards the British presence.

The second event shifting attitudes on Southeast Asia was the end of Confrontation. On the night of 1 October 1965, a series of events later described as an attempted coup by the Partai Komunis Indonesia (PKI) in Djakarta lead the Indonesian military to take government and pursue the elimination of thousands of PKI members throughout the country. This take-over initiated a slow approach to the West under Indonesia's new leader in the background, General Suharto, with secret negotiations between Malaysia and Indonesia in April 1966 leading to an official end of Confrontation in August that year.

For the British government, the coup did not immediately lead to a shift of policy, more so as news of the developments in Indonesia only poured into the West slowly.[13] At the same time, the British Cabinet was convinced that a defence cut, willingly or forced by economic developments, was imminent.[14] Whereas the British White Paper published on 22 February 1966 emphasised the country's interest to stay in Southeast Asia, it proved a distinctive moment in British global thinking as it announced the withdrawal from Aden, and un-

[11] Quoted in: *Pickering*, Britain's Withdrawal, 139.
[12] *Benvenuti*, Cold War and Decolonisation, 248–254.
[13] *Subritzky*, Confronting Sukarno, 174–177.
[14] *Benvenuti*, British Military Withdrawal, 196.

derlined the British position to not become involved in any significant overseas commitment in the future without allied cooperation.[15] Nevertheless, although the Paper indicated the need for alternative contingency planning, because of its vague character, it pleased its allies while it led to severe criticism from the British services.[16]

The ambiguity of policy continued into 1967, despite the decision to withdraw British troops from Borneo in October 1966 following the end of Confrontation.[17] The British Defence White Paper, published in early 1967, dismissed the strained economic situation again and underlined yet once more Britain's overseas commitments. Ultimately, it enabled opponents within the British Cabinet to push even stronger for a thorough review of Britain's military presence. In April 1967, this pressure resulted in the cabinet decision to start planning for a partial withdrawal of troops until 1970, followed up by a complete withdrawal in the mid-1970s.[18] New planning considered dispatching forces from Europe, leading to the shift from a military 'presence' in the region to a military 'capacity' or 'capability' to assist in regional conflicts.[19] It fell to Secretary of State for Foreign Affairs George Brown to discuss these plans with Britain's allies at the SEATO Council Meeting in Washington in April 1967.

During these discussions, Brown received strong reactions from all sides, which seemed to indicate that Australia, New Zealand and the USA were noticing for the first time the full extent of Britain's East of Suez plans.[20] Over the following months, Tasman policymakers dedicated their efforts to challenge the British plans. At the same time, they realised the complexities of various competing positions within London. None of the allied approaches proved successful, as the British government announced its decision for a gradual withdrawal from 80 000 to 40 000 servicemen by 1971 and a complete withdrawal by the mid-1970s on 18 July 1967.[21]

Despite allied resistance, a further acceleration of the British decision came in late 1967 when another balance of payments crisis forced the British government to devalue the British Pound from 2.80 to 2.40 US Dollars, resulting in an immediate increase of defence costs by 50 million British Pounds.[22] Addition-

[15] *Dockrill*, Britain's Retreat, 155.

[16] *Pham*, Ending "East of Suez", 84 f.

[17] *John Darwin*, The Empire Project. The Rise and Fall of the British World-System 1830–1970, Cambridge 2009, 643.

[18] *Pickering*, Britain's Withdrawal, 157 f.

[19] *Sue Thompson*, British Military Withdrawal and the Rise of Regional Cooperation in South-East Asia, 1964–73, Basingstoke 2014, 108–110.

[20] See for a general report of the talks with Brown NAA A9861 3/12/77/8 Part 2B, AEmb. Washington 1558, 19.4.1967; ANZ ABHS W4628 7148, Box 120, LONB 106/7, Part 2, NEmb. Washington, 20.4.1967.

[21] Supplementary Statement on Defence Policy, Cmnd 3357, 18.7.1967, London H. M. S. O., July 1967, 5.

[22] *Benvenuti*, Anglo-Australian Relations, 107 f.

ally, the decision to withdraw from the Gulf of Aden made in July proved to be disastrous when local powers revolted against the remaining British troops and forced them into hasty withdrawal.[23] As a consequence, those in the British Cabinet in support of a definite end to Britain's role East of Suez finally gained a majority. Under the leadership of new Chancellor Roy Jenkins, the British Cabinet decided on a complete withdrawal from Southeast Asia by March 1971, a date that was only moved to December 1971 after a last-minute intervention by Lee Kuan Yew. Although Britain's allies again protested the plans, Britain made its decision public on 16 January 1968.[24] While the decision indicated the steps for withdrawal, it also expressed Britain's willingness to "retain a general capability based in Europe" that could be deployed to Southeast Asia "as, in our judgement, circumstances demand".[25] Yet further steps taken, such as the intended renegotiation of the AMDA and the cancellation of an order of fifty F-111 aircraft, underlined Britain's decision to cut its defence position East of Suez.[26]

As much as they were a challenging episode for the self-perception of Britain, the defence reviews under the Wilson government spanning from summer 1965 to early 1968 proved as a crucial, divisive period in its relations to Australia and New Zealand. Cooperation among the allies still relied heavily on the shared security framework established during and after the Second World War. Further on, it had been strengthened in connection to similar threat assessments of the Southeast Asian region, as Britain and its partners had agreed that communism and instability could threaten Australia's and New Zealand's national security, Southeast Asian states and the global Western position. Britain's decision to withdraw fundamentally questioned those shared premises of cooperation. Its policy to stay seemed even more questionable when it applied another time for entry to the EEC in May 1967.[27] The choice of British defence presence overseas and integration into Europe resulted again in a dichotomy between a world or global role and a European role.[28]

Consequently, the discussions between Britain and its allies reflected on known frameworks of imperial cooperation, as well as on regional and global orders. On the (post-)imperial level, Australia and New Zealand, as well as

[23] *Hyam*, Britain's Declining Empire, 396.

[24] For a detailed account of the accelerated withdrawal decision in late 1967 see *Jeffrey Pickering*, Politics and 'Black Friday'. Shifting Power in the Cabinet and the Decision to Withdraw From East of Suez, November 1967–January 1968, in: Twentieth Century British History 12/2, 2002, 144–170.

[25] Public Expenditure in 1968–69 and 1969–1970, Cmnd. 3515, London H. M. S. O., January 1968, 5.

[26] *McDougall*, Wilson Government, 238.

[27] *Helen Parr*, Britain, America, East of Suez and the EEC. Finding a Role in British Foreign Policy, 1964–67, in: Contemporary British History 20/3, 2006, 403–421.

[28] *Benvenuti*, Anglo-Australian Relations, 121 f.

Canada, asked now if the East of Suez plans were related to the general demise of British world power (Chapter 4.1). Furthermore, the debate touched on the future outlook of the Southeast Asian region and feasible concepts of interaction and commitment, a debate related to the regional level of considerations (Chapter 4.2). Lastly, all three countries determined if and how Britain's decision challenged their policy of involvement and forward defence as it questioned the purpose and legitimacy of a continued Western military presence from a global perspective (Chapter 4.3).

4.1 Experiencing Anger and Regret – The Potential Loss of a British Link

In the Summer of 1965, British High Commissioner to Australia W. P. Oliver used his valedictory note to remind officials back home of the strong emotional ties Australians held with Britain. He therefore advised against any British consideration for withdrawal: "[…] Australians would feel isolated indeed without the expectation of the comradeship in adversity of the Britons in whose company they have fought the two wars which constitute so great a part of Australian history and national identity."[29]

Oliver's remarks came on the heels of renewed rumours that Britain was considering substantial defence cuts in Southeast Asia. A few weeks earlier, New Zealand's High Commission in London had noted Britain was assessing its indefinite stay in the region: "The only vital interest which the United Kingdom has in the Far East is in fact the protection of Australia and New Zealand, and we can hardly expect them to carry out this responsibility if we do not play a bigger part."[30] The question of burden-sharing was still a crucial issue in the discussions between Britain and its allies. While admitting that a bigger contribution could be made, Wellington urged its London High Commission to encourage British officials in retaining a presence based on arguments of a special relationship: "New Zealand, we suggest, is entitled to a better financial treatment than foreign governments which are not joined with the United Kingdom in a common defence effort against the same antagonists."[31] Similarly, Australian officials recommended to underline in talks with British officials the obligation "to assist in close defence of Australia and New Zealand, should the occasion arise (This would be the reverse of action by Australia and New Zealand in two world wars)".[32]

[29] TNA DEFE 11/637, Valedictory Despatch by W. P. Oliver (BHC Canberra), 8.7.1965.

[30] ANZ ABHS W4628 7148, Box 119, LONB 106/5, Part 1, Note for File (NHC London), 17.6.1965.

[31] ANZ ABHS W4628 7148, Box 119, LONB 106/5, Part 1, Wellington to NHC London 1827, 21.6.1965.

[32] NAA A1209 1965/6124, Note by Defence Department, 17.6.1965.

The insistence on a shared historic effort which demanded a continued and close allegiance was one of the most powerful rhetoric strategies for dominion officials to pursue. It already became apparent in the early stages of negotiations since Britain largely legitimised its presence with the defence obligation to Australia and New Zealand. Conversely, officials from these countries could claim a historical legacy or responsibility in return for their service and allegiance to the British war efforts, particularly during the World Wars.[33]

4.1.1 1965/1966 – Years of Conflicting Emotions?

Rumours of a British defence review increased with the split of the Malaysian Federation in the Summer of 1965. The following quadripartite talks occurred in an atmosphere of considerable suspicion voiced by Australian and New Zealand officials. Some had already criticised the pessimistic tone of a paper the British government had circulated before the meeting, which seemed to draft the situation in Southeast Asia as bad enough to justify a retreat, even in contradiction to assessments made for the region a few years earlier.[34] Similarly, the indication that Britain was considering a negotiation with Indonesia caused alarm among Australian and New Zealand officials.

Yet both countries differed on the appropriate response to the British plans. While Australian officials urged for high-level meetings, New Zealand's Keith Holyoake objected to sending a special envoy to the meeting[35], and later showed himself in strong personal belief of British assurances. During the ANZUS Council meeting in 1966, he opposed Australian and American confrontational approaches: "He wondered if there were not more dangers in taking steps which might be interpreted as doubting this decision than to staunchly assert a belief in its validity."[36] Holyoake's attitude relied on the concept of moral obligation. He exposed a conviction of continued British interests that could be derived from the British assurances for protection, a conviction he shared with a lot of New Zealanders and a substantial group of Australians. He also dismissed the need for an explicit approach to the issue, certainly out of fear that the British might review the issue more fundamentally, an approach also shown in ANZUS talks with the Americans.

Conversely, Australians developed a strong mistrust for British actions and perceived those as a betrayal of Commonwealth values. In contrast to New Zealanders, they insisted more strongly on inclusion within British strategic thinking and reviews. In general, as the memoirs of Minister for Air Peter

---

33 *Millar*, Australia in Peace and War, 144.

34 NAA A3211, 1969/1847, Part 2, ADEA to AHC London 4669, 7.9.1965.

35 NAA A1838 682/4, Part 5A, AHC Wellington 432, 6.9.1965.

36 ANZ ABHS W5533 22128 Box 92, CBA 50/8/2, New Zealand Report on ANZUS Council Meeting, 30.6./1.7.1966.

Howson[37] reveal, Australian policymakers were more divided in their attitudes. Some assumed the assurances made by the British government on a continued presence were valid; others urged to expect a British retreat. Some found themselves between both positions expecting the British to bluff to get their allies to contribute more. Oscillating between trust and suspicion, these schools of thought would remain throughout the following discussions and manifested themselves among different groups of policymakers.

In the quadripartite talks, Australian resistance was backed by New Zealand and most importantly the USA, where officials underlined they would link their financial support for the weak British Pound Sterling to a continued British presence in the Far East.[38] British officials grudgingly obliged the allied opposition. Meeting with Denis Healey afterwards, Alexander Downer experienced the conversation as the "first time I have heard a British Minister being critical, to me, of our policy or of your own personal attitude".[39] Similarly, other Australian officials in London reported an unusual reticence among their British counterparts.[40] Experiencing a division of interest also affected British officials who started to examine Australian and New Zealand suspicions and insecurities. Following the quadripartite talks, some papers even argued with the experiences of 1942. Because of the tensions, missions from both countries advised to appreciate these insecurities: "[…] we should continue to keep guiding them firmly by example, we must keep them well informed on our policy and we must religiously consult them on all matters which might affect them."[41] While these examinations supported Australian demands for closer cooperation, other officials like British High Commissioner Charles Johnston urged a thorough review of the special Anglo-Dominion relationship to distinguish between allied collaboration and self-interest. For instance, Australians would take the close links with Britain in equipment and logistics for granted while purchasing American equipment: "This frame of mind, which is of course a survival from our imperial heyday, may be flattering to our self-esteem but operates against our material interest."[42] On both sides, officials notably started to examine the scope and strength of (post-)imperial cooperation against national interests, yet a clear distinction remained difficult.

The quadripartite talks on Singapore's secession had introduced a certain element of insecurity and suspicion on the British defence planning. These insecu-

[37] *Peter Howson/Don Aitkin* (Ed.), The Howson Diaries. The Life of Politics, Ringwood 1984, 181.

[38] *Jones*, Conflict and Confrontation, 288 f.

[39] NAA A1838 TS3006/10/4/1, Part 1, Alexander Downer (AHC London) to Robert Menzies, 20.9.1965.

[40] NAA A3211 1969/1847, Part 2, AHC London 9416, 22.10.1965.

[41] TNA DEFE 11/637, Comment by Rear Admiral Davies (BJSLS Canberra), 15.10.1965.

[42] TNA DO169/487, Johnston (BHC Canberra) to CRO, 24.9.1965.

rities even transpired into Canadian debates, where officials expressed doubts regarding the British position and the region following a withdrawal. When Harold Wilson visited Ottawa in December 1965, he proposed for Canada to contribute to a collective force in the region that would allow Britain to reduce its defence spending. While Lester Pearson supported this idea, he nevertheless made clear it should be followed up by countries with larger interests in the area.[43]

In Australia and New Zealand, British visits were now accompanied by media speculation. When Denis Healey visited Canberra in early February 1966, the New Zealand *Northland Times* suspected the British government to merely inform Australia and New Zealand of its decision for withdrawal, a treatment similar to colonial times.[44] Other papers called Healey's visit out as diplomatic make-believe.[45] As expected, the talks evolved in a strained atmosphere. Healey himself adopted a provocative mixture of threat and shaming to both fend off allied requests for inclusion in British considerations and to press for burden-sharing.[46] New Zealand officials reported how Healey "commented somewhat oddly they were not prepared to be alone as they had been in the 1960s against Indonesia. No-one in England in the 1970s [...] [would] be prepared to take on alone a sophisticated opponent 10 000 miles away".[47] To Britain's allies, being committed to Malaysian defence since the mid-1950s, this must clearly have been a strange statement that bordered on an insult of their efforts. Additionally, Healey further upset counterparts by indicating that Britain could use its retreat from the region as a bargain in negotiations with Indonesians.[48]

The heated discussions came to a pinnacle on the next day when Healey reiterated a well-known accusation against Australians as 'dragging their feet' on greater burden-sharing. If they would not agree to contribute to said planning soon, Healey indicated – as New Zealand sources reported – that "many of his colleagues would say 'b----- them'. The Australian Ministers took exception to this remark and McEwen in particular pointed out with some asperity that Australia had not said 'b----- you' to Britain in 1914 or in 1940 and could not accept that this should be the basis of the relationship when considering the 1970's".[49] Healey's sharp comment revealed discussions would not be restricted to a friendly exchange of opinion. In a review of the conference, NSEA Alister McIntosh referred to Healey's outburst as symbolising how strained re-

[43] LAC RG25 A-3-c, Vol. 10042, 20-1-2-BRIT, Part 1, Memorandum on the Meeting between Lester Pearson and Harold Wilson (19.12.1965), 20.12.1965.
[44] "Are Some More Equal than Others?", Northland Times, 13.1.1966.
[45] "UK Asian Defence Cuts", Canberra Times, 19.1.1966.
[46] *Benvenuti*, Parting of the Ways, 586 f.
[47] ANZ ABHS W4628 7148, Box 119, LONB 106/5A, Part 2, NHC Canberra 91, 1.2.1966.
[48] Ibid.
[49] ANZ ABHS W4628 7148, Box 119, LONB 106/5A, Part 2, New Zealand Report on Defence Talks in Canberra, 14.2.1966.

lations were: "[…] when a Britisher has the effrontery to borrow an Australian term and fling it back, this is taken as very bad form indeed."[50]

Despite the intensity of discussions, the British White Defence Paper published at the end of February 1966 seemed to acknowledge allied fears of a premature withdrawal. Afterwards, Harold Holt thanked Harold Wilson for this "sound, indeed historic, decision which you will never regret".[51] Drafting Wilson's response, British officials themselves showed insecurities regarding Australian attitudes. After crossing out 'I trust' and 'I hope', Wilson's reply flatly stated: "I take it that you are not contemplating a reduction in your forces there."[52] Officials were no longer willing to rely on traditional formula previously used in Commonwealth communications, and replaced trusting ambiguity with emotional sincerity.

Rhetoric and references combined, the defence talks in early 1966 set the tone for discussions to follow. At the same time, they did not result in substantial rethinking within Australian and New Zealand official circles; instead, they pushed for quadripartite talks with the USA. They expected that British reluctance to commit to a substantial defence role in Southeast Asia would clash with growing American considerations for the instability of the region. Some New Zealand officials showed themselves sceptical of quadripartite talks and pointed to previous experiences with American evasion of joint planning. Meanwhile, Holyoake showed himself satisfied by the British assurances, and believed British officials "were bluffing with a view to getting Australia and New Zealand to foot more of the bill".[53]

Both the scepticism for American cooperation and the reliance on British assurances angered Australians, who felt that New Zealand left it up to them to "make the running"[54] in any new defence arrangement. Australian officials struggled with considerable uncertainty about the British plans. As Canberra instructed their posts, "None of us knows at this stage precisely what Britain wants, how strongly they will press for what they want, and whether the Americans will move some way to meet them if pressed."[55]

Resulting both from anticipation and suspicion of British moves, Australians clashed again with British officials in June 1966. When reports had emerged in the Australian press that the British Labour Party (BLP) had endorsed the retreat East of Suez on its party convention in May 1966, Australians demanded a

[50] NLNZ MS-Papers-6759-356, McIntosh (Wellington) to Templeton (NHC London), 10.2.1966.

[51] TNA PREM 13/890, Part 2, Harold Holt to Harold Wilson 25.2.1966.

[52] For the different drafts for Wilson's message see TNA PREM 13/890 Part 2 (final message sent on 2.3.1966).

[53] NAA A1838 TS682/4, Part 8, AHC Wellington 93 10.2.1966.

[54] ANZ ABHS W4627 950, Box 4505, 434/8/1, Part 10, NDEA to NHC Washington 247, 15.3.1966.

[55] NAA A1838 682/4, Part 9, ADEA to AHC Wellington 175, 3.3.1966.

clarification of this move from Wilson.[56] Initially, Holt had considered sending a message to Wilson and already prepared a press statement, but his Secretary John Bunting tried to convince him otherwise:

"Any message to Mr. Wilson, no matter how drafted, will convey that we hold him or his Government in some kind of doubt. At least this will give him the impression that you have something less than full confidence in him (and as between Prime Minister to Prime Minister I would wish to avoid that), but more than that, I fear that it might give him an opening."[57]

Similarly, officials like Paul Hasluck were convinced that such a public move could upset Australian confidence by implying a British withdrawal was imminent.[58]

Ultimately, Holt instructed Alexander Downer to meet with Wilson.[59] To his staff, he insisted that he needed to request clarification from the British government, otherwise this would result in "a disastrous erosion of the assurances which the British had given to us about their future presence in South East Asia".[60] In contrast to Bunting's recommendations, Holt expected his insecurity to be of some kind of validity to British officials. Upon meeting with Wilson, Downer explained his visit with Australian concerns for a continued British presence, emphasising that "the Australian government felt deeply, and especially because of their great attachment to Britain, that any British Government that abandoned this policy would rapidly reduce Britain to the status of a second-rate nation".[61] As Downer reported, Wilson replied that his government would differ from the Australian government in its faith of a continued presence in Southeast Asia, "but none the less he agreed with me when I pointed out the moral value of Britain remaining firmly established at Singapore for as long as possible".[62]

While Downer concluded that the matter was put to rest with this meeting, Holt's staff appeared eager to smooth over the gravity expressed in the Australian appeal.[63] John Bunting had indeed realised the damage done to the Australian reputation among the British government as he urged Holt on several occasions to not make the exchange between both governments public, given that this could further undermine Britain's trust.[64] Several press reports had in-

56 NAA A1209 1966/7335, Part 1, Harold Holt to Alexander Downer (AHC London), 1.5.1966.

57 NAA A1209 1966/7335, Part 1, John Bunting to Harold Holt, 31.5.1966.

58 NAA A1209 1966/7335, Part 1, Paul Hasluck to James Plimsoll, 27.5.1966.

59 NAA A1209 1966/7335, Part 1, Harold Holt to BHC London 3125, 31.5.1966.

60 NAA A1209 1966/7335, Part 1, Note for File by Lawler (APMD), 30.5.1966.

61 TNA DO 169/444, Report on Talks between Harold Wilson and Alexander Downer, 1.6.1966.

62 NAA A1209 1966/7335, Part 1, Downer (BHC London) 5295, 1.6.1966.

63 TNA DO 169/444, BHC Canberra 759, 1.6.1966.

64 NAA A1209 1966/7335, Part 1, John Bunting for Harold Holt, 2.6.1966 and Note for File by Bunting, 3.6.1966.

deed blamed Holt's political style for the tensions with Britain over the issue.[65] Holt himself felt the need to explain his request to Downer after the episode: "[…] you know me well enough to realize that I do not set in motion action of the kind with which we have just been dealing unless I judge that there is good cause for it."[66]

Meanwhile, Australian and New Zealand policymakers themselves continued to doubt the British long-term policy. Despite the British White Paper, New Zealand officials judged in June 1966 that a withdrawal, given the financial and political difficulties Britain was facing, was only a question of time.[67] Following the BLP episode, Charles Johnston reported from Canberra that both public and government believed that "the United Kingdom will let Australia down".[68] He also underlined the intensity and emotionalism the debate recently adopted: "Since this is not a rational deduction it cannot be disposed of entirely by rational argument."[69] As British Foreign Secretary Michael Stewart was currently in Australia, Johnston recommended including some sort of soothing reference to Australia's protection in one of his upcoming statements. His prepared draft underlined the traditional obligation Britain felt towards Australia's security: "I should like to say that it is unthinkable that if Australia were the victims of aggression Great Britain would not come to her assistance. This is not a question of treaties or legal obligations: it is unthinkable that a British Government or the British people would do otherwise."[70] Johnston's suggestion, however, posed difficulties for some British policymakers as it could be too specific a statement. One defence official pointed out that the last time such a statement was made was under Anthony Eden in 1955, "Since then however, HMG have been at pains to play down any obligations to help a Commonwealth country against aggression merely because it is a Commonwealth country."[71] He feared such a statement could result in similar demands for assurance from other Commonwealth countries. For the CRO, however, a statement along the drafted line made sense as it would reflect British opinion. In their view, the speech could ultimately serve to remind Australians that they had a responsibility to uphold their end of the agreement "by providing the facilities which we shall need in their country".[72] An insistency on historical cooperation could be understood

65 See e. g. "Still East of Suez", The Bulletin, 11.6.1966.

66 NAA A1209 1966/7335, Part 1, Harold Holt to BHC London (Downer) 3185, 2.6.1966.

67 ANZ ACIE 8798 EA1 234, 59/2/209, 59/2/209, Part 1, Memorandum for Talks with Harold Holt on British Defence Policy in the Far East, n. d. (June 1966).

68 TNA PREM 13/890, Part 2, BHC Canberra (Johnston) to CRO (Palliser) 915, 26.6.1966.

69 Ibid.

70 TNA PREM 13/890, Part 2, BHC Canberra (Johnston) to CRO (Palliser) 915, 26.6.1966.

71 TNA PREM 13/1454, Part 3, Peduzie (BMD) to Palliser (CRO), 28.6.1966.

72 TNA PREM 13/1454, Part 3, "Statement by the Foreign Secretary in Canberra: Attitude of the United Kingdom in the Event of Aggression against Australia", Brief for Harold Wilson, 28.6.1966.

as a demand for future burden-sharing. The British Cabinet endorsed the idea to let the special Anglo-Dominion relationship work in Britain's favour:

"In further discussion it was suggested that to link our readiness to go to the help of Australia with the readiness shown by them to come to our help in two World Wars would be appropriate: it would reflect a widespread sentiment, would convey the idea of our sending forces to help rather than stationing them in the area and would provide a means of distinguishing our relationship to Australia and New Zealand from our relationship to other Commonwealth countries, since we would not wish to give a similar undertaking to them."[73]

Cabinet advised Stewart to include an amended version of Johnston's proposal that pointed even sharper to past defence cooperation: "But as Australia and New Zealand came to the help of Great Britain in two world wars it is unthinkable that if Australia and New Zealand were the victims of aggression Great Britain would not similarly come to their assistance."[74] This particular reference was used by Stewart in a speech at the Australian Institute of International Affairs on 30 June 1966. Here, he explained the recent political decisions Britain had taken and how they might affect its relations with Australia. In his concluding words, he addressed the audience on the question of British obligation to Australian defence. After stating the lines proposed by the CRO, he concluded: "So you can take it from me that we have neither the wish nor the intention to turn our backs on the world East of Suez."[75]

Stewart's statement was widely welcomed by Australian and New Zealand officials as an assurance of Britain's contribution to forward defence.[76] At the same time, however, Australian officials were not willing to rely on this verbal assurance. They understood his remarks on Britain's protection were not specified to a presence in Southeast Asia.[77] Furthermore, as his statement had been an offer to calm down public recriminations on both sides, the emotions attached to the East of Suez issue did not vanish. Officials like Paul Hasluck objected to his remarks as patronising towards Australia's independence.[78] The various, emotionally charged attitudes on defence discussions remained a bone of contention on several following incidents. During a visit to Washington a month later, Harold Holt upset British officials when he repurposed Stewart's

---

[73] TNA CAB 148/25, Record of Defence and Overseas Policy Committee Meeting, 29.6.1966, quoted in: *S. R. Ashton/Carl Bridge/Stuart Ward* (Ed.), Documents on Australian Foreign Policy. Australia and the United Kingdom 1960–1975, Barton 2010, 175–176.

[74] TNA PREM 13/1454, Part 3, Palliser to BHC Canberra, 29.6.1966.

[75] TNA PREM 13/1454, Part 3, Speech given by Michael Stewart at the AIIA, Canberra, 30.6.1966.

[76] Report on ANZUS Council Meeting, 30.6./1.7.1966, ANZ ABHS W5533 22128, Box 92, CBA 50/8/2.

[77] *Goldsworthy*, Losing the Blanket, 166.

[78] Summary on ANZUS Council Meeting 1.7.1966, quoted in: *Benvenuti*, Parting of the Ways, 589.

statement by commenting that Australia's growing alliance with the USA was the result of Britain 'turning its back on the world'.[79] New Zealand officials in Canberra reported Holt not only offended Harold Wilson by his strong emphasis on the American allegiance, but also because he had shared parts of his discussions with Wilson with the press. To them, this was a clear sign that Australian officials were struggling "rather clumsily for the appropriate balance between firmness and sympathy with which to prosecute its dialogue with London".[80] Already before, CRO official Saville Garner had pointed to Stewart's assurances before telling Australian staff that "if it wasn't for our concern for Australia's interests and protection, Britain would be out of the Far East, lock, stock and barrel and as quick as a flash".[81]

Despite Stewart's statement, perceptions of a growing divergence between British assurances and its lack of resources to uphold the commitments could not be erased.[82] However, his remarks on Britain's obligation established themselves as a reference over the further course of negotiations and developments. In April 1967, after George Brown's revelations for withdrawal, Wilson reassured Holt that Stewart "spoke for all of us", Britain's intention was still "to stand by Australia as Australia stood by us in two world wars".[83] Additionally, Stewart's assurance could draw some legitimacy from a continuously close relationship among lower levels of policymakers. Australian and New Zealand officials regularly received some comfort and sympathy from British counterparts on their position in Southeast Asia. During the various ensuing stages of the East of Suez discussion, it became apparent that not only Australian and New Zealand policymakers were divided on the actual need to cut Britain's military presence overseas, but also British policymakers.

Throughout the debates of 1966, British officials also sought advice from Canada on Commonwealth cooperation and burden-sharing. In March 1966, British official Geoffrey Arthur confided to Canadian High Commission staff that he could not engage in a "further agonizing reappraisal of Britain's military role"[84] if a Conservative government would be elected. Such attitudes were shared with Canada because of its status as a close yet unaffected bystander of the discussion. With its limited interest in Southeast Asian defence, but traditional working relationships in other areas of joint security, officials could take Canadian counterparts into confidence.

---

[79] *Benvenuti*, Anglo-Australian Relations, 85 f.

[80] ANZ ABHS W4628 7148, Box 120, LONB 106/7, Part 1, NHC Canberra, 4.8.1966.

[81] NAA A1209 1966/7335, Part 1, AHC London to Bunting, 12.7.1966.

[82] "The SEATO Rites", The Bulletin, 9.7.1966; "Facing up to the East-of-Suez retreat", The Australian, 17.11.1966.

[83] TNA PREM 13/1455, CO to BHC Canberra 842, 20.4.1967.

[84] LAC RG25 A-3-c, Vol. 10282, 27-1-2-BRIT, Part 1, CHC London, 11.3.1966.

However, Canadians also shared some concerns with Australians and New Zealanders over Britain's future capabilities for international cooperation. In foreign policy and diplomacy, they witnessed similar changes in the traditionally close alliance with Britain. The feeling of a rift in Anglo-Canadian relations came in early 1966. In the years before, Canadian officials had reported on several incidents, where not only interests were at odds, but where the British also seemed to have dismissed or ignored the Canadian position. While minor frictions had existed over the defence framework in Southeast Asia, larger differences related to areas of cooperation such as the ICSC and NATO.[85]

In talks with British High Commissioner Henry Lintott, CSSEA Paul Martin indicated in April 1966 he felt that in Anglo-Canadian relations, "there did not seem to be quite the degree of frankness or confidence which should exist".[86] He complained that the British government had missed to inform Canadians on certain issues, or would simply take their position for granted. Martin himself recalled this period in his memoirs: "Something was lacking. I could not put my finger on it, because I knew it had more to do with the appearance than the substance of our political relationships."[87] Canadians witnessed a shift in their close relations with Britain, but they could not yet determine the underlying causes or outcome.

CDEA's Commonwealth Division soon followed up the request expressed by Martin to substantially review the departmental relations to Britain.[88] As no major change had taken place in cooperation recently, the review should address current arrangements that could have helped to create "a general atmosphere of grievance".[89] While indicating that relations with British officials were generally good and that they could not trace a specific problem, other divisions confirmed a palpable decline in relations with Britain.[90] The Defence Liaison (1) Division reported on some difficulties in information sharing and cooperation but explained that historical ties with Britain – in contrast to other countries – would lead to expectations for better relations.[91] Another explanation was laconically offered by the Latin American Division: "[…] this is probably a reflection of the decline of Britain as a world power in both the economic and political sense and the progressive weakening of the Commonwealth

---

[85] LAC RG25 A-3-c, Vol. 10042, 20-1-2-BRIT, ICSC Memorandum by Far Eastern Div., 5.2.1964, and NATO Ext. to CHC London, 12.11.1964.

[86] LAC RG25 A-3-c, Vol. 10042, 20-1-2-BRIT, Talks between Paul Martin and BHC Henry Lintott, 25.4.1966.

[87] Quoted in: *Hilliker/Donaghy*, Canadian Relations, 39.

[88] LAC RG25 A-3-c, Vol. 10042, 20-1-2-BRIT, Commonwealth Div. to various divisions, 26.4.1966.

[89] Ibid.

[90] LAC RG25 A-3-c, Vol. 10042, 20-1-2-BRIT, Reply by Far Eastern Div., 9.5.1966; Disarmament Div., 6.5.1966; and African & Middle East Div., 10.5.1966.

[91] LAC RG25 A-3-c, Vol. 10042, 20-1-2-BRIT, Defence Liaison (1) Div., 6.5.1966.

through its miraculously flexible evolution to the point where there is little left but the grin of the Cheshire cat."[92] Officials already felt Britain's changing international status affected their relationship without necessarily creating heated arguments like in Australia and New Zealand.

Meanwhile, the Deputy High Commissioner at Canada House, Geoffrey Murray, had drafted a similar paper on the state of relations between both countries.[93] Murray felt impelled to write such a paper after what he witnessed as personal differences between Michael Stewart and Paul Martin which seemed symptomatic "that in 1966 Canada does not share the same respect and confidence which may have existed at an earlier time in our relations with the United States and Great Britain".[94]

In his attached review[95], Murray identified a growing divergence of outlooks in both countries starting in the late 1950s. Witnessing a change in the global order of powers, decolonisation and "the humiliating fiasco of Suez [...] the British began to have far-reaching doubts about their real status and role on the international stage." Therefore, Britain had been more and more willing to disregard old affiliations for new realities: "'Old friends' including 'kith and kin' are being compared – often unfavourably – with new associates whose essential interests may be closer to those of present-day Britain." Canada, on the other hand, had become more aware of the limits of international influence since the late 1950s while paying more attention to the crucial issue of its own national unity in the face of biculturalism. As both sides now realised that they were increasingly supporting national interests rather than working together on a shared (post-)imperial outlook, this would result in "dismay about the disintegration of old ideas, old values, old relations and an old order of things." While Murray could not offer an immediate solution to this widening gap, he concluded: "Whatever the cause, there is no room for complacency about the need for early answers which can help to set Canadian-British relations on a new course toward the goals of cooperation, confidence and cordiality which history entitles conscientious people on both sides of the Atlantic to expect."

In Ottawa, in its summary of division responses, the Commonwealth Division underlined the continued similar outlook on policy with Britain: "[...] in terms of substantial policy differences our problems today with Britain are neither numerous nor more serious than any other periods."[96] It further expressed the generally good conditions of cooperation, but recommended some

---

[92] LAC RG25 A-3-c, Vol. 10042, 20-1-2-BRIT, Latin American Div. (Pick), 27.4.1966.

[93] *Hilliker/Barry*, Canada's Department of External Affairs Vol. 2, 323.

[94] LAC MG31 E83, Box 13, Geoffrey Murray (CHC London) to USSEA Marcel Cadieux, 14.5.1966.

[95] For the following see LAC MG31 E83, Box 13, "Britain and Canada 1966", Paper attached to Geoffrey Murray (CHC London) to CSEA Marcel Cadieux, 14.5.1966.

[96] LAC RG25 A-3-c, Vol. 10042, 20-1-2-BRIT, Memorandum to CSSEA, 14.6.1966.

improvement in consultation and exchange practice with the establishment of a joint committee.[97] This proposal was equally supported by Murray in London. Additionally, regular visits of ministers should be increased in both countries. Ultimately, it fell to the Canadian Department of Trade to introduce such a committee, a step that led to some frustrations for the CDEA as it feared losing influence against the rivalling department.[98]

Just as in Australia and New Zealand, officials saw a growing divergence of interest between Canada and Britain. While this was perceived as a natural evolution following Britain's retreat from its former Empire, officials did not accept the demise of close cooperation in foreign policy resulting from this decline. Like Australia and New Zealand, Canadians were opposed to the demising quality of consultation and cooperation that resulted from Britain's new focus on national interests.

4.1.2 1967 – "The Shock of a Family Separation"

While Canadians reviewed the larger picture of (post-)imperial cooperation, Australian and New Zealand officials continued to focus on the question of Southeast Asian defence cooperation with Britain. In late 1966, Australian Liaison Staff in London reported again on an unusual denial of access to information in British services: "Regrettably in this slightly strained atmosphere there is an increased reluctance to provide information, comment is embellished by personal views and prejudices, and the practice of being given a quick look at COS Minutes appears to be temporarily at abeyance."[99]

Indeed, British defence thinking had been in motion again for some time, following the official end of Confrontation in August 1966.[100] As the defence review continued in early 1967, Australian officer Frank Hassett concluded that the unusual restrictive access in the British Ministry of Defence (BMD) could be related to the unpopular reception of the upcoming defence review by Britain's close allies: "In such circumstance it is not surprising that there is a well co-ordinated 'wall of silence' regarding future policy not only within Defence, but within the top echelons of the Services also."[101] He requested to approach upper service ranks in order to file a complaint and press for more information, and ended his letter with a slight nostalgic warning: "In short, what I am saying is that the days when we are deeply and intimately involved are

---

97 LAC RG25 A-3-c, Vol. 10042, 20-1-2-BRIT, CHC London, 14.6.1966.

98 LAC MG31 E83, Box 13, Geoffrey Murray (CHC London) to Basil Robinson, 2.3.1967.

99 NAA A1945 73/1/63, Australian Joint Service Staff (AJSS) London (Gladstone), 4.11.1966.

100 NAA A1945 73/1/63, Letter by AJSS (Hassett), 4.10.1966 and Letter by AJSS (Hassett), 11.10.1966.

101 NAA A1945 73/1/63, AJSS London (Hassett) to Canberra, 2.2.1967.

passing and that this is being reflected in the amount of information we are being given."[102]

Hassett's regretful remarks indicate Australians still stuck to the principle of close consultation and information-sharing, and expected the British to act accordingly. Britain's apparent silence was seen as a violation of usual norms of close cooperation, an obstruction of the practice of Commonwealth consultation. With information-sharing being temporarily suspended, George Brown's revelations for withdrawal at the SEATO meeting in Washington a few months later were anticipated by many as a "fait accompli"[103] and were surrounded by rumours and suspicion. Before the SEATO meeting, Charles Johnston therefore urged his supervisors in London that without "a genuine process of consultation"[104], British decisionmaking could have a seriously damaging effect on the relationship with Australia.

When George Brown informed American, Australian and New Zealand representatives about Britain's intention to cut its defence by half up to 1970 and withdraw entirely by 1975, Britain's allies reacted with disbelief and dismay. Both Hasluck and Holyoake showed themselves shocked, and Hasluck engaged in what Brown called "emotional arguments (though he did not become emotional himself – he was calm and friendly throughout) about the value of a British world role and a British presence on the mainland".[105] In Canberra, Charles Johnston met a visibly moved Harold Holt who told him that Brown's revelations had come as a shock to Australia.[106] From Washington, Hasluck urged Holt to send a message to Wilson indicating Australia's objections based on shared sentiment and identity: "Those of family sentiment and dangers undergone together in the past no less than practical considerations make us want a continuance of British strength by our side."[107] Australian feelings were further nourished by the suspicion that British officials had "virtually already made up their minds"[108] about their withdrawal from Southeast Asia. In London, Alexander Downer told British Cabinet Member James Callaghan that "in unfolding their new defence proposals to us they had hit us between the eyes".[109]

With such strong recriminations, Australian officials tried to convince British officials to review their plans for a withdrawal, again with the insistence on traditional forms of cooperation. Reporting to Canberra, Alexander Downer in-

[102] Ibid.

[103] NAA A1209 1966/7335, Part 2, John Bunting to Harold Holt, 17.4.1967.

[104] TNA Prem 13/1455, Charles Johnston (BHC Canberra) to CO 622, 18.4.1967.

[105] TNA FCO 46/54, BEmb. Washington to FO 1277, 19.4.1967.

[106] TNA FCO 46/54, BHC Canberra (Johnston) to CO 635, 21.4.1967, and BHC Canberra (Johnston) to CO 636, 21.4.1967.

[107] NAA A9861 3/12/77/8, Part 2B, AEmb. Washington 1600, 20.4.1967.

[108] NAA A1838 TS691/1/1, Part 1, AEmb. Washington 1764, 28.4.1967.

[109] NAA M1003 (Alexander Downer Papers), DEFENCE EAST OF SUEZ, AHC London 5326, 3.5.1967.

sisted Australia should press for its right to be included in British policymaking: Officials should avoid giving "the impression that we are not overconcerned, that we are easily converted to this new British defence thinking, and that we really do not care very much whether the British withdraw from Asia".[110] Downer and others felt encouraged by voices from within the British government and offices that indicated a continued identity of interest and sentiment with Australia and New Zealand. In Kuala Lumpur, the Defence Adviser to the British High Commission criticised the British plans as purely politically motivated and urged Malaysian, Singapore and New Zealand officials to "hit the British hard"[111] to revise their plans. One Australian telegram from London proposed to put the British government into a shameful position by offering financial support that would emphasise the emotional ties between both countries:

"There is a good deal of sentiment in Britain for continuing to work closely with Australia and our offer would underline the importance we attach to the continuing British military presence. The faint blush of shame that the British might feel need not be to our disadvantage. Even if not accepted, an Australian offer could increase the pressure on the British to modify their plans."[112]

Conversely, other officials called for a more constructive approach, most of all Downer's Deputy Thomas Critchley. Immediately after the Washington talks, he wrote a lengthy report back to Canberra showing himself sceptical on chances to change the British minds, yet he agreed that statements should tacitly underline the close ties between Britain and the former dominions: "Although there is little concern for South-East Asia, there is a good deal of sentiment for Australia and New Zealand."[113] Mediating lines were also presented by Australian politicians. Already after his talks in Washington, Hasluck proposed to be more conciliatory in messages to Wilson: "Our best line may be to find ways to influence or persuade British rather than to scold them."[114] While ADEA officials agreed with their minister on a more tacit approach[115], officials from the Australian Prime Minister's Department (APMD) underlined the need to appeal to British linked to its imperial role: "The British public needs to feel that we value them because they are Britons, for their moral wealth and for their achievement. We must make this our message."[116]

Similarly, New Zealanders considered the use of sentiment. As Australians, they had experienced on multiple occasions the close confidence of British offi-

110 NAA M1003, DEFENCE EAST OF SUEZ, AHC London 5206, 2.5.1967.

111 ANZ ABHS W4628 7148, Box 120, LONB 106/7 Part 2, NHC Kuala Lumpur 267, 21.4.1967.

112 NAA A9861 3/12/77/8, Part 2B, AHC London 6008, 16.5.1967.

113 NAA A9861 3/12/77/8, Part 3, AHC London (Critchley) 4804, 24.4.1967.

114 NAA A1838 TS691/1/1, Part 1, AEmb. Washington 1562, 19.4.1967.

115 NAA A1209 1966/7335, Part 2A, Note for ASEA, 24.4.1967.

116 NAA A1209 1966/7335, Part 2A, Note for Secr. APMD by Allan Griffith, 26.4.1967.

cials who seem to struggle with the plans of their government.[117] When Deputy Prime Minister John Marshall flew to London for talks in June 1967, his brief therefore underlined that New Zealand's advocacy for a continued close military cooperation rested "partly on the almost undefinable nature of the relationship between Britain and New Zealand".[118] Representatives in London were briefed in similar terms, and advised to underline in talks with the British the need to uphold a commitment that "is one of the major remaining Commonwealth links which gives life and vigour to the whole Commonwealth relationship".[119]

Some British counterparts reacted sympathetically to such pleas, with some officials using similar arguments in an assemblage of shared war effort, moral obligation and mutual trust, as a reply by Brown to Downer shows:" '[…] you can trust us; we will always look after you. You don't need undertakings from us signed on the dotted line. We won't let you down.'"[120] Brown's remarks forcefully evoked images of a close relationship that was still based on unwritten rules and values. However, the majority of policymakers were opposed to engaging in a talk of sentiment and repudiated further concessions to their allies. With a hint to the quadripartite talks in 1965, an internal memo stated: "We have once already in the past two years allowed the Americans and the Australians to twist our arms and force us to backtrack. If we let them do it again, we shall not […] increase their respect for us but only their suspicion – which is already intense."[121] Some officials warned New Zealand counterparts that if they would not offer "something more than impassionate pleas to stay for ever"[122], Britain would continue with its plans.

In talks, indeed no progress was made aside from recriminations and pleas. With little apparent regards for their allies, the British government announced its plans for complete withdrawal by the mid-1970s on 18 July 1967. Again, Australians and New Zealanders reacted with regret and anger. Referring to Britain's traditional role in the region, Holt wrote Wilson:

"We see the United Kingdom as having taken historic decisions to reduce its world role and contract, to a significant degree, from the kind of international responsibility Brit-

[117] See e. g. NHC Singapore 204, 25.4.1967, in ANZ ABHS W4628 7148, Box 120, LONB 106/7, Part 2.

[118] ANZ ABHS W5631 22310, Box 193, PAR 222/1/1, Part 2, Brief for Dep. Prime Minister, 31.5.1967.

[119] ANZ ABHS W4628 7148, Box 120, LONB 106/7, Part 2, Brief for London Talks, 31.5.1967.

[120] NAA M1003, DEFENCE EAST OF SUEZ, AHC London 5326, 3.5.1967.

[121] TNA PREM 13/1455, Memorandum for Britain's Approach to Quadripartite Discussions, 12.5.1967.

[122] ANZ ABHS W4628 7148, Box 120, LONB 106/7, Part 2, NHC London 2664, 30.5.1967.

ain has carried for many, many years […] Some of the basic assumptions on which the foreign policies of our two countries have been based – at least in relation to this area of the world – seem to us to have been destroyed, and we must re-think our whole situation."[123]

In New Zealand, Keith Holyoake reiterated his regrets about the British decision and his doubts about Southeast Asian stability. Moreover, he deplored the loss of the logistic framework Britain had provided so far for New Zealand forces.[124]

Among the public, the atmosphere created by the insistence on sentimental ties led to various reactions to the British decision. The *New Zealand Herald* called Britain's announcement the "end of an era in world affairs"[125]; looking at the Australian debate it described the feelings surrounding the decision as "the shock of a family separation [which] is tinged with a mixture of both sadness and indifference".[126] Other newspapers sided with Britain, e. g. the *Christchurch Star* asked 'Doesn't Anyone like Britain any more?'[127], an attempt to raise sympathy for Britain's position as struggling under financial pressures.

These outlined public statements were all torn between regrets over Britain's decision and a certain understanding for its motives, resulting in commiseration over Britain's demise as a world power. Australian cartoonist Les Tanner had captured these feelings a few months earlier with a cartoon in *The Bulletin* (Fig. 1). It depicted Britannica doing a striptease in front of Harold Holt, Lee Kuan Yew and Tunku Abdul Rahman, all visibly distressed by the performance. Their plea "Please adjust your dress before leaving", referring to Britannica's sparse clothing, as she wears only an undergarment labelled "East of Suez", could either be understood as plea for proper coverage of Britain's East of Suez position or a gracious, less humiliating retreat.[128] As the cartoon suggests, Britain's allies anticipated and deplored the former imperial power was not able to cover its military commitments, and watching the British struggle seemed to be similarly painful.

Australian and New Zealand statements made before and after 18 July 1967 indicate the identity dilemma many of them felt during the discussions on Britain's retreat East of Suez. On the one hand, many continued to believe in an alliance with and allegiance to Britain, which would demand sympathy and support for any British policy, regardless if it was advantageous for their own position. On the other hand, the element of trust was bruised by Britain's appar-

[123] NAA A1838 TS691/1, Part 11, Harold Holt to Harold Wilson, 14.7.1967, in: *Ashton/Bridge/Ward*, DAFP, 222–223, 223.

[124] ANZ ABHS W4628 7148, Box 121, LONB 106/7, Part 3, Keith Holyoake to Harold Wilson, 7.7.1967.

[125] "British Abdication East of Suez", New Zealand Herald, 20.7.1967.

[126] "British no more, Australia seeks an image", New Zealand Herald, 21.7.1967.

[127] "Doesn't Anyone like Britain any more?", Christchurch Star, 24.7.1967.

[128] *Les Tanner*, "Please Adjust Your Dress Before Leaving", Thc Bullctin, 6.5.1967.

Fig. 1: Les Tanner, "Please Adjust Your Dress Before Leaving", The Bulletin, 6.5.1967.

ent disregard for shared institutions, such as consultation and moral obligation. Officials could be upset British officials had not been frank about the degree of economic or political pressure. *The Australian* aptly summarised the conflicting emotions after the British decision: "They are decisions that will strike home sharply and emotionally for many Australians – and no less so for the fact that we have known for a long time that they had to be made."[129]

Following the British announcement, Australians and New Zealanders shifted strategies by approaching the issue with cautious expressions. The Australian Cabinet decided "as much as possible should be made of the assurances which the British messages and White Paper contain as to the careful timing of the withdrawal and as to the continuing part which Britain will have in the Far East".[130] As a complete withdrawal was only envisaged in an unspecific way for the 1970s, officials like Holt hoped for local developments or diplomatic efforts to influence British thinking in the meantime.[131] In New Zealand, NSEA George Laking urged that Thomas McDonald would continue as High Commissioner in London for another term, "during what will obviously be a very vital and sticky period".[132] Furthermore, departmental caution and pessimism in both countries were increased by another set of British considerations, namely its renewed interest in seeking entry into the EEC made public in early May 1967.

129 "Let's get a move on!", The Australian, 20.7.1967.

130 NAA A5619 C22, Part 1, Cabinet Decision 473, 18.7.1967.

131 NAA A2908 D25, Part 2, Press Briefing given by Harold Holt, 19.7.1967.

132 NLNZ 92–258 (George Laking Papers) 03/25, George Laking to Thomas Macdonald, 11.10.1967.

All three former dominions had been left by the first EEC discussions with the impression Britain eventually would seek entry again.[133] As a result, officials tried to grasp the degree of interdependence of both policy fields, EEC and East of Suez, when British considerations for a second bid became known. Around the quadripartite talks in autumn 1965, British officials had proposed to establish a "gentleman's agreement"[134] to cover both trade and defence relations in order to share the defence burden. During subsequent discussions, Australian and New Zealand officials learned their British counterparts increasingly considered trade opportunities as a prerequisite to its continued presence in Southeast Asia. In February 1967, the Australian Liaison Staff in London reported that British services were severing their attitude towards Australia because of a new EEC interest.[135] Days before the SEATO meeting, Australians in London also wondered if press leaks on a British military withdrawal could have been tactically placed to test allied reactions in the face of an upcoming EEC bid.[136]

As a consequence, Britain's allies tackled the strong link between economic and defence interest and underlined in talks with the British the need for a political view on the bases. At the same SEATO meeting, Dean Rusk was the first to ask George Brown if his government intended to "strip its Asian decks and get closer to Europe".[137] Although Brown denied this interdependence, officials sensed a connection between both sets of issues in the following.[138] From London, the New Zealand High Commission commented: "If Britain's European venture prospers, interest in extra-European affairs is bound to shrink. Either way, […] the days of the East of Suez policy are numbered."[139]

The New Zealand government was particularly worried about any implication a British EEC entry could have for its huge dependence on Commonwealth preferential trade. Although New Zealand had focused on diversification of trade after Britain's first EEC bid, the transition of its economy was still underway. In that situation, the dual interdependence with the British economy and defence arrangements was even more troubling, as the *Auckland Star* put it poignantly: "[…] if Britain is not going to buy our butter after she joins the Common Market we will not have enough sterling to pay 29 million for a British built frigate."[140]

---

133 *Benvenuti*, Anglo-Australian Relations, 112–115.

134 NAA A4940 C4279, AHC London 8668, 5.10.1965.

135 NAA A1945 73/1/63, AJSS London (Hassett), 31.1.1967.

136 NAA M1003, DEFENCE EAST OF SUEZ, AHC London 4443, 18.4.1967.

137 ANZ ABHS W4628 7148, Box 120, LONB 106/7, Part 2, Record of Meeting between Keith Holyoake, Harold Holt, Dean Rusk and George Brown, 20.4.1967.

138 LAC RG25 A-3-c, Vol. 8600, 20-1-1-12, Part 4, CHC Canberra (Menzies) 583, 27.4.1967.

139 ANZ ABHS W4628 7148, Box 120, LONB 106/7, Part 2, NHC London to NEmb. Washington, 4.5.1967.

140 *Ian Templeton*: "Revised Defence Priorities Don't Please Services", Auckland Star, 13.6.1967. The article referred to a frigate New Zealand had ordered from Britain. Following

In contrast to New Zealand, Australia decided to prioritise their strategic interests and opted against turning the discussions on the EEC into a "second front"[141] with Britain. For Australia, a British EEC entry was considered less threatening than in the early 1960s as it had diversified its trade in the meantime, most of all with Japan.[142] However, Australian officials were still concerned by the implications of a British entry into Europe for them and the Commonwealth, leading to an approach to Canadians in the hope of joining diplomatic forces with them against Britain.[143]

Although Canadians opposed a joint approach to influence Britain, they shared concerns about the link between East of Suez and British interests to enter the EEC. A Canadian memo in early 1967 judged the EEC bid to be a crucial issue: "If Britain moves closer to Europe there could be variations of emphasis but it would surely be in Canadian interest not to allow these to develop into some form of 'continentalism' on both sides of the Atlantic."[144] Integration into Europe was clearly linked to tendencies in isolationism, something opposed by Pearson's internationalist outlook. But while they experienced similar moments of suspicion and non-consultation in frameworks such as NATO[145], Canadians refrained from actively influencing Britain to review its decision. Pearson's government had decided early in its tenure that the ultimate decision on the EEC entry would lay with Britain.[146]

A thorough reflection on the dual implications of a British withdrawal from Southeast Asia and an entry into the EEC was prevented by yet another French veto against British entry in November 1967. Nevertheless, Britain's EEC bid had its implications for the East of Suez discussions. The issue had put Americans on the spot as they were opposed to a British withdrawal, but welcomed Britain's EEC application as a valuable step of European integration. Ultimately, they favoured Britain's turn to Europe, indicating their prioritisation of European integration in contrast to Britain's continued role in Southeast Asia.[147] The loss of American opposition against a British withdrawal further diminished Tasman chances to press Britain for a change of policy.

Britain's January decision, Holyoake notified Harold Wilson that his government had to reconsider the purchase, ANZ ABHS W4627 950, Box 4506, 434/8/1, Part 18, NDEA to NHC London 448, 7.2.1968.

[141] NAA A1209 1967/7117, Part 2, Lawler to Holt, 27.4.1967, quoted in: *Benvenuti*, Parting of the Ways, 592.

[142] *Ward*, British Embrace, 246 f.

[143] LAC RG25 A-3-c, Vol. 10660, 23-1-AUSTL, CHC Canberra 706, 16.5.1967.

[144] LAC RG25 A-3-c, Vol. 10042, 20-1-2-BRIT, Memorandum on Britain and Europe, n. d. (early 1967).

[145] LAC MG31 E83, Box 13, Geoffrey Murray (CHC London) to Basil Robinson, 28.4.1967.

[146] *MacLaren*, Commissions High, 510 f.

[147] *Jones*, Decision Delayed, 589 f.

4.1.3 1968 – The End of an Era

Following the British announcement in July 1967, officials in the Australian departments demanded a more active strategy in response to the British decision: "In any case, simply to wait for the British to tell us what they are going to do seems insufficient. [...] We are in no position to pursue these matters effectively until we know what we want to do ourselves."[148] However, for the remainder of 1967, the Australian government decided against a clear policy. Instead, politicians continued to rely on British assurances that their views would be taken into consideration. As earlier emotional charges had not resulted in a British revision of its plans, outspoken critics like Alexander Downer were now advised to soften their statements on the issue and were informed that Australia was inclined "to accept the British decisions without much demur, with recognition that only some dramatic development in the area is likely to have significant effect on them".[149]

Nevertheless, officials still hoped to influence Britain's decision based on personal relationships with British officials who indicated opposition to their government's plans. One British official went as far with New Zealand representatives as to suggest their special confidence overruled even British circles: "[...] there are some things we'd rather trust with you people than with other Whitehall Departments."[150] But despite these favourable relations, neither Australian nor New Zealand approaches could prevent the acceleration of the British timetable for withdrawal confirmed in January 1968. The British financial situation had become alarming after the government was forced to devalue the British Pound on 28 November 1967. After observing the debate in the House of Commons, Australian Staff Hassett assessed the devaluation as the "death blow to what little British determination previously remained to retain a military capacity capable of playing a significant role outside of Europe".[151] While witnessing Britain's difficulties, potential negotiations were complicated by the disappearance of Harold Holt on 17 December 1967. For Australia and New Zealand[152], the uncertainty and, ultimately, change of leadership had profound effects on further dealings with Britain.

---

[148] NAA A1838 TS696/1, Part 3, Anderson to Acting ASEA, 2.11.1967.

[149] NAA A1209 1966/7335, Part 6, Harold Holt to Alexander Downer, 27.7.1967, quoted in: *Benvenuti*, Parting of the Ways, 595.

[150] ANZ ABHS W4628 7148, Box 121, LONB 106/7, Part 3, NHC London 5556, 21.11.1967.

[151] NAA A9861 3/12/77/8, Part 4, Hassett (AJSS London) to Australian Secretary of the Department of Defence, 29.11.1967.

[152] An article by the newspaper *Dominion* suggested in summer 1968 that Holyoake had considered resigning but was so profoundly shaken by Holt's disappearance and the British decision in January 1968 that he decided to continue his premiership; "Battle of wits in SE Asia", Dominion, 10.6.1968.

In early 1968, British Secretary of State for Commonwealth Affairs, George Thomson, visited Wellington and Canberra to discuss further British deliberations on defence. When Tasman officials were informed of his visit, they already expected an acceleration of Britain's withdrawal plans, and felt confirmed by various press leaks.[153] A likely turn in Britain's policy was also seen in its renewed interest in European integration depicted by the EEC bid, despite de Gaulle's veto.[154] New Zealanders therefore suspected that Thomson's visit would serve the purpose to announce the accelerations "under the façade of consultation".[155] In Australia, officials equally complained about the "shabby Thomson exercise".[156] They had also been advised by British services not to let the opportunity pass to voice their frustrations, "the harsher the better".[157]

In preparations for the meetings, New Zealand officials equipped themselves for a last insistence on shared imperial ties. Presenting a summary of all assurances given by British officials up until early 1968[158], George Laking recommended underlining "That the government would regard complete withdrawal by 1 April 1971 as a going back on all the British have said to us in the last 18 months about their intention to honour their commitments and to withdraw in an orderly fashion".[159] In his talks with Thomson, Holyoake showed sympathy over Britain's economic difficulties, but shared his shock over the British decision and insisted on its traditional obligation.[160]

Australians also drafted briefs that listed for another time all the arguments speaking against an early withdrawal from the region. During the talks, Cabinet Member Alan Hulme criticised that Thomson's visit was not "in the nature of real consultations in keeping with the traditional spirit of Commonwealth partnership; he [Thomson] seemed to have come merely to tell the Australian government what had been decided".[161] While they argued similarly to New Zealanders by insisting on British assurances given, Australians also depicted Britain's plans as a betrayal. The acceleration was unacceptable, even more

---

[153] ANZ ABHS W4628 7148, Box 121, LONB 106/7, Part 3, NHC London, 8.1.1968.

[154] ANZ ABHS W4627 950, Box 4506, 434/8/1, Part 17, Brief by George Laking for George Thomson Visit, 5.1.1968.

[155] ANZ ABHS W4628 7148, Box 121, LONB 106/7, Part 3, NDEA to NHC Kuala Lumpur 1, 2.1.1968.

[156] NAA A1838 TS696/1, Part 6, Brief for George Thomson visit, n. d. (Jan 1968).

[157] NAA A9861 3/12/77/8, Part 5, AJSS London to AMD, 4.1.1968.

[158] ANZ ABHS W4627 950, Box 4506, 434/8/1, Part 17, Summary of British Comments on the Far East Presence since June 1966, 9.1.1968.

[159] ANZ ABHS W4627 950, Box 4506, 434/8/1, Part 17, George Laking to Keith Holyoake, 9.1.1968.

[160] TNA FCO 24/91, Record of Meeting between George Thomson and the New Zealand Cabinet, 11.1.1968.

[161] TNA FCO 24/91, Record of Meeting between George Thomson and the Australian Cabinet, 12.1.1968.

so as officials felt that their acceptance of the July decision had already been a compromise.[162]

While the emotions expressed during the discussions with Thomson did not alter Britain's plans, the repercussions of the official decision made public on 16 January 1968 were felt both in Britain and the former dominions. Shortly before the publication, Denis Healey described the upcoming announcement as a 'watershed moment' in British history; a term picked up by the New Zealand High Commission in London as apt.[163] Previously, Thomson had reported "a sense of sadness rather than anger" among Tasman officials over "what they clearly regarded as the ending of an era".[164] Following the British decision, it was again Alexander Downer who found the sharpest words for the British decision. Meeting with British service officials on the day of the announcement, he called it "a day of shame, disgrace and dishonour".[165]

The perception of a watershed moment had also poured into the Tasman public. New Zealand's *Dominion* titled 'The Day Britain let us down' and spoke of "a bitter lesson of untrustworthiness of the United Kingdom Government", leading to the drastic question "Can we trust Britain again?"[166] In a similar article, the *Evening Post* made headlines with 'Twilight of an Empire' and assessed the emotions felt in the country after the announcement: "Brought to an abrupt realisation that the apron strings which she has grasped for so long are soon to be severed, New Zealand is hurt and disappointed, and very uneasy concerning what the future holds for a small, vulnerable country that increasingly must stand on its own feet."[167]

Although these references indicate the January announcement was seen as a definite decision, both Australians and New Zealanders still hoped to influence the British defence plans. With the right approach, New Zealanders expected "for our friends in the [British] Government to manoeuvre in directions more favourable to our needs, even within the policy now laid down".[168] The hope for support in British ranks was also sustained by statements of support from outside the traditional circle of British policymakers. In February 1968, Australia House received a letter from the London Chamber of Commerce, which expressed its sympathy for the Australian position and underlined "our mutual ties are much too deep to permit this situation to rupture permanently our relationship with you".[169] Around the same time, Alexander Downer reported on a

[162] ANZ ABHS W4628 7148, Box 121, LONB 106/7, Part 3, NHC Canberra 39, 10.1.1968.
[163] ANZ ABHS W4628 7148, Box 121, LONB 106/7, Part 3, NHC London 229, 16.1.1968.
[164] TNA FCO 24/92, BHC Wellington 78, 12.1.1968.
[165] NAA A3211 1969/1846, Part 3, AHC London (Downer), 17.1.1968.
[166] "The Day Britain let us down", Dominion, 18.1.1968.
[167] "Twilight of an Empire", Evening Post, 18.1.1968.
[168] ANZ ABHS W4628 7148, Box 121, LONB 106/7, Part 4, NHC London, 9.2.1968.
[169] NAA A1838 370/1/3, Part 2, London Chamber of Commerce to AHC London, 13.2.1968.

speech given by Prince Philip at the New Zealand Society in which he stressed Britain would always come to Australia's and New Zealand's help – "bases or no bases, carriers or no carriers, F.111s or no F.111s".[170] Feeling confirmed in his perceptions, Downer framed Prince Philip's speech as being "symptomatic of much which is being said privately in London these days. […] Wherever I go I find deep anger, and shame, at the government's decision last month".[171]

Such statements from governmental outsiders were partly underpinned by official British statements of a continued principle of moral obligation.[172] However, these symbolic statements seemed increasingly hollow, given that British policymakers pursued plans for withdrawal by practical arrangements in the following months.

The demise of British world power, represented by the decision in January 1968, created difficulties for the whole 'Old' Commonwealth, including Canada. On the eve of the British Pound devaluation in late 1967, Lester Pearson received the Freedom of the City of London. He used the occasion to give various statements on the special relationship Britain still had with Canada, but also with other parts of the world: "Britain, with its wisdom, and its experience; with the sense of moderation and justice of its people; has a vital and indispensable role to play in the world today and tomorrow."[173] Further on, he celebrated the Canadian nation as a product of British values that proved flexible and tolerant to changing times and circumstances. Ultimately, he referred to the current change in Anglo-Canadian relations: "Our formal relationship, I know, is different than it once was. Kipling's daughter has now left home. But I can testify that our kinship is unimpaired and our friendship remains deep and enduring."[174] With a change in British policy in plain sight, Pearson's address was designed to reassure the public and officials alike that despite the current difficulties Britain faced, it could still rely on its Canadian partners.

As the British East of Suez plans did not immediately present Canada with any strategic inconvenience, the decisions taken in July 1967 and January 1968 received minor coverage. In general, Canadians followed the arguments for withdrawal outlined to them by British officials. Moreover, because of their small role in the region, officials did not consider taking a larger role in Anglo-Dominion discussions.[175] However, the increasing dichotomy between a Euro-

[170] NAA A1838 67/1/3, Part 3, AHC London 2346, 9.2.1968.

[171] Ibid.

[172] NAA A1838 67/1/3, Part 3, Press Conference by British Secretary of State for Commonwealth Affairs George Thomson, 10.1.1968.

[173] LAC MG31 E47 (Arnold Smith Papers), Vol. 3, Notes for Speech by the Right. Hon. Lester Pearson at Luncheon in London, 27.11.1967.

[174] Ibid.

[175] LAC RG25 A-3-c, Vol. 8402, 20-AUSTL-1-3-NZ, Part 3, CHC Canberra 1529, 5.10.1967.

pean and a British world role troubled Canadian officials similar to Australian and New Zealand counterparts. Preparing material for Wilson's visit to Ottawa in early 1968, Canadian High Commissioner to London Charles Ritchie indicated the abolition of overseas responsibilities was strongly linked to successful integration into Europe.[176] He later criticised the rigidity of this political decision: "They were likely people who in the course of the house cleaning became possessed with a frenzy of throwing out things only to find later on that they had thrown out very valuable things in the process."[177] Canadians were equally unsettled by the swift change in British foreign policy outlooks. In a lengthy Canadian briefing paper on Britain[178], both the East of Suez withdrawal and Britain's turn to Europe were interpreted as expectable and inevitable developments in the light of Britain's changing global position. Nevertheless, the brief deplored any potential damages done to the Commonwealth by Britain's retreat from a world role. Support for the Commonwealth was deemed essential, because its dissolution would "be a serious loss for Canada for reasons both of emotion and practical international utility".[179] The various briefs indicate a deep concern for the future of frameworks linked to a British set of values.

However, the regret over shifting relations was not followed up by concise policy reviews since the changes were linked to transformations within Canada. As historian C. P. Champion has outlined on the discussions under Lester Pearson, questions such as non-British immigration or a new flag would uphold the idea of being British in a larger framework of liberalism and internationalism.[180] Following this perception, the transformation of the former British Empire was a larger background to more pressing issues that confronted Canada on a domestic level, especially with Quebec.[181] In a broader review of Canada's foreign policy, CSSEA Paul Martin had called foreign affairs increasingly as a uniting practice: "In formulating Canadian policy, we must attempt to derive the maximum benefit for all Canadians from the possibilities which our international contacts open to us."[182] In fact, Canadian newspapers interpreted Pear-

[176] LAC RG25, Vol. 10663, 23-3-1968, CHC London 684, 7.2.1968.

[177] LAC RG25, Vol. 10663, 23-3-1968, CHC London 1177, 5.3.1968.

[178] LAC RG 25-A-4, Vol. 3171, 36-1968/3, Special Task Force on European Country Studies – Western Europe – Britain.

[179] Ibid., 85.

[180] *Champion*, Strange Demise, 157–195.

[181] Over the course of the 1960s, the Quebec province, representing the largest part of Franco-Canadian society, demanded both greater independence as well as the recognition of a separate identity that could mount in its extremist forms to a call for separatism. For further analysis of the influential role of Quebec on the period covered by this study I gladly refer to the work of my colleague Sebastian Koch, *Sebastian Koch*, Identitätskrisen nach dem Ende des Britischen Empire. Zur kulturellen Neu-Verortung in Kanada, Australien und Aotearoa Neuseeland, Tübingen Forthcoming [2022].

[182] *Paul Martin*, New Dimensions in Canadian Foreign Policy. Speech given at the University of New Brunswick, 16.5.1967, in: External Affairs 19/5, 1967, 194–199, 195.

son's speeches in London more as an indirect attack on Charles de Gaulle for his interference with Canadian affairs earlier that year, rather than being directed at the state of Anglo-Canadian relations.[183] While tentative references to national interests would come fully to fruition under Pierre Trudeau, Canadians continued to perceive most of the discussions on Britain's withdrawal from Southeast Asia as deplorable yet inevitable development that had to be reviewed on a regional level.

4.2 Experiencing Urgency and Uncertainty – The Dismantling of Regional Security

Britain's first considerations for withdrawal also came for Australians and New Zealanders at a time of considerable unease about regional developments. In 1965, aside from the escalation in the conflict between Indonesia and Malaysia, Vietnam remained the largest trouble spot, with three coups in the course of late 1963 to early 1965, escalating further into an unsettling conflict with global implications.

Against this backdrop, Tasman officials strongly objected to British considerations of withdrawal as inappropriate and premature. Not only were Australian and New Zealand intelligence and strategic assessments of the region contradicting British reviews, but their policymakers also underlined how Britain had urged for a defence commitment to Malaysia with contrary assessments only a few years earlier. During consultations, Britain and its ANZAM partners challenged each other on the question of Britain's tenure in the face of political instability. Again, these discussions were largely influenced by suspicion and mistrust resulting from secrecy over individual plans, belated consultation and other negotiation tactics from both sides.

In addition to declining imperial cooperation, dominion officials linked the British withdrawal from Southeast Asia closely to a dismantling of their regional defence structure. With a strategic policy relying strongly on forward defence, Australian and New Zealand officials feared for a power vacuum in the region. Additionally, Britain provided the shared logistical and institutional framework in Malaysia, most dominantly for the CSR. While the region itself gained growing importance as a category during discussions, suggestions for an alternative British presence on the Australian mainland were largely repudiated, especially on the political level.[184] To push for a continued British presence, Australian officials pointed to the historic legacy and responsibility Britain had

[183] See e.g. "Keep hands off Canada, PM warns", Globe and Mail, 28.11.1967; Guy Cormier: "M. Pearson retour de Londres", La Presse, 29.11.1967.

[184] *Benvenuti*, Anglo-Australian Relations, 74 f.

as a regional power. Together with Canada, by adopting arguments of British exceptionalism, they also underlined the benefit of a continued British commitment as part of a Commonwealth framework.

4.2.1 Undermining Forward Defence – Discussions on an Alternative Base in Australia

In summer 1965, Australian Liaison Officer Geoffrey Hartnell indicated a changing atmosphere among policymaking circles in London. Reporting on talks with British officials, Hartnell sensed the government under Wilson was coming closer to an inevitable turn in defence policy over economic and political pressures. He described a tense, anxious outlook among officials:

"– it is being as if the shutter of an injection [sic!] seat could be pulled down in hoping not to move. There are many reasons for this – partly antipathy to the US, a natural dislike of assuming an inferior role and financially the conflict between the requirements of the Welfare State and a world power. But in any event the Defence Review has brought the UK to another cross roads in her Far East Defence policy."[185]

Hartnell called for an Australian initiative to prevent Britain from further questioning its traditional presence in Southeast Asia: "I am certain that it is far better to grasp the nettle at a time of our own choosing, rather than to let it sting us when we are not prepared for it."[186] Singapore's secession from Malaysia only a couple of weeks later served as said ejector seat, or an "accelerator"[187] for British thinking on its presence in Southeast Asia. With an eye on the British memo circulated before the meeting which promoted negotiations with Indonesia, Australian officials concluded the British "now seem to acknowledge that there is no easy way of ending it on acceptable terms, and that for the British themselves to be suspected of seeking actively to promote a settlement could start a slide into all the worst consequences we are trying to avoid".[188]

During quadripartite talks, Australians and New Zealanders objected to British plans to end Confrontation by approaching Indonesia, and feared any publicity given to such considerations.[189] These concerns were shared by the Americans[190], and even Canadians recommended caution in regards to the Southeast Asian region, as a British retreat would open up "a host of long-term policy questions about the future of Malaysia, Indonesian external policy, the Austra-

[185] NAA A1945 73/1/55, AJSS (Hartnell) to AMD, 14.6.1965.

[186] NAA A1945 73/1/55, AJSS (Hartnell) to AMD, 5.7.1965.

[187] NAA A1838 TS3006/10/4/1, Part 1, "Future Relations with Malaysia and Singapore", Brief for Quadripartite talks, n. d. (Sept. 1965).

[188] Ibid.

[189] ANZ ABHS W5422 950, Box 34, 111/3/3/15, Part 8, Report by Keith Holyoake on the ANZUS Council 1965, 28.6.1965.

[190] NAA A1838 682/4, Part 5A, AEmb. Washington 3030, 1.9.1965.

lian and United States role in Southeast Asia, and the peace and stability of the area generally".[191] With strong allied protest, British officials were divided on how much they should take their allies into confidence in their future planning. British Commander-in-Chief Far East (CINCFE) John Grandy objected to any plans for further consultation as potentially damaging: "[…] if we let news of this get out before our plans are really and truly fixed and then decide after all that we cannot afford it, or we find that then AUS/NZ/AM boys aren't with us for some reason or other, we would, to my mind, have unnecessarily put ourselves into a pretty poor position."[192] At the same time, British officials used their contacts in London to convey their confusion over the allied disregard for their economic and political struggles. As Hartnell reported, "There is a suggestion that as we live closer to the South East Asian scene we have come to take Singapore for granted and do not appreciate that factors beyond British control will determine the tenure of their stay. This, of course, implies a lack of understanding by the UK of our position but this has always been present".[193] Hartnell's report implies that both sides deplored what they perceived as a misunderstanding of the other's position. As he anticipated the antagonism only to grow, Hartnell advocated a positive approach to Britain, including talks on contingency planning for a British retreat to an alternative site in Australia. This proposal had been floated by British planners since 1962, yet most Australian officials objected to such considerations because they feared it to be an overture to a complete British withdrawal.[194]

Uncertainty and mistrust continued to cloud Australian considerations. Paul Hasluck called his staff for a review of the whole defence relationship with Britain: "I have an uncomfortable feeling, rather than a definite opinion, that we have not got a great deal of clarity, certainty, and realism in our views at the moment as we had two months ago."[195] Australian considerations in the aftermath of the quadripartite talks illustrate how officials started to review their own premises for a continued British presence in Southeast Asia. This was not the first time they considered a defence and strategic review, but it was the first time when such a reappraisal rooted in views contrary to British outlooks. Additionally, conflicting emotions on the right course of action emerged from fears that any constructive approach to Britain might be taken as an opportunity for withdrawal. As a result, contingency planning and the alternative of a British base in Australia became a controversial issue. While some officials like Hartnell sup-

[191] LAC RG25 A-3-c, Vol. 8917, 20-INDON-1-3-MLSIA, Brief for the Visit of Harold Wilson, 14.12.1965.

[192] TNA DO 169/439, CINCFE Grandy to BHC Kuala Lumpur (Head), 21.9.1965.

[193] NAA A1838 682/4, Part 5A, Geoffrey Hartnell (AJSS London), 20.9.1965.

[194] *Andrea Benvenuti*, The British are "Taking to the Boat". Australian Attempts to Forestall Britain's Military Disengagement from Southeast Asia, 1965–1966, in: Diplomacy & Statecraft 20/1, 2009, 86–106, 94 f.

[195] NAA A1838 682/4, Part 5A, Memorandum by AMEA Paul Hasluck, 1.10.1965.

ported a closer look at potential bases off the Southeast Asian region, potentially in Australia, other officials like Keith Shann objected to such a step. Reporting from Indonesia, Shann saw any retreat from the area as encouraging "a stepping up of confrontation, a very grave weakening of the whole of Western position in the area, including that of the Americans in Vietnam and the endangering not only of our strategic position, but, in the end, of Britain's investment".[196]

Supporters of alternative planning emphasised the need for continued British cooperation that might assist the former 'mother country' in its current struggles. Additionally, they underlined the danger of driving the British out of Southeast Asia altogether if they showed no willingness to make concessions. Conversely, opponents to alternative planning stressed the continuous need for Britain in the area as its presence fulfilled a specific role. Amidst these differences, both sides agreed on the uncertainty of future developments in the region because of the unpredictable outcome of the Vietnam War. Ultimately, the Australian government opted to wait for further British planning and dismiss joint planning for an alternative site in Australia.

Meanwhile, New Zealanders, like their Australian counterparts, doubted the British arguments for a timely withdrawal and insisted on continued British support of forward defence.[197] When Harold Wilson wrote Keith Holyoake and Robert Menzies in late September that "Time is not on our side, either as regards our tenure in Singapore or the continuation of confrontation"[198], Holyoake replied that time was really the essence in continuing a Western defence effort for as long as possible.[199] Menzies showed himself even less willing to consider joint planning, stiffened in his position by departmental advice through John Bunting: "Our policy, on the other hand, is that Britain stays there as long as she can, including, if necessary in humiliation."[200] Menzies adopted Bunting's recommendations in his reply to Wilson and urged the British to stay indefinitely in Southeast Asia, "even in adversity".[201] This particular line angered British officials such as Denis Healey: "It is one thing for our allies to think that we should not get out of Singapore merely to save money; it is another for them to imply we ought to stay there (and could stay there) regardless of the practical and political difficulties which will mount up against us if current trends continue."[202]

---

[196] NAA M1003 (Alexander Downer Papers), MALAYSIA-SINGAPORE, AEmb. Djakarta (Shann), 8.9.1965.

[197] See e. g. ANZ ABHS W4628 7148, Box 119, LONB 106/5, Part 1, NDEA to London 2673, 2.9.1965.

[198] ANZ ABHS W4628 7148, Box 119, LONB 106/5, Part 1, Harold Wilson to Keith Holyoake, 25.9.1965.

[199] ANZ ABHS W4627 950, Box 4505, 434/8/1, Part 10, Keith Holyoake to Harold Wilson, 14.10.1965.

[200] John Bunting to Robert Menzies, 19.10.1965, quoted in: *Goldsworthy*, Losing the Blanket, 164.

[201] TNA PREM 13/889, Robert Menzies to Harold Wilson, 22.10.1965.

[202] TNA PREM 13/889, Denis Healey to Harold Wilson, 1.11.1965. Some Australian poli-

Instructed to seek clarification on the issue, Charles Johnston could not convince Menzies to accept British assessments of a likely deterioration between Malaysia and Singapore. Instead, Menzies underlined local willingness to host British troops indefinitely. Following this meeting, Johnston felt that he had not dealt with "rational people"[203] as both Menzies and the present Paul Hasluck insisted on the British to stay. Furthermore, Menzies referred during the talks to Churchill's decision to remain in Tobruk in 1942, a historic example that should show British prime ministers could uphold an undesirable or unpopular military presence.[204] Menzies' reference indicates how Tasman officials would continue to frame Britain's specific role as part of the region and forward defence. In further communications with Wilson, Menzies underlined "Britain's presence and military strength on mainland South East Asia (and perhaps, consequently, Australia's and New Zealand's) is sanctioned by tradition and by arrangements with a free popular Government".[205]

Rhetoric strategies and arguments emphasising Britain's regional obligation were continued during Healey's visit in early 1966. Shortly before his arrival, the Australian Cabinet restated its objection to any planning for bases in Australia, and called for quadripartite plans to ensure that "any scaling down in Britain's global commitments did not involve reductions which imperilled Australian security".[206] ASEA James Plimsoll repeated these points in his brief for the Healey talks:

> "The objective should be to get into Mr. Healey's head the idea that everything is not lost in Singapore; that the best thing of all is to continue to have a physical presence in Malaysia and Singapore, and that nothing else is as good for us; and that we should be thinking of positive measures to enable us to stay, rather than basing our thinking on a conclusion that withdrawal by 1970 is almost inevitable."[207]

The following talks confirmed that both sides differed on the potential regional threats. Suspicion had also been created by informal approaches of British officials beforehand, who had indicated a willingness to review their commitment, regardless of allied opposition.[208] In talks with Healey, John McEwen brought Australian misgivings to the point when he asked Healey if "the British would like to go, or intended to go, regardless of duress".[209]

---

cymakers were equally confused by the reference; NAA A1838 682/4, Part 5A, Gordon Jockel to Thomas Critchley (AHC Kuala Lumpur), 29.10.1965.

203 TNA PREM 13/889, BHC Canberra (Johnston) to CRO 1428, 24.11.1965.

204 Ibid.

205 TNA PREM 13/889, Robert Menzies to Harold Wilson, 19.1.1966.

206 NAA A1838 682/4, Part 7, Cabinet Decision 1465, 10.1.1966.

207 NAA A1838 TS682/4, Part 8, Brief by Plimsoll, 30.1.1966.

208 NAA A1838 TS682/4, Part 8, ASEA James Plimsoll on Talks with New Zealand and British Officials, 28.1.1966.

209 NAA A1209 1965/6595, Part 3, Record of Discussions with Denis Healey 1.2./2.2.1966, quoted in: *Ashton/Bridge/Ward*, DAFP, 144–157.

Consequently, Australians doubted the use of further studies on an alternative base amidst uncertainty regarding British plans[210], and reiterated their objection to an alternative site in the following. They told British counterparts "there would be considerable political problems for any Australian Government in accepting large British Army bases on Australian soil and, furthermore, subsidising them substantially, unless the forces they housed had a clearly defined and (to the Australian eye) sensible role".[211] Australians also expressed their concerns over the potential embarrassment and domestic pressure with their troops fighting in Vietnam while British troops were stationed in Australia.[212]

Nevertheless, British officials continued to insist on further allied planning, leading to requests from Australian diplomats to consider the British plans. In London, Thomas Critchley recommended a flexible position regarding an alternative site in Australia to allow further negotiations with the British:

> "In any case I feel strongly that we should take every opportunity to commit the British on their East of Suez policy while we have the opportunity and that this should include commitments to bases in Australia. […] If I could judge the feeling here correctly, a great deal could depend on sentiment. I would hope that we could make the British feel that they are genuinely wanted in Australia and that we are prepared to make our contribution towards their being there."[213]

In a twist of Critchley's recommendation, Canberra placed its tactics in the following on a British attachment to the Southeast Asian region. Officials strongly framed their resistance to an alternative site on regional British bases as being irreplaceable, both in a strategic and cultural sense. At the same time, they hoped to bring both Britain and the USA into quadripartite talks, to determine their allies' strategic policy on the region and to engage the USA in exerting pressure on Britain.[214]

Allied differences only grew at the end of Confrontation. While negotiations between Malaysia and Indonesia were underway, Harold Wilson sent a message to both Robert Menzies and Keith Holyoake, stating that Britain intended to keep its presence until the end of the conflict.[215] Given the auspicious regional talks, NSEA Alister McIntosh asked in an internal memo: "[…] one wonders what was the point of making a statement with such a limited commitment."[216] Following McIntosh's recommendations, Holyoake therefore un-

[210] NAA A5619 C22, Part 1, Report by Defence Committee in Preparation for Denis Healey Visit, n. d. (January 1966).
[211] ANZ ABHS W4628 7148, Box 120, LONB 106/7, Part 1, NHC Canberra, 4.8.1966.
[212] NAA A1838 682/4, Part 9, Gordon Jockel to Thomas Critchley, 19.5.1966.
[213] NAA A9861 3/12/77/8, Part 2A, Thomas Critchley to Gordon Jockel, 2.6.1966.
[214] *Benvenuti*, Parting of the Ways, 587.
[215] ANZ ABHS W4627 950, Box 3762, 201/2/3/1, Harold Wilson to Keith Holyoake, 3.8.1966.
[216] ANZ ABHS W4627 950, Box 3762, 201/2/3/1, Memorandum by Alister McIntosh, 12.8.1966.

derlined the need for Britain to stay regardless of Confrontation in his reply to Wilson: "[…] we do hope that you will continue to share the view that our mutual security interest in the area goes well beyond the ending of confrontation and that forces in base facilities should, if possible, be maintained there for a long time to come."[217] Again, both sides felt deliberately uninformed over the objectives of the other side, an unusual feeling in contrast to close consultation experienced earlier.

4.2.2 Questioning the Local Repercussions on the Strategic Framework of Southeast Asia

In April 1967, Washington hosted both the annual SEATO Council Meeting and the Vietnam Contributors' Meeting. As both events occurred concurrently, they showed contemporaries how far Britain and its allies were drifting apart on regional security policy. While the Vietnam contributors discussed further resistance to North Vietnamese aggression, the SEATO meeting, including George Brown's revelations, exposed the growing fractures in Western defence.[218] Brown's announcement was both expected as some had seen the writing on the wall, and unexpected as in the weeks before British officials like Denis Healey had made reassuring statements.[219] During the meeting, Brown implied that Britain was contemplating a withdrawal not just due to local sensitivities, but also because of failing Western strategy: "The problems in Southeast Asia were of a comparatively new type – subversion and guerrilla warfare – and he [Brown] questioned whether military means were the best way of combating them."[220]

The ANZUS powers felt compelled to challenge the British position, not only on the question of local attitudes towards the bases, but also on the apparent rejection of forward defence. Referring to Brown's remarks, Australian Minister Peter Howson noted in his diary that local powers would not object, but welcome the Western presence as an effort to raise standards of living.[221] His comments resembled earlier statements in which Australians claimed a better understanding of the region due to their proximity and interventionist policy. This claim of hegemonic knowledge of local attitudes furthered differences between Britain and its ANZAM partners, both on the question of future strategic policy and needed commitments. To challenge Britain's opposition to local

[217] ANZ ABHS W4627 950, Box 3762, 201/2/3/1, NDEA to NHC London 3180, 15.8.1966.

[218] ANZ AAEG W3252 6956, Box 9, TKY 50/9/9, Part 6, Report on SEATO Council Meeting, 15.4.1967.

[219] ANZ ABHS W4628 7148, Box 120, LONB 106/7, Part 1, NHC London, 8.3.1967.

[220] ANZ ABHS W4628 7148, Box 120, LONB 106/7, Part 2, Record of Meeting between Keith Holyoake and George Brown, 18.4.1967.

[221] *Howson/Aitkin*, Howson Diaries, 292.

bases, Australia and New Zealand used their diplomatic contacts and defence cooperation to collect independent information to disprove British arguments, a strategy already used on frictions within ANZAM cooperation during Confrontation. They also coordinated efforts to challenge the British plans. Prior to April 1967, Australians had already advised Malaysians to insist with Britain to keep ground forces in the region.[222] Through these various efforts, officials realised Malaysians and Singaporeans had come to appreciate the ANZAM and Commonwealth defence framework and seemed equally opposed to a British retreat.[223]

At the same time, Australian and New Zealand officials argued on regional sensitivities when they pressed British officials to reconsider publicity surrounding British retreat plans. The Singapore secession of August 1965 led to cautions against any Four Power discussion that could indicate both to Malaysia and Singapore as to Indonesia indecision over future allied strategy.[224] With Britain's withdrawal plans, Australian and New Zealand officials were concerned any publicity could deeply disturb regional relations in favour of subversive forces.[225] As British bases relied strongly on local acceptance, officials were quick to point to the adverse effect of any planning that could be leaked and taken as a British willingness to leave the region.

Yet publicity could also come as an advantage. When John Marshall flew to London in June 1967, New Zealand officials feared by keeping the British plans in secrecy, "[…] we would be prevented from publicly speaking out against it, while the British would be free to proceed with implementing their plans for a complete withdrawal, untroubled by any public criticism at home or abroad".[226] Officials clearly thought of a community of Britishness among officials, but also amongst the public who could support allied resistance once the British plans were revealed.

Torn between these two objectives, public statements were designed in an ambivalent manner. While they vigorously expressed their anger over Britain's withdrawal in narratives appealing to imperial sentiments, the Australian Cabinet decided in favour of cautious public statements regarding local reception:

"It was agreed first that comments in the statement should be pitched towards restraint so as to avoid unnecessary scare or upset in Singapore and Malaysia, and second, that for policy reasons in relation to Britain, as much as possible should be made of the as-

---

222 NAA A2908 D25, Part 1, ADEA to Posts (AHC Kuala Lumpur 1340), 18.3.1967.

223 ANZ ABHS W4628 7148, Box 120, LONB 106/7, Part 2, NHC Singapore 208, 28.7.1967.

224 ANZ ABHS W4628 7148, Box 119, LONB 106/5, Part 1, NDEA to NHC London 2713, 6.9.1965.

225 Record of Meeting between Harold Wilson and Harold Holt, 13.6.1967; in: *Ashton/Louis*, East of Suez, 114–118, 116.

226 ANZ ABHS W5631 22310, Box 193, PAR 222/1/1, Part 2, Brief for Deputy Prime Minister, 31.5.1967.

surances which the British messages and White Paper contain as to the careful timing of the withdrawal and as to the continuing part which Britain will have in the Far East."[227]

With a strong stance on Britain's previous statements, Tasman officials could hope to guard some of the insecurities created by the British announcement, both at home and in the region. Trust in Britain's assurances could help bridge the gap of uncertainty created by the instability of the region, an argument that could be equally put to the British. Consequently, Harold Holt also told the Australian press his government's statement on Britain's decision was "being rather lacking in Oomph"[228] as any overdramatic statement might undermine local confidence.

Still, officials pushed the argument of an already destabilised region. Shortly before the July White Paper, Holyoake wrote to Wilson that New Zealanders saw "no ground for confidence that by the mid-1970s South-East Asia will have ceased to be an area of instability, or that Communist China will have ceased to exert a major disruptive influence".[229] He further insisted that "the psychological gap between land-based forces and forces over the horizon is very real"[230], therewith pointing to the British considerations for a general capacity as a replacement for stationed troops. Holyoake's remarks on the psychological need for a British element in the CSR were linked both to the deliberations on an alternative base in Australia as to the growing British resistance to committing to SEATO. In early 1966, Britain had already suggested meeting their SEATO commitments by dispatches of mobile forces from Britain rather than by stationing forces in the region.[231] The question of a continued presence was particularly crucial as most of the logistical support for New Zealand forces was provided by the British. In the last resort, a British retreat could also delegitimise the legal basis for both Australia and New Zealand to station troops under the arrangement of AMDA, making a renegotiation of this arrangement necessary.

Concerning British suggestions for a general overseas capacity, Australian and New Zealand officials questioned the feasibility of a dispatch of troops from Britain. A report from the Liaison Staff in London mocked recent British struggles to implement such a mobile force: "It is of some amusement that one of my contacts [...] had a very heavy cold when I saw him yesterday as a result of a day of visits with the Minister of Defence (Administration) to a number of derelict barracks, which had not been occupied since the war, but which are now being assessed for rehabilitation."[232] The British difficulties only strength-

227 NAA A5619 C22, Part 1, Cabinet Decision 473, 18.7.1967.

228 NAA A2908 D25, Part 2, Press Briefing given by Harold Holt, 19.7.1967.

229 ANZ ABHS W4628 7148, Box 121, LONB 106/7, Part 3, Keith Holyoake to Harold Wilson, 7.7.1967.

230 Ibid.

231 ANZ ABHS W4628 7148, Box 119, LONB 106/5A, Part 2, NHC London 795, 1.3.1966.

232 NAA A1945, 73/1/63, AJSS London, 28.4.1967.

ened Australian beliefs that a turn away from Southeast Asia was a wrong decision, and they were supported by British service attitudes in their opposition. British defence officials told Australian counterparts that they were convinced that Britain could not retreat from Southeast Asia "except at the price of complete chaos"[233] and therefore estimated the earliest possible retreat in 1972, if not the mid-1970s. Similar views were shared by British service representatives in Southeast Asia.[234]

Equipped with tacit recommendations from British military officials, Australians and New Zealanders centred their arguments around the CSR. Here, they were able to adopt arguments of sentiment as the 28th Brigade was seen by many as the epitome of Commonwealth cooperation. Similar to emphasising British contributions in providing a political and diplomatic framework, they underlined the historic role Britain had played in establishing the forces.[235] Visiting London, John Marshall was advised to underline the departure of British forces would "destroy the successful Commonwealth partnership in the defence of Singapore and Malaysia which has been an exercise in peacekeeping in the best sense of the term".[236] In talks with Healey, Marshall therefore described the CSR as the "most practical demonstration of the permanent Commonwealth, the hard core of old countries that would always remain. It provides emotional as well as rational encouragement, and its loss would be real and damaging".[237] ANZAM and the continued presence of the CSR were deemed as key elements in negotiations with the British, and Australian officials highlighted a continued British element in the CSR as both fulfilling its defence obligations for the Commonwealth and under SEATO.[238]

Again, positive connotations of British exceptionalism fused the discussion. One ADEA brief suggested to appeal to Britain's "sense of duty" to Malaysia and Singapore: "We should exploit the fact that these are countries which have been formed and shaped by Britain, which have particularly strong security links with Britain and a strong sense of a continuing association with Britain."[239] To avoid charges of nostalgia or colonialism, officials drew a clear distinction between a former imperial role and a continued British presence as forward-looking: "This future British role can be presented as in important re-

233 NAA M1003, DEFENCE EAST OF SUEZ, AHC London 4014, 7.4.1967.

234 ANZ ABFK W5807 7281, Box 174, 226/7/24, Part 1, 226/7/24, Record of Meeting with CINCFE Michael Carver, 19.5.1967.

235 NAA A2908 D25, Part 1, AHC Singapore 962, 24.5.1967.

236 ANZ ABHS W5631 22310, Box 193, PAR 222/1/1, Part 2, Brief for Deputy Prime Minister John Marshall, 31.5.1967.

237 TNA FCO 24/284, Report of Meeting of John Marshall and Denis Healey, 12.6.1967.

238 NAA A1209 1966/7335, Part 4, "Britain's East of Suez", Defence Committee No. 32/1967, 15.5.1967.

239 NAA TS3006/10/4/1, Part 3, Working Paper "Australian Policy on British Defence Policy East of Suez", n. d. (May 1967).

spects a modern and acceptable development from the imperial past, as a more limited and constructive role (tied to the preservation of stability, national development, etc.) and as a lesser burden and larger partnership with the Commonwealth countries."[240]

Equipped with such positive connotations, some officials hoped to depart from a narrow threat-based narrative surround Southeast Asia altogether. In a meeting of the Australian Defence Committee (ADC), James Plimsoll recommended abandoning the argument of moral obligation: "He [Plimsoll] thought that the Australian government should not put its case in terms of fear of a direct threat to Australia, for example by invasion. Such arguments would not be convincing, and in any case merely lead Mr Brown to say that if Australia was attacked it could be sure of British help."[241] Instead, representations should focus on the constant uncertainty surrounding the area and the valuable regional role Britain had played in the past. Plimsoll was challenged by other members who argued many people in Britain would still support the East of Suez role, "not to defend Malaysia or for some general strategic purpose, but because they felt that Britain ought to give defence support to Australia and New Zealand because of ties of kinship and because of our contribution in two world wars".[242]

Ultimately, the ADC recommended shifting the focus back from the Australian mainland to a British role in Southeast Asia:

> "Our case should not be presented as deriving from fears for our own physical security. Our assessment is that there is little risk of a direct threat to Australia in the foreseeable future and we should make this plain, particularly as some British statements about coming to Australia's aid in the event of attack suggest that they believe this to be our prime pre-occupation. […] We can continue to stress the impossibility of foreseeing what the position in Asia will be in the seventies and all the political consequences, uncertainties and re-calculations which would immediately begin to flow from a decision taken and announced now for a complete withdrawal by 1975."[243]

The ADC perceived the insistence on moral obligation as a dead end, as it could be sufficiently satisfied with a British base in Australia. It would be the uncertainties in the region that would demand a British presence, therefore it made sense to embrace the instability of the region as an argument.

In the following, Australians avoided further talks on an alternative site in Australia. Due to both Australia's apparent reluctance and Britain's economic difficulties, the option of an alternative site was eventually dropped, although references continued until the end of 1967.[244]

---

[240] Ibid.
[241] NAA TS3006/10/4/1, Part 3, Report of the ADC Meeting, 17.5.1967.
[242] Ibid.
[243] NAA A9861 3/12/77/8, Part 2B, Minutes by ADC, 19.5.1967, 10 f.
[244] See e. g. NAA A9861 3/12/77/8, Part 4, NHC London, 30.11.1967.

4.2.3 "And we are left out in the cold"[245] – Disorientation and Uncertainty Following the British Decision 1967/68

Following the announcement in July 1967, Australia and New Zealand hoped to gain time by proposing adjustments of a regional role to Britain. As they had focused on local links during the first half of 1967, officials from both countries continued to point to a Commonwealth setting rather than a British setting. Yet cooperation among them as with local powers remained limited. The fear of precipitating a British withdrawal would remain the key factor inhibiting further cooperation, since discussions of new regional defence arrangements were doubted as "weakening, not strengthening, [of] the British sense of commitment and participation".[246] Furthermore, closer local contacts were still partially blocked by a biased Eurocentric outlook among Australian and New Zealand politics. Perceptions of the Asian 'Other' still defined most of the foreign policy applied to the region.[247] As they felt confirmed in their outlooks by the continuous tensions and rivalries between Malaysia and Singapore, officials believed that a British presence was still warranted. Moreover, their decline to join Lee's intervention in London in January 1968 shows that Tasman decisionmakers continued to underestimate the influence and capacity local leaders could bring to the negotiation table.[248]

In general, regional cooperation was still strongly linked to Britain's role at the centre of it. In a brief prepared following the British decision in July 1967, New Zealanders assessed their consecutive commitments to the Malaysian region essentially as help to the British, which also explained the dependence on British facilities.[249] The following approaches to Britain stressed time and again how Britain's presence was irreplaceable and how damaging its retreat would be for the regional balance. In talks with George Thomson, Keith Holyoake underlined Britain could not be replaced by either the USA or Australia, and emphasised the (post-)imperial unity between two distant countries when he addressed New Zealand's perception of being abandoned:

> "Holyoake said that he had always regarded New Zealand as half a dozen English counties joined to the mother country by 12 000 miles of sea. It was only since the end of World War II that New Zealand had accepted the idea of a defence obligation to Southeast Asia rather than the Middle East or Europe, and public opinion was only gradually accepting the idea that New Zealand's destinies lay in this part of the Pacific."[250]

---

245 Quote from "Urgent Look at Defence", Dominion, 23.1.1968.

246 NAA A4940 C4626, Comment by APMD, 27.9.1967.

247 See *Gurry*, Identifying Australia's 'Region', 21–25.

248 *George Westbrook*, Foreign Policy Review. January–June 1968, in: Australian Quarterly 40/3, 1968, 92–103, 92.

249 ANZ AAFD W3738 811, Box 1312, CAB 222/1/1, "New Zealand Defence Policy" (D (67) 10), 11.09.1967.

250 TNA FCO 24/91, Record of Meeting of Keith Holyoake and George Thomson, 11.1.1968.

While his senior advisers George Laking and Chief of Defence Staff Leonard Thornton questioned Thomson on the strategic consequences of Britain's withdrawal, Holyoake took the role of the elderly statesman grieving the loss of a special relationship between both countries that had produced a specific mental mapping. Similar emotions of abandonment and anxiety created by the British decision were also expressed in the greater Tasman public. A few weeks after Britain's announcement on 18 January 1968, the *New Zealand Listener* described the decision as resulting in a "sense of impending nakedness":

"By folding the flag the British are, in a sense, unveiling for us the latent dangers of Asia. […] By 1971 we shall be far closer to the Asian reality than ever before. There are perils ahead, but there may be more value than many people imagine in having to live more dangerously than seemed necessary when Britain stood between us and a world we barely knew."[251]

As the editorial suggested, the British plans increased the feeling of exposure to a dangerous neighbourhood. Regional insecurity was also voiced by the *Canberra Times*: "Geographically we are where we were; strategically and psychologically we are entering a new experience, and it is not surprising that we should be uncertain of our role and our responsibilities."[252]

Newspapers also assessed the implications for the region. Pointing to previous assurances, the *Auckland Star* bemoaned the end to what should have been an indefinite military presence:

"Perhaps inevitably, there are bitter, if pointless, recriminations here against the British who only a year ago gave Kuala Lumpur, Singapore, Canberra and Washington the firmest public and private assurance that they would maintain some sort of South East Asian military presence as long as their hosts made them welcome which could have been almost for ever so far as the Governments of Singapore and Malaysia were concerned."[253]

By referring to Southeast Asian attitudes, newspapers did not only offer points of identification for domestic audiences, but they could also remind the British of their positive local reception.

In the months following the British decision, Australian officials felt confirmed in their feelings of loss when they talked to British service personnel.[254] The sympathy expressed by British services such as the CINCFE seemed to offer avenues for continued cooperation.[255] Moreover, the gravity and rigidity of Britain's decision inscribed in Tasman officials a kind of urgency which resulted in a more activist approach to Britain. As some Australian officials feared losing a certain momentum created by the British announcement, they pressed

---

[251] "Folding the Flag", New Zealand Listener, 2.2.1968.
[252] *T. B. Millar,* "Where do we stand?", Canberra Times, 19.1.1968.
[253] "Nobody willing to step in", Auckland Star, 26.2.1968.
[254] ANZ ABHS W4628 7148, Box 121, LONB 106/7, Part 4, NHC London, 2.2.1968.
[255] NAA A9861 3/12/77/8, Part 5, AHC Singapore 599, 5.3.1968.

Britain for an early Five Power Meeting with Malaysia and Singapore. Talks also seemed warranted in the face of Britain's unapologetic attitude in spite of allied protests. In preparation for SEATO and ANZUS talks in April 1968, Australian officials reviewed the current crisis of trust: "There is currently a serious problem of confidence. Britain has been forced by economic pressures and domestic politics to go back on a series of undertakings."[256] While it suggested finding a way of restoring the lost confidence, the brief also recommended clarifying Britain's future plans for cooperation.

As a result, a strong emotional charge developed both from the regional instability and the regret over British 'foul play' during negotiations. Keith Holyoake expressed these sentiments during the SEATO Council meeting in Wellington: "Britain has assured us […] that a substantial military capability based in Europe and Britain will remain and can be deployed as circumstances demand. I hope I am not just playing with words when I single out the word 'can'. I wish that the word 'will' had been used instead of the word 'can'."[257] Such comments targeted Britain's position as dishonest and potentially harmful to New Zealand interests, but also pressed for disclosure of long-term plans.

Meanwhile, officials also looked into ways of symbolically communicating their anxiety about regional developments. Already shortly after Britain's January decision, New Zealand official Ralph Mullins drew upon the *Ecclesiastical History of England* by the Venerable Bede. Summarising the tale of the Roman withdrawal from Britain that left only Hadrian's wall to defend the British against Scottish and Picts, Mullins concluded with a paragraph from the *History*:

> "'Hereupon a timorous guard was placed upon the wall, where they pined away day and night in the utmost fear.' One hopes that this is not a forecast of the Australian/New Zealand garrison role in Malaysia after the British withdrawal. […] Altogether not a very happy precedent whichever way you look at it."[258]

His script was ultimately used at the Five Power Meeting in June 1968, where Holyoake engaged with George Thomson in a 'battle' of historic analogies. Holyoake challenged Thomson on latter's reference that New Zealand had developed into a "modern, vigorous nation" after the British withdrawal of garrisons in the late nineteenth century, despite "public outcries all over the country that this was the end of the British Empire, that Britain was turning its back on her sons".[259] Dryly, Holyoake replied that "His party had not studied what

[256] NAA A1838 2461/13, Part 2, Brief for the Australian Delegation to Wellington, 27.3.1968.

[257] ANZ AAEG W3252 6956, Box 9, TKY 50/9/9, Part 6, Report by New Zealand Delegation of SEATO Council Meeting, 17.4.1968.

[258] ANZ ABHS W4627 950, Box 4506, 434/8/1, Part 18, Note for File (Mullins), 28.2.1968.

[259] ANZ ABHS W5400 20358, Box 96, KL 102/1/9, Part 2, Record of Five Power Defence Talks held in Kuala Lumpur, 10./11.6.1968.

his countrymen said 90 years ago during the period of the Maori wars. […] he supposed there was some value in looking backwards for guidance".[260] Holyoake's remarks were clearly intended to communicate his country's feeling of exposure, and his regret over losing New Zealand's traditional ally and partner, Britain. Britain's insistence on setting up a mobile force could be linked to the Roman Wall and the Maori Wars: without a physical presence, New Zealand would have to face 'alien' aggression alone.

This episode of historical analogies also indicates how much policymakers of both sides engaged in a shared (post-)imperial frame of symbolic reference. Following the Five Power talks, the British High Commissioner in Kuala Lumpur W. Bentley thanked the New Zealand High Commission staff for forwarding the quotes of Bede, and replied with a quote from Dryden's *The Double Dealer*: "Be kind to my remains, and oh, Defend, (Against your judgement) your Departed Friend."[261] Passing Bentley's communication to Wellington, New Zealand official D. H. Hunn underlined with good humour the reference to Britain being a 'double dealer'.[262] Similar analogies can be found in the Australian context, where historical references were equally used to underline regrets over the British decision. *Australian* cartoonist Bruce Patty adopted the quote "Once more into the breech [sic], dear friends" from Shakespeare's *Henry V* to subtitle a cartoon (Fig. 2) showing a visibly battered Holt being shoved into a cannon by a military labelled "UK Withdrawal Forces" while his British badge had been crossed out.[263]

The cartoon could also serve as a metaphor for the perceived imbalance between Australia's continued efforts in the region, and Britain's reluctance to fully commit under a shared set of values. Another factor crucially played into such perceptions of divergence: the ongoing Vietnam War. Britain's withdrawal not only exposed the Vietnam contributors to potential regional instability, but it also undermined, on a global level, their legitimisation for being committed to Vietnam as Western powers.

Before the last chapter deals with these doubts and uncertainties amidst the global exposure of the Western military effort in Southeast Asia, a section on Canada's role during the East of Suez discussions seems appropriate to examine the scope and limits of this discussion.

---

[260] Ibid. On the discussions surrounding the retreat of Britain's last regiment from New Zealand in 1870 see *W. David McIntyre*, Imperialism and Nationalism, in: Geoffrey W. Rice/William Hosking Oliver (Ed.), The Oxford History of New Zealand. 2. publ., Auckland 1992, 337–347, 340.

[261] ANZ ABHS W5400 20358, Box 96, KL 102/1/9, Part 4, W. Bentley (BHC Kuala Lumpur) to D. H. Hunn (NHC Kuala Lumpur), 31.7.1968.

[262] ANZ ABHS W5400 20358, Box 96, KL 102/1/9, Part 4, D. H. Hunn (NHC Kuala Lumpur) to Ralph Mullins (NDEA), 19.8.1968.

[263] *Bruce Petty*, "Once more into the breech, dear friends …", The Australian, 20.7.1967.

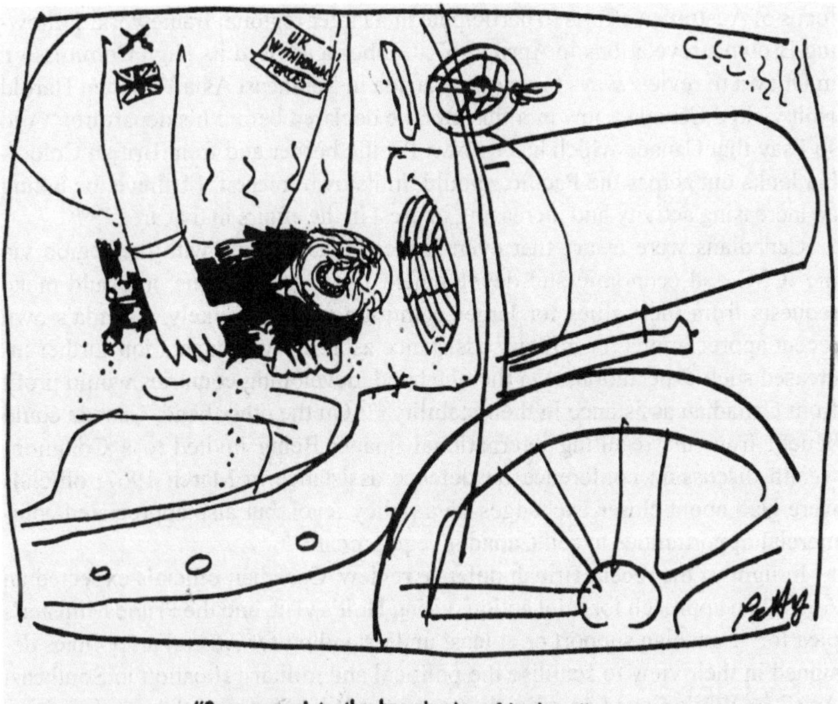

"Once more into the breech, dear friends..."

Fig. 2: Bruce Petty, "Once more into the breech, dear friends ...", The Australian, 20.7.1967

4.2.4 Canada and East of Suez

Throughout the discussions on East of Suez, Canada was only involved as an observer. While it engaged with the other former dominions or Britain in discussions on the implications of withdrawal, Canadian officials stuck to a theme of non-commitment. Despite Canadian concerns for regional instability, the British decision did not result in a similarly charged atmosphere of regret and anxiety as in Australia and New Zealand.

In early 1966, Canadian High Commissioner to Australia Arthur Menzies was approached by Paul Hasluck to discuss plans for a regional defence alliance. Hasluck explained that Australian officials would look into the possibility of an allied military planning body that would include Canada, aside countries such as India and Japan. After the meeting, Menzies deemed Hasluck's approach as indicating that the "Australian government regards Canada as a close associate in essential security matters."[264] Indeed, Canada increasingly moved into the

[264] LAC RG25 A-3-c, Vol. 8842, 20-AUSTL-1-3, Part 3, CHC Canberra (Menzies) 27, 13.1.1966.

focus of Australian efforts to participate in a larger regional framework. Following Brown's revelations in April 1967, Canberra advised its High Commission in Ottawa to review ways to engage Canada in Southeast Asia.[265] When Harold Holt visited Canada a few months later, he declared before his departure: "And so I say that Canada which has its own Pacific border and from British Colombia looks out across the Pacific, should, in its own interest, I believe, be taking an increasing activity and increasing interest in the affairs in that area."[266]

Canadians were aware that even if their engagements with the region via the ICSC and economic and development ties were cautious, it would make requests from their allies for larger commitments more likely. Canada's own recent appreciations for military assistance as a field of cooperation further increased such expectations. On the one hand, developing countries would profit from Canadian assistance in their stability.[267] On the other hand, Canada could benefit from the resulting international image: Being invited to a Commonwealth discussion conference on defence assistance in March 1967, officials were glad about closer exchanges on a policy level, but also appreciated commercial opportunities to sell Canadian equipment.[268]

In light of the recent British defence review, Canadian officials expected an Australian approach for joint action during Holt's visit, and the Prime Minister's plea for "Canadian support or at least understanding for Australian policies designed in their view to stabilise the political and military situation in Southeast Asia".[269] While Canadian officials recommended referring to the usual position of their country's limited regional interests, Holt was similarly advised by the Australian staff in Ottawa that a Canadian inclusion in any form of security alliance was highly unlikely. Canadians would only focus on peacekeeping missions and would perceive their commitment to the ICSC as a sufficient contribution to the Western effort in Southeast Asia. If all, the brief recommended using the visit to inform Canadians on Australia's commitment to the Vietnam War because Canada, "even at top levels, is tending to lose sight of what the war is really about".[270]

A similar approach to Canada was also considered by New Zealand officials. In an internal meeting, Holyoake remarked that "Canada, like New Zealand, had tended to look to Europe and the Atlantic community but that during the next hundred years, however, he hoped that more attention would be given to

[265] NAA A1838 229/9/1, Part 3, CDEA to CHC Ottawa, 23.4.1967.

[266] NAA M4295, File 20, Press Conference given by Harold Holt in Ottawa, Canada, 5.6.1967.

[267] LAC RG24-B-2, Vol. 21577, 5-2-5040-12, "Military Assistance to Non-NATO countries", n. d. (8.9.1966).

[268] LAC RG25 A-3-c, Vol. 11393, 27-4-CWLTH, Directive by CMD, 9.3.1967.

[269] LAC RG25 A-3-c, Vol. 8600, 20-1-1-12, Part 5, "Australia and the Far East", Briefing Paper (Far Eastern Div.), n. d. (18.5.1967).

[270] NAA A1838 229/9/9/3, Part 1, AHC Ottawa 251, 12.5.1967.

Asia and the Pacific".[271] The meeting further underlined that use could be made of appealing to Canada's role in the ICSC as a stabilising contribution to the region. However, the sources reveal little about such approaches from New Zealand to the Canadian government.

Instead, other groups pushed for an initiative: Shortly after Britain's announcement of withdrawal in January 1968, Keith Holyoake received a letter from Canadian members of the Mackinac College in Michigan, USA. Regarding Britain's decision, the letter expressed support for New Zealand's policy in Southeast Asia and called for a Commonwealth conference on security that should include Canada: "[we] believe that Canada needs and would respond to such a new national purpose which would give all Canadians a sense of unity and common destiny and that responsible involvement in Asia, in concert with Australia, New Zealand, Singapore and Malaysia would fire their imagination."[272] In his reply, Holyoake echoed the Canadian line objecting any military activity: He told them that Canada was already committed, urging that they should not "under-estimate the value of the contribution which Canada is already making in Asia".[273] Furthermore, it would be imprudent to invite Canada to any conference devoted only to military efforts.

While official Canadian concern for direct implications of Britain's withdrawal was thin, approaches like the one made by the college members indicate a certain public unease about Canadian detachment from the issue, which was also voiced within Canada. When Harold Wilson visited Ottawa in February 1968, he was asked during a television broadcast about the consequences of his government's decision: "There is a very great concern in this country [...] as to who will replace Britain in the areas from which she has removed herself."[274] Like Holyoake, Wilson reiterated Canadian lines on alternative ways of stabilisation, e. g. employing development assistance.

During discussions, most requests to Canada were answered with reference to Canada's military assistance to Malaysia. Notably, Canadian High Commissioner to Kuala Lumpur, John Hadwen, would become an influential figure in balancing and framing Canada's non-committal response to the uncertainties Malaysia and Singapore faced after the British announcement. However, his position seemed at times contrary to official Canadian attitudes in Ottawa, partly because his personal opinion seemed to be tainted by local experiences. In one of his lengthy reports, he insisted that no one being present in the region could

271 ANZ ABHS W4627 950, Box 1409, 56/2/3, Part 2, Minutes of EA Committee, 12.7.1967.

272 ANZ ABHS W5422 950, Box 3, 111/1/3/1, Part 13, Daniel Law (Mackinac College Michigan, USA) to Keith Holyoake, 1.2.1968.

273 ANZ ABHS W5422 950, Box 3, 111/1/3/1, Part 13, Reply by Keith Holyoake to Daniel Law (Mackinac College Michigan, USA), 26.2.1968.

274 "Face the Nation", CBS Broadcast of Interview with Harold Wilson, 11.2.1968, LAC RG25 A-3-c, Vol. 10042, 20-1-2-BRIT.

fail to recognise the damaging influence and cause for conflicts by communist subversion.[275] With an eye on Britain's impending retreat, Hadwen reviewed Canadian options for assistance in the region in early 1968. He expected an increase, not a decrease, of tensions in the area inspired by Chinese communism. If Canada feared such a scenario, he recommended committing to defence alliances soon: "It may well be that we are approaching a situation in South and Southeast Asia in which there will have to be similar defensive arrangements and similar economic assistance to that provided Europe in the face of the immediate post-World War Two Russian menace."[276] Consequently, he later advised the establishment of a defence assistance program based on Canadian foreign affairs principles, "because of our geographical relationship to the countries around the Pacific and the historical Commonwealth association with Singapore, Malaysia, Australia and New Zealand particularly".[277]

Hadwen's recommendations went beyond Canada's official position of non-involvement. Probably anticipating adverse reactions from his supervisors, he therefore balanced his suggestions by proposing inclusion of Malaysia and Singapore as part of development efforts, and added that his proposals were in no way "any suggestion that the result would be a 'commitment' or 'obligation' of a military treaty nature".[278] Departmental insecurities towards the East of Suez debate were also illustrated by parallel discussions concerning a potential, ultimately declined Canadian naval visit to Malaysia and Singapore. As Ottawa's Commonwealth Division recommended:

> "Even any enquiries at this time for a Canadian visit to either Port Swettenham or Singapore could only be interpreted as representing an armed forces interest in the area by the populations of the two countries, and would certainly encourage requests from those two countries for us to assume some of the defence responsibility vacated by the British."[279]

Similar precautions were taken when Harold Wilson visited Ottawa in February 1968. As a Canadian brief on the recent British decision highlighted, Canada should refrain from giving the appearance it might be interested in a new commitment. Instead, it should point to its current aid projects in the region and Canada's limited interests. Therefore, the brief advised that since both countries were not immediately interested in the region anymore, both could talk openly about "what Britain can do diplomatically to fill the vacuum".[280]

---

275 LAC RG25 A-3-c, Vol. 8600, 20-1-1-12, Part 6, CHC Kuala Lumpur (Hadwen) 68, 29.2.1968.

276 Ibid.

277 LAC RG25 A-3-c, Vol. 10285, 27-1-2-MLSIA, CHC Kuala Lumpur, 3.5.1968.

278 Ibid.

279 LAC RG25 A-3-c, Vol. 10054, 20-1-2-MLSIA, Part 2, Commonwealth Div. to USSEA, 16.1.1968.

280 LAC RG25 A-3-c, Vol. 8903, 20-BRIT-1-3-E.Suez, Part 1, Brief (Commonwealth Div.), 8.2.1968.

Instead of security cooperation, Canadians focused on their military assistance program to Malaysia and established a similar program for Singapore. In discussions, officials emphasised such assistance would not only improve relations with the region, but also with Australia and New Zealand as it would indicate a "sympathetic interest in the stability and security of the region which is of vital concern to Australia in particular and of course to New Zealand".[281] However, Hadwen himself admitted that their support for Malaysia could cause an embarrassing misuse by local contacts to exert pressure on the British: "We will have to develop a technique of accepting what is legitimate as a tribute to Canada but avoid an improper use of Canada purely as an example from which to criticize the British."[282]

In a way, also Canada found itself mediating between British and regional interests; similar to Australia and New Zealand, it was afraid to jeopardise its relations with Britain. Large parts of the concerns stemmed from supra-regional discourses on colonialism and hegemony that should be discussed in the following.

4.3 Experiencing Doubt and Fear – Global Implications of Britain's Withdrawal

Aside from framing their concerns in the context of a former imperial relationship and regional security cooperation, Australia and New Zealand also struggled with the potential global implications of a British withdrawal. Since regional stability was crucially linked to geopolitical shifts of the Cold War, contemporary assessments could refer to many issues challenging the region:

> "The causes of instability are diverse and include: political and economic readjustment to the withdrawal of western rule; conflict of national interests; minority problems, which are acute in several states, notably those arising from the presence of Chinese minorities; the search for national identity and new state policies; growing political awareness and desire for a higher standard of living; the division and weakness of the area under the shadow of the powerful Communist China and exposed to other external pressures; and the suitability of many areas for guerrilla tactics."[283]

Aside from Chinese subversion, which received special coverage in threat assessments throughout the 1960s, factors such as competing nationalisms and ethnic tensions were linked to regional instability. As a consequence, references

281 LAC RG25 A-3-c, Vol. 10054, 20-1-2-MLSIA, Part 2, Brief (Commonwealth Div.), 28.3.1968.

282 LAC RG25 A-3-c, Vol. 10054, 20-1-2-MLSIA, Part 2, CHC Kuala Lumpur (Hadwen), 8.4.1968.

283 ANZ ABHS W5242 950, Box 33, 85/1/1, Part 12, "Defence Review 1968: Missions of Forces", Defence Council Memorandum by NMD (DO (68) 25), 25.3.1968.

to Southeast Asia as 'the Balkans of Asia' emerged, a reference that drew both on threat perceptions of communism and cultural otherness.[284] At the same time, Britain's withdrawal from other parts of the Empire illustrated the immediate dangers of a political vacuum.[285]

Despite growing awareness for local elements of instability, many policymakers in Australia and New Zealand still considered Chinese communism as the underlying gear for most of the local conflicts. In contrast, British officials increasingly underlined the overall demise of a Chinese threat and promoted a military withdrawal from the region as timely. The strategic divergence was matched by a normative rift in the English-speaking alliance. Together with the USA, Australia and New Zealand continued to support the domino theory by a policy of forward defence, while Britain and Canada were at the forefront of Western countries that called for a regional review of security and China's role in it.

Throughout discussions of withdrawal, British insistence on coexistence with China and its proposal for alternative regional orders indicated a shift in perspectives on regional and global security being interdependent. Similarly, Britain's stance on a non-committal position regarding the Vietnam War enforced Australian and New Zealand perceptions it was retreating from the Western containment alliance, both strategically and morally. In contrast, Australian representatives like High Commissioner Kenneth Bailey insisted on regional conflicts causing global repercussions: "The immediate threat to Australia's national and regional security is that presented by aggressive Asian communism, and it is this threat that is also the most serious danger to world security."[286]

Therefore, resistance to a British withdrawal not only became visible in the strategic discussions related to defence arrangements such as SEATO, but also in debates concerning China and Vietnam. Australian and New Zealand officials objected to the timing of withdrawal as they perceived the region still in the grip of uncertainty and instability caused by communist influence and subversion. Their fears were increased when the British questioned the benefit of a military presence, particularly ground forces, as physical deterrence in an age of nuclear threat and guerrilla subversion. Moreover, local and international recriminations targeted the bases as symbols of Western supremacy, a further factor contributing to doubts on what overall was more and more perceived as a precarious Western military presence.

---

[284] Such analogies had been drawn since the late 1950s, but seemed even more fitting over the deterioration in Vietnam; LAC RG25 A-3-b, Vol. 4731, 50062-40, CHC Canberra (MacDermot), 21.9.1959; LAC RG25, Vol. 10663, 23-3-1968, Brief for Commonwealth Prime Ministers' Meeting, 4.12.1968.

[285] *McCourt*, Britain's "East of Suez Role", 461.

[286] NLA MS4622, Box 5, File 36, Note for Patrick Shaw as Australia's Permanent Representative to UN, n. d. (1967).

On similar postcolonial issues, traditional institutions, including the Commonwealth, seemed to enter a distinct crisis of their own over a divide between 'Old' and 'New' members. Similarly, decolonisation was negotiated within the UN framework. These crises were discussed across all three former dominions, and were closely related to a changing normative framework of international relations pointing increasingly to national self-determination, equality and the abolition of Western Cold War outlooks.[287] In the face of constant Southeast Asian instability despite substantial Western efforts, attitudes towards forward defence and containment began to change. British officials now mentioned concerns for 'white faces' and indicated a willingness to consider neutralism as a long-term solution. The state of regional security was increasingly assessed against local conditions of development and progress. The concerns for decolonisation effects, for example the imbalance of votes in the UN or the tensions in the Commonwealth, were also brought to a focus in Southeast Asia, even more so as the deterioration in Vietnam created unprecedented anti-Western sentiments around the world.

In negotiations with Britain over a military withdrawal, Tasman officials largely framed their concerns by pointing to the region as a global theatre and therefore a responsibility of the West. From this focus, a two-sided presentation developed. On the one hand, officials underlined the necessity of Western containment strategy, both because of a continued Chinese threat as because of differences among Southeast Asian neighbours that would prevent a robust regional response to any attack. On the other hand, they underlined the positive aspects of Asian cooperation and the local sympathy for Western, but specifically British engagement. In contrast, Canadians again approached regional and global considerations differently. While they did not negate regional implications, they were more concerned with global implications of Chinese isolation and therefore framed regional developments more as symptoms than causes of a larger conflict. Consequently, they refrained from regional intervention while trying to take on issues on a supra-regional level.

4.3.1 Dealing with a Continued Chinese Threat

Following the end of Confrontation, dominion officials faced a growing British unease over threat assessments related to Southeast Asia. Aside from the continuing uncertainties about Indonesia that particularly haunted the Australians[288], it was the growing divergence on the nature of the communist threat

[287] *Denis Stairs*, Reviewing Foreign Policy, 1968–70, in: Don Munton/John J. Kirton (Ed.), Canadian Foreign Policy: Selected Cases, Scarborough 1992, 189–204, 192.

[288] For a contemporary assessment of Australia's attitude towards Indonesia see *Peter J. Boyce*, Australian Attitudes to Security, in: Thomas B. Millar (Ed.), Australian-New Zealand Defence Co-operation, Canberra 1968, 16–34, 23–25.

which caused most tensions, with controversial and sometimes emotional discussions. During his visit to Malaysia and Singapore to discuss implications of Britain's latest defence considerations in April 1967, Denis Healey targeted Australian insistence on a continued Chinese threat and mocked the notions of fear in Australian discussions: "'And, if I may say your Prime Minister, for whom I have considerable respect, is a bit inclined to cry wolf.' After a pause he added 'even if the wolf is 95 percent there!'"[289] In the following, he insisted that Australia was too concerned with a Chinese threat when it was so far away from the Asian mainland. To Australians, Healey's remarks might have caused some irritations given his previous assurances on shared British attitudes regarding China, where he had confirmed the support of containment strategy in early 1966.[290] Back then, High Commissioner Charles Johnston had also warned London officials to understand that any move towards China would be met by fear in Australia:

> "This is an issue on which Australians of all shades of opinion feel deeply. Unless it is very carefully handled it could have a deplorable effect on our relations with this country. We may think that the Australian attitude about local threats to our bases is a typical piece of slap-dash optimism: 'She'll be right, mate.' But for us, sitting on the other wide [sic!] of the world far away from the turmoil of Asia, to tell the Australians that we do not think Singapore necessary for their defence is as they see it coming dangerously close to saying 'I'm all right, Jack.'"[291]

Johnston's warning came after British officials indicated to their allies that they wished to find a form of coexistence with China.[292] As Johnston predicted, a year later, Australian officials felt betrayed by Britain, which now emphasised the need to globally come to terms with China's position and dismissed notions of a regional threat.

Tasman policymakers were concerned over these breaches to the Western containment strategy, not least because their own policy on China was increasingly criticised. Australian Leader of the Opposition Arthur Calwell condemned the official policy of establishing trade relations without Chinese recognition as distorted.[293] His successor Gough Whitlam, after making headlines as the first Member of Parliament (MP) to openly support recognition in the mid-1950s, suggested in talks with Canadians joint action to overcome the international isolation of China.[294] In New Zealand, critics also demanded recognition after the country had established trade relations with the Communist regime in the

[289] NAA A9861 3/12/77/8, Part 2B, AHC Singapore 739, 25.4.1967.

[290] NAA A1209 1965/6595, Part 3, Summary of Discussions of Australian Cabinet with British Defence Secretary Denis Healey, quoted in: *Ashton/Bridge/Ward*, DAFP, 144–157, 154.

[291] TNA DO 169/439, BHC Canberra (Johnston) to CRO 1430, 25.11.1965.

[292] *Nicholas Tarling*, The British and the Vietnam War. Their Way with LBJ, Singapore 2017, 173 f.

[293] LAC RG25 A-3-c, Vol. 8842, 20-AUSTL-1-3, Part 1, CHC Canberra 142, 2.4.1964.

[294] LAC RG25 A-3-c, Vol. 8842, 20-AUSTL-1-3, Part 4, CEmb Bangkok, 8.1.1968.

1950s.[295] Despite the position of non-recognition, the Tasman departments themselves never abandoned conceptional work searching for a coexistence with the Communist regime. However, officials in both countries concluded the time was not right to make changes.[296] From a broader perspective, it was both political resistance as well as an anti-communist public majority that ultimately inhibited a policy change.

Therefore, given their closeness, Australian and New Zealand officials were worried when Canadian officials resumed their efforts for recognition of China in the mid-1960s. In talks with ASEA James Plimsoll in October 1965, Canadian officials had called a Chinese admission to the UN inevitable in the next few years. In contrast, Plimsoll insisted on a postponement, given the current developments in Vietnam and the critical implications for Taiwan.[297] A couple of months later, Australian High Commissioner Kenneth Bailey used a speech at the Canadian Institute for International Affairs (CIIA) to emphasise Australian concerns amidst Canadian plans. While he admitted that the West had to find a way of accommodation with China in the long run, Bailey underlined the need to militarily resist Chinese aggression in the region by outside powers in the meantime.[298] By comparing Southeast Asia to 1940s Europe, Bailey equated Australia's commitment in Southeast Asia to Canada's commitment to NATO.

Despite such efforts, Canadians were not willing to follow the proposed containment strategy. Instead, in a speech at the Banff Conference of World Affairs, Paul Martin reiterated Canada's traditional outlook on Asia. "[E]ven when our role has not been a major one and our interests have been indirect"[299], Canada had come to realise the danger to world peace arising from the conflicts in Southeast Asia. Therefore, it would continue commitment for a solution-finding of these conflicts by peacekeeping operations, such as the ICSC, but nobody should expect "dramatic actions on Canada's part".[300] Nevertheless, Martin introduced a new political objective that might have seemed dramatic to Canada's Western partners: Canada would be interested in coming to terms with China by supporting its admission to the UN, as long as this position would not threaten the existence of Taiwan.

Alarmed over this and further public statements, Australian representatives approached Canadian counterparts to emphasise that Canada's plan of recog-

---

295 *Buchanan*, Banned by Tides, 178.

296 ANZ ABHS W4628 7148, Box 119, LONB 106/5A, Part 2, Report on Meeting between NSEA Alister McIntosh and ASEA James Plimsoll, 9.5.1966.

297 NAA A1838 229/10/4/3, Part 2, AHC Ottawa 619, 16.10.1965.

298 *Kenneth Bailey*, Australia, Asia and World Security. Address given at CIIA and Dalhousie University, 12.5.1966, in: Dalhousie Review 46/3, 1966, 295–304, 301.

299 LAC RG25, Vol. 3072, File 10: "Canada's Asian Policy". Speech given by Paul Martin at the Fourth Annual Banff Conference on World Affairs, Banff, Alberta, 26.8.1966.

300 Ibid.

nition could dangerously affect Australia's security.[301] In a lengthy telegram related to the issue, the High Commission in Ottawa explained some of the difficulties in making Australia's concerns known to Canadians:

> "We had mentioned to some of them that there was an Australian impression that Canada might perhaps be approaching this whole question overmuch as a theoretical exercise, whereas for Australians living actually in the region and in close proximity to China this was very much a matter of bread and butter and bullets."[302]

The report continued that within the CDEA, there would be a couple of experts such as Arthur Menzies or Chester Ronning, who were raised in China, and therefore had a personal interest in obtaining improved relations with China. Ultimately, the CDEA would also draw knowledge from its ICSC role:

> "[…] there is a certain pride here in the Department's record in Indo-China. A good third of Canada's Foreign Service Officers have served in one of the three Indo-Chinese countries […] and it has been put to us that the Canadian Department of External Affairs perhaps has more Indo-Chinese expertise than does the Australian Department of External Affairs."[303]

With a military commitment to Vietnam resting on convictions of defending both the region and Australia against communist aggression, the Canadian attitude was likely met with anger by Australian staff. Although they observed the Canadian public statements mainly as a fulfilment of public demands, Australians were concerned talk of recognition might eventually lead to political action.[304] They had difficulties adjusting to Canada's changing policy, and these difficulties were only enforced by the planned British withdrawal at hand.

This also became apparent in New Zealand's thinking. In preparations for the London quadripartite talks in October 1966, New Zealand policymakers prepared briefs on the Western image in Southeast Asia and Communist China. While they admitted that regional powers might object any idea of "'ganging up'"[305] by Western alliances, officials nevertheless underlined the need for a continued policy of containment. British forces were needed to "deny this area to Communism, although there is no essential Western interest requiring that the countries of the area be aligned in a pro-Western sense".[306]

As the comment shows, New Zealand understood its continued forward defence both serving its own security interests and its relations with anti-com-

---

301 NAA A1838 229/10/4/3, Part 2, AHC Ottawa 559, 25.11.1966.

302 NAA A1838 229/10/4/3, Part 2, AHC Ottawa 775, 23.11.1966.

303 Ibid.

304 NAA A1838 229/10/4/3, Part 2, AHC Ottawa 565, 29.11.1966.

305 ANZ ABHS W4628 7148, Box 119, LONB 106/5A, Part 2, "Western Image in South-East Asia", Brief for London Quadripartite Talks, n. d. (28.9.1966).

306 ANZ ABHS W4627 950, Box 1409, 56/2/3, Part 2, Remarks by I. Stewart to External Affairs Committee, 13.7.1966.

munist and nonaligned countries in the region. In contrast to Australia, New Zealand sources indicate a larger disposition to consider alternative concepts for regional order that would benefit the global course of the Cold War. Additionally, New Zealanders were equally informed about Canadian initiatives for Chinese recognition[307], but refrained from an openly critical stand similar to the Australian reaction.

When a renewed British interest for neutralisation in Vietnam became known in early 1966, New Zealand officials considered the possibilities of this approach. In his assessment, George Laking balanced the advantages of both approaches: "Containment of China may involve some risks, and a good deal more expense than we care for; but neutralization by withdrawal might well prove to hold greater dangers than these for our security."[308] Following this assessment, neutralisation was repudiated as "a gesture of appeasement of Communist China".[309] Ultimately, New Zealanders were just as guided as Australians by American attitudes towards the issue. Additionally, the status of Taiwan remained unsolved, standing in the way of any approach to Communist China. Both countries promoted the idea of a two-China solution parallel to continued calls for forward defence.

British officials therefore correctly assumed their allies would hardly accept neutralisation, particularly Australia, as it seemed too strongly influenced by "what they see as unchanging facts of geography".[310] Canadians also noticed how much the other two countries appreciated China by national security premises, with Australia perceiving China "as a regional rather than a world problem".[311] While both Britain and Canada postponed alternative approaches to regional order, Britain's desire to abandon the Western containment position increasingly revealed itself to its ANZAM partners. In April 1967, Australian Liaison Staff Hassett reported from London of growing resistance to commitments among British services who had objected to Australian concerns over the situation in Southeast Asia, and had wondered if Australia was not unnecessarily involved in countries like "Vietnam, which were a very long way from Australia", claiming that "some form of domination of them by China was inevitable in the very long term".[312] As they were opposed to any large-scale com-

307 ANZ ABHS W5579 6958, Box 184, NYP 3/40/3, NHC Ottawa, 8.2.1966.

308 ANZ ABHS W5631 22310, Box 193, PAR 222/1/1 Part 2, NEmb. Washington, 2.8.1966.

309 ANZ ABHS W4628 7148, Box 119, LONB 106/5A, Part 2, "Communist China: Threat to South-East Asia", Brief for London Study Group, 26.9.1966.

310 TNA DO 169/444, "Indo-Pacific Policy", Paper by the Planning Committee (PC (66) 16), 7.4.1966.

311 LAC RG25 A-3-c, Vol. 8600, 20-1-1-12, Part 5, "Australia and the Far East", Briefing Paper for Harold Holt Visit, n. d. (18.5.1967).

312 NAA A1945 73/1/63, AJSS London (Hassett), 3.3.1967.

mitment outside Europe in the future, Hassett indicated that his protest had no effect on his counterparts:

"You have heard all this before (I remember Mountbatten saying something very much on the lines [...] as far back as the early fifties) but it is interesting to know that this line of thinking still persists in well informed, high level circles, notwithstanding all our own and other nations' utterances on the subject over a number of years."[313]

To Hassett and others, British remarks on Chinese domination paired with the opposition to any overseas commitment must have seemed contradictory in itself. With membership in SEATO, but also in NATO, Britain still belonged to anti-communist security alliances, which considered military intervention a viable tool. Yet attitudes increasingly differed and especially clashed on Vietnam. When Wilson proposed a Commonwealth peace mission to Vietnam in 1965, Australians refused to withdraw an already dispatched artillery to give credibility to this initiative.[314] New Zealanders gave their support to Wilson's initiative, but privately shared their misgivings about Britain's insistence on finding a solution to the conflict as Co-Chairman of the Geneva Accords.[315]

Public pressure on the Australian and New Zealand governments on Vietnam only enforced the issue. Already by late 1965, Keith Holyoake received a letter from a private citizen who questioned the need for European troops in Malaysia.[316] In his reply, Holyoake insisted a military presence was part of New Zealand's alliance obligations, and emphasised Malaysia and Singapore welcomed the European troops as they were not able to defend themselves.[317] The ensuing escalation in Vietnam only added pressure on the committed countries, who reacted with sharp pleas for solidarity among their Anglo-Saxon allies. Just as Wilson shared with Americans his concerns about the growing anti-imperialist voices in Britain objecting to any further presence overseas[318], Australians and New Zealanders increased their criticism of Britain's detachment from the conflicts in the region, especially from Vietnam. In talks with British officials in autumn 1966, Gordon Jockel strongly protested the British proposal to seek an end to the Vietnam War by negotiations. Instead, he insisted on the specifics of Asian communism that would demand a military response: "It is very tough and lays great emphasis on guerrilla warfare. The West will therefore have to

313 Ibid.

314 *David McCraw*, The Demanding Alliance. New Zealand and the Escalation of the Vietnam War, in: Australian Journal of Politics & History 34/3, 1988, 307–319, 309.

315 ANZ ABHS W4628 7148, Box 119, LONB 106/5A, Part 2, Malcolm Templeton (NHC London) to Jack Sheperd (NEmb. Washington), 29.7.1966.

316 The original letter of Mr. Hekkenberg could not be found but Keith Holyoake's reply indicates the questions and criticism posed by the letter; ANZ ABHS W5422 950, Box 3, 111/1/3/1, Part 13, Reply by Holyoake to Citizen Hekkenberg, 24.12.1965.

317 Ibid.

318 Report of Talks of Harold Wilson with Dean Rusk, 10.6.1966, quoted in: *Ashton/Louis*, East of Suez, 92–94.

use power to achieve its ends [...] A ceasefire would be the worst solution to the conflict [...]."[319] Around the same time, Jockel gave a talk at the Imperial Defence College, where he reiterated his opposition to negotiations. He called for an approach sensitive to local conditions and developments, and charged outside powers as falsely applying prefabricated theories: "I suspect that these needs of empiricism make this a difficult area for those concerned with general theories or patterns of relationships or with planning and policy projection."[320] He emphasised stability could only be reached by fostering resistance and confidence among local governments in the face of the communist threat.

Australian statements increasingly drafted a dichotomy between the efforts taken by them and other committed powers and the unresponsive attitude of most Western European countries, Britain included. Returning from a trip to Europe in April 1966, Hasluck declared his visit had been dedicated "to bring home to Western European Governments the importance to *them* of what is happening in the Far East, and in particular the consequences to *them* of Chinese Communist aggressive expansion against any of its neighbours".[321] A few months later, Holt addressed a London audience along similar lines:

> "I bring to a European audience a view from 'Down Under' where perhaps the perspective looks rather different than the view taken from this point of distance. We see the struggle going on in South Vietnam, not merely as one in resolving an issue in that disturbed, complex country, but as one affecting South East Asia generally and, indeed, ultimately Asia as a whole perhaps even finally the peace and economic progress and stability of the world as a whole."[322]

Such statements should underline how strongly Australians disagreed with Britain on the global threat of Asian instability. Additionally, these statements pointed to the growing deterioration of the Anglo-American 'special relationship' over Vietnam.[323] Over the increasing antagonism between the USA and Britain, Australian officials hoped to guard the Anglo-American unity on Southeast Asian security, not least to safeguard the system of spatial responsibilities covering Malaysia and Vietnam. Already in May 1965, Paul Hasluck told Michael Stewart "of the acute embarrassment in which we would be placed if we were supporting in two separate but inter-related fields two allies if they were in any serious disagreement".[324] With Australian officials, American counterparts

319 ANZ ABHS W4628 7148, Box 119, LONB 106/5A, Part 2, Report on London Study Group (3./4.10.1966), NEmb. Washington, 26.10.1966.

320 LAC RG25 A-3-c, Vol. 8842, 20-AUSTL-1-3, "The Australian View on South East Asia", Speech given by Gordon Jockel to the Imperial Defence College Canberra, 5.9.1966.

321 Speech by Paul Hasluck in the AHoR, in: CNIA 37/4 (April 1966), 190–198, 190.

322 NAA M4295 (Harold Holt Papers), 20, Press Conference given by Harold Holt at Australia House, 7.6.1966.

323 ANZ ABHS W5533 22128, Box 92, CBA 50/8/2, Report on ANZUS Council Meeting, 30.6./1.7.1966.

324 NAA A1838 67/1/3, Part 3, AHC London 3662, 7.5.1965.

like Robert McNamara did not hide their misgivings as the USA would "not tolerate a situation where it was the only one making real sacrifices for Asian defence".[325]

As the moralisation of Vietnam only fuelled the antagonism, dominion officials were aware a British withdrawal would undermine the concept of spatial responsibilities in the region, just as it would also increase the normative gap between Vietnam contributors and non-involved members of the English-speaking alliance.[326]

The divide of the alliance had also become apparent in American-Canadian relations. Over the issue of Vietnam, disagreement between both countries excelled the usual frame of cordial disparity to an atmosphere of open resentment. By the mid-decade, Canadians had grown weary of American escalation and ignorance for ICSC attempts to mediate the conflict. In 1965, Lester Pearson used a speech at Temple University, Philadelphia, to call for a suspension of the American bombing of North Vietnam and was subsequently scolded by Lyndon B. Johnson in an unprecedented manner.[327] His speech was an indication of the growing Canadian helplessness concerning US policy, as the American bombing had also resulted in the withdrawal of Canadian truce bodies in the region and therewith effectively ended the work of the ICSC.[328] Moreover, Canadian officials were appalled to find out Americans still suspected the Chinese to be fighting in Vietnam, something they constantly argued against in their commission work.[329]

Tensions only grew in the following year when Martin advocated Chinese admission to the UN, which caused a sharp reaction of Dean Rusk: "Let me be rude. If Canada had troops in Vietnam, I would be more sympathetic to your dilemma. But the fact is that Canada has no risks to bear in the situation."[330] Americans perceived their commitment to Vietnam as contributing to the Free World effort that also benefitted Canada. Hence, they objected to Canada's determination to be a mediating voice in the conflict. Like their ANZUS partners, Americans were upset by Canada's 'holier-than-thou' attitude to a conflict they perceived as crucial to global security. Together with Australia and New Zea-

---

325 ANZ ABHS W4628 7148, Box 119, LONB 106/5A, Part 2, NEmb. Washington 299, 16.4.1966.

326 ANZ ABHS W4628 7148, Box 119, LONB 106/5A, Part 2, Malcolm Templeton (NHC London) to Jack Sheperd (NEmb. Washington), 29.7.1966.

327 *John English*, Speaking Out on Vietnam, 1965, in: Don Munton/John J. Kirton (Ed.), Canadian Foreign Policy: Selected Cases, Scarborough 1992, 135–152.

328 *Douglas A. Ross*, In the Interest of Peace. Canada and Vietnam 1954–1973, Toronto 1984, 23.

329 *George Roberts*, My War, 1965, in: Arthur E. Blanchette (Ed.), Canadian Peacekeepers in Indochina, 1954–1973: Recollections, Ottawa 2002, 112–116, 115 f.

330 Quoted in: *John English*, Lester Pearson and China, in: Paul M. Evans/Michael B. Frolic (Ed.), Reluctant Adversaries: Canada and the People's Republic of China 1949–1970, Toronto 1991, 133–147, 143.

land, they also struggled with the outspoken moralisation of Vietnam in Canadian debates, which started to influence their own domestic debates.[331] Although Pearson kept its Vietnam criticism and Canada's China policy in line with American attitudes in the following, the growing gap in Western security thinking on the Southeast Asian theatre had become apparent.

4.3.2 "All the Way with LBJ" – Western Containment Strategy in Demise

The criticism over Vietnam and Britain's withdrawal plans contributed to a larger Australian interest in the American alliance. In 1965, a paper drafted by the Policy Planning Group under Garry Woodard indicated the departmental desire for a thorough analysis of current relations. The paper concluded Australia's relations with the USA would currently be more intimate and extensive than with Britain, given their shared long-term interest for strategic planning in Southeast Asia, and called the ANZUS Council "a unique forum for the frank exchange of views on foreign and defence policy on a regular basis", with "no arrangements [...] for regular Anglo-Australian exchanges at the same level".[332] Similar appreciations for the American alliance were reached in New Zealand, where policymakers like George Laking drafted the American relationship along lines comparable to Anglo-New Zealand relations. Discussing various treaty commitments in 1965, New Zealand officials assumed that American thinking in ANZUS could replicate the Commonwealth relationship:

> "It is a more formal means of achieving an intimate relationship and that with the United Kingdom evolved naturally out of historical and constitutional development. The range of our contacts with the United States does not reach anything like that with the United Kingdom, but the closeness of the relationships especially in the defence field is similar."[333]

New Zealand policymakers seemed less united on the American alliance than their Australian counterparts. One reason was the lack of conviction in the success of the military intervention in Vietnam that had accompanied New Zealand commitment early on. Most officials reluctantly accepted the Vietnam contributions as the price to pay for American protection, but little support for American moral reasoning existed inside and outside the departments.[334] Additionally, remoteness and parsimony were still strong advisers in policymaking, and were paired with the continued trust given to British cooperation.[335]

---

[331] *Vucetic*, Anglosphere, 93.

[332] NAA A1838 682/4, Part 6, "Australia's Relations with the United States and the United Kingdom", Draft by Policy Planning Group (Woodard), 27.10.1965.

[333] ANZ ABHS 5242 950, Box 68, 87/32/1, "New Zealand Position and Responsibilities in ANZAM, SEATO and ANZUS", Briefing Paper, 29.7.1965.

[334] *Rolfe*, New Zealand Defence Policy, 52.

[335] See e. g. Frank Corner (NEmb. Washington, 15.9.1967), quoted in: *Robert Rabel*, New Zealand and the Vietnam War. Politics and Diplomacy, Auckland 2005, 213.

Another issue was the continued hardship for decisionmaking created by the American alliance. On different occasions, Johnson did not inform his Australian and New Zealand counterparts on planned military operations in Vietnam. Over Australian insistence on better consultation in late 1965, Americans showed some understanding but emphasised their limits "if one had to consult a list of allies".[336] When Americans did not inform its ANZUS partners on the resumption of bombing of North Vietnam after the SEATO meeting in June 1966, the New Zealand broadcast *Lookout* criticised the apparent indifference to the issue among New Zealand officials, and underlined the need for consultation: "[…] it's of special importance here because, as a part of the South East Asian neighbourhood, we shall have to live with the consequences of American action here long after American troops have been withdrawn."[337]

Another crucial factor was the growing criticism of American interventionism, which affected the military positions in the region. On the escalation in Vietnam, Tasman officials were not only aware of the potential critical discussions in the Western world, but also feared growing resistance of local leaders to the use of military bases.[338] As troops stationed in Malaysia and Vietnam were rotated, public discussions increasingly considered both theatres as interdependent. Even if the negative reputation of Vietnam troops could taint the CSR's image, Australians and New Zealanders still hoped their Malaysian commitment, linked to a British presence, would foster a better understanding of their Vietnam contribution as part of the 'Free World' effort. Not least because of the American reputation, a continued British presence was therefore warranted or even preferred, as Keith Holyoake told Michael Stewart in 1966: "The British were preferable 'policemen' to the Americans in unstable areas, […] on account of their 'semi-retired' status."[339]

Ultimately, Britain's indifference to the Vietnam War also presented an identity dilemma for Australia and New Zealand. Given the strong reference to shared values with the former 'mother country', it was difficult for Tasman officials to legitimise their commitments in a charged public debate that focused on the morality of the war. The dilemma was further increased by Canadian foreign policy. Pursuing quiet diplomacy and constraint, Canadians indicated to their allies that there was scope to dissent with American policy even as a close ally. In both Australia and New Zealand, opposition groups started to use Canada's position to call for similar policies of constraint in their countries.[340] In both cases,

336 US State Assistant Secr. of Defence John McNaughton in Talks with James Plimsoll, NAA A9861 3/12/77/8, Part 2A, AEmb. Washington 3670, 21.10.1965.

337 *Arnold Entwisle*, "SEATO Council Meeting", Lookout Broadcast, 2.7.1966.

338 ANZ ABHS W5400 20358, Box 108, KL 103/6/3, Part 1, Wellington to NHC Kuala Lumpur 169, 21.2.1967.

339 ANZ ABHS W4627 950, Box 1409, 56/2/3, Part 2, Minutes of EA Committee, 6.7.1966.

340 LAC RG25 A-3-c, Vol. 8842, 20-AUSTL-1-3, Part 3, CHC Canberra 222, 7.5.1965; LAC RG25 A-3-c, Vol. 8871, 20-NZ-1-3, Part 2, CHC Wellington 327, 13.9.1965.

sources indicate the Canadian government was cautious in not undermining the position of the current governments, while sticking to its own principles on both issues. Only a few Canadian observers advocated closer cooperation among the former dominions, such as former diplomat John Holmes who saw the Commonwealth as a supportive framework for the allied efforts in Southeast Asia.[341]

To appeal to Canadians as to British officials, Australians and New Zealanders increasingly drafted their commitment to Vietnam as one of peacekeeping, and pointed to shared values and obligations. Notably, Harold Holt stepped forward with strong verbal support for the American policy in Vietnam, most notably with his famous statement of being "all the way with LBJ"[342] during a visit to Washington in June 1966. Here, he spoke of Australia's commitment to Vietnam and Malaysia as support for the global "crucial struggle for human liberty"[343] that would stand in direct tradition to its commitment in the World Wars. He also insisted that SEATO was applying a "domino theory in reverse"[344] to allow countries in the region to prosper behind a shield provided by the alliance.

Consequently, New Zealand and Australian officials framed a future British presence as an effort of assistance and defence welcomed by local forces. In parts, they drew on the successful image British forces had received for their role played in both the Emergency and in Confrontation, and adopted the argument of a 'better' Western influence exerted by British military intervention, in contrast to American aggression in Vietnam.[345] Tasman officials were also convinced that the USA needed a British presence to counteract criticism of its Vietnam intervention. As Australians had already judged in early 1966 that "Any prospect that the British would abandon their presence in South East Asia must tend to embarrass and undermine present United States policy"[346], George Brown's revelations a year later enforced fears over disunity within the English-speaking alliance. Harold Holt explained this position to the Australian press when he cautioned them to write about Brown's statement: "While the United Kingdom is in the area America feels less embarrassed about continuing to exhibit its own presence substantially in the area than it would if it were the only non-Asian power of consequence left on or around the mainland of Asia."[347]

---

341 *John W. Holmes*, A Canadian's Commonwealth. Realism Out of Rhetoric, in: The Round Table 11, 1966, 335–347, 346.

342 *Harold Holt*, "All the way with LBJ". Speech at a state reception, White House, Washington D.C., 30.6.1966, in: Sally Warhaft (Ed.), Well May We Say …: The Speeches that Made Australia, Melbourne 2004, 123–124, 124.

343 Address by Harold Holt to the National Press Club, 30.6.1966, in: CNIA 37/6 (June 1966), 321–325, 322.

344 NAA A1209 1965/6251, Part 1, Opening Statement by Harold Holt at the 11th SEATO Council Meeting, 27.6.1966.

345 *A. L. Burns,* Letter to Editor: Mature and flexible policies, Canberra Times, 27.1.1966.

346 NAA A5619 C22, Part 1, FADC (Decision No. 33), 30.1.1966.

347 NAA A9861 3/12/77/8, Part 3, Press Briefing by Harold Holt, 26.4.1967.

Britain's plans revealed in April 1967 would indeed mark a further demise in the Anglo-American 'special relationship' that was also palpable to the dominions. Commenting on the disunity, a memo prepared by the New Zealand High Commission London in October is worth quoting in length:

"It seems likely that the immense upsurge in American power and assumption of global responsibilities led not only to a diminution of United States reliance on Britain but also to diminution of American respect for Britain as the latter divested itself of an Empire and began, in a typically uncertain manner, to search for a new role in the world. […] The fact of the matter is however, not so much that the British have been unwilling to pay the price, but that in military and economic terms they have not been able to pay it and that, after years of indecisiveness, a British Government is actively pursuing the twin policies of entering Europe and abandoning Britain's historical role as a 'world policeman'. […] Having clung to an illusion for so long, the British should not be surprised (though many are) if sections in Congress and among the American people – which do not have the same understanding as the Administration does of Mr. Wilson's difficulties with his left-wing over issues like Vietnam and defence spending – look askance at their withdrawal from Aden, Malaysia and Singapore and show no sympathy for a Britain that must appear in American eyes to be so devoid of an appreciation of what the Americans are trying to do in Vietnam and elsewhere in Asia."[348]

As the comment indicates, New Zealanders, as Australians, shared some of the American concerns and misgivings about Britain's retreat as an abdication from a world role.

Tasman officials feared Brown's announcement would cause a domino reaction, where further governments would decide to withdraw their troops as well. Gordon Jockel told Canadians that Brown's statements had destroyed Australian and American hopes that Britain "maintain as convincing a façade as possible 'even if they had to do it with mirrors'".[349] Fears of a domino effect increased over 1967 when representatives in North America reported on new tendencies of neo-isolationism in the American congress that could result in a complete American retreat from Southeast Asia soon.[350] Already during Confrontation, American unwillingness to back the ANZAM effort in Malaysia had indicated to Australian and New Zealand officials they could increasingly face difficulties in receiving support for a commitment after Britain left. Although such fears had been mollified by Americans at the ANZUS Council in 1967[351], doubts about American backing remained. In fact, New Zealand's Embassy already reported in late 1967 that the US government increasingly expected Southeast Asian countries to resolve conflicts themselves[352], a prelude to the Guam Doctrine announced under Nixon two years later.

[348] ANZ ABHS W4627 950, Box 3762, 201/2/3/1, NHC London, 31.10.1967.

[349] LAC RG25 A-3-c, Vol. 8600, 20-1-1-12, Part 4, CHC Canberra (Menzies) 583, 27.4.1967.

[350] LAC RG25 A-3-c, Vol. 8842, 20-AUSTL-1-3, Part 3, CHC Canberra 1599, 19.10.1967.

[351] NAA M1003, DEFENCE EAST OF SUEZ, ADEA to AHC London 3550, 3.5.1967.

[352] ANZ ABHS W4627 950, Box 4506, 434/8/1, Part 17, NEmb. Washington, 15.12.1967.

While both New Zealanders and Australians struggled between the British and American alliance, the latter intensified their rhetoric in support of Western intervention in Southeast Asia. On 12 April 1967, a few days before the SEATO meeting in Washington, Paul Hasluck spoke to Australian veterans of the Pacific War about the need to commit to Southeast Asia, and criticised the trend in Western thinking to consider a retreat: "Hence I would argue that a withdrawal from Asia or a lack of interest in Asia today is isolation in its most foolish form. Withdrawal from or lack of interest in Asia are very close to being withdrawal or lack of interest in world affairs."[353] In light of Brown's disclosures at the SEATO meeting, New Zealand officials in Canberra could later call Hasluck's statement the "deliberate first shot in the Australian counter-attack".[354] However, in the wake of growing anti-war protest movements and Britain's determination to leave the region, parts of the Australian press doubted Hasluck's approach[355], and Canadian officials in London reported that his remarks had both damaged his reputation at the Foreign Office and a chance for British support in Vietnam.[356]

Despite little success with British officials, Tasman policymakers continued to draft regional conflicts as a global responsibility, in order to overcome narratives of geographical distance that would make the retreat of remote powers such as Britain or the USA more plausible. Again, they engaged the argument of being better suited to assess the threat because of their proximity to the theatre. In October 1967, Paul Hasluck took the opportunity for such a statement at the UN:

> "We have chosen to take a side, but we are certainly not less willing or less capable of joining in a debate about the morality or the purposes of the war than are those who have not chosen to take any sides or than those who have chosen to favour some other side. We are no less honourable than those who have made no decision at all. Indeed, we may be better equipped to talk because, as well as having applied a moral test to our own actions, we have a closer and more intimate knowledge of situations and events than those who have no first-hand experiences of the war and of the countries affected by it."[357]

He further asked about the righteousness of Western involvement in the World Wars, contrasting it to the recent Western unwillingness to defend countries threatened by aggression in Southeast Asia. Ultimately, he underlined Southeast Asia as a theatre of global importance: "I also ask whether some of us may be forgetting the realities of the world in which we live. Unfortunately, this

[353] Address by Paul Hasluck at the First Conference of the Veterans of Asian-Pacific Wars, 12.4.1967, in: CNIA 38/4 (April 1967), 163–164, 163.

[354] ANZ ABHS W4628 7148, Box 120, LONB 106/7, Part 2, NHC Canberra, 22.4.1967.

[355] "Forward into Asia", Age, 21.4.1967.

[356] LAC RG25 A-3-c, Vol. 8600, 20-1-1-12, Part 4, CHC London 2288, 28.4.1967.

[357] Statement by Paul Hasluck, 13.10.1967, in: CNIA 38/10 (October 1967), 419–426, 419.

is still a world in which peace is kept and security is maintained by military power."[358]

Within Australia, political statements targeted Britain even more openly. Already in early 1967, Liberal MP John McLeay had vigorously expressed his anger:

"I was very disappointed when the Socialist Government of Great Britain decided to give us virtually no support in our efforts to assist the people of South Vietnam. We have gone to the assistance of Great Britain militarily on at least five occasions. I well remember the phrase, which I think was used by Sir Robert Menzies: 'When Britain is at war, we are at war.' But now when we seek to take a stand in Vietnam and thereby make our small contribution to prevent another world conflict, not only the mother country but also the whole of Western Europe are at pains not to be involved with us."[359]

After the British announcement in July 1967, Liberal MP William Haworth criticised the decision as one diametral to the historic foundations of the Anglo-Australian relationship:

"I can just recall Australia being told in 1914, and I very well remember our being told in 1939, that what happened in Europe must affect the future of Australia and New Zealand. I believed that to be true then just as it is true today that what happens in Asia must affect the future of Britain and Europe. […] I must say there are nasty implications in the idea that Britain will now be happy to let other people do the peace keeping while she gets on with the cash register keeping. If the United Kingdom cannot do anything for the economic and social projects envisaged by her allies for this part of the world, she can at least leave her troops in the area and maintain her bases."[360]

Rather than pointing to the American effort to protect the 'Free World', both statements referred to a British betrayal of its traditional moral obligation towards Australia. In their view, the shared commitments during the World Wars would have sanctioned another shared commitment in Vietnam. At a time when the Vietnam contributors increasingly received international criticism for the escalation of the war, politicians like Haworth expected Britain to side with Australia because of its shared background and values. Australians and New Zealanders felt visibly challenged by the split in the Anglosphere over British and Canadian reservations to their Vietnam commitments.

Following Britain's final decision in January 1968, the arguments of global responsibility were again linked to the historic experiences of joint intervention in Europe. During George Thomson's visit to Australia, John McEwen told him that "Australia had gone to Belgium, Greece and Gallipoli readily; these places were a long way away. In Vietnam Australia did not ask for British troops, but

358 Ibid.

359 Statement by the Member of Parliament John McLeay in the AHoR, 2.3.1967, CPD 9/1967, 321–324, 322.

360 Statement by the Member of Parliament William Haworth in the AHoR, 31.8.1967, CPD 35/1967, 664–670, 666.

they did not even have Britain's voice".[361] Again, officials based their arguments on a shared framework whose values had been established throughout previous commitments undergone together. With a reference to the World Wars, officials also hoped to integrate the Vietnam War into a historic continuity of resisting totalitarianism. In the depiction of global responsibility, parallels between World War Europe and contemporary Southeast Asia seemed appropriate. In talks with Saville Garner, ASEA Plimsoll drew a direct line to Britain's current commitment: "Australia in the past had made a contribution to global security, and we felt that Britain had a continuing obligation in return to us."[362]

After the British decision, analogies of historic responsibility were also drawn by some Canadian colleagues: In one of his reports, Canadian High Commissioner John Hadwen predicted that the region might be challenged by China and communism in the next fifteen years, as Europe had been during and after the war.[363] He therefore called for some kind of assistance to the countries in the region to create confidence that would help them resist communism.[364] Yet Hadwen followed most of the departmental thinking back in Ottawa when he focused on the social rather than political implications of communism. As he witnessed the discussions on Britain's withdrawal decision on the spot, he differed from his Tasman colleagues by accepting the British decision as an appropriate reaction to local developments.[365] Despite his admiration for British regional policy, Hadwen welcomed the decision in allowing local governments to consider and develop their own strengths and national identities.

4.3.3 At European Crossroads – Questioning White Presence in Southeast Asia

The historic reference to Europe in the 1940s and 1950s was a way of addressing concerns that Southeast Asia could become a theatre of global dimension, and found its way in various assessments such as the 1966 New Zealand Defence Review: "We must prepare ourselves for a long period of living as a nation with the kind of sustained tension that until recent years was regarded as peculiar to Europe."[366] The comparison was a two-fold argument: On the one

[361] TNA FCO 24/91, Record of Meeting between John Gorton and George Thomson, 12.1.1968.

[362] NAA A9861 3/12/77/8, Part 5, Note for File on Talks of James Plimsoll with Saville Gardner, 11.1.1968.

[363] LAC RG25 A-3-c, Vol. 8600, 20-1-1-12, Part 6, CHC Kuala Lumpur (Hadwen) 68, 29.2.1968.

[364] LAC RG25 A-3-c, Vol. 8600, 20-1-1-12, Part 6, CHC Kuala Lumpur (Hadwen), 14.3.1968.

[365] LAC RG25 A-3-c, Vol. 8600, 20-1-1-12, Part 6, CHC Kuala Lumpur (Hadwen) 68, 29.2.1968.

[366] ANZ AAFD W3738 811, Box 1321, CAB 224/1/1, Part 1, Cabinet Document (CP (66) 384), 13.5.1966.

hand, it helped insist with the British that their presence was warranted as a contribution to a global struggle for peace. On the other, the reference to Southeast Asia as Europe was a powerful metaphorical argument that could challenge the discursive antithesis between Europe and Southeast Asia already established with Britain's EEC bid at the beginning of the decade.

Tasman efforts to object to Britain's integration into Europe as being diametral to Western efforts for global peace were also related to the British retreat from the Commonwealth. With issues such as the Rhodesian conflict, the mid-1960s saw the growing challenge of international norms of anti-imperialism and anti-racism, which particularly targeted Britain. Given their background as former white settler colonies, the dominions felt equally challenged by demands for racial equality. Additionally, the introduction of the Commonwealth Secretariat unsettled many policymakers as the organisation seemed to replace old unwritten practices and values with an institutionalised body. The first Commonwealth Secretary-General Arnold Smith became a symbol of the "'de-Britannicizing' of the Commonwealth"[367], even more so as he oversaw the transition of Canadian Commonwealth policy away from a narrow British-led framework. Ultimately, Canada, because of its international record of peacekeeping and mediation, could further pursue a mediatory role as a bridge between the 'White' and 'Non-White' Commonwealth. In contrast, Australia and New Zealand faced greater difficulties over the new agendas of the organisation, both because of their military commitments in Southeast Asia and because of their discriminatory immigration policies.

Being aware of Britain's contested position within the Commonwealth, officials from all three countries anticipated a British review of its overseas commitments. When they realised that British officials expected similar repercussions against their bases as experienced in other parts of their former Empire, Australians tried to draft the cases of Malaysia and Singapore differently.[368] In July 1967, Australian politician Peter Nixon underlined that both Malaysia and India had emphasised their interest in a continued British presence: "This is not the Prime Minister of Australia speaking; this is the Prime Minister of Malaysia, a very prominent Asian. This is the view of both the Malaysian Prime Minister and the Indian Foreign Minister. It is in the face of all this that the United Kingdom has taken the decision to withdraw."[369] Such arguments insinuated that there was an underlying legitimacy for a British presence created by the Commonwealth framework, which could draw further credibility particularly from non-white members of the organisation welcoming such a presence.

[367] *McIntyre*, Significance of the Commonwealth, 56.
[368] NAA A1838 682/4, Part 5A, McIntyre to AMEA, 11.10.1965.
[369] Statement by the Member of Parliament Peter Nixon in AHoR, CPD 33/1967, 17.8.1967, 247–250, 249.

However, officials were unsure if Britain was interested in a continued lead in the Commonwealth in general. Already following Britain's defence review in 1965, New Zealand officials had questioned Britain's desire to retain a role worthy of a global Commonwealth:

"The whole question does of course raise the issue whether Britain intends to continue to play a world role (albeit a reduced one) or whether it is resigning itself to a purely European vocation, in the manner of France. If the latter is the case, the future of the Commonwealth as an entity seems murky indeed."[370]

The discussions on Britain's presence East of Suez further contrasted a European role with a British global role. For Australia and New Zealand, a European role clearly would mean a loss of influence. Privately, Thomas Critchley thought that Britain's desire for flexibility expressed in its announcement in April 1967 "would be excessive to the point of flabbiness and that Britain could find herself, like France, free to say a great deal, but with nobody taking much notice".[371] During the final stages of negotiation in early 1968, Paul Hasluck challenged George Thomson when he indicated that Britain's withdrawal would make it in Asia "something less than that of Italy and a little more than Sweden".[372]

The choice between Europe and the world was enforced by discussions on the necessity and legitimacy of a Western military presence in contrast to alternative regional orders. Over international criticism of military involvement, the escalation of the Vietnam War stirred debates that communist groups had not necessarily been influenced by outside powers, but could have a national basis of support among the population. As a result, Western containment could be challenged by claims of national self-determination. Even before, the British had to consider the implications of 'European' or 'white' forces as distinct of indigenous troops over Indonesia's charges of neo-colonialism. Following the official end of Confrontation in summer 1966, British officials therefore increasingly argued for a withdrawal of their forces not only based on economic and strategic factors, but also on ideological grounds. In talks with Americans a year earlier, Denis Healey warned of the political implications of a continued presence: "We should think more carefully about the dangers that continued intervention in the affairs of Southern Asia by blond Caucasians with guns may be politically counterproductive."[373] In 1966, Wilson implied in talks with Dean Rusk that he watched with concern the criticism against the British bases "as a symbol of the Kiplingesque quality of our Far Eastern policy".[374]

---

370 ANZ ABHS W4628 7148, Box 119, LONB 106/5, Part 1, NDEA to NHC London 1827, 21.6.1965.

371 NAA A9861 3/12/77/8, Part 3, AHC London 4804, 24.4.1967.

372 TNA FCO 24/91, Record of Meeting between John Gorton and George Thomson, 12.1.1968.

373 TNA DEFE 13/115, 5.10.1965; in: *Ashton/Louis*, East of Suez, 7–11, FN 11.

374 TNA PREM 13/890, Record of Meeting between Harold Wilson and Dean Rusk, 10.6.1966; in: *Ashton/Louis*, East of Suez, 92–94, 94.

Confronted with this trend in British thinking, Australian and New Zealand officials feared for their forward defence position, both on a strategic and a moral level. The spatial rhetoric of deviance used for Europe and Southeast Asia only enforced with Australian and New Zealand officials they were losing an important ally in a culturally alien surrounding. Such perceptions had received a major incentive with Brown's statement in Washington in April 1967. Aside from economic and strategic factors, Brown expanded Britain's motives with a moral or ideological argument when he linked recent considerations for withdrawal to the ongoing Vietnam War: "When the heat goes off in Vietnam it will go somewhere else; he [Brown] had a strong feeling that at that point white faces on Mainland Asia would become very recognisable (and, by implication, unacceptable)."[375]

With Brown's remarks, the question of 'white faces' came to form the core of a discussion concerning the entire Western presence in the region. From a broader perspective, the question of local opposition touched on the whole question of Western containment strategy and forward defence. However, in contrast to the concerns which had been voiced in talks on Malaysian or Singapore resistance to forward defence forces, e. g. under SEATO, the implication of general resistance to white troops forced officials to fundamentally review foreign bases at times of anti-imperialism and racial divides.

Following Brown's statement, Australians tried to determine the depth of British conviction concerning this argument. Hasluck himself asked his staff after the talks to examine if Brown's remarks indicated "that the British position had become or was becoming untenable or merely that Britain was tired of being unpopular".[376] From London, New Zealand staffer Malcolm Templeton commented on Brown's position: "This no doubt sound as screwy to you as it does to me; but it remains a fact that a good many influential people in Whitehall see no reason why Britain should spend its resources supporting, in an obviously subsidiary role, an American policy which in their contention is wrong anyway."[377]

Immediately following the Washington talks, Holt urged that Wilson should question the basis of the British concerns, and pointed to the beneficial role Britain could still play in the region:

"I also believe that, although this may seem to run against the current of a lot of modern thinking, Asia, for a successful transition to strength, stability and peaceful progress, will continue to need the moral, material, and even military help that the United Kingdom, the United States and countries like my own, Canada and New Zealand can give."[378]

[375] NAA A9861 3/12/77/8, Part 2B, Report of Talk between George Brown and Keith Holyoake, AEmb. Washington 1558, 19.4.1967.

[376] NAA A9861 3/12/77/8, Part 2B, AEmb. Washington 1585, 20.4.1967.

[377] ANZ ABHS W4628 7148, Box 120, LONB 106/7, Part 2, NHC London to Jack Sherd (NEmb. Washington), 4.5.1967.

[378] TNA FCO 46/53, Harold Holt to Harold Wilson, 21.4.1967, in: *Ashton/Bridge/Ward*, DAFP, 186–187, 186.

Holt clearly referred to an Anglosphere of cooperation, while at the same time he separated Britain's unique character from those of its allies to underline the need for a continued 'British' presence. In order to convince Britain of the desirability to stay indefinitely, Holt also underlined the "century of Asia".[379] This image fell in line with his other promotions for a better understanding of the region. During his tenure as Prime Minister, he was able to depict his leadership as one of 'discovering' Asia. His public approach was welcomed by many for the breakaway from conservativism and Eurocentric outlooks embodied by Robert Menzies.[380] Returning from a tour to Asia in 1967, Holt stated:

"This Australia of ours is a vast island continent inhabited largely by people of British or European stock and with a heritage of national freedom, personal liberty and the institutions of a British parliamentary democracy. But geographically we are part of Asia, and increasingly we have become aware of our involvement in the affairs of Asia."[381]

For the first time, an Australian Prime Minister endorsed the concept of Asian identity; however, Holt's insistence on a known set of British values motivating the approach to Asia emphasised continuity: "I believe that Asia is now the crucial area of the struggle to preserve the values of independence, liberty and social justice, for which we have fought in two global wars."[382]

Australian promotion of a positive image of the region again served to highlight their proximity which would translate into them possessing a better knowledge of the local contexts than other powers. In addition, such arguments were designed to counter the presented 'white faces' criticism and should attract a specific British interest to continue an active role in the region. Already in 1966, Holt had urged Wilson to consider a British presence for its own interest, "Britain should not miss out on the 'exciting possibilities' afforded by this great region of the world".[383] In 1967, APMD official Peter Bailey recommended to deal with British withdrawal plans, but also Canadian distancing, by underlining opportunity,

"that in the countries of the Indian Ocean that progress has hardly started. But this is not a reason for pulling out so much as for keeping up the effort, for acting responsibly. For American and Canadian audiences the message is 'Go West, young man!' – that Asia is the new frontier of today, and that to look back is to deny the trust imposed on us by the past."[384]

---

379 *Alexander Downer*, Six Prime Ministers, Melbourne 1982, 91.

380 ANZ ABHS W5503 7148, Box 250, LONB 69/8, Part 1, NHC Canberra 15.2.1966; on the argument of continuity between Menzies and Holt see *Mads Clausen*, 'Falsified by History'. Menzies, Asia and Post-Imperial Australia, in: History Compass 6/4, 2008, 1010–1023.

381 Speech by Harold Holt in the AHoR, 12.4.1967, in: CNIA 38/4 (April 1967), 140–145, 140.

382 Ibid.

383 LAC RG25 A-3-c, Vol. 8842, 20-AUSTL-1-3, Part 3, Record of Meeting of Harold Holt and Harold Wilson, CHC London 1248, 25.7.1966.

384 NAA A1209 1966/7335, Part 4A, Peter Bailey for Prime Minister Harold Holt, 9.6.1967.

Similarly, Australian and New Zealand officials presented recent attempts of regional integration as promising developments. The mid-1960s indeed saw signals of genuine regional cooperation, which differed from the regional alliances sustained by outside powers of the 1950s.[385] In 1966, after a proposal by South Korea, the anti-communist framework of Asian-Pacific Cooperation (ASPAC) had been introduced. Although doubts about longevity of the alliance remained, Australia and New Zealand joined ASPAC, "partly to signify their acceptance of their new-found Asian destiny".[386] They hailed the organization as opportunity to "foster a sense of regional consciousness among the governments of Asia and a common approach to the problems of the region".[387] The most promising grouping, however, seemed the Association of Southeast Asian Nations (ASEAN), which was introduced just a few months later. As New Zealand sources indicate, its establishment promised regional stability as it included former adversaries Malaysia, Singapore and Indonesia.[388] However, officials were also cautious as ASEAN appeared determined to remove external influence in the long run. New Zealanders pointed out that ASEAN defined foreign bases in its preamble as temporary constructions, thus providing a basis "upon which the association could conceivably move in directions uncomfortable for the United States and ourselves".[389]

Both confronted with local hostilities among Southeast Asian countries and the uncertainty about future outlooks, Australia and New Zealand insisted that a regional defence framework provided by Western powers, including Britain was needed as long as those regional initiatives were embryonic in size.[390] A New Zealand brief therefore recommended to publicly support the regional character of the organisations but to insist with Asian leaders that "in the absence of the Western military guarantee there would be little scope for any Asian independence".[391]

Nevertheless, the argument of regional progress and opportunity was pushed with British officials, with attempts to draft Britain's traditional role as a unique stabilising force. One Australian note commented on the right presentation of this argument as one of historic responsibility:

---

385 *Thompson*, British Military Withdrawal.

386 ANZ ABHS W4627 950, Box 770, 1/2/27, Part 5, Division Heads' Meeting, 27.7.1967.

387 Australian officials cited in 'Regional Cooperation in Asia', New Zealand Foreign Ministry, 25.5.1972, quoted in: *Halvorson*, Australia in Asia, 92.

388 See the New Zealand assessment on the developments in ANZ ABHS W4628 6952, Box 9, SIN 251/1/7, NDEA to Posts, 6.11.1967.

389 ANZ ABHS W4628 6952, Box 9, SIN 251/1/7, NDEA to Posts, 6.11.1967.

390 ANZ ABHS W4628 6952, Box 9, SIN 251/1/7, "Regional Cooperation", Brief for New Zealand-Japan Talks, 2.5.1968.

391 ANZ ABHS W5400 20358, Box 88, KL 101/5/1, "Regional Development", Brief for Four Power Information Conference, 9.11.1966.

"The security of the area of course is vital to Australia but the area promises, with the wisdom and assistance that Britain has given in the past, to emerge notwithstanding temporary signs of strain into an area of real stability. It is a flash point in the world at this time but so were Korea and Berlin in the 1950s."[392]

A focus on a specific 'British' presence was in parts connected to continued scepticism that the USA was not accepted to fill such a role, as New Zealand diplomat Reuel Lochore highlighted: "For social and political reasons, and because of the implied infringement of sovereignty, no Asian country can really welcome the presence of American forces on its soil."[393] The need for genuine British elements was further emphasised over the question of replacing British forces with Gurkha troops. Holt rejected this proposal in talks with British services in June 1967: "The Australians had no complex about the use of Gurkhas, but if there were no British soldiers in the Commonwealth Brigade an asset of great psychological value would have been lost. It did not require great numbers of them; a few British soldiers and a larger number of Gurkhas would do."[394] Similarly, New Zealand officials dismissed the proposal in negotiations as they felt it did not represent the same political outlook as a British presence.[395]

The resistance to Gurkhas exposed continued racialised thinking on the region. At the same time, Australian and New Zealand officials strongly opposed the racialised categories presented in the 'white faces' argument. In Washington, Keith Holyoake urged Brown to review this position: "If this thesis was advanced publicly as a reason for the British withdrawal it would imply that the newer countries such as Australia and New Zealand, who did not enjoy Britain's traditional position in the area, would be even less welcome."[396] From the beginning of discussions, Australia and New Zealand, as non-Asian powers, clearly feared the implications for their own troops stationed in the region. As they framed Brown's statement in a racialised global order, Australia and New Zealand had to question their own basis of being committed as white powers in Asia. For them, the issue sharpened their own antagonism of cultural and geographical belonging. Additionally, they had to wage the implications of local opinion. In discussing the potential replies to Brown's remarks, New Zealand staff in Malaysia urged to present their opposition without notions to fear: "[...] we are likely to create the impression we feel in danger of being cut off from our white brethren and left to face South East Asia alone – which will help neither

392 NAA A1209 1966/7335, Part 2A, Note for ASEA, 26.4.1967.

393 ANZ ABHS W5631 22310, Box 193, PAR 222/1/1, Part 2, NEmb. Bonn (Lochore), 11.4.1967.

394 TNA PREM 13/1323, Meeting of Harold Holt with the British Defence Ministry, 14.6.1967, in: *Ashton/Bridge/Ward*, DAFP, 206–211, 209.

395 ANZ ABHS W4628 7148, Box 121, LONB 106/7, Part 3, NHC London 3680, 26.7.1967.

396 TNA PREM 13/1455, Record of Quadripartite Ministerial Discussion at AEmb. Washington, 20.4.1967.

our present case nor our longterm position."[397] Such an approach demanded a balanced presentation, and the emotional dilemma was not lost on British officials like Denis Healey: "[…] for Britain a continued presence in the Far East was simply a matter of policy, for Australia and New Zealand it was a matter of survival."[398]

Brown's 'white faces' comment touched on Australian and New Zealand self-perception as Western nations who were committed in an Asian neighbourhood. It therefore revoked feelings of difference and threat, something even the positive descriptions of Asia failed to overcome. The conflict was reminiscent of the difficulties experienced during Confrontation, when Malaysia's international image seemed better served by a Commonwealth, rather than a British, defence presence. How strongly the issue was related to Australia's self-perception as an Anglo-Saxon nation was emphasised by Charles Johnston on the eve of Brown's statement:

"[…] this is a red rag to the Australian bull. […] financial necessity they can understand – also, if it happened the need to leave Singapore and Malaysia because of local political opposition. What they do not accept is that we should withdraw because of some theoretical reason about relations between the West and South East Asia, an area which they claim to understand far better than we do."[399]

After addressing in a separate message the emotions Holt had shown during their first meeting after Brown's comments, Johnston returned to the question of 'white faces' in another telegram and urged his officials to consider the consequences of continued exploitation of this argument:

"I would however like to advise very strongly indeed that in our further discussions with the Australians on defence we should not use [the] 'white faces' argument again. I suggest that in this delicate issue it is important for us to keep both theory and emotion out. […] In these circumstances for us to go on talking about white faces suggest to their mind that we care more about sentiment and ideology than about their national survival."[400]

As Johnston emphasised, references to 'white faces' could lead to emotional Australian reactions that were caused by fear for their own security. To Australia as to New Zealand, the continuous struggle of reconciling their geographical with a cultural or ethnic identity was brought to the point by highlighting their white background. They suspected British officials to consider a withdrawal to please international and especially Afro-Asian opinion, and sought local support to reject this position. When Healey visited Kuala Lumpur for talks in

[397] ANZ ABHS W4628 7148, Box 120, LONB 106/7, Part 2, NHC Kuala Lumpur 301, 8.5.1967.

[398] ANZ ABHS W4628 7148, Box 119, LONB 106/5A, Part 2, New Zealand Report on Defence Talks in Canberra, n. d. (February 1966).

[399] TNA FCO 46/54, BHC Canberra (Johnston) to CO 636, 21.4.1967.

[400] TNA FCO 46/54, BHC Canberra (Johnston) to CO 656, 25.4.1967.

late April 1967, he spoke of Anglo-Saxon troops leaving the Asian mainland. The New Zealand High Commission staff reported on the following: "Quaintly enough Yeo [Beng Poh] took the term to include Americans and British only, and we did not disabuse him."[401] As they received the response that Malaysia and Singapore would welcome a continued white presence, Tasman officials sought to present this case accordingly with British counterparts.[402]

An Australian review of Britain's decision in July 1967 underlined the various objectives fuelling the announcement for withdrawal. According to the review, aside from economic, financial and political considerations, Britain had also decided to withdraw based on the following reasons:

"(iv) The growth of political opposition to overseas military establishments because of: (a) ideological considerations (national self-determination, and 'white faces'); (b) emotional considerations (casualties from conflicts in the Middle East and South East Asia); (c) the indefinite duration of colonial wars; (d) Western failures in 'colonial' wars; (e) their international unpopularity, particularly given the changed array of forces in the United Nations."[403]

The author of the review, Rowen Osborn, expected the British decision to be as much based on frustrations over its challenging role in the Commonwealth and decolonisation issues as for economic considerations and the political interest in Europe. As a result, he did not believe in a change of attitude despite allied protest:

"Although there is undoubtedly in Britain a strong sense of community with and moral obligation towards Australia and New Zealand, there is no real feeling that we are a part of South East Asia, or that we are in danger from either China or Indonesia. There is if anything a feeling that we are, on this subject, too inclined to cry wolf. There is also no doubt in some circles in Britain a feeling, that if we are exposed, we have merited it through our immigration and Viet Nam policies. There is too, the feeling that we have not in the past contributed our fair share to the cost of defending the Malaysian area."[404]

Here, Osborn touched on a multitude of issues paving the way of Anglo-Australian difference, including the question of threat assessments or burden-sharing. Moreover, his comments indicate how much Australia understood the British decision for withdrawal as a departure from previously shared 'racial' or 'colonial' concepts that would determine an appropriate engagement with the region. In sum, Osborn's report indicates how misunderstood Australians felt by their former 'mother country' over a variety of policies, and how ideological allegations dominated the debate.

---

401 ANZ ABHS W4628 7148, Box 120, LONB 106/7, Part 2, NHC Kuala Lumpur 289, 29.4.1967.

402 NAA TS3006/10/4/1, Part 3, "Australian Policy on British Defence Policy East of Suez", ADEA Working Paper, n. d. (May 1967).

403 NAA A1838 TS 691/1, Part 13, Note by Osborn, 22.8.1967, in: *Ashton/Bridge/Ward*, DAFP, 230–237, 230.

404 Ibid.

Shortly after Brown's statement, Denis Healey remarked in talks with New Zealanders that "Brown had been silly to use these words to white Asians such as ourselves".[405] His comment, just as Brown's remarks, point to the difficulties Australians and New Zealanders had in locating themselves within the region while perceiving themselves as Anglo-Saxon, European and/or White. Within Australia, many still criticised the positivist attitude Harold Holt took towards the region and doubted the new description as 'Asian' Australia or New Zealand. Political observers such as Professor J. D. B. Miller expected Australians to struggle with their geographical identity for a long time to come: "Australia will not become 'part of' Asia […] Nothing can make Australia Hindu, Muslim, or Buddhist; nothing can bring it to adopt Asian family or caste systems; nothing can make it give up English; nothing can make it stop eating what it eats or reading what it reads."[406]

Criticism of an Asian identity also underlined the continuity of ideological, biased perceptions held in both countries. In a cartoon printed by the *Australian*[407] (Fig. 3), Prime Minister Harold Holt is seen mingling with a group of 'underdeveloped Asians' (India's Prime Minister Indira Gandhi, Lee Kuan Yew and Tunku Abdul Rahman) when he is approached by Harold Wilson carrying the 'White man's defence burden', a reference to Rudyard Kipling.[408] The cartoon's subtitle states Holt's reply to Wilson: "What d'ya mean take over, I'm one of them now, haven't you heard?" As the caricature suggests, Holt's approach to Asian countries still seems guided by hierarchical, prejudiced thinking on their status of development. Furthermore, the cartoon indicates his approach could primarily be a strategy to avoid further defence commitments.

The developments in Southeast Asia forced people from both countries to assess their shortcomings for the understanding of Asia, including those on an institutional level. Gordon Jockel, one of the most influential Australian policymakers engaged in discussions on the correct policy on Asia, took a professional sabbatical in 1967, indicating awareness for some limitations of his knowledge. During his leave, he visited the Department of International Relations at Australian National University (ANU), followed by research visits to the USA and Hong Kong – all to obtain a better understanding of China.[409] His intend-

[405] ANZ ABHS W4628 7148, Box 120, LONB 106/7, Part 2, NHC Kuala Lumpur 275, 26.4.1967.

[406] *J. D. B. Miller*: "Australian Policy in Asia", n. d. (1968), found in: LAC RG25 A-3-c, Vol. 8842, 20-AUSTL-1-3, Part 6.

[407] *Aubrey Collette*, "What d'ya mean take over", The Australian, 20.7.1967.

[408] Rudyard Kipling initially wrote the poem "White Man's Burden" for the Crown Jubilee of Queen Victoria in 1899, but it soon came to represent both British and American imperialism and Eurocentric ideas of superiority and the civilizing mission; *John Philip Jenkins*, White Supremacy. URL: https://www.britannica.com/topic/white-supremacy. Accessed September 5, 2019.

[409] "A (distant) study of the Chinese puzzle. Our Gordon Jockel visits a 'Think Tank'", Sydney Morning Herald, 6.6.1967.

Fig. 3: Aubrey Collette, "What d'ya mean take over", The Australian, 20.7.1967

ed stay at ANU illustrates how problematic the demand for Chinese knowledge had been handled by the ADEA so far. At ANU, Jockel met former public servants Stephen FitzGerald and Gregory Clark, who had both left the Department in the previous years in protest of Australia's official policy on China. Both moved on to become influential public voices in favour of recognition and engagement. While Stephen FitzGerald would become Australia's first Ambassador to China in 1973, Clark would publish a book called *In Fear of Asia* in 1967, in which he targeted both Australia's attitude towards China and its commitment to Vietnam. He ultimately called for a revision of Australia's foreign policy: "Few Western countries have been less the target of Chinese hostility than Australia. Few countries, Western or non-Western, are more hostile to China than Australia."[410] His judgement came at a time when such reviews were only commencing over the British withdrawal. With the developments over the next few years, however, they would gain substantial scope and speed at the turn of the decade.

---

410 *Gregory Clark*, In Fear of China, Melbourne 1967, 161.

4.4 Conclusion of Part 4

Upon his departure from Canberra in 1971, British High Commissioner Charles Johnston recollected as one of the most challenging episodes during his term the 'white faces' debate:

"For us to tell them that we were withdrawing our forces, and to offer them instead a piece of trendy left-wing theology […] accentuated the flibbertigibbet impression which […] our country all too often gave. […] We […] appeared as a giddy butterfly flitting unsteadily round the fringe of world politics. It was a heart-breaking period for British representatives on this side of the globe."[411]

Like so many others, Johnston experienced the debate on Britain's decision to withdraw East of Suez as an emotional and challenging time. His recollections relate to similar assessments of the issue as a watershed moment that struck the relationship between Britain and the former dominions.

As the analysis of discussions surrounding Britain's withdrawal plans from 1965 to 1968 reveal, the whole East of Suez discussion was characterised by an emotionally charged atmosphere that perpetually questioned the Anglo-Dominion relationship.[412] This climate resulted from fractions within the framework of personal affiliation, shared backgrounds and values. At the same time, the high degree of informal, symbolic talk during negotiations that engaged historical analogies or sentimental arguments underlined how close and frank both sides still perceived their relations.[413] For Australia and New Zealand, appeals to a shared war experience or a moral obligation were deemed effective, as policymakers in both countries felt a profound affiliation to Britain and expected an appreciative British response. At the beginning of discussions, they were confirmed in their strategies when British officials like Michael Stewart assured that close relations sanctioned a British obligation: "[…] of course our close relationship with Australia and New Zealand carries with it moral responsibilities in the field of defence."[414]

However, the course of negotiations shows a decline in the efficacy of arguments of kith and kin. The support or understanding for Britain's declining ability to stay in Southeast Asia was increasingly linked to a position of rationality, while the voices of regret and dismay were more and more connected to the image of irrationality, nostalgia and sentiment. In the course of discussions, pleas for sentiment therefore became less effective as they lost credibility both in the former dominions as in Britain. However, distinctions of 'sentiment' vs

411 TNA FCO 24/1072, Valedictory Dispatch of Charles Johnston, 2.4.1971, quoted in: *Lloyd*, Diplomacy With a Difference, 257.

412 *Kristensen*, In Essence Still a British Country.

413 *Goldsworthy*, Losing the Blanket, 8 f.

414 Statement by Michael Stewart at the National Press Club Australia, 26.6.1966, in: CNIA 37/6 (June 1966), 390–392, 390.

'rationality' were mainly created to serve political attitudes. Australian and New Zealand officials still argued from respective Anglo-Australian or Anglo-New Zealand outlooks that cherished the British connection, and continued working with premises derived from British values. The endurance of traditional concepts of moral obligation or a confidential relationship in those debates underpinned ideas of continued close cooperation. Therefore, the various, concurrent strands of British assurances and declarations of incapacity to uphold their presence were difficult to entangle for policymakers who still believed in concepts of mutual confidence and assistance. At the same time, emotional attachment made the regrets of policymakers like Frank Hassett, Alexander Downer or Keith Holyoake more understandable as they felt they truly witnessed the decline of a close partner or relative.

Likewise, those sources invalidate arguments that such emotional or sentimental approaches were only used as a rhetoric strategy. Rather than being directed as an act of talk that should motivate or stimulate compassion or empathy among the public[415], the simultaneous occurrence of such arguments in a highly professional and confidential space leads to assumptions that those arguments strongly appealed to a shared British background or belonging. As the discussions reveal, the argument was symbolically charged by large support for said close relationship and moral obligation through strong residents of imperial imagination on both sides.[416] One manifestation is the insistence on consultation as a (post-)imperial practice among close partners. Without such a continued mindset, its use would have been called out as nostalgic practice by all participants of the discussion. Instead, it lingered on for most of the discussions as a valid argument in a shared framework of British thinking.

Therefore, when we look at the reports going back and forth between the metropole London and the periphery, we do not need to distinguish too much if the emotion was truly felt or just an instrumentalising, appealing act of speech. Even if they did not feel in a similar way, the very essence of understanding said emotions illustrated to all officials involved the degree of imperial affiliation and belonging. The East of Suez discussions present themselves as a last imperial lesson, the confirmation that Britain, Australia and New Zealand constituted a transnational British emotional community. Both sides could engage in talks that confirmed and perpetuated ideas of a (post-)imperial framework, a British orbit they shared on foreign policy. Given its role as an observer who was able to decode the symbolic communication over disagreements between Britain and Australia and New Zealand, even Canada engaged in such discussions.

---

415 See on this argument e. g. political scientist Murray Edelman wo distinguishes between appealing speech in the public space and negotiating talk in non-public spaces, *Murray J. Edelman*, The Symbolic Uses of Politics, Urbana 1964.

416 *Subritzky*, End of Empire, 217.

The emotional appeals by officials like Harold Holt or Keith Holyoake, as well as the outbursts of Paul Hasluck or Alexander Downer, were a way of addressing the apparent rift between British and dominion outlooks. When we acknowledge dispositions like Britishness were heavily supported by sentiment, the loss of Britain's partnership in Southeast Asia caused collective struggles that were articulated by emotions of fear, anger, regret and bitterness. Despite anticipating the withdrawal, Britain's actual decision destroyed for many the idea of a British world community.[417] These feelings were not only enforced by different paths taken in foreign policy, for example on Vietnam, but also with the abandonment of shared institutions derived from imperial cooperation. Institutions such as the traditional consultation within the Commonwealth constituted a practice of trust; their demise therefore created the feeling of uncertainty among policymakers on both sides. To Australians and New Zealanders, the decline of shared institutions and outlooks became even more excruciating in talks with sympathetic British counterparts, particularly in service ranks, which equally deplored a British retreat. This perspective also adds new layers to the characterisations of British policymakers such as Denis Healey or George Brown, who could be considered supporters of an East of Suez policy[418], yet clashed with Tasman counterparts on various occasions.

However, the variance of emotion forecasted a future shift of attitudes among policymakers. While individuals like Alexander Downer vehemently opposed the British plans, others saw his emotional approach as outdated and one of "the old white Commonwealth".[419] Additionally, Downer was more a politician rather than a civil servant, meaning his views had to be counterbalanced on numerous occasions by external affairs officers and advisers.[420] The validity of Downer's feelings is not put in question; it is rather the question of how wide his sentiment was shared among policymakers and the public. Even though he ranked at the extreme end of a scale of Britishness, it nevertheless makes sense to assume that policymakers across the dominions all understood the emotional struggle of adapting to a framework without British support, including the more detached Canadians. At the end of 1966, Geoffrey Murray insisted from London that Canadians, in their determination to follow new foreign policies, should not sacrifice the good, intimate relations with Britain.[421] In his reply to Murray, Basil Robinson urged him to support Canada's new directions in foreign policy, even in the face of British recriminations: "Change which goes against the grain is always hard to accept."[422]

---

417 *Kristensen*, In Essence Still a British Country, 51.

418 *James*, Global Britain's Strategic Problem, 179 f.

419 LAC RG25, Vol. 10663, 23-3-1968, CHC Canberra 912, 4.6.1968.

420 NLA TRC 4903, Interview with William Pritchett by Garry Woodard, 28.10.2002/4.2.2003, 147.

421 LAC MG31 E83, Box 13, Geoffrey Murray to Basil Robinson, 18.11.1966.

422 LAC MG31 E83, Box 13, Basil Robinson to Geoffrey Murray, 21.11.1966.

Most of Murray's communications with Ottawa were related to Anglo-Canadian differences in Commonwealth dealings; an area where also Australia and New Zealand experienced frustrations. As the emotional statements throughout the discussion showed, the apparent lack of consultation and trust saddened both sides. Additionally, the way Britain came to its ultimate decision for withdrawal by 1971 indicated to many the real end of former imperial power, it symbolised the "unpredictably rapid decline of British influence and inflicted an unnecessary loss of great-power dignity, the fig-leaf that had made the end of Empire acceptable at home and less revealing abroad".[423] The duality of EEC and East of Suez as policy options increased the perceived dichotomy between a British European role and a British World role which had already come up during political debates in 1960–1963. People in the former dominions could mourn the loss of Britain's world role, and they expressed their regrets in the language of the Empire.[424]

These emotions were only enforced when discussions turned to scenarios of abandonment in an alien environment, feelings that intensified in the face of a potential simultaneous American withdrawal. At the same time, uncertainty resulted from a distinct ambiguity about the USA as an ally, both regarding the shape of the American alliance as its growing divergence from British policy.[425] The strong reactions to the British decision therefore might be interpreted as the individual or collective struggle with feeling abandoned by familiar structures and affiliations. Even if diplomats and public servants were less weary of the dissolution of British ties, they nevertheless supported or acquiesced to the official rhetoric of regret.

Furthermore, they shared concerns about the uncertain future of Southeast Asia. A good example is a recollection provided by Australian diplomat William Pritchett. He recalled how he tried to review the British decision with colleagues in July 1967:

> "Gordon Balkers, the deputy secretary of defence in charge of this area, the thinking on this, and Gordon Jockel, who was then the divisional head of South East Asia, came over to my place one Sunday afternoon […] and we had tea and we tried to discuss the issue. What should we do? What should Australia do? It was a very lightweight discussion. We just, you know, didn't have an answer. So they went home."[426]

For officials like Pritchett, the uncertainty surrounding Southeast Asia produced varying emotions of perplexity and regret amidst the British withdrawal. Even if he admitted he knew a British withdrawal was imminent long

[423] *Darwin*, Britain's Withdrawal, 156.

[424] *Neville Meaney*, Australia and the World, in: Neville Meaney (Ed.), Under New Heavens: Cultural Transmission and the Making of Australia, Port Melbourne 1989, 379–450, 431.

[425] *McLean*, British Colony, 73–75.

[426] NLA TRC 4903, Interview with William Pritchett by Garry Woodard, 28.10.2002/4.2.2003, 122.

before the decision was taken[427], he and others had no answer to the question of a revised defence framework without Britain. Being brought up with a strong mindset of imperial imagination, many officials in Australia and New Zealand felt challenged by the British withdrawal in adapting to a new outlook based on their geographical rather than their historical or cultural identity. The discussions on Southeast Asia and, in a larger global framework, the role of Communist China brought all three countries to extend their mental maps to the region. As a result, spatial categories of a regional or global framework slowly replaced the previous imperial map. While Canada's Cold War alliance with the USA enforced the focus on North America and Europe, Australia and New Zealand considered the space around Southeast Asia and the Pacific as a new area of international affairs. These different paths were pursued with different mindsets of adaption; while Canada pursued its geographical identity largely in accord with its cultural identity, both Australia and New Zealand struggled with what they perceived as an antagonism between geographical and cultural identity. As Australian High Commissioner Kenneth Bailey described it aptly at the time, every country's foreign policy is shaped by history and geography, "factors that all move in the same direction. In Australia they do not".[428] This problem of reconciliation Canadians only experienced over domestic conflicts: Given the growing dissent of Quebec with federal policies, Canada had to balance the alignment with American politics with alternative models of detached engagement such as peacekeeping or diplomacy of constraint.[429]

For Australia and New Zealand, the struggle of reconciling a cultural with a geographical identity manifested in the East of Suez discussions. Most apparent were the underlying insecurities of identity during the discussions on Brown's 'white faces' comment. At the same time, the discussions on the future of regional developments opened discussions on a positive relationship with the region and established first contacts of cooperation. British insistence on a need to withdraw indicated to Tasman officials that their presence was now no longer perceived as support of British forces, but a potential commitment independently of previous arrangements. This was even more underlined by discussions on Australia's and New Zealand's regional identity in contrast to a 'European' Britain. Holt's premiership therefore indicated a state of transition.[430] In his statements, he not only emphasised Australia's new focus on Asia, but also underlined the need to overcome the loss of British elements in Australia's outlook. Furthermore, Holt was responsible for adjustments in the field of im-

427 Ibid., 121.
428 *Bailey*, World Security, 295.
429 *Vucetic*, Anglosphere, 86 f.
430 See on this argument also *Halvorson*, Australia in Asia, 89 f.

migration, aboriginal emancipation and national culture that indicated a retreat from Britishness.[431]

Ultimately, however, long-lasting apprehensions of the Asian region were hard to overcome, especially as officials like Holt showed such discomfort about the loss of British ties. Statements on Asia made during the late 1960s indicate that any approach was determined more by jet travel and warfare technology decreasing the distance to the Asian continent than by an honest interest in co-operation with the neighbouring countries north of the Tasman dominions.[432] Aside from resistance to local cooperation, e. g. with Gurkhas, this was in both countries further emphasised by continuous policies of white immigration.[433] Nevertheless, Holt's premiership had unconsciously departed from traditional foreign policy, as commentator Bruce Grant wrote following Holt's disappearance: "More by temperament and political instinct than by calculation, he was a catalyst of the major forces at work on Australia's destiny in this century."[434]

In reaction to the criticism of the Western presence and related British considerations for withdrawal, Tasman officials reacted with a strong emphasis on the need for continued Western containment. Especially in the Australian case, this also meant strong support for the American effort in Vietnam. Australia and New Zealand also had to come up with a certain convincing image for a Western presence in the region, not only since they would lose legitimisation and credibility over Britain's retreat, but also because they feared backlashes as the only nations in the region with a majority of population originating from European, white ancestors. Additionally, a position of military intervention was still considered the only viable option to react to regional instability. At the same time, the strong objection to Britain's military and moral retreat from the conflicts in Southeast Asia highlights how much both countries still endorsed the imperial agenda of a British civilising mission. From this perspective, their resistance to retreat from a policy of forward defence can be linked to other fields where imperial attitudes were still displayed, such as immigration policy, their relationship with indigenous people or their relations with Pacific nations.

All arguments of the East of Suez debate combined reveal a certain discomfort shared among the former dominions regarding the British plans. At the same time, the insecurity was caused by ongoing regional conflicts and continued Cold War tensions. Yet especially the issue of Chinese recognition already exposed differences in the framing of Southeast Asia and the related military presence. Questioning the basis of forward defence and Cold War intervention, the East of Suez discussions initiated a fundamental review process in defence and foreign policy that would stretch beyond the decision taken in 1968. Fol-

---

431 *Curran*, Power of Speech, 54–57.

432 Ibid., 59.

433 *Meaney*, End of 'White Australia', 179 f.

434 *Bruce Grant*, "Holt and Asia", Age, 22.12.1967.

lowing the British decisions, the focus of reviews would shift from an appeal to a British change of policy to the questioning of own rationales, leading to a departure in foreign policy and security, not only in Australia and New Zealand, but also in Canada.

Part 5

Consolations and New Beginnings – Foreign Policy Re-Orientation Going into the 1970s

"Until the Second World War we had hardly known that South East Asia existed. Since that time we had switched our defence commitment from Europe and the Middle East to South East Asia. All this was a slow process but there was a growing consciousness among New Zealanders of a Pacific and South East Asian future. These 'successive shocks' make us conscious of Britain's position in the world and our own and we have to find a way of coping with these changing circumstances."[1]

After the British decision in January 1968, public discussions as well as official considerations among policymakers in Australia and New Zealand were filed with nostalgia, regret and uncertainty. Like Keith Holyoake, many officials felt they had to cope with a rapid change in policy thrown at them by the British. At the same time, discussions focused on the question of what could follow the British framework: "After Britain, Who?"[2] So far, strategy in both countries had centred around the cooperation with 'great and powerful friends' and was based on principles of forward defence. The British retreat not only put this strategic position under scrutiny, but it also put several frameworks of foreign policy and defence into question. With the Southeast Asian region in turmoil, public and official demands for policy review only grew.

The general atmosphere of public debate on foreign policy was also palpable in Canada, where the cautious, ambivalent governmental approach to American Vietnam policy had resulted in public resentment. Particularly young Canadians wished for their government to adopt a more independent position in international affairs. Similarly, Canadian officials, like Australians and New Zealanders, had to assess the implications of a shifting international framework in which Britain would only be one among other partners. All three countries had to consider how the British retreat from a world role would affect ties and principles of cooperation, security alliances and their general outlook of foreign policy.

In a larger development, a thorough review of foreign policy was also called for by a new generation of policymakers entering office at the end of the dec-

---

[1] Keith Holyoake in talks with George Thomson, ANZ ABHS W4628 7148 Box 121, LONB 106/7, Part 3, Record of Talks of Keith Holyoake and George Thomson, 11.1.1968.

[2] This was the name of a panel discussion with notable political scientists and experts like Alistair Buchan and Bruce Miller in the *New Zealand Listener*, "After Britain, Who?", New Zealand Listener, 9.2.1968.

ade. Within a couple of years, diplomats who had laid the very foundation of foreign policy in the post-war years were succeeded by officials who had little to no relations to this (post-)imperial framework.[3] Both in and outside of the departments, the first post-war generation would bring new values and principles which would redefine the thinking on and practice of foreign policy.[4] The change of generation brought a remarkably young and educated audience to the forefront. In 1965, 38.5 percent of the Australian population was under 20 years old.[5] In Canada, the population at universities had more than doubled from 1957 to 1967.[6]

This new generation increased public attention to foreign policy issues in all three countries. The debates surrounding the Vietnam War had politicised large parts of society, not only young people, but also groups previously marginalised by or outside of politics.[7] As a result, the war ended the consensus on foreign policy largely unchallenged since the end of the Second World War. New controversial issues of military service and new forms of protest and political confrontation embedded the discussion of foreign policy into a larger social context. At the same time, academic discussions and new academic policymakers would fuse into the departments.[8] Similar developments in other Western states bound Australian, Canadian and New Zealand protests into a global context, with only the time of protest peaks lagging shortly behind Western Europe movements.[9]

In parts, new stimuli also came from a more diverse society. With only minor adjustments to overwhelmingly British immigration in the 1950s and 1960s, the end of the decade finally saw a lift of the curfew of White immigration policies.

---

[3] *Greg Donaghy*, "A Sad, General Decline?": The Canadian Diplomat in the 20th Century, in: Robert Bothwell (Ed.), Canada Among Nations, 2008: 100 Years of Canadian Foreign Policy, Montreal 2014, 41–60, 52 f.

[4] *Shirleene Robinson/Julie Ustinoff* (Ed.), The 1960s in Australia. People, Power and Politics, Newcastle 2012; *Paul Litt*, Trudeaumania, Vancouver/Toronto 2016.

[5] *Edwards*, Nation at War, 16.

[6] *Jack L. Granatstein*, Canada 1957–1967. The Years of Uncertainty and Innovation, Toronto 1986, 211.

[7] *Jason Flanagan*, The Vietnam War at Home and Abroad, in: Shirleene Robinson/Julie Ustinoff (Ed.), The 1960s in Australia: People, Power and Politics, Newcastle 2012, 199–216; *Peter Pierce*, 'Never Glad Confident Morning Again': Australia, the Sixties and the Vietnam War, in: Jeffrey Grey/Jeff Doyle (Ed.), Vietnam: War, Myth and Memory: Comparative Perspectives on Australia's War in Vietnam, Crows Nest 1992, 69–80.

[8] One prominent example was the Canadian key adviser to Pierre Trudeau, Ivan Head, who joined his staff after being active at debates at the University of Alberta; *John English*, Two Heads Are Better Than One: Ivan Head, Pierre Trudeau and Canadian Foreign Policy, in: Greg Donaghy/Kim R. Nossal (Ed.), Architects and Innovators: Building the Department of Foreign and International Trade, 1909–2009, Montreal 2009, 239–252.

[9] *Edwards*, Nation at War, 177 f.; *Robert Rabel*, Vietnam and the Collapse of the Foreign Policy Consensus, in: Malcolm McKinnon (Ed.), New Zealand in World Affairs: Vol. 2: 1957–1972, Wellington 1991, 40–63.

In all three countries, immigration from Non-British countries was replacing the old bonds to home.[10] In Canada, French Canadians entered public discussions over Quebec Separatism, but also became more visible in public offices. As a third group, indigenous people fought for larger representation in national policies. All groups combined appropriated a space in political discourse that resulted in a broadening of discussions on national foreign policy.[11]

This shift in demographics reversely created expectations for political change. Around the turn of the decade, Labo(u)r or Liberal governments in all three countries could generate enthusiasm and anticipation for reform. In Canada, Pierre Trudeau received an unprecedented level of media attention as his unconventional style of politics contrasted largely with his predecessors.[12] In Australia and New Zealand, both Gough Whitlam and Norman Kirk campaigned their elections under the slogan "It's time", indicating the considerable atmosphere of surfeit with the current conservative governments.[13] All three politicians ultimately embodied the public demand for new, visionary policy initiatives.

Such calls were sustained by developments in international affairs, where a window of opportunity seemed to open up for those willing to see it, most of all with a change in US policy. In March 1968, Lyndon B. Johnson surprised America's allies with his announcement for a cessation of the bombing of North Vietnam and his decision to not run for another term as American president. Johnson's announcement followed on the heels of American defeat in the Tet Offensive, which not only gave support to Vietnam War critics but also resulted in a serious questioning of American ability to win the war.[14] Johnson's successor, Richard Nixon, used his term to introduce a series of decisions that would further shift American policy in the region, cumulating in the Guam Doctrine of summer 1969, in which he indicated an American desire for regional powers to solve conflicts among themselves.[15] A further shift in US policy was introduced in July 1971 when Nixon announced his intentions to seek relations with China.

This shift in American politics unsettled Australia and New Zealand after the strategic pressure already caused by Britain's announcement. However, recrim-

[10] *Jatinder Mann*, "Leavening British Traditions": Integration Policy in Australia, 1962–1972, in: Australian Journal of Politics & History 59/1, 2013, 47–62.

[11] *Pierce*, Australia, the Sixties, 72.

[12] *Litt*, Trudeaumania; *Robert Wright*, Trudeaumania. The Rise to Power of Pierre Elliott Trudeau, Toronto 2016.

[13] *Robert Rabel*, The World Turned Upside Down? New Zealand Politics Until 1984, in: Richard W. Baker (Ed.), Australia, New Zealand, and the United States. Internal Change and Alliance Relations in the ANZUS States, New York 1991, 89–108, 94.

[14] *John Murphy*, Harvest of Fear. A History of Australia's Vietnam War, Boulder 1993, 198.

[15] Remarks by Richard Nixon to Reporters in Guam, 25.7.1969, quoted from *James Curran*, Unholy Fury. Whitlam and Nixon at War, Carlton 2015, 104.

inations against the USA were soon overtaken by events and processed by new arrangements. One of these new arrangements was the Five Power Defence Arrangements (FPDA), officially established in fall 1971. Before, after a series of consultations during 1968, Australia and New Zealand decided to keep a joint force in Malaysia and Singapore after Britain's withdrawal, a decision made public in early 1969. This commitment was buttressed by a new British government under Edward Heath in 1970, who offered to participate in a Five Power arrangement and a limited military force.[16] While the FPDA would lack many of the strengths previous arrangements had, they nevertheless mitigated some of the concerns over the British and American withdrawal.[17] The Guam Doctrine was also processed under the impression of a growing international appreciation for regionalism depicted by the success of ASEAN, but also changing discourses on China. Other Western countries, including Canada, had worked on integrating the PRC into the international community by bilateral approaches to China. Nixon's new course was therefore integrated into a new paradigm of regionalism and global Cold War détente.

The multitude of developments and changes spanning from the late 1960s to the early 1970s added to the general perception in Australia and New Zealand that both countries needed to adjust their frameworks of foreign policy, defence and strategies. In the following, reviews touched on their future perception as a nation without close British ties, their position in the region and, ultimately, their position in a world where Britain was more a European than a global power. Similarly, under the impression of a new government of Pierre Trudeau, Canada engaged in a profound foreign policy review that assessed the Canadian policy previously based on the Western alliance.

In the wake and aftermath of the East of Suez negotiations, considerations within the former dominions pointed in two directions. On the one hand, Britain's decision to withdraw pressed on the dominions the need for a more self-reliant foreign and defence policy. Self-reliance was understood as being based on a strong independent national stance, with notions of their current policies lacking such independence and maturity.

On the other hand, officials retreated from arguments of historic affiliation, sentiment and Britishness. These arguments seemed to have failed in negotiations with Britain, similar to threat assessments made on Southeast Asia. In opposition to such arguments, both officials and outside observers called for a more rational approach to foreign policy that would enable an independent position. Within the region, moral obligations and previous unwritten arrangements should be replaced by more solid, treaty-based arrangements. All fields were

[16] *McDougall*, Australia and the British Military Withdrawal, 191 f.

[17] *Andrea Benvenuti/Moreen Dee*, The Five Power Defence Arrangements and the Reappraisal of the British and Australian Policy Interests in Southeast Asia, 1970–75, in: Journal of Southeast Asian Studies 41/1, 2010, 101–123.

combined in discussions on appropriate concepts of a 'national', independent foreign policy. During and following the East of Suez discussions, alternative models without a British presence in Southeast Asia were discussed that ultimately allowed to cope with the British decision.

Throughout those years, all three countries considered forms of international commitment that relied less on Britain and more on other institutions (such as the Commonwealth) or an own 'national' interest in international affairs. Moreover, a certain dichotomy between Britain and the 'nation' was established during the discussions that resulted from the demise of British power, the advent of new policymakers and a changed demographic. These discussions will be dealt with in Chapter 5.1. The readjustment following the British decision also resulted in a transition from the previous framework of great power alliances to a multilateralist foreign policy.[18] In all three former dominions, the concepts of regional and global responsibility helped shape new partnerships, commitments and self-perceptions detached from the former British framework. These new outlooks will be analysed on a strategic, more regional-focused level in Chapter 5.2, and a value-based, supra-regional level in Chapter 5.3.

5.1 Towards a New Nationalism in Foreign Policy and Defence

Over the experiences in dealing with the British over East of Suez, many Australian and New Zealand policymakers started to challenge the concept of Commonwealth cooperation based on trust and mutual obligation. Similarly, Canada reviewed the need for continued British ties in a period of serious uncertainty which stemmed from changes in British and American foreign policy. Official and public debates now questioned the foundations of cooperating with the Western allies, a policy established in the post-war period. Britain was no longer a 'mother', the USA no longer a 'brother' or 'cousin'. Over the question of foreign policy and diplomacy, but also over the idea of forward defence and intervention, all three countries assessed their former security frameworks. For the first time, Australia and New Zealand came to fundamentally review their defence concept as detached from any greater, more powerful ally. At the same time, the analogy of family ties was now applied among the dominions themselves, estimating how much of previous modes of cooperation they could transfer onto their closest partners in the 'Old' Commonwealth.

---

[18] *Gary Smith/Dave Cox/Scott Burchill*, Australia in the World. An Introduction to Australian Foreign Policy, Oxford 2005, 95.

5.1.1 Public and Departmental Discussions on a More Self-Reliant Foreign and Defence Policy, 1967–1968

Despite large departmental support for it, doubts in a sentimental approach to Britain over East of Suez started to show after July 1967. In the emotionally charged atmosphere following Britain's first decision, the *Listener* asked its readers "'Who do we think we are?'".[19] So far, sentiment had prevented an adjustment to the world New Zealand was living in. According to the editorial's author, this had not been a wrong position if sentiment coincided with self-interest. But with Britain's interest diverging and no "close relative" around, not even Australia, sentiment would be bad guidance in future operations: "There can be no sentimental response to anything as nasty and as complicated as the war now raging in Asia. If we are to be part of it, it must be on the basis of reason and cold calculations."[20] In one of the following issues, a reader, who called himself a "loyal New Zealander", applauded the spirit of this article and urged to use current issues with Britain as an opportunity to "replace sentiment by clear thought and a tightened belt".[21] The editorial underlines how public criticism grew as British officials seemed to be unresponsive to arguments of kith and kinship.

Similar apprehensions towards sentiment were voiced in the Australian public. In reporting on the difficulties particularly older Australians showed in adapting to a changed relationship with Britain, the *Australian Financial Review* commented: "Regarded in human terms, some of the confuse emotionalism which now surrounds the whole subject of Anglo-Australian relations would suggest a very neurotic state of mind bordering on paranoia."[22] The newspaper blamed Australians not to have seen the signs of Britain's turn to Europe and discarded the entire emotional base of the discussion that was exemplified by representatives such as Alexander Downer: "The continued campaign to denigrate Britain's policy towards Europe is at best neurotic and at worst cynically self-seeking."[23]

Most critical comments targeted the government's insistence on emotions, especially the sentimental ties towards Britain. As the New Zealand *Sunday Times* judged, these emotions were increasingly regarding as inhibiting an activist approach: "The 'regret' the Prime Minister expressed at Britain's decision to halve its military forces in Singapore and Malaysia is a useless reaction, and

---

19 "Who Do We Think We Are?", New Zealand Listener, 11.8.1967.

20 Ibid.

21 *George Jennings*, Letter to Editor on Editorial "Who Do We Think We Are?", New Zealand Listener, 1.9.1967.

22 "A Case for Dr Freud?", The Australian Financial Review, 23.10.1967.

23 Ibid.; see also *Stuart Ward*, Sir Alexander Downer and the Embers of British Australia, in: Carl Bridge/Frank Bongiorno/David Lee (Ed.), The High Commissioners: Australia's Representatives in the United Kingdom, 1910–2010, Barton 2010, 145–163, 153.

too typical of the way we are facing reverses."[24] To the public, their officials had missed the opportunity to focus on Australia's and New Zealand's position in regards to the British development, relying for too long on ideas of shared obligations and ties. Many comments judged the departmental work as having failed to make timely arrangements: "If Canberra really was surprised by the modest and well-heralded British plans for a withdrawal of forces east of Suez, then its foreign affairs machinery can only be described as a disaster."[25] Such public criticism was paralleled by attacks from the political opposition. In July 1967, Gough Whitlam criticised Holt's government for its passivity regarding the British reviews, given "[…] the signs have been clear for a very long time".[26]

In New Zealand, political opposition was less outspoken as Leader of Opposition Norman Kirk agreed with Keith Holyoake's government in his support of British ties. Although he had tentatively welcomed the British decision as an opportunity to revise the objectives of a presence in Southeast Asia[27], he stuck more than his Australian counterpart to traditional alliance-based defence structures. When the New Zealand Labour Party (NLP) voted in May 1968 against membership in SEATO, Kirk and other party leaders were quick in defending the alliance. Similarly, he also resisted party motions that favoured an early retreat from Malaysia.[28]

The public criticism corresponded in parts to departmental demands for policy review. In Australia, senior public servants such as James Plimsoll or John Bunting urged Australian ministers to consider what Australia's policy would be in reaction to the British defence plans.[29] In most of these requests, autonomy over Australia's policymaking and a need for principles of foreign policy in times of uncertainty were the main arguments.

In New Zealand, an internal paper had already called in 1965 for a readjustment of foreign policy and defence objectives. Given the uncertainty created by signs of a British withdrawal from the area, foreign policy should focus on national rather than alliance objectives: "[…] if this geographically and racially divided country were ever to be attacked by the dissolvent processes which

24 "East of Suez", Sunday Times, 23.7.1967.

25 "New look in political arrogance", The Australian Financial Review, 28.7.1967.

26 NAA (Sydney), M157 (Gough Whitlam Papers), Box 38/27, Malaysia, Press Statement by Gough Whitlam, 19.7.1967.

27 "Good Move Says Kirk", New Zealand Herald, 20.7.1967.

28 *David McCraw*, Staying in Singapore? New Zealand's Third Labour Government and the Retention of Military Forces in Southeast Asia, in: New Zealand Journal of Asian Studies 14/1, 2012, 1–17, 3.

29 NAA A1838 TS3006/10/4/1, Part 4, Plimsoll to Hasluck, n. d. (~ Aug. 1967); for Bunting's various requests for clarification of Britain's position see NAA A4940 C1473 Part 3, Bunting to Holt, 25.8.1967 or Bunting to Holt, 28.9.1967.

have often succeeded elsewhere, many may wish that attention had been given to pointing out not only what was bad but also what must be defended."[30] Therefore, "It would be a strengthen for New Zealand, in the search for an identity which the British withdrawal into Europe imposes upon her, to have certain nationally accepted, fixed points."[31] This particular paper resurfaced in the policy discussions following Britain's decision in early 1968, indicating the increased level of departmental thinking on the issue.[32]

Aside from departmental briefs, diplomatic petitions accompanied the policymaking process. Former and current diplomats called for a review of longstanding principles of foreign policy.[33] These calls were backed by public requests for better diplomatic representation in Southeast Asia. "Woe-fully inadequate representation"[34], as the *Evening Post* described it in November 1967, would not help to establish New Zealand's distinct position in the region. Similarly, the traditional conduct of being represented by either Britain or Australia in areas where New Zealand had no own post was now criticised.[35] Equally, doubts about current policy practice were voiced by defence officials. Aside from criticism of ad-hoc planning, it was mostly the reliance on the British logistic framework that caused frequent discussions in the defence departments.[36]

The following considerations increasingly linked the New Zealand presence to questions of self-sufficiency and independence. Already in 1966, a broadcast had urged the New Zealand government to spend more on defence, not only to keep New Zealand's alliances, but also to please growing demands of nationhood.[37] In March 1967, George Laking compared the developments in Asian nationalism as paralleling "a smaller revolution in our own country. I mean our own awakening to full nationhood."[38] He further emphasised how recent devel-

---

[30] ANZ ABHS W4628 6957, Box 21, SAI 63/1/1, Part 1, "New Zealand Foreign Policy", Paper by J. V. Wilson, 1965.

[31] Ibid.

[32] See further documents on New Zealand's foreign policy in ANZ ABHS W4628 6957, Box 21, SAI 63/1/1, Part 1.

[33] "Changing Perspectives for New Zealand in Asia", Speech given by George Laking, 13.3.1967 (found in ANZ ABHS W4628 6957, Box 21, SAI 63/1/1, Part 1); further discussions among civil servants and diplomats in ANZ ABHS W5631 22310, Box 193, PAR 222/1/1, Part 2.

[34] Evening Post, 14.11.1967, quoted in: *James Kember*, New Zealand Diplomatic Representation in Southeast Asia: The 1950s and 1960s, in: New Zealand Journal of Asian Studies 11/1, 2009, 385–401, 385.

[35] ANZ ABHS W5402 18069, Box 119, BRU 64/1/6, NHC Canberra, 17.6.1968.

[36] ANZ AAFD W3738 811, Box 1312, CAB 222/1/1, "New Zealand Defence Policy", NDEA Paper (D (67) 10), 11.9.1967.

[37] *J. L. Roberts*: "Defence of New Zealand", New Zealand Broadcast "Lookout", 29.1.1966, found in: ANZ ABHS W4628 7148, Box 117, LONB 106/3 Part 1.

[38] ANZ ABHS W4628 6957, Box 21, SAI 63/1/1, Part 1, "Changing Perspectives for New Zealand in Asia", Speech given by George Laking, 13.3.1967.

opments such as Britain's imminent retreat from Southeast Asia had instilled a sense of urgency to come to a more self-reliant foreign policy outlook.

Laking's references on the question of nationhood, reiterated in further speeches, were picked up by newspapers. In July 1967, the *Listener* presented a domestic transition from a British to a more self-reliant cultural framework as being driven by international developments: "We are learning the hard way that there are powerful countries and overseas financial interest ready to push us around if we let them. […] Our response to the pressures being exerted will determine our destiny (And if we really must have one) our national character."[39] The already mentioned editorial *Who do we think we are?* had tried to make sense of events along similar lines: "[…] perhaps we shall have to confront the prospect of a sad and permanent decline in our fortunes before we completely replace sentiment with reason, the capacity to react with the ability to respond. Perhaps after all, we are not quite a nation. If not, we must hurry to become one."[40] Both editorials revealed the growing link drawn between rationality and independence, and corresponded to ideas of national cohesion in the face of outside pressure.

In reverse, arguments of kith and kin were increasingly linked to immaturity. In January 1968, a reader of the *Listener* expressed his anger, not at the British, "but the politicians who have been happy to disguise their lack of foresight by staking their hopes for the future on the motherland they sentimentally idealize."[41] Others argued that because of the sentimental attachment, policymakers had dismissed demands for alternative defence arrangements. The *Christchurch Star* judged:

"New Zealand has not yet realised how drastically this country will be affected by the British withdrawal to Europe. The sense of complacent security, based on British might, has been so deep-seated since the earliest days of European settlement that its pending disappearance has plunged this country into a state of traumatic shock, one symptom of which is reluctance, even in the highest places, to look the facts squarely in the face."[42]

Increasingly, public comments criticised that officials had taken the British relationship for granted. Similarly, also Australian media demanded an adjustment in foreign policy. Here, the newspaper *Bulletin* published a series calling for a new, more rationalised approach to British relations shortly after the January decision. As the tensions over recent British foreign policy had been caused by the preferential treatment of affairs with Britain, the High Commissioner in London should now "approach his appointment as if Britain were Thailand, or Nigeria, or Korea – a country that is different from his own, that he must

39 "A Surfeit of Self", New Zealand Listener, 17.11.1967.
40 "Who Do We Think We Are?", New Zealand Listener, 11.8.1967.
41 *Owen Gager*, Letter to Editor, New Zealand Listener, 23.2.1968.
42 "Prime Minister's Job", Christchurch Star, 2.3.1968.

study for its peculiarities, and toward which he must maintain a certain detachment".[43] The *Bulletin* featured another article which reviewed options for improvement in Anglo-Australian relations. Instead of "old sycophancy", Australians should adapt "a skilful use of honesty rather than flattery" so British elites "are not condescending to us but see us as cousins".[44] Traversing different areas of foreign policy, the author closed his article with a call for constitutional detachment that would include symbols such as the national flag, anthem and even the Queen:

"[…] the change in Australian attitudes to Britain that began when Singapore fell in 1942 has accelerated in the last few years, and particularly in the last few months. However, while it is now something on which most people are likely to agree at a cocktail party, there is still a slowness to contemplate the full implications of our mutual drifting away. It may only be when the forms and ceremonies of Australian national life are completely de-Anglicised that we shall fully act as a nation that understands where in the world it is."[45]

As these articles argued, rather than continuing in an unequal relationship, Australia's international interests would be better served with an independent national outlook. This outlook should be defined as independent of Britain. The British decision and Southeast Asia as an area of commitment seemed to offer the chance to establish an own identity, with papers like the *Sunday Telegraph* celebrating this opportunity: "While we painfully find out that the withdrawal of the British from Malaysia will pose us for the first time in our history with difficult problems which we must decide entirely for ourselves, we now have the ability to make at least limited commitments on our own initiative."[46]

The growing link between an opportunity to establish independent policies and a national identity also became visible in the rhetoric of new Australian Prime Minister John Gorton. After his election following the tragic loss of Harold Holt, Gorton soon received a reputation for being both non-conformist and individualist, and in a symbolic distinction from his predecessors he called himself "Australian to the bootheels".[47] His open scepticism towards the British ties certainly caused diplomatic concern, as he confused counterparts such as British High Commissioner Johnston with blunt statements on a "drifting apart"[48] of the Anglo-Australian relationship. Upon meeting Alexander Downer in early 1969, he told the Australian High Commissioner:

"Britain […] had become for Australians a foreign country: we must treat her as such. Historically, the score was even. We had been settled, and developed, behind the shield of

[43] "Our man in London: be hard-headed" (Comment by 'Observer'), The Bulletin, 27.1.1968.
[44] "Backing away from Britain?", The Bulletin, 2.3.1968.
[45] Ibid.
[46] Editorial quoted in: TNA FCO 24/189, BHC Canberra 658, 20.5.1968.
[47] *Downer*, Six Prime Ministers, 114.
[48] TNA FCO 24/189, BHC Canberra (Johnston), 1.8.1968.

the Royal navy for one hundred and twenty years. In return we had volunteered unstinted support during the two World Wars, as well as earlier colonial wars in the nineteenth century. Now the British were withdrawing all military support as well as moving towards Europe economically and politically. The old links were breaking: sentiment alone could not sustain our association."[49]

Downer disagreed with this assessment, and was relieved when Gorton seemed to change his attitude during his visit to London.[50] Nevertheless, Gorton reiterated this position when he told Wilson during talks that Australia would treat the relations with Britain as similar to those with other foreign countries.[51]

Gorton's attitude towards Britain was strongly influenced by what would become known as 'new nationalism', a political rhetoric calling for a more self-reliant national identity. Over the course of his term, he proclaimed that Australia would need a new self-definition: "For so long we stood not really as a nation in our own right, but as a nation the people of whom spoke of 'home' and meant another nation, meant Great Britain [...] it is essential that we should develop a feeling of nationhood [...] I hope you will all help me in the years ahead to foster this feeling of real nationalism."[52] On another occasion, he spoke of the need to instil "a real sense of Australianism".[53] At the same time, Gorton's statements lacked a clear idea of what kind of Australian nation he envisaged, a fact noted by influential observers such as Donald Horne.[54] Gorton followed Holt's policies of lessening restrictions to non-European immigration and supporting the Australian arts[55]; however, he had no cohesive picture to offer for Australian nationhood. Therefore, it makes sense to follow Coral Bell's assessment of his term: "It seems appropriate that a period of ambivalences was under the governance of a man who often seemed to be in two minds (and to swing rather rapidly between the two), and who was certainly the most unexpected and 'maverick' of Australia's post-war prime ministers."[56]

The term 'maverick' certainly also applied to Canada's new Prime Minister Pierre Elliott Trudeau who entered office a couple of months after John Gorton in June 1968. Like no leader before him, Trudeau symbolised the departure into a new era of politics, both on a domestic and international level. During his campaign, he met expectations with a programmatic call for a foreign policy fo-

[49] Quoted in: *Downer*, Six Prime Ministers, 115.

[50] *Ward*, Alexander Downer, 155.

[51] TNA FCO 24/284/1, Meeting of Harold Wilson with John Gorton, London, 7.1.1969, in: *Ashton/Bridge/Ward*, DAFP, 293–297.

[52] The Bulletin, 5.10.1968, quoted in: *Curran/Ward*, Unknown Nation, 6.

[53] Quoted in: *Curran*, Power of Speech, 63.

[54] Donald Horne: New Nationalism; quoted in: *James Curran*, The "Thin Dividing Line". Prime Ministers and the Problem of Australian Nationalism, 1972–1996, in: Australian Journal of Politics & History 48/4, 2002, 469–486, 473.

[55] *Mann*, Leavening British Traditions, 53.

[56] *Bell*, Dependent Ally, 80.

cusing on national interests: "We wish to take a fresh look at the fundamentals of Canadian foreign policy to see whether there are ways in which we can serve more effectively Canada's current interests, objectives and priorities."[57] While this call for national interests was also designed as a robust response to the issue of Quebec separatism[58], Trudeau initiative for a new international direction was largely motivated by misgivings on the previous foreign policy, and would also cover the Anglo-Canadian relationship.

When it came to the British relationship, Trudeau's attitudes were remarkably different from his predecessors. His experiences and networks established during his studies at the London School of Economics apparently did not engrain the same sense of Britishness as similar experiences did in Lester Pearson.[59] With the departure of Pearson, CDEA officials bemoaned the loss of one of the true experts on the Anglo-Canadian relationship: "[...] a person who, by training and by nature, was able to follow events in Britain and interpret them for himself; he did this both as a professional diplomat who had served in London and as an historian imbued with a deep sense of British constitutionalism."[60] Just as Gorton in Australia, Trudeau would also introduce new policymakers who would share most of the demographic appearance of their predecessors while being less devoted to the British relationship.[61]

This shift in Canadian priorities was also communicated to British officials. In talks with new CSSEA Mitchell Sharp in October 1968, British High Commissioner Colin Crowe learnt that Canada welcomed a revised, less sentiment-based relationship with Britain, as Sharp indicated with reference to the new Canadian flag: "The Union Jack in the corner of the old flag had distorted attitudes towards the United Kingdom in this country but now we could look at each other in a much more clear-eyed and equal way."[62] Sharp also baffled British official Paul Gore-Booth when he asked that the more Britain "could treat Canada as a country with whom we had close relations but of a kind of similar to our relations with other countries, the better it would be for both sides".[63] Gore-Booth challenged Sharp's request by stating that Canada would still assume a

57 Speech given by Pierre Elliott Trudeau, Statements and Speeches 68/17, 29.5.1968, quoted in: *Bruce Thordarson*, Cutting Back on NATO, 1969, in: Don Munton/John J. Kirton (Ed.), Canadian Foreign Policy: Selected Cases, Scarborough 1992, 174–188, 174.

58 *Mary Halloran/John Hilliker/Greg Donaghy*, The White Paper Impulse. Reviewing Foreign Policy Under Trudeau and Clark, in: International Journal: Canada's Journal of Global Policy Analysis 70/2, 2015, 309–321.

59 *MacLaren*, Commissions High, 514.

60 LAC RG25 A-3-c, Vol. 10042, 20-1-2-BRIT, Commonwealth Div. to various divisions, 4.3.1968.

61 *Donaghy*, Canadian Diplomat, 52 f.

62 TNA FCO 68/38, BHC Ottawa (Crowe), 24.10.1968.

63 TNA FCO 63/28, Paul Gore-Booth to Denis Allen (FCO), 16.11.1968. Sharp's request was buttressed by public demands for such a new footing of relations, see e. g. *Charles Lynch*, "Advantages in Being Equal", Ottawa Citizen, 3.12.1968.

special position in Britain's outlook: "[...] there is a regard for Canada arising from history which is not the same as our sentiments towards, say, Italy."[64]

British officials realised that Canadians were eager to set their relationship with Britain on a new footing. Consequently, officials like Crowe called for a review of Anglo-Canadian relations:

"Both of us insists that the old parental relationship has gone and that we treat each other as equals, but neither of us has tried to think out what sort of relationship should succeed the old. It seems to me that we have tended to take each other for granted and therefore have been mutually hurt and stressed when one has done something which the other has not liked."[65]

The similarities to arguments discussed in Australia and New Zealand on taking the 'Old' Commonwealth relationship for granted are remarkable. As Crowe assessed the implications of a new Canadian outlook that has less regard for special ties with Britain, he agreed in parts with Sharp to consider the relationship as based on 'rational' principles constituted with every other foreign country: "We should aim for an ordinary relationship plus instead of an old Commonwealth relationship minus as it were. I suggest this would be to our benefit both psychologically and in giving us a clearer idea of our objectives. We need to brush the tears from our eyes – they tend to blur the sight."[66]

Crowe outlined this argument further in a following report. While there existed several ties to Britain, officials should consider the impact of recent diverging attitudes: "Day to day consultation, bilaterally and in the multilateral organizations remains close, and mutual trust still pervades the relationship. Mutual understanding and agreement, on the other hand, have long ceased to be automatic, even on matters of major interest."[67] To keep Canada committed, e.g. to the Atlantic Community, Crowe recommended focusing on Britain's own interests: "This may mean on occasions a stiffer defence of our interests in Canada than has been customary in the past."[68] With these arguments, Crowe aligned himself with recent thinking in other parts of the former British Empire, not least in Australia and New Zealand, that discharged emotional appeals to common bonds as outdated and inefficient.

At the same time, his remarks indicate a certain unease about deprioritising Commonwealth relations for national interests. The difficulties in choosing between Commonwealth and Britain had also shown within the organisation. Throughout the 1960s, British officials had felt wrongfully charged over their position on African decolonisation, and concluded that emotions within the organisation would only prove politically harmful. As a consequence, they de-

64 TNA FCO 63/28, Paul Gore-Booth to Denis Allen (FCO), 16.11.1968.

65 TNA FCO 63/28, BHC Ottawa (Crowe) to Denis Allen (FCO), 28.11.1968.

66 Ibid.

67 TNA FCO 68/38, BHC Ottawa (Crowe) to Denis Allen (FCO), 9.12.1968.

68 Ibid.

emphasised the sentimental relationship within the institution.[69] In parts, this change of attitude was entwined with the merger of the CRO and FO, where officials argued that Commonwealth relations were no longer privileged and intimate and therefore could be conducted under one roof dedicated to all foreign affairs.[70] Further reviews like the Duncan Report published in 1969 also pointed away from a British world role and focused on ties towards Europe.[71]

Following this British 'pragmatisation' of international relations, Australia and Canada took administrative steps themselves. The Canadian government decided in 1971 to transfer its United Kingdom desk from the Commonwealth to the European Division, causing anger with officials such as Charles Ritchie, who opposed the CDEA's position that "Britain was considered peripheral to our interests and placed in an 'And others' category".[72] In Australia, the administrative transfer of Australia House from the APMD to the ADEA was discussed since 1971. When officials like Alexander Downer, and parts of the APMD protested this step, new Prime Minister William McMahon chose a compromise. While the APMD would control specific features such as the relations with the Crown and the Commonwealth, the remainder of relations was transferred to the ADEA.[73]

Australia's announcement on the future authority of Australia House in October 1972 coincided with Britain's third and successful bid for EEC entry.[74] How much relations had already changed between Britain and its former dominions was now indicated by largely muted reactions to this step, contrasting the heated reactions to Britain's previous applications. Both Canada and Australia adopted the official position that the decision ultimately lay with Britain, but that they nevertheless would wish for a safeguard of their national interests. Only New Zealand would continue to advocate strongly for an appreciation of its economic difficulties.[75]

5.1.2 *Involvement or Isolationism after the British Withdrawal?*

Aside from departmental restructuring and calls for foreign policy reviews, policymakers considered a defence review as equally urgent in the face of a Brit-

---

69 *Lloyd*, Us and Them, 24.

70 TNA FCO 77/3/1, Saville Garner: "The Future of the Commonwealth Office and Foreign Office: A Personal View", 2.2.1967, quoted in: *Cullen*, Kenya and Britain, 41.

71 *John W. Young*, Twentieth-Century Diplomacy. A Case Study of British Practice 1963–1976, Cambridge 2008, 42–45.

72 Charles Ritchie to CUSSEA, 29.3.1971, quoted in: *MacLaren*, Commissions High, 516.

73 *Ward*, Alexander Downer, 159–161.

74 ANZ ABHS W4627 950, Box 3812, 203/3/6, Part 2, Press Statement by Australian Prime Minister William McMahon, 25.10.1972.

75 For the contextualisation and analysis of the dominions' attitude to the third EEC bid I am happy to refer to the work of my colleague Clara Seltmann; *Seltmann*, Butter, Wut und Tränen.

ish retreat. Although some officials had tried to initiate a discussion on forward defence in the years before[76], a thorough discussion was only commenced following the British decision in January 1968. Now, two positions dominated the discussion. Adopting an isolationist perspective, one side was soon summarised under the term 'Fortress Australia'[77], subsuming different notions of territorial defence to denounce Australia's forward defence policy. It was opposed by a policy of continued intervention that supported an active overseas policy under the labels of forward defence and containment.

In late-1968, the journal *Australia's Neighbours* featured a joint editorial on both positions. One side was represented by political scientist Max Teichmann, who argued for a withdrawal from Southeast Asia. He favoured armed neutrality, a concept which, aside from criticising the American position of containment, subsumed ideas of allowing defence expenses only for Australia's own protection.[78] The other side in support of forward presence was advocated by journalist and political scientist Bruce Grant. To Grant, forward presence would mean the continued support for non-communist governments in a general effort for regional stability. However, he also linked it to a review of Australia's security policy.[79] While both academics differed on the use of military presence in the region, they nevertheless agreed on the need for a review. Desired was a more independent foreign and defence policy that was less determined by, as Teichmann coined it, "the All the Way-Where you go, we go, policy"[80] in support of Britain and the USA.

Similarly, among the departments, attitudes on forward defence were divided. A tendency for staying on was visible in overseas missions in the region and within the armed services. Australia House, the APMD and the ADEA were more concerned with the ongoing political discussions and therefore chose a cautious or opposed position to underwrite a continued presence. In politics, John Gorton again represented the ambiguities shown in the defence discussions. Following the British decision for withdrawal, he had unsettled Australian policymakers when he gave support to a 'Fortress Australia' policy instead of forward defence.[81] His controversial statements on defence, ranging from

[76] See e.g. NAA A1209 1965/6124, Paper on the British Defence Review by AMD, 17.6.1965.

[77] The term was equally used by New Zealand policymakers, a further indication of how interwoven continental defence was perceived by both countries.

[78] *Max Teichmann*, Australian Defence: Two Views, 1968. II. Disengagement, in: Australia's Neighbours 4/52–53, 1968, 4–8; see also *M. Grattan*, Armed Neutrality – A Foreign Policy for Australia, in: Australian Quarterly, Dec. 1968, 44–56, 46 f.

[79] *Bruce Grant*, Australian Defence: Two Views, 1968. I. Regional Role, in: Australia's Neighbours 4/52–53, 1968, 1–4.

[80] *Teichmann*, Australian Defence, 4.

[81] *Matthews/Ravenhill*, Adrift in an Alien Sea, 174; *Westbrook*, Foreign Policy Review, 94 f.

an "Israeli-type"[82] of continental defence force to his awkward charming of Richard Nixon by stating that "wherever the United States is resisting aggression [...] then we will go Waltzing Matilda with you"[83] in 1969, represented the disorientation in the highest office on how Australia perceived both its defence premises and the necessary framework of alliances and self-reliance.

Official uncertainty and indecision also reflected in departmental ranks, with some officials demanding a swift and thorough review of Australia's security concepts: "The fundamental question for Australia is whether we intend to play a positive and sustained part in shaping arrangements for security in Asia, notwithstanding the British disengagement."[84] Other officials pointed to the complexities of the issues involved: "The determination of new policies may take some little time, especially as I got the impression that the full implications of what is happening have not yet been really assessed."[85] During an ADC meeting in May 1968, James Plimsoll emphasised the lack of direction in policy-making circles, specifically on how to reconcile the various strands of public demands with a substantially 'new' outlook that should follow Britain's withdrawal.[86]

Australian policymakers felt the pressure to review their strategic framework, a position confirmed by the annual *Strategic Basis for Australian Defence* paper published in August 1968:

> "[...] we could hardly assert that this forward defence concept represents an independent strategy of our own. Rather it has been a case that we have deliberately, doubtless in our own interests and perhaps inescapably, tied Australia to the strategy of others. We have had such a tradition first to fit comfortably into British strategy and more recently in that of the US."[87]

Despite these doubts, officials recommended continuing a policy of flexibility for the time being. The demand for such flexibility had also been the outcome of changes in American policy after the Tet Offensive in spring 1968. Johnson's announcement for a halt of bombing as well as the American military defeat unsettled Australian officials.[88] In addition, the following shift in US policy served deep-seated fears of American isolationism. As Peter Howson noted in his diary: "[...] to my mind it's the first step of the Americans moving out of South east Asia and [...] within a few years, there'll be no white face on the

[82] *Curran*, Unholy Fury, 90; *Murphy*, Harvest of Fear, 203.

[83] Quoted in: *Edwards*, Nation at War, 202.

[84] NAA M3787, File 53, "Australia's Role in Asian Security", Australian Cabinet Submission No. 8, 24.1.1968.

[85] NAA A1838 229/9/9/2, Part 2, Draft Letter Paul Hasluck to Paul Martin, n. d. (February 1968).

[86] NAA A1838 TS677/3, Part 12, Report by James Plimsoll on ADC Meeting, 10.5.1968.

[87] "Strategic Basis of Australian Defence Policy 1968" (DC No 27/1968), ADC Report, 14.8.1968; in: *Ashton/Bridge/Ward*, DAFP, 284–286, 286.

[88] *Edwards*, Nation at War, 192 f.; *Horner*, Strategic Command, 287.

Asian mainland [...] from now on, and to a much greater extent, we shall be isolated and on our own."[89]

Again, officials feared to be left alone in the area, even more so as they were still waiting for an American response to the British withdrawal plans. After they had left a list of questions with American officials in July 1967 that should enable an American confirmation of Australia's commitments in Malaysia and Singapore under the ANZUS umbrella, the Australian Embassy Washington only received answers in late January 1968. While Americans were unwilling to underwrite the security of Australian troops in the region, they expressed their appreciation for a continued Australian role:

"Although Australia (and New Zealand) cannot either assume the full responsibility of the British or fully replace the military capabilities which will be withdrawn, we believe that continued arrangements for augmenting Malaysian and Singapore forces with Australian (and New Zealand) armed forces would both have a valuable stabilizing influence within the region and symbolize outside concern with the area."[90]

The ambivalence of that statement was neither lost on Australian nor New Zealand officials. Latter felt they had yet again witnessed a failed Australian approach for closer cooperation.[91]

Other New Zealand briefs supported the doubt in any deeper American interest in the issue. Following Britain's January decision, New Zealand's Embassy in Washington underlined that it had often emphasised the importance, but also the lack of intimacy in the relations with the USA, especially as US officials were not willing to share information: "The result, in the case of Australia and New Zealand, is a shallow relationship from which understanding of our problems and a real impulse to assist is often missing. [...] One can take too cosy and nostalgic a view, but on the whole the British did take us into their confidence."[92] For New Zealanders, relations with Britain still served as a role model, despite recent frictions. Moreover, the triangular relationship in ANZUS combined with Australian neglect for Tasman coordination had produced a New Zealand perception of holding a junior position within the alliance.

As the American shift came on the heels of the British decision in early 1968, New Zealand officials addressed the lack of consideration for allied interests: "There are ties of sentiment: but we have had in the recent weeks a useful reminder of their intrinsic strength. Certainly if the British were not influenced in their decision by the past we have even less reason to think that the forward-looking Americans might be."[93] Clearly, these officials doubted the rela-

[89] *Howson/Aitkin*, Howson Diaries, 415.

[90] NAA M3787, File 53, AEmb. Washington 261, 18.1.1968.

[91] ANZ ABHS W4627 950, Box 4506, 434/8/1, Part 18, Memorandum for Keith Holyoake by George Laking, 1.2.1968.

[92] ANZ ABHS W5422 950, Box 34, 111/3/3/15, Part 7, NEmb. Washington 84, 18.1.1968.

[93] ANZ ABHS W5422 950, Box 34, 111/3/3/15, Part 7, NDEA Paper, 11.3.1968.

tions with both countries; in the case of the USA, they furthermore suspected Americans to hold information back, especially on Vietnam. Such suspicions would be ultimately vindicated when the Pentagon Papers were published in the summer of 1971, revealing the lack of information the ANZUS partners received on the long-term American policy over the years.[94]

Like Australians, also New Zealanders discussed continuing forward presence with confusion and switching positions due to doubts in their partners' agendas. Here, officials were equally challenged by notions of isolationism produced in domestic debates. In a speech given in May 1967, George Laking strongly repudiated calls for international retreat and underlined that New Zealand was "not an inward looking nation": "It may have something to do with our past as part of a world-wide empire; it may be because in two world wars and many other smaller conflicts we have sent our young men across the world to fight in the defence of others."[95] Similarly, officials like Malcolm Templeton strongly advocated for a continued forward defence in "an age of shrinking geography", and argued isolationism would limit "the politico-strategic means we and our allies have to influence developments."[96] However, New Zealand's public attitude seemed to favour a position of isolation, with several newspapers promoting a 'Fortress Australia' policy by pointing to the continued instability of the Southeast Asian region.[97] Moreover, political commentators could use strong emotional strands of distance and remoteness in the New Zealand fabric to support a policy of isolation or "unarmed neutrality".[98]

While policymakers had been challenged on forward defence before, it was with the British decision in January 1968 that public criticism of the concept grew substantially. In April 1968, commentators used the annual SEATO Council Meeting being hosted in Wellington to criticise the government's policy. Aside from various critical newspaper articles[99], a protest movement organised the *Peace, Power and Politics Conference* as an alternative space of foreign policy debate.[100] Afterwards, former government officials and political scientists entered the public discussion, among them the former New Zealand Secretary of Defence (NSD) Jack Hunn. In an article for the *Listener* in May 1968,

---

94 NLNZ 92–258, 04/16, Ralph Mullins to George Laking, 2.8.1971.

95 ANZ ABHS W4628 6957, Box 21, SAI 63/1/1, Part 1, "Development of Foreign Policy", Speech by George Laking to the Royal Commonwealth Society Christchurch, 10.6.1967.

96 ANZ ABHS W5242 950, Box 34, 85/1/1, Part 13, Templeton to New Zealand Defence Liaison Staff (NDLS) London (Robertson), 26.6.1968.

97 "Ill-Prepared for Vital Defence Decisions", Auckland Star, 10.6.1968.

98 *Alan Robinson*, Trends in Australian-New Zealand Relations, in: Australian Quarterly 41/1, 1969, 43–51, 44.

99 "SEATO has very Limited Uses", Auckland Star, 1.4.1968; Nicholas Turner: "Is SEATO Just a Paper Tiger?", Evening Post, 6.4.1968.

100 *McKinnon*, Independence and Foreign Policy, 202.

Hunn challenged New Zealand's premises of alliance security: "Cool analysis leaves one with an uneasy feeling that our defence strategy, however valid it may have been in the past, is both impracticable and provocative for the future."[101] Instead, he proposed to abandon SEATO and to focus on a constructive role in the UN and the cooperation with Australia. At the same time, he supported integrating the ANZUS treaty as part of a "qualified alignment"[102], a general alliance with the USA and other Western powers that would not automatically result in military commitments.

Hunn's public statement resulted in various responses. One reader hailed his article for the injection of "a healthy dose of realism into a situation where official obfuscation and double think largely prevailed before".[103] Others welcomed his 'constructive defence' as an invitation to reach a continental defence in conjuncture with Australia.[104] Critics of his suggestions essentially pointed to the continued need for Western security in the face of Asian instability. One reader called his proposal for 'Fortress Australia' unrealistic, given New Zealand's population size: "It would be indeed a very thin white line of heroes who would have to defend this area in association with something like the Canadian/United States D. E. W. (Defence Early Warning) line."[105] Journalist Ian Templeton criticised Hunn's apparent lack of concern for a Chinese threat, or the crucial lessons in New Zealand history: "Australia and New Zealand missed by hair's breadth being attacked in 1941 – and we certainly did not have the forces ready to cope alone with a direct attack."[106]

What transpires throughout the discussion surrounding Hunn's and other policy statements are various strands of thought on New Zealand's foreign policy. For one, New Zealand was engaging in a fundamental review of its own position in regional strategic concepts, a fact not lost on Australia and Canada.[107] Most of these discussions dwelled on the fact that New Zealand's relative size and its limited resources made a genuinely independent defence policy exceptionally hard to achieve, if not impossible. At the same time, critics like Hunn could dominate public debates, a fact that indicates both a lack of public confidence in official concepts of foreign policy as well as missing governmental voices to gather support for forward defence.

In Australia and Canada, department officials were equally challenged by former colleagues in their policy towards Southeast Asia. In Australia, form-

---

[101] *J. K. Hunn*, Constructive Defence, New Zealand Listener, 31.5.1968.

[102] Ibid.

[103] H. W. Youren to Editor, New Zealand Listener, 21.6.1968.

[104] *A. T. Arthur*, New Zealand Defence Policy, National Programme "Looking at Ourselves", 8.6.1968; found in: ANZ ABHS W4628 7148, Box 117, LONB 106/3, Part 1.

[105] McKinnon to Editor, New Zealand Listener, 25.6.1968.

[106] *Ian Templeton*, "Forward Strategy for NZ in Asia", Christchurch Star, 24.6.1968.

[107] "New Zealand's Forward Defence Plan to be changed", Canadian Press, 8.8.1968, found in: ANZ ABHS W5242 950, Box 34, 85/1/1, Part 13.

er departmental members such as Gregory Clark or Macmahon Ball[108], as well as historians such as Manning Clark and Geoffrey Serle, criticised the government's take on national defence as solely laying within great power alliances.[109] In Canada, former diplomats Escott Reid, Douglas LePan, and A. F. W. Plumptre issued a public call for a ceasefire in Vietnam in 1967.[110] The massive expansion of academic literature on foreign policy in the 1960s had also been acknowledged by the establishment of a section for academic relations within the CDEA in 1967.[111] There was little domestic opposition to Canada's non-committal position on Southeast Asia, a fact regularly drawn upon by critics of military intervention in Australia and New Zealand.[112] Yet all three governments faced growing criticism over their relations with the USA, Australia and New Zealand for their military support in Vietnam, Canada for its acquiescence to it. Here, vocal anti-Americanism matched Vietnam protest movements and criticism of neo-imperialism in other Western countries at the end of the 1960s.

As a result, public expectations for a change in foreign policy were visible throughout election campaigns in many Western countries. In Canada, they found their match with Pierre Trudeau, who developed into an intellectual 'poster boy' for other liberal politicians to follow. Not only did he enter office with a provocative criticism of current diplomatic and foreign policy practice[113], but his endorsement of controversial policy goals such as the recognition of China or nuclear disarmament also seemed to strike a nerve, especially with a young audience. In and outside of Canada, his term was anticipated as a transformative moment in Canadian foreign affairs, including its relations with the USA.

After entering office, Trudeau indeed invited a fundamental review of Canada's foreign and defence policy that would span two years up to the mid-1970s.[114] While this review expressed a new zeitgeist of foreign affairs, it was also a reaction to external developments. Like Australians and New Zealanders, Canadian officials realised the end of Western post-war reconstruction in the late 1960s,

[108] See e. g. William Macmahon Ball: "Australia's Role in Asia", Roy Milner Memorial Lecture Melbourne, Melbourne, 1.11.1967; found in: NLA MS7851 (Macmahon Ball Papers), Box 24, Series 9, Folder 50.

[109] *Ralph Pettman*, The Radical Critique and Australian Foreign Policy, in: Peter J. Boyce/J. R. Angel (Ed.), Independence and Alliance: Australia in World Affairs 1976–80, Sydney 1983.

[110] *Greg Donaghy*, Tolerant Allies. Canada and the United States, 1963–1968, Montreal 2002, 172; *Reid*, Radical Mandarin, 372 f.

[111] *Stairs*, Reviewing Foreign Policy, 195; *P. Dobell*, Canada in World Affairs, 1971–1973, Toronto 1985, 9 f.

[112] For example used by Gough Whitlam; *Curran*, Unholy Fury, 86.

[113] *Donaghy*, Canadian Diplomat, 50 f.

[114] *John English*, Just Watch Me: The Life of Pierre Elliott Trudeau. 2. Ed., Toronto 2009, 57–69; *Ivan L. Head/Pierre Elliott Trudeau*, The Canadian Way. Shaping Canada's Foreign Policy 1968–1984, Toronto 1995.

leading the focus away from Europe to other world areas.[115] While Canada's reviews of foreign policy pushed for the implementation of national interests, the corresponding defence reviews questioned the use of continued military commitment, most of all to NATO.[116] As they challenged previous alliance policies and brought departmental outsiders to contribute to the review process, the Trudeau government reacted to a crisis of professional culture that was also visible in Australia and New Zealand. In New Zealand, following Hunn's *Constructive Defence* article, one reader expressed resentment towards civil servants and their attitudes being mostly unknown to the public.[117] At the same time, public protest now focused on projects endangering New Zealand independence, such as the OMEGA project in 1968.[118] With strong public criticism, officials felt attacked by "a public who did not seem to believe that we can have the capacity for exercising independent judgement based on New Zealand's own national interests, since New Zealand was not continually striking 'independent' (i. e. anti-American) public attitudes".[119] Officials bemoaned that especially a younger audience would see them essentially as an American ally, with criticism of their role in Vietnam now spreading over to other issues of foreign policy.

5.1.3 Where to Turn in the Anglosphere? – Alternatives to a British or American Outlook

Caused by the public criticism and doubts about their policy framework, officials in all three countries reassessed their partnerships within the Anglosphere. Departmental briefs and reports on bilateral relations had been regular before, but now they were fed by the feeling of urgency and demand for alternatives. As Australian journalist Ian Moffitt commented, "Cousins with little interest in one another, who come together tentatively at family funerals"[120], they now felt the need to review their familiar relations. Had they all 'taken each other for granted' all this time?

Equally, all three countries were aware they shared similar effects and experiences in a transformative phase. When Pierre Trudeau published the out-

[115] *Stairs*, Reviewing Foreign Policy, 191.

[116] *Danford William Middlemiss/Joel J. Sokolsky*, Canadian Defence. Decisions and Determinants, Toronto 1989, 5.

[117] *Reader M. Weatherall* to Editor, New Zealand Listener, 21.6.1968.

[118] OMEGA was a worldwide navigation system for ships and aircraft under American control. In the late 1960s, the USA approached both the Australian and New Zealand government for a potential site for a transmitter, and ultimately chose a site in Australia. On New Zealand's governmental difficulties to handle the public protests against the project see "NZ's Omega Affair", Canberra Times, 20.7.1968.

[119] ANZ ABHS W4627 950, Box 770, 1/2/27, Part 6, Division Heads' Meeting, 9.8.1968.

[120] Ian Moffitt, The Australian, 25.5.1968, quoted in: *Lorne Kavic*, Canada and the Commonwealth. Sentiment, Symbolism and Self-Interest, in: Commonwealth Journal 65/257, 1975, 27–49, 43.

come of his foreign policy review in a colourful six-booklet publication with the title *Foreign Policy for Canadians* (FPC) printed in summer 1970, Australian and New Zealand officials observed the process and result carefully. While the substance and long-term scope of the booklets were limited[121], it was their proclamation of Canadian goals in foreign policy, such as social justice, equality and quality of life, which indicated a departure in policy thinking.[122] British High Commissioner George Whitehead explained that the value of the publication did not lay in its content,

> "[…] but in the process of analysis and self-education which the Review has imposed on Canadian officials and ministers, in regard to Canada's national interests, Canada's position in the present world, so different from that when the last review of foreign policy was conducted at the end of the war, the limitations on Canada's freedom of action in the world and what she can expect to achieve broadly in pursuit of her national interests and inclinations, within those limits."[123]

Since the paper indicated a turn away from traditional alliances, the New Zealand High Commission Ottawa commented that the review "does appear to mark the end of that unique era of internationalism which was the nation's trademark".[124]

While former Canadian policymakers, starting with Pearson himself, were opposed to the goals laid out by the review[125], Australia and New Zealand could welcome a new Canadian emphasis on the Pacific. Already before, Pierre Trudeau had announced that Canada would take "its ringside seat on the Pacific"[126] with an active policy. A year later, the Canadian Minister of Trade Jean-Luc Pepin toured the Pacific and fashioned the trip as a clear breakaway from old trade relations with Britain and the USA: "We are not saying goodbye to Europe, but the embrace is getting cooler."[127] While officials like Canadian High Commissioner John Hadwen celebrated Pepin's tour as a successful entry into the region[128], New Zealand officials hoped for closer relations between both countries, primarily to mitigate some of the consequences of the British and

---

121 *Halloran/Hilliker/Donaghy*, White Paper Impulse.

122 *Thordarson*, Cutting Back, 174f.; *Robert Bothwell/Jack L. Granatstein*, Trudeau's World. Insiders Reflect on Foreign Policy, Trade, and Defence, 1968–84, Vancouver 2017, 129.

123 TNA FCO 7/1773, Dispatch by BHC Ottawa (Whitehead), 26.8.1970.

124 ANZ ABHS W5761 6952, Box 123, SIN 337/1/1, NHC Ottawa 249, 26.6.1970.

125 Quoted in: *Jack L. Granatstein/Robert Bothwell*, Pirouette. Pierre Trudeau and Canadian Foreign Policy, Toronto 1990, 34.

126 Address given by the Right. Hon. Pierre Elliott Trudeau, 10.5.1968, quoted in: LAC RG25-B-12, 36-For.P.-Cda+Pac.

127 *Fraser Robertson*: "Looking into Business. Pepin's Tradewinds blow Westward Ho", Globe and Mail, 1.5.1969.

128 Trinity College Private Papers F2307, Series 2, Box 2, Diary Vol. 3, John Hadwen to CSSEA Mitchell Sharp, 30.4.1969.

American retreats.[129] Various documents indicate that New Zealand policymakers desired a more significant Canadian interest in the region as it appreciated the shared values and outlooks between both countries, even more so as Canada could serve as a positive countermodel to the close Australian neighbour.

Given the uncertainties in the wake of Britain's retreat, New Zealand officials also sought ways to assess the depth of relations with its closest geographical ally. With growing Tasman links in trade, tourism, culture and migration[130], the shared commitments in Southeast Asia and Britain's pending withdrawal increased expectations for closer cooperation. While both countries agreed on their coordination of planning for Malaysia and Vietnam[131], the idea of closer cooperation clashed with considerations for self-reliance and independence. Given that overseas posts reported on outside perceptions of Tasman defence as inseparable[132], officials from both countries saw national distinction as equally important. Especially New Zealand, which considerably relied on Australian logistics and cooperation over integrated elements in Malaysia and Vietnam, sought ways to emancipate itself from the subordinate role. In what can be described as a friendly rivalry, both countries engaged in close operational relationships while they tried to establish distinct national positions.[133]

Most of the ambiguities of the cross-Tasman relationship became visible in the discussions on a political merger between both countries. This idea resurfaced during the British defence negotiations and was addressed by Australian High Commissioner to Wellington, David McNicol, in a lengthy report. While both governments would essentially dismiss the idea of a merger, he reported that influential individuals such as John McEwen or Arthur Calwell had supported a Tasman federation time and again in previous years. Despite these earlier proposals, McNicol was struck by the current insistence by federation supporters that a merger was inevitable and necessary because of Britain's turn to Europe: "The cold message of Britain's desire to enter the EEC and of her intention to withdraw from South-East Asia is increasingly being received here. A consequential reflex for the New Zealander is to turn to his closest and more powerful neighbour."[134]

---

129 ANZ ABHS W5579 6958, Box 184, NYP 3/40/4, Part 1, Memorandum for Visit of Keith Holyoake to USA and Canada, 3.9.1969.

130 *Alan Burnett*, New Zealand Policies Towards Australia 1960–1972, in: The Australian Quarterly 45/1, 1973, 78–91; *Robinson*, Australian-New Zealand Relations.

131 See joint message of Harold Holt and Keith Holyoake to Harold Wilson in ANZ ABHS W4628 7148, Box 121, LONB 106/7, Part 3, NHC Canberra to London 254, 4.10.1967.

132 ANZ ABHS W4628 6957, Box 21, SAI 63/1/1, Part 1, NEmb. The Hague (Cunningham), 13.6.1967.

133 *Ian McGibbon*, New Zealand's Vietnam War. A History of Combat, Commitment and Controversy, Wollombi 2010, 216–222.

134 NAA A1838 370/1/19/1, Part 1, AHC Wellington (D. W. McNicol), 30.11.1967.

As the issue received a further stimulus by the British withdrawal announcement in January 1968, McNicol noted that the idea of a merger was "more widely discussed by the press and radio and in public forums than at any time we can recall".[135] His reports were matched by New Zealand articles calling for a more activist approach to cooperation with Australia. When both governments announced in January 1968 that they would form an ANZAC battalion for Vietnam, the *Auckland Star* expected the integration only to be the beginning of closer cooperation that potentially could lead to a merger.[136] *The Press* underlined the interdependence of both countries' foreign and defence policy, and dismissed notions of independence if it would only please political sentiment: "National identity in the field is less important than the efficient pooling of resources."[137]

Yet these national sentiments inhibited more extensive cooperation. When journalist E. W. Tipping visited New Zealand for a *Melbourne Herald* editorial in January 1968, he sensed continued suspicions for Australian motives leading up to the highest ranks, including Prime Minister Keith Holyoake. Tipping advocated taking the recent British decision as a chance to sort out differences between both countries: "Right now. Not next year, or in 1972."[138] Other editorials followed with similar recommendations to take the opportunity created by the British announcement.[139] Meanwhile, Australian officials internally warned of a fall-out of relations between both countries: "For a generation […] we have taken our relationships with New Zealand too much for granted, and have, as a community, at times conduct ourselves in such a way as to antagonise New Zealand's citizens."[140]

Both sides clearly saw their defence as interdependent, but Australians gave lesser attention to New Zealand defence concerns. Due to its relative size, Australians could not only push its defence priorities in cooperation, but also assumed that New Zealand counterparts would follow suit on critical strategic issues. In contrast, New Zealanders were inhibited by fears that the country could become a satellite, province, or colony of Australia. The *Evening Post* provokingly titled an editorial "Can Australia be a mother to us?"[141], answering the question with an ambiguous 'no' that hailed wartime cooperation, but called for New Zealand independence in peacetime. Asked about a merger in March 1968, New Zealand Leader of Opposition Norman Kirk said he was "sick and tired of this humbug" and he would expect Australia to behave as a "mother-in-law" if federation would

---

135 NAA A1838 370/1/19/1, Part 1, AHC Wellington (Savingram 3/68), 15.3.1968.

136 "The Anzacs – again", Auckland Star, 10.1.1968.

137 "ANZAC Battalion", The Press, 12.1.1968.

138 *E. W. Tipping,* "The Kiwi who wants to be alone", Melbourne Herald, 22.1.1968.

139 *Douglas Brass,* "A chance for Mr Gorton to get down to specifics", The Australian, 27.3.1968.

140 NAA A1838 370/9/3, Memorandum for File by Kelly, 30.11.1967.

141 "Can Australia be a Mother to Us?", Evening Post, 27.7.1967.

actually take place.[142] Both NLP and New Zealand National Party (NNP) voted in 1968 against unity with Australia[143] – despite the absence of any concrete planning for a merger, indicating to observers such as the Australian High Commission Wellington how prominent this issue had actually become.[144]

Over the coming years, the idea of a merger remained in a state of vague reference while New Zealanders continued to struggle with its implications. A paper written by the New Zealand High Commission Canberra in 1972 underlined the feeling of being at Australia's mercy: "[…] we are stuck with each other in an enclave to the south of Asia. (The psychology of this acceptance should not be underrated.) It is also a fact of life that we need the Australians more than they need us."[145]

The discussions on a merger highlighted how both countries feared for their independence in policymaking, but how they also regarded the other as an inalienable part of any future outlook. Increasingly, officials now transferred rhetoric previously directed towards Britain to underline the interdependent, close relationship between the two countries. When George Laking spoke of a growing "businesslike aspect" in foreign policy with Britain, he simultaneously spoke of "a deep, if seldom expressed, sense of kinship"[146] with Australia. From the position of a bystander who understood the intricate relationship of former sister dominions, Canadian officials still judged external pressures as too low to force both countries into a federation:

"Nevertheless there is no serious emotional pressure to unite, little of the feeling of togetherness in the face of Asia which must increasingly characterize the feelings of white South Africans and Rhodesians in the face of Black Africa. New Zealanders feel isolated and unquestionably look to Australia for relief from this isolation but this is a far cry from saying that New Zealanders yet feel a need to be part of Australia."[147]

Canadian judgement would turn out to be correct. While the intellectual concern for cross-Tasman relations created a vast output of papers, practical arrangements for more significant cooperation on foreign affairs were unavailing. The Defence Supply Agreement established in 1969 would remain the only treaty between both countries and only resulted from military need.[148] In 1972, an

[142] Quoted in: NAA A1838 370/1/19/1, Part 1, AHC Wellington 293, 27.3.1968.

[143] NAA A1838 370/1/19/1, Part 1, AHC Wellington, 17.5.1968 and AHC Wellington (Savingram 15/68), 8.8.1968.

[144] NAA A1838 370/1/19/1, Part 1, AHC Wellington (Savingram 15/68), 8.8.1968.

[145] ANZ ABHS W5533 22128, Box 154, CBA 89/1/1, "Australia-New Zealand Relations", Draft by the NHC Canberra, 26.5.1972.

[146] ANZ ABHS W4628 6957, Box 21, SAI 63/1/1, Part 1, "New Zealand Foreign Policy in the Face of Change", Address given by George Laking to the Royal Overseas League, 8.6.1971.

[147] LAC RG25 A-3-c, Vol. 8402, 20-AUSTL-1-3-NZ, CHC Wellington to CUSSEA, 1.3.1968.

[148] *Burnett*, New Zealand Policies Towards Australia, 81.

Australia-New Zealand Consultative Committee on Defence would follow. In general, however, the trend of contributing to similar alliance frameworks and following similar defence interests with simultaneous indecision on direct defence cooperation would continue in both countries, despite the renewed pressures over Britain's decision to withdraw.

5.2 Towards a New Regional Framework of Security and Cooperation

"Australia in the last few years has begun to realise that she is a Pacific power and obviously her interests, both economic and political, must primarily be in the Pacific area. The fact that Australia now looks more to the North than to the West is a perfectly natural development and not one that affects our close and intimate relations with her."[149]

As the introductory quote from a British brief indicates, the East of Suez discussions fell in a time of greater Australian awareness for its regional position. As already discussed, this was the result of the profound regional transformations that both accompanied and resulted from the British decision. Britain's announcement in January 1968 only precipitated the severe setback for US operations in Vietnam in the following months, creating overall the impression of a dramatic turn of Western strategy in Southeast Asia. At the same time, slow transformative processes had opened alternative regional assessments. While the conflict in Vietnam was still raging, surrounding countries made remarkable progress in economic growth and regional integration. The slow American retreat from the area, further depicted by Nixon's Guam Doctrine, strengthened this regional reordering.

However, given the duality of British and American considerations for retreat, Australasians had difficulties in adapting to these regional changes. A reorientation towards the region was linked to a series of previously doubted policy shifts that included a potential demise of relations with Britain. Moreover, the question of communist threat lingered on, creating considerable anxiety among policymakers who had relied on and believed in the containment of communism for a long time.

Over Britain's retreat, Australasian officials not only were forced to review their security principles, but they also had to implement post-withdrawal arrangements. As their contributions had been small compared to their 'great and powerful allies'[150], both Tasman nations now had to decide if they were will-

[149] TNA FCO 24/188, Brief on British-Australia Relations, Sept/Oct. 1967.

[150] By 1967/1968, Australia was committed with around 2 000 service personnel in Malaysia and around 8 000 servicemen of all three services in Vietnam; *Millar*, Anglo-Australian Partnership, 82; "The Great Retreat", Age, 20.7.1967. During Confrontation, around 1 400 New Zealand servicemen served in Malaysia. Being dispatched from the battalion in Terendak,

ing to foot the bill themselves. Given the practical difficulties of regional security, the outcome of this planning was moreover determined by local attitudes, the position of Malaysia and Singapore and, in a second tier, the neighbouring Southeast Asian countries. For the first time, Australia and New Zealand had to acknowledge the role of these nations as independent actors. As a result, officials realised in parts for the first time their own regional responsibility without Britain. The notions of a 'mature' nation being able to act independently of Britain was now applied to the question of regional security. In contrast to the Australasian commitment to Vietnam that had been taken on without Britain, the question of a continued presence after the British withdrawal from Malaysia included now the uncertainty of US policy. Given the transformation of British and American policy, officials and the greater public were now aware that their own commitment would mean a certain substitute of the great powers in the area, something they had previously rejected in talks with the British. However, in the process of reviewing this position, some commentators saw the use of presenting this decision as an indication of both countries' ultimate detachment from the British security umbrella, and their adoption of an independent role in the region. Similarly, Canada took the British decision as an incentive to assess its engagement with Southeast Asia, particularly focusing on military and development assistance and its general interest in the Pacific.

5.2.1 "Sindausthailaysia!" – Establishing a Regional Strategic Framework after Britain's Departure, 1967/68

Already in April 1967, when British plans for withdrawal started to take shape, the Australian Cabinet reviewed the continuation of the defence aid program to Malaysia and Singapore worth AUD 25 million allocated until 1970. The Cabinet submission presented on this issue called the aid essential to foster regional stability, to encourage a continued British presence and to help Malaysia and Singapore to establish their own forces. The discussion had come at a time when Britain already indicated financial difficulties and Canada and the USA were not willing to become engaged in the region. Therefore, "Australia has become, more or less by default, Malaysia's principal current source of defence aid, a fact which has doubtless given rise to some expectation of continuing Australian assistance".[151]

In the following, over discussions on continuing their own commitment after a British withdrawal, those policymakers favouring retention underlined the need to give credibility to Australia's role detached from a British pres-

various artillery and infantry units (100–200 troops) served with Australian forces in Vietnam, with a peak of 543 troops serving in Vietnam in 1968; *McGibbon*, Forward Defence, 29–31.

[151] NAA A4940 C1473, Part 3, Cabinet Submission 197, 10.4.1967.

ence, while supporters of a withdrawal stressed potential risks of staying without Britain.[152] Ultimately, Cabinet rejected an extended defence program, but decided on the continued presence of Australia's forces for the time being, at least to allow tentative planning on the future of the troops.[153]

Accordingly, Australian officials urged New Zealanders to stay in Southeast Asia during a bilateral meeting in October 1967.[154] Like Australians, New Zealanders had started to assess potential departures from British-centred cooperation through local requests for defence aid. In April 1967, officials judged continued military assistance necessary as any reduction could be interpreted "both by the British and the Malaysians and the Singaporeans as a weakening of our active interests in the problems of the area".[155] When British plans for withdrawal became apparent, service officials and external officials were divided on the retention of forces. While defence officials demanded to commence military planning on the premise of a continued presence, NDEA officials drafted a paper that challenged this premise.[156]

In contrast to Australian considerations, which deferred any fundamental review for the time being, New Zealand examinations already assessed the advantages and disadvantages of a continued presence. The issue felt more pressing as New Zealanders struggled with the indicated dismantling of ANZAM, resulting in the withdrawal of logistic support from Britain.[157] As a consequence, early New Zealand considerations hoped for larger American support, but were set back by vague American statements only supporting a continued ANZAC presence in Malaysia as a "statement of intent".[158]

Meanwhile, both Australia and New Zealand coordinated their approaches to Malaysia and Singapore. Fundamental to all Tasman discussions were concerns that a continued contribution to Malaysian and Singaporean defence could develop into an unfavourable commitment. Therefore, the Australian Cabinet decided that preliminary decisions should be communicated in "a limited and provisional attitude", which would not "at this stage amount to a firm intention to continue an Australian military presence".[159] ASEA James Plimsoll under-

[152] A support for withdrawal was proposed e. g. in NAA A1838 TS3006/10/4/1, Part 4, Note by Osborn, n. d. (Aug. 1967); support for staying was expressed e. g. by ASEA James Plimsoll, NAA A1838 TS696/1, Part 1, "Notes on some political points arising in consideration of the implications of British defence decisions" (James Plimsoll to Paul Hasluck), 25.8.1967.

[153] NAA A4940 C1473, Part 3, FADC Meeting, 25.8.1967.

[154] NAA A4940 C4658, Points for Talks with Keith Holyoake, n. d. (September 1967).

[155] ANZ ABHS W4627 950, Box 4667, 455/7/3, Part 1, NSD to Keith Holyoake, 6.4.1967.

[156] ANZ AAFD W3738 811, Box 1312, CAB 222/1/1, "New Zealand Defence Policy", NDEA Brief (D (67) 10), 11.09.1967.

[157] ANZ ABHS W5400 20358, Box 91, KL 102/1/4, Part 2, NHC Singapore, 21.7.1967 and Far East Command (UK), 16.8.1967, with Record of the CINCFE Meeting (10.8.1967).

[158] William Bundy in talks with Frank Corner, ANZ ABHS W4628 7148, Box 121, LONB 106/7, Part 3, NEmb. Washington 890, 16.10.1967.

[159] NAA A4940 C1473, Part 3, Cabinet Decision 771, 11.12.1967.

lined any continued presence should be characterised as "an entirely new type of commitment, namely an independent and direct commitment of forces, including land forces, to the national defence of two foreign states".[160] Not only the self-reliant character of such a commitment seemed to constitute a precedent. Without Britain, also the Commonwealth frame seemed to lose weight as a powerful reference since Malaysia and Singapore were now considered 'foreign' countries.

The issue of a new defence framework also extended to AMDA. In fact, the defence arrangement had been in constant debate since the secession of Singapore. Now, with a British retreat, AMDA was likely abolished, renegotiated or replaced by another agreement. Yet officials from both countries hoped to keep AMDA for as long as possible. However, officials within the region urged to use the momentum to take an active role, even more so as any rejection of discussions could upset relations with Malaysia and Singapore.[161] From Singapore, Australian High Commissioner Alfred Parsons advocated to grasp the new-won influence over developments in the region:

> "As you rightly say, no one knows (or should be brash enough to predict) what the future holds in South-East Asia, but many people are searching around and are receptive to new ideas.[…] We have as much at stake as anyone in what emerges in terms of the military security of Asia in the next few years, but we may not always have the same opportunity to influence developments as we do in the present state of flux."[162]

However, such recommendations were subdued by an official policy avoiding early negotiations. Both countries feared that any approach to Malaysia or Singapore would encourage long-term arrangements.[163]

Nevertheless, calls for an active regional policy were renewed half a year later, after the British decision in early 1968. Now, newspapers supported overseas opinions by emphasising the opportunity for an independent role in regional cooperation. The *Sydney Morning Herald* commented that Australia had "for the first time a clean slate on which to write an Australian policy towards our northern neighbours".[164] Equally, the *Canberra Times* demanded a new approach to Australia's defence role: "[…] "above all, it needs a new definition of itself – a new self-image as a growing force in Asia, capable of both the sacrifices and the skill which leadership demands."[165]

---

160 NAA A1838 TS3006/10/4/1, Part 4, James Plimsoll to Paul Hasluck, n. d. (August/September 1967).

161 NAA A1838 TS696/1, Part 3, AHC Kuala Lumpur 2236, 27.10.1967.

162 NAA A1838, TS3006/10/4/1, Part 4, Alfred Parsons to William Pritchett, 6.9.1967.

163 ANZ ABHS W4628 7148, Box 121, LONB 106/7, Part 3, NDEA to NHC Kuala Lumpur 613, 22.9.1967.

164 "UK Withdrawal is a Defence Watershed", Sydney Morning Herald, 15.1.1968.

165 "Pressure to step into Britain's shoes", Canberra Times, 18.5.1968.

However, officials still felt uncertain about long-term developments[166], especially over the parallel escalation in Vietnam. The Tet Offensive infused the debate on potential similar developments in the Malaysian area. Furthermore, as the Malaysian commitment had been used before to fend off American requests for further troop contributions to Vietnam, both countries feared that an early withdrawal from Malaysia/Singapore could provoke new American requests. Consequently, the decisions taken in 1968 pointed to the need for forces for the time being, to sustain regional stability, foster cooperation and back the American position.[167]

Since Britain's decision suggested a departure from the concept of forward defence, Australian and New Zealand officials increasingly underlined the need for Malaysian and Singapore defence rather than Western containment. This rhetoric was contrasted by continued doubts about new defence arrangements without Britain. During tripartite talks in Wellington in March 1968, Australians and New Zealanders reiterated their resistance to any new defence arrangements. Visibly irritated, CINCFE Carver probed them on this position: "[…] if you do not intend to take on a commitment why should you continue to maintain forces in a country?"[168] While they felt they had undertaken commitments with European partners – which they deemed trustworthy – in SEATO and ANZAM before, the new commitments were unprecedented in their composition, given that neither Britain nor the USA would participate. Although British officials underlined their intention to back an ANZAC commitment[169], Tasman officials were left in doubt about any future framework.

Leading up to the Five Power talks in June 1968, officials in both countries reviewed the pros and cons of staying in the region. Among the arguments in favour of staying were the diplomatic and political opportunities in the region, the option of reentry for Britain and the American sympathy for such a presence. Arguments speaking against a presence were the concerns for an open-ended commitment, each country's limited capacity to militarily act alone, and the lack of clear American support for such a commitment. In balance, both countries supported a continued presence until 1971, but noted that current uncertainties would prevent a long-term decision.[170]

---

[166] The uncertainties about the British, American and Australian position were summarised in ANZ ABHS W4628 7148, Box 121, LONB 106/7, Part 4, NDEA Memorandum for Prime Minister, 8.2.1968.

[167] NAA M3787, File 53, "Implications for Australia of British Defence Decisions", Australian Cabinet Submission No. 7, 23.1.1968.

[168] ANZ ABHS W5400 20358, Box 96, KL 102/1/9, Part 2, Report of Meeting between British, Australian and New Zealand officials, 9.4.1968.

[169] ANZ ABHS W5400 20358, Box 96, KL 102/1/19, Part 2, Memorandum for File (NHC London), 29.3.1968.

[170] ANZ ABHS W5400 20358, Box 96, KL 102/1/9, Part 2, Draft for Statement by Keith

Although they could not agree on an immediate strategy, both countries hoped to keep AMDA for as long as possible, not least because differences between Malaysia and Singapore prevented planning for local defence cooperation. To advocate for the retention of AMDA, Australians resorted again to historical arguments during the Five Power talks in June 1968: "We want rather to continue in the imprint of the past where arrangements both with regard to the process of consultation and the acceptance of obligations have been characterised by a spirit of informality and mutual trust."[171] While the statement may have seemed like an indication of Australia's continued interest in close consultation with the British, it was also a rhetoric strategy to fend off any new – written – arrangements that would bind Australia to Malaysia's defence.

The historic arguments and narratives presented in the Five Power talks would serve as a last depiction of imperial imagination. This image of familiar talks was further nurtured by a forthcoming British attitude that would help phase out some of the anger and regret created by Britain's decision for withdrawal.[172] Although the talks did result in few substantial agreements, many officials felt reassured by the British determination shown during the meeting. According to New Zealand Chief of Defence Staff (NCDS) Leonard Thornton,

> "Viewed against their impressive assurances of 'continuing interest and concern' these apparently forthcoming contributions placed the British delegation in a strong position at the outset and to some extent pre-empted the line of attack which might have been followed by other delegations, notably the Australians and ourselves."[173]

Other sources equally underlined that the British representatives had shown themselves assuring enough to dispel some of the suspicion created by the previous incidents of missed consultation, and offered a perspective for future cooperation.[174]

Perceptions of continued British support were further enhanced by discrete assurances from the British service side. Following the talks in June, British Chief of General Staff (BCGS) Geoffrey Baker indicated to New Zealanders that he would, without consulting British ministers, aim at keeping one brigade in special training for Southeast Asia.[175] From London, Critchley reported of

Holyoake under Agenda Item D at Five Power Conference, 10.6.1968; NAA A9861 3/12/77/8, Part 6, "Australian Military Presence in Malaysia/Singapore", Australian Cabinet Submission 81, 9.5.1968.

171 NAA A1838 696/1/9, Part 1, Australian statement for Five Power Talks, n. d. (May/June 1968).

172 *McCourt*, Britain's "East of Suez Role", 468.

173 ANZ ABHS W4627 950, Box 4507, 434/8/1, Part 21, Report by NCDS Thornton, 19.6.1968.

174 LAC RG25 A-3-c, Vol. 8903, 20-BRIT-1-3-E.Suez, Part 2, CHC Kuala Lumpur, 14.6.1968.

175 ANZ ABHS W5400 20358, Box 96, KL 102/1/9, Part 3, NHC London, 24.6.1968. One

assurances he received for continued British interest, and urged to make the most of British offers to participate in joint training and exercises.[176]

Aside from intermediate considerations that still included British elements, some officials like the former Australian Ambassador to Indonesia Keith Shann used the momentum of departmental reviews to push for a new, even greater regional role:

"Our role seems to me to be one of holding the ring in our immediate area amongst countries who know us, respect us, and trust us, while they do not necessarily fully trust their own neighbours, and may, if there is not a real and significant Australian contribution, seek to make provision independently for their own safety – something which they cannot afford, and which is unnecessary if Australia is seen to fill the vacuum. […] We can, if we set our minds to it, be the unquestioned leader of a rather cosy, and pretty secure grouping, Sindausthailaysia! – The 'Aust' stands for 'Australasia'."[177]

Shann could stress the progress Australia has made with regional partners through the recently established security networks and commitments, a position also voiced by other officials who underlined the growing interdependence of Australia's future and the region's developments.[178] Such visions of Australian regionalism were also presented by outside commentators such as Bruce Grant, who underlined the nexus between Australia's regional position and its ability to perceive itself as a nation, and the strength it could derive from local appreciations. To him, the retention of forces in the region was a "calculated risk"[179], which despite some disadvantageous effects could enhance Australia's relations with both the region and its powerful allies, as well as its own definition as a nation.[180] While he presented local countries as having little in common with the European outlook of Australia, he nevertheless thought the commitment itself offered opportunities for Australia to establish an identity, both based on the form of commitment it would take as based on local attitudes towards Australia. By presenting a continued commitment as a calculated risk, Grant advocated an activist, operable approach to questions concerning the future of the region: Australians should not fear any unfamiliar threat, but should move into a conscious position on potential consequences.

Nevertheless, Shann and Grant belonged to a minority group supporting a clear commitment to the region. Meanwhile, a large departmental uncertainty inhibited an unambiguous affirmation of a continued presence. Instead of embracing a new regional position, the following months saw a remarkable

---

handwritten note commented on Baker's unusual promise with "No wonder they say war is too important to be left to the generals".

176 NAA A1838 TS696/1/9, Part 3, Critchley to Gordon Jockel, 27.9.1968.

177 NAA A1838 TS677/3, Part 12, Keith Shann to Gordon Jockel, 29.6.1968.

178 *Halvorson*, Australia in Asia, 88 f.

179 *Bruce Grant*, Pacific Signposts. 3) Shattered Images, in: Meanjin 27/3, 1968, 261–272, 272.

180 *Bruce Grant*, Australia's Defence Policy, in: Quadrant, Jan–Feb 1969, 37–41, 41.

passivity on Australian decision-making.[181] Over hostilities and suspicions between Malaysia and Singapore, but even more so over the difficulties in Vietnam, both Tasman governments confirmed retention of forces until 1971 in September 1968, but dispelled any further planning ahead.[182]

As the Tasman dominions tried to sort out their own security and defence premises detached from Britain, Canada had witnessed the British decision largely from the sidelines. Still, Canadian officials devoted some thinking to potential repercussions on their security framework. A CDEA memo prepared in late 1968 called the British withdrawal in combination with the uncertain US position in Vietnam and Thailand disturbing, yet this would not suggest "that we follow the Australian pattern of committing combat forces to the region as we have in Europe, but rather that we consider providing more assistance".[183] Instead, officials should vaguely consider "whether as a Pacific country we do not have a role to play in this area".[184]

Such recommendations matched the emphasis of a Pacific policy under Pierre Trudeau, and was music in the ears of regional diplomats such as John Hadwen. In summer 1968, Hadwen proposed to assist Malaysia with military advisers.[185] In a lengthy report to Ottawa, he contrasted previous Canadian policy towards the area of Southeast Asia with a stronger emphasis on development assistance and, given the already existing ties with Malaysia, the recommendation to extend military assistance in both material and personnel. In discussions about a potential Canadian role in the region, Hadwen again urged in May 1969 to consider military equipment and training as assets in supporting non-communist governments in the region.[186] He also used Pepin's tour through the Pacific to review the multitude of opportunities encountered in the region, including the question posed by many locals: "Why weren't Canadians here yesterday?".[187]

Although there is not much in Canadian sources to be found if Hadwen's recommendations were actively endorsed, his call for a more active policy was sustained by larger departmental studies. With more frequent visits of Pacific leaders such as John Gorton or Keith Holyoake to Canada, the Canadian Far Eastern Division advised on a policy review in early 1969. The review should

181 This was also criticised by some newspapers, e. g. "As we were", Sydney Morning Herald, 13.6.1968.

182 *Edwards*, Nation at War, 200.

183 LAC RG25 A-3-c, Vol. 8903, 20-BRIT-1-3-E.Suez, "Duplication of British Withdrawal from 'East of Suez'", CDEA Paper, 10.12.1968.

184 Ibid.

185 LAC RG25 A-3-c, Vol. 10317, 27-8-AUSTL, CHC Kuala Lumpur (Hadwen) 602, 24.7.1968.

186 LAC RG25 A-3-c, Vol. 10092, 20-CDA-9-FE, Notes by Blair Seaborn on a Meeting of Indochina Commissioners (Saigon, 23.4.1969), 21.5.1969.

187 Trinity College Private Papers F2307, Series 2, Box 2, Notes prepared by John Hadwen for Jean-Luc Pepin's Speech in Vancouver, 2.5.1969.

cover the expansion of regional contacts, but should also assess how Southeast Asia, as a theatre crucial for the global balance of power, could be stabilised other than by military means.[188] Aside from offering Canadian experience in truce and peacekeeping operations, the review's author, Canadian High Commissioner to Australia Arthur Menzies, recommended regional networks of defence assistance, both "to limit Big power military influence in Southeast Asia"[189] as to foster regional self-determination.

Both Hadwen and Menzies aptly walked the tightrope of Canada's non-committal position on Southeast Asian involvement that had been ingrained for decades. On the one hand, they looked for loopholes in the definition of military assistance that was provided by Canada's pride in peacekeeping operations. They clearly adopted arguments similar to those presented by Australian and New Zealand representation, such as regional instability and the opportunity for a unique Canadian engagement. On the other hand, they were quick to discharge any notion they might support military intervention.

Both diplomats were also able to draw on departmental considerations on military assistance, which underlined this form of relief as crucial in supporting emerging nations on their path to self-reliance and independence. In summer 1969, one Canadian brief argued that military forces, given their position in the political hierarchies of most countries under consideration, were "for better or worse [...] an extremely important factor in the life of the developing countries".[190] At the same time, the brief cautioned to carefully review every case for military assistance. The resulting list of eligible countries was therefore short – no communist countries, no countries that were currently fought over by East or West, and no countries "in which military assistance on a significant scale might be interpreted as an implied Canadian commitment or willingness to help safeguard the security of the country in question (unless the government wishes to imply such a willingness, as a deterrent to the country's neighbours)".[191] The last category of undesirable commitments clearly stemmed from previous experiences. Disadvantageous parallels were drawn to the discussions on Malaysian assistance during Confrontation[192]; similarly, officials also feared another supervisory commitment similar to the ICSC.[193] As a re-

188 LAC RG25 A-3-c, Vol. 8615, 20-1-2-ASIA/PACIFIC, Part 1, Briefing Points by Far Eastern Div., 25.3.1969.

189 LAC RG25-B-12, 36-For.P.-Cda+Pac., "Canada and the Pacific", Policy Paper, Dec. 1969.

190 LAC RG24-B-2, Vol. 21577, 5-2-5040-12, Memorandum by CDEA (Interdepartmental Military Assistance Committee), 11.7.1969.

191 Ibid.

192 LAC RG25 A-3-c, Vol. 8600, 20-1-1-12, Part 6, Defence Liaison (1) Div. to Commonwealth Div., 12.2.1968.

193 LAC RG25 A-3-c, Vol. 8600, 20-1-1-12, Part 6, Far Eastern Div. (Seaborn) to Commonwealth Div., 12.2.1968.

sult, the responsible Commonwealth Division cautioned on any larger involvement in regional security: "There is a thin line between tendering advice and assuming responsibility for the results of diplomatic activity consequent upon advice."[194]

Accordingly, most Canadian officials resisted further involvement in the region, not only in the field of military cooperation, but also in areas of information and intelligence sharing. One example was the repeatedly declined invitation by Australia and New Zealand to participate in forums to share information on the region.[195] Instead, Canadian officials continuously stressed that their regional interest would markedly differ from the interest of their Western allies in the region.[196]

5.2.2 Australia and New Zealand on Ground Forces and ANZAC Cooperation, 1968/69

Over the Summer of 1968, notions of a self-reliant defence outlook increased in Australian and New Zealand discussions. Following the Five Power talks, the *Adelaide Advertiser* hailed the opportunity for Australia to become a regional player: "This is a significant date for Australia. It brings us into South-East Asia as a principal, as an initiator of decisions instead of as a young executive of British and American policies."[197] In New Zealand, a broadcast programme judged that the Five Power talks would stress the topic of independent defence: "I think there'll be a growing realization that our defence depends on us and us alone – and when I say us I mean Australia as well".[198]

Indeed, the aftermath of the Five Power talks was devoted to the question of long-term strategy following the British withdrawal after 1971. While discussions on air and naval forces soon reached agreements, it was the question of ground forces that would cause considerable tensions between Australia and New Zealand. Here, difficulties of navigating into a post-British regional security framework were exposed the strongest. On the one hand, as previous discussions on 'white faces' had already indicated, officials placed considerable value

194 LAC RG25 A-3-c, Vol. 8903, 20-BRIT-1-3-E.Suez, Part 1, Circular from Commonwealth Div., 12.3.1968.

195 See the departmental discussions on the participation at the Four Power Conference on Cooperation of Information Activities after Canada had been invited by New Zealand and Australia, LAC RG25 A-3-c, Vol. 8600, 20-1-1-12, Part 7, Commonwealth Div. to Information Div., 8.9.1969.

196 LAC RG25 A-3-c, Vol. 8600, 20-1-1-12, Part 7, Commonwealth Div. to Information Div., 8.9.1969.

197 Adelaide Advertiser, 10.6.1968, quoted in: NAA A1838 TS696/1/9, Part 2, Digest of Press Opinion, ADEA to AHC Kuala Lumpur 1660, 12.6.1968.

198 *A. T. Arthur,* "New Zealand Defence Policy", National Programme "Looking at Ourselves", 8.6.1968, found in: ANZ ABHS W4628 7148, Box 117, LONB 106/3, Part 1.

on the retention of ground forces as a psychological deterrent. In an age of increasingly elaborate and modern warfare, they were still appreciated for their symbolic value as a physical presence. Moreover, officials perceived ground forces as potential tripwires: deemed as more vulnerable, an attack on them would attract great power support or protection under defence alliances such as ANZUS. Yet these advantages could also be judged as disadvantages: Specialists deemed ground warfare as outdated, and stationed troops could also cause political difficulties as negative tripwires sparking off internal conflicts and local insurgencies. These questions of strategic and/or political purpose of ground forces and the question of appropriate stationing of these forces were a major cause of friction between the Tasman governments. The debate would also expose what kind of relationship both countries had envisaged with Malaysia, Singapore, and the broader region.

Immediately after Britain's first decision in July 1967, an Australian meeting in Kuala Lumpur covered potential issues for Australia's own presence if a transfer of forces from bases in Malaysia to Singapore was considered. Referring to the rivalry between Malaysia and Singapore, High Commissioner Alfred Parsons recommended dividing Australia's forces evenly to satisfy both countries. Turning to the question of the appropriate size and shape of forces after the British withdrawal, some military officials judged land forces as unreasonable since an Indonesian threat was unlikely. They were rebutted by officials like Parsons who explained with an eye on the ongoing negotiations with Britain, "it was contrary to the views advanced by Australian authorities in recent months that the lack of ground forces made a treaty commitment less credible".[199] In a way, officials felt bound to the arguments presented to the British during negotiations on a withdrawal East of Suez, and supported the retention of ground forces to underline Australia's determination in serving local security frameworks.

The division of attitudes on ground forces was similar in New Zealand. The main concern for New Zealand officials was the risk of being drawn into counter-insurgency or an open-ended commitment, as one paper noted in April 1968: "A decision to maintain a small ground force element would not keep options open, but would rather represent a significant decision difficult to reverse in future."[200] In response, representatives in the region like New Zealand High Commissioner to Kuala Lumpur Doug Zohrab argued for retaining ground forces as a sign of New Zealand determination and activism, and called ground forces a "fundamental characteristic of the South East Asian theatre".[201] Zohrab also ad-

[199] NAA A1838 213/1, Part 2, Meeting of High Commissioners in Kuala Lumpur, 25.8.1967.

[200] ANZ ABHS W5400 20358, Box 96, KL 102/1/9, Part 2, NDEA Paper, 30.4.1968.

[201] ANZ ABHS W5400 20358, Box 96, KL 102/1/9, Part 2, Draft by NHC Kuala Lumpur, 20.5.1968.

vocated a more courageous policy amidst potential issues: "South East Asia will continue to simmer, even occasionally to boil on one place or another, and we will not help the situation by going."[202] To him, the question of ground forces was the first test of New Zealand's identification with the region.

Most opposition to a continued presence was nourished by the continued tensions between Malaysia and Singapore. Keith Holyoake and Paul Hasluck had already discussed the risk of being dragged into an internal conflict in March 1968.[203] In Australia, AMD Alan Fairhall cautioned about the underlying risks of a retention of ground forces: "Whatever may be the limits we place on Australian involvement in insurgency problems we must reckon that Malaysia and Singapore would be expecting our forces to be available for use in insurgency situations beyond those limits."[204]

With Malaysian-Singapore differences already inhibiting considerations, discussions between Australia and New Zealand were further hampered by varying attitudes towards future purposes: While Australia was more concerned with the strategic implications of ground forces for its alliance framework[205], New Zealand increasingly focused on the implications on its relations with local governments. Australia only added to cross-Tasman tensions on the issue by being secretive about its plans for the region, despite an agreement for joint study regarding the future base for the ground forces, resulting in various appeals from New Zealand representatives in Canberra and an official request for clarification by Keith Holyoake.[206]

Given their different priorities, the frictions between both countries flared up over the future location of the forces. With Britain's retreat from the CSR, the base in Terendak would soon become an expensive asset to keep. Aside from Terendak, further options were Singapore or Penang close to the Royal Australian Airforce (RAAF) base Butterworth. While Australia increasingly preferred a transfer of its units to Singapore, New Zealand officials wished to keep Terendak as an indication of a balanced presence in both Malaysia and Singapore. Although being sympathetic with Singapore, the NDEA feared that the move would further isolate Singapore within the area as a host to Western forces, and could antagonise Indonesia.[207]

In contrast, Australian officials had already followed from the Five Power talks that a continued presence in Terendak was unfeasible because of the Brit-

[202] Ibid.

[203] ANZ AAFD W3738 811, Box 1312, CAB 222/1/1, Part 1/2, Report of Talks of Keith Holyoake with Paul Hasluck, 12.2.1968.

[204] NAA A5619 C22, Part 2, Cabinet Submission 282, Report by Alan Fairhall on Five Power Defence Talks, 12.8.1968.

[205] NAA A5619 C22, Part 2, Cabinet Minute Dec. 543, 19.9.1968.

[206] ANZ ABHS W4628 7148, Box 121, LONB 106/7, Part 5, Memorandum for Cabinet by Keith Holyoake, 16.9.1968.

[207] ANZ ABHS W4628 6957, Box 23, SAI 68/1/1, Memorandum by NSEA, 29.11.1968.

ish withdrawal of logistics.[208] A fact-finding mission sent to the region in November 1968 reported that Terendak would be too expensive and could result in potential difficulties over sharing facilities with Malaysians.[209] However, ADEA officials protested a move to Singapore as seriously endangering the "sense of continuity, confidence and stability"[210] provided to Malaysia by the Australian forces in Terendak. James Plimsoll tried to convince ASD Henry Bland and other military authorities that a retention of forces would indicate to Malaysia a willingness to support the country in its efforts against communism.

As much as Australian mandarins tried to side with New Zealand counterparts[211], the Australian government pushed a transfer through. On 15 December 1968, AMD Fairhall introduced a Cabinet submission in which he called the further stationing in Terendak unconceivable. Aside from costs, the shared housing with Malaysian forces presented an issue: "Problems of command and control and disciplinary problems flowing from differences in race, language, customs, pay and standards and sharing facilities would, in the view of our Chief of Staff Committee, make sharing Terendak an unattractive military proposition."[212] Commenting on these references to potential racial tensions with Malaysians, New Zealanders made their disagreement with the Australian position known: "[…] we on the other hand, whilst agreeing there would be difficulties calling for adjustments and tolerance, see this as a useful and appropriate military experiment in regard to our future relations in the area."[213]

As the Australian Cabinet ultimately decided on a move to Singapore[214], New Zealanders could indeed feel overruled and dismissed in their position stated on various occasions. Ultimately, Holyoake accepted the decision grudgingly: "Given the overriding importance of cooperation with Australia, we have virtually no option, in the last analysis, but to accept the Australian position and make the best of it."[215] Throughout discussions, New Zealand felt that Australia had also expressed little sympathy or sensitivity for local attitudes, an opinion also shared by Australian representatives abroad. When instructed to convey the decision to Malaysian officials, Australian High Commissioner Allan Eastman asked Canberra to reconsider its short message: "I feel that this is far too

[208] NAA A5619 C22, Part 2, Cabinet Submission 282, Report by AMD Alan Fairhall on Five Power Defence Talks, 12.8.1968.

[209] NAA A1838 TS696/1/9, Part 4, Alfred Parsons (AHC Singapore) to Gordon Jockel, 14.11.1968.

[210] NAA A1838 TS696/1/9, Part 4, Note for File by Lance Joseph, 2.12.1968.

[211] ANZ ABHS W4627 950, Box 4028, 253/3/6/2, Part 5, Memorandum for Prime Minister, 12.12.1968.

[212] NAA A5619 C22, Part 3, Cabinet Submission 436 (by Allen Fairhall), 15.12.1968.

[213] NAA A1838 TS696/1/9, Part 4, Note by NDLS Canberra, 17.12.1968.

[214] NAA A5619 C22, Part 2, Cabinet Minutes Dec. 781, 18.12.1968.

[215] ANZ AAFD W3738 811, Box 1316, CAB 222/3/1, Part 2, Keith Holyoake to Cabinet, 2.1.1969.

off-hand for such an historic decision which is so open to misinterpretation by good and bad alike."[216]

When the decision was made public in early January 1969, many newspapers were equally critical. In New Zealand, the news was met with traditional anti-Australianism that evoked feelings of inferiority, conversely producing sympathies with the Southeast Asian countries, for example by the *Evening Star*: "The men with the slide-rules and computers in Canberra have not in the past appreciated the psychological and political importance of a small force in Asian eyes, and the real impact it could have without ever firing a shot in anger."[217] Anger was also expressed in the Australian press. In *The Bulletin*, Harvey Stockwin called the announcement "a disaster. For one thing, coming as it did by itself after all the doubt and uncertainty, it gave no long-term reassurance (which by now has become necessary), thus inviting speculation that it was a prelude to withdrawal".[218] Other Australian newspapers criticised that Gorton's announcement of the decision, shortly before the important Commonwealth Prime Ministers' Meeting in January 1969, could have been drafted more soliciting and positive towards its Commonwealth partners in the region.[219]

The Australian decision indeed created diplomatic difficulties for both Tasman nations with Malaysia. Australian High Commissioner Eastman reported after the decision of a Malaysian "sense of grievance at the absence of 'reasonable prior consultation and explanation' (which they had come to regard as an established convention between us)".[220] His New Zealand colleague Zohrab paralleled the decision to the British announcement for withdrawal a year earlier, and called for "utmost flexibility, imagination and understanding"[221] to repair the damaged relations.

Both Australia and New Zealand understood that Malaysia and Singapore linked them to previous British arrangements, something they sought to avoid. On a deeper level though, Malaysian reactions exposed valuable strands of Commonwealth cooperation defined by traditional consultation concepts. Despite Britain's departure, officials had to consider the use of safeguarding such a Commonwealth framework. While officials could celebrate the fact that Australia and New Zealand had decided independently on a regional commitment for the first time[222], the episode nevertheless left both countries with important lessons for future cooperation.

---

[216] NAA A1838 TS696/1/9, Part 4, AHC Kuala Lumpur 3060, 28.12.1968.

[217] "New Zealand Defence Role in SEA", Evening Star, 23.12.1968.

[218] *Harvey Stockwin*, "Retreat from Malaysia", The Bulletin, 18.1.1969.

[219] See Australian Press Digest in ANZ ABHS W4628 7148, Box 121, LONB 106/7, Part 6, NHC Canberra 13, 6.1.1969.

[220] NAA A1838 TS696/1/9, Part 5, AHC Kuala Lumpur (Eastman) 367, 1.2.1969.

[221] ANZ ABHS W4628 7148, Box 121, LONB 106/7, Part 6, NHC Kuala Lumpur (Zohrab) 9, 7.1.1969.

[222] ANZ ABHS W4628 7148, Box 121, LONB 106/7, Part 5, NDEA to NHC Kuala Lumpur 820, 28.12.1968.

For one, New Zealand officials clearly felt side-lined as junior partners by the Australian dominance in decisionmaking, especially from the APMD.[223] After experiencing similar differences in ANZUS, the episode enforced calls for a New Zealand policy driven by national interests rather than cross-Tasman cooperation. Moreover, the decision indicated a more general lack of Australian appreciation or understanding of local attitudes. The racialised argument against shared housing in Terendak paralleled arguments used during discussions on larger security measurements at Butterworth.[224] In contrast, New Zealand officials pursued considerations for stationing troops with a greater sensitivity towards local attitudes.

The episode also exposed frictions within Australian policymaking circles: With Canadians, Gordon Jockel shared his frustrations about the missed opportunity for better regional relations, commenting that "if Australia saw its future in close cooperation with countries of South East Asia then forces and families should learn to live with Asians".[225] He also resented how the Australian government had informed Malaysia of its decision, "in self-interested nationalistic manner we resent in others, we simply told the Malaysians of our intentions".[226] Equally, the New Zealand High Commission Canberra judged the decision as representing a growing strength in nationalist policy introduced by John Gorton, who would not care "whether there is an appearance of consultation or not with other interested parties. But the disturbing thing about Mr Gorton's brand of nationalism is that it looks too much like withdrawal from contacts with other countries".[227]

The announcement on a troop transfer would not be the last tense episode in Australian-Malaysian relations during 1969. While officials like Gordon Jockel tried to mediate the nationalist rhetoric adopted by Gorton in talks with Malaysians[228], the Australian Prime Minister provoked further tensions by underlining on various occasions that any new defence arrangement would not cover East Malaysia. At the Five Power Meeting in June 1969, Gorton referred to the recent communal riots in Malaysia the month before to speak out in favour of only covering the security of 'Malaya'.[229]

---

223 ANZ ABHS W5533 22128, Box 12, CBA 22/2/1, NHC Canberra, Annual Report on 1968/69, 31.3.1969.

224 *Sean Brawley/Mathew Radcliffe*, Losing the Blanket, Building a Fence: Australian Anxiety and the End of Military Colonialism in Malaysia, in: The Journal of Imperial and Commonwealth History 45/6, 2017, 1026–1048.

225 LAC RG25 A-3-c, Vol. 8842, 20-AUSTL-1-3, CHC Canberra 27, 9.1.1969.

226 Ibid.

227 ANZ ABHS W4628 7148, Box 121, LONB 106/7, Part 6, Millen (NHC Canberra) to Mullins (NDEA), 8.1.1969.

228 ANZ ABHS W5400 20358, Box 97, KL 102/1/9, Part 6, NHC Kuala Lumpur 171, 13.3.1969.

229 ANZ ABHS W4628 7148, Box 121, LONB 106/7, Part 7, Opening Statement of John Gorton, 19.6.1969, NHC Canberra, 27.6.1969.

Among Western countries, the riots had served the re-emergence of long-standing perceptions of Southeast Asia as fundamentally destabilised by ethnic, political and cultural differences and tensions.[230] Despite the opposition to Gorton's political style, New Zealanders and also Canadians[231] therefore agreed to some parts with the apprehensions Australians held about any future defence arrangement in Malaysia and Singapore. They were equally concerned that Malaysia or Singapore could take any commitment as a simple takeover from the British. At the same Five Power Meeting, Keith Holyoake was however able to present his country's regional policy in more consoling terms, underlining that New Zealanders were aware and accepting "that we can be affected by what happens in South-east Asia and that we must be concerned with developments there".[232]

5.2.3 Australia, Canada and New Zealand as Asian-Pacific Nations

Shortly after Australia's and New Zealand's announcement to maintain troops after Britain's retreat in March 1969, the *New Zealand Herald* published a cartoon highlighting a change in regional policy (Fig. 4). Under the title *Stepping Stones*[233], cartoonist Gordon Minhinnick showed prime ministers John Gorton and Keith Holyoake holding hands and attempting a walk over the hot stones of 'Foreign Policy'. On the other side, Malaysia's Tunku Abdul Rahman and Singapore's Lee Kuan Yew are seen waiting, ready to welcome the two prime ministers. While the hot stones may refer to the recent difficulties of both Tasman governments in agreeing on their future joint strategy, they are also indicative of the struggles both countries endured on the path of better relations with the region. With the title *Stepping Stones* referring to public statements on Asian invasions made in the decades before, Australian and New Zealand new policy now seemed to represent a reverse direction: It was the task of the Tasman nations to make their way over to the Southeast Asian nations.

The decision taken in early 1969 to retain forces after 1971 was indeed a major step for Australia and New Zealand in the direction of establishing a distinct role in the region. They agreed to keep two separate yet connected battalions, resulting in the stationing of around 2 000–2 500 servicemen in total.[234] Even if officials were not able or willing to replace Britain, they perceived a

---

[230] *Peter J. Boyce*, The Bonds of Culture and Commonwealth in Southeast Asia, in: Journal of Southeast Asian Studies 2/1, 1971, 71–77.

[231] LAC MG26 O7, Vol. 259, 313.45, Brief for Visit of Pierre Trudeau to Pacific Area, n. d. (4.5.1970).

[232] ANZ ABHS W5400 20358, Box 97, KL 102/1/9, Part 6, Report on Canberra Five Power Meeting, 19./20.6.1969.

[233] *Gordon Minhinnick*, Stepping Stones, New Zealand Herald, 7.3.1969.

[234] *Bruce Juddery*, "Regional five-power 'posse' takes shape", The Canberra Times, 6.8.1970.

Fig. 4: Gordon Minhinnick: Stepping Stones, New Zealand Herald, 7.3.1969 (Source: New Zealand Herald/Photo/NZME/Gordon Minhinnick)

regional commitment as an indispensable factor to Australia's and New Zealand's own security. While this resembled earlier appreciations for regional development, the activist approach and the larger appreciation for local attitudes indicated a departure from previous concepts of foreign policy and defence. Comments such as Minhinnick's cartoon celebrated the fact of a larger cooperation, including the one across the Tasman.

Now, their shared location close to the Asian mainland became a necessity and opportunity for both countries to act on. With the announcement for a continued presence in February 1969, Gorton could oppose the arguments of instability Britain had endorsed to legitimise its withdrawal: "We reject this utterly. It is contrary to our historical actions in Korea, in Vietnam and in the region of which I speak, and it is contrary to our future interest."[235] The decision was also praised as an empowering sign of maturity and departure from inferior status in previous alliances. Officials like Alan Watt could call Gorton's announcement "historic. It is an important decision taken by an independent nation to maintain a military presence in the area for use in defined circumstances, without an automatic guarantee […] of military support by a Super or Major Power if the Australian forces concerned get into difficulties."[236]

[235] Statement by John Gorton in AHoR, 25.2.1969, found in: LAC RG25 A-3-c, Vol. 10282, 27-1-2-AUSTL.

[236] "ANZUS Treaty, Past, Present and the Future", Conference Paper by Alan Watt pres-

In a speech in March 1969, Keith Holyoake highlighted the fundamental changes of the regional policy taking place over Britain's retreat. Before, his staff had promoted such a speech to counter "the J. K. Hunns and the advocates of neutralism and Fortress Australia".[237] They recommended he should include "realism, confidence, and a sense of New Zealand nationalism"[238] in his speech, which Holyoake followed up by putting recent developments into a historic perspective. Until recently, New Zealanders had "been content because they believed that New Zealand was tagging along behind Britain and that this was the obvious – the 'loyal'– thing to do".[239] Now with the British gone and an emerging national consciousness, all New Zealanders would have to consider if they were willing to continue commitments established under a British umbrella: "It is in the knowledge of the past that we can turn to the question that we as a nation must answer today: in the new situation emerging today, will our basic policies continue to be sound and in the national interest?"[240]

Advocating a policy of regional involvement and allied cooperation, Holyoake pointed to past decisions for orientation: "We did not choose in 1939 that Nazi Germany should attack Poland, we did not choose in 1950 that North Korea should attack South Korea; we did not choose that there should be a Malayan communist guerrilla emergency, or Indonesia's Confrontation policy, or the Vietnam war. We faced a situation in which those wars existed."[241] Holyoake strongly interlinked strands of historical experience and present regional instability to create a consistency in New Zealand's outlook on regional security. At the same time, he presented the decision to retain troops as one of moral obligation or responsibility. These arguments previously put forward with British officials now seemed to resonate with a domestic audience: Newspapers such as the *New Zealand Herald* subsequently supported Holyoake by calling the retention of force "a significant step in the evolution of nationhood".[242] Simultaneously, the NDEA advised its diplomatic posts in the region to underline "our own national role as a country of the Asian/Pacific region"[243] and urged representatives to establish and deepen their Southeast Asian contacts.

Yet these repurposed arguments for commitment sought to establish an updated role in the region. Both Australian and New Zealand officials increas-

ented at ANU (Conference on Australia-New Zealand Relations), 23.2.1970, LAC RG25 A-3-c, Vol. 8842, 20-AUSTL-1-3, CHC Canberra 486, 30.7.1970.

[237] ANZ ABHS W4627 950, Box 4507, 434/8/1, Part 23, NDEA to NHC New Delhi 52 (Laking), 31.1.1969.

[238] Ibid.

[239] ANZ ABHS W4628 7148, Box 116, LONB 106/2/7, Part 5, "A Defence and Foreign Policy for New Zealand", Speech given by Keith Holyoake at the NIIA, 7.3.1969.

[240] Ibid.

[241] Ibid.

[242] "Maturity in Foreign Policy", New Zealand Herald, 7.3.1969.

[243] ANZ ABHS W5400 20358, Box 97, KL 102/1/9, Part 6, NDEA to NEmb. Djakarta, 27.3.1969.

ingly understood the importance of regional cooperation as an alternative to previous alliances dedicated to containment. While the independent defence relations with Malaysia and Singapore indicated new national confidence, in 1969, commentators were anxious that both countries would not repeat the mistakes of their predecessors in the region. The *Auckland Star* recommended that the ANZAC powers should avoid a firm commitment: "The relationship must be intimate but informal enough not to be regarded as a threat by any country in the area with whose destiny we are now involving ourselves as independent nations."[244] Similarly, AMD Fairhall cautioned to balance the need of sustaining relations with Malaysia and Singapore against creating a restrictive framework: "We must achieve this contact short of systematized arrangements, formal or informal: only thus can we hope to avoid creating a sense of Australian responsibility and an expectation of commitment."[245]

Increasingly, discussions also underlined the need for local governments to deal with conflicts themselves. This request for local self-reliance correlated with the change in US policy in July 1969, when Richard Nixon indicated a larger American unwillingness to become involved in Asian conflicts. Although his predecessors had made similar statements before, the emphasis of regional self-reliance and the denial of military assistance related to communist aggression in the Guam Doctrine set a precedent.[246] Nixon's announcement was embedded in a larger shift in US policy that had in parts been anticipated by Australian and New Zealand observers[247], especially as the American intervention in Vietnam had turned into such a controversial commitment.

While Nixon's announcement was mainly a pragmatic, balance-of-power oriented reading of regional security, it nevertheless instilled a certain urgency and distress in Australian and New Zealand foreign policymaking.[248] As opposition and media could charge the government for missing signs of changing US attitude, some officials like Australia's Ambassador to Washington Keith Waller read the statement as precipitating a "major withdrawal from the whole area west of Hawaii".[249] The uncanny reference to the term 'East of Suez' indicates how much officials still framed their outlook on regional security in terms of great power alliances. Yet these frameworks were shifting. While officials like Gordon Jockel would wish for the USA to play "the 'policeman' in Asia"[250], they nevertheless underlined the need for Australia to come to terms

244 "Flexible Defence Role in Malaysia", Auckland Star, 26.2.1969.

245 NAA A5619 C22, Part 3, Cabinet Submission 622 (by AMD Allen Fairhall), 10.6.1969.

246 *Thompson*, British Military Withdrawal, 135.

247 ANZ AAFD W3738 811, Box 1316, CAB 222/3/1, Part 2, Memorandum by NMEA Keith Holyoake to Cabinet, 2.1.1969.

248 *Andrea Benvenuti/David Martin Jones*, With Friends Like These: Australia, the United States, and Southeast Asian Détente, in: Journal of Cold War Studies 21/2, 2019, 27–57, 30.

249 AHC Washington, (26.2.1970), quoted in: *Curran*, Unholy Fury, 106.

250 LAC RG25 A-3-c, Vol. 8842, 20-AUSTL-1-3, CHC Canberra 378, 25.2.1969.

with its own national security objectives. Equally, the New Zealand Embassy Washington welcomed the American announcement to help New Zealand decide for what reasons it was staying in the region: "Is our interest really stability in Southeast Asia, or is it more simply and fundamentally just denying ground to the enemy?"[251] The Embassy came to no clear recommendation, but highlighted how most allies would expect New Zealand to stay in the region.

Uncertainty following the Nixon Doctrine also transpired in the discussions on Five Power defence that ran parallel. While Britain had underlined its continued interest in the region, the meeting of 1969 finally agreed to set a date to abolish AMDA, and to replace it with a Five Power Declaration.[252] The direction of British policy did not substantially alter when the Conservatives under Edward Heath were elected a year later, despite his condemnation for the British decisions in 1967/1968 as "'a flagrant breach of pledges'".[253] Moreover, as Australians and New Zealanders witnessed Heath's bid for EEC entry within days of his election, they understood that a British turn to Europe was no longer a piece of party politics, but an accepted bipartisan goal in British thinking. This perception would be only enforced when witnessing Britain's general reluctance to become further engaged in the Commonwealth.[254]

As a result, Tasman officials had mixed feelings when new British Secretary of Defence Lord Carrington indicated Britain's desire to retain a limited military presence during a visit in 1970. They appreciated the decision not for military reasons, but for the political and psychological value for regional stability. At the same time, officials linked the new arrangement to the rapid transformation of the regional security framework:

> "It is now two and a half years since the announcement of a firm British decision to withdraw by the end of next year and the countries of the area have, by and large, got so used to the idea of the British leaving and to accepting the basic reasons for their departure, that it is difficult to imagine that the decision could in fact be reversed."[255]

Even more so, officials were cautious that "the renewal of the British presence [could] lead to notions of self-contained 'Commonwealth' military community and induce inward-looking attitudes among our people in the region".[256]

---

251 ANZ ABHS W5400 20358, Box 97, KL 102/1/9, Part 6, NEmb. Washington 1343, 28.7.1969.

252 *Thompson*, British Military Withdrawal, 140.

253 Quoted in: *Andrea Benvenuti*, The Heath Government and British Defence Policy in Southeast Asia at the End of Empire (1970–71), in: Twentieth Century British History 20/1, 2009, 53–73, 58.

254 *Benvenuti/Dee*, Five Power Defence Arrangements, 102 f.

255 ANZ ABHS W4628 6950, Box 9, OTT 88/1/1, Memorandum on New Zealand Defence Policy after East of Suez, n. d. (August 1970).

256 Quoted in: *Andrea Benvenuti*, Shifting Priorities: Australia's Defence Ties to Britain in the Aftermath of Empire, in: History Compass 2, 2004, 1–11, 5.

In parts, British officials reacted to and therewith enforced these cautious, ambivalent attitudes. During his visit, Lord Carrington underlined that Britain would enter a new defence structure as "one partner among five equal partners".[257] Similarly, Heath picked up his predecessor's policy to replace AMDA with a more loose-knit arrangement. Ultimately, the communique issued after the Five Power discussions in April 1971 expressed the desire to establish arrangements that would not impose "undue strain or obligation on any party"[258], and resulted in a consultation agreement that had fewer teeth for joint action than the previous AMDA. It only declared that

"in the event of any form of armed attack externally organized or supported or the threat of such attack against Malaysia or Singapore, their Governments would immediately consult together for the purpose of deciding what measures should be taken jointly or separately in relation to such attack or threat."[259]

The altered character of arrangements was further indicated by vague, undefined positions regarding the Borneo territories and the inclusion of SEATO forces.[260]

Under FPDA, Australia, Britain and New Zealand decided to establish a shared force under the acronym ANZUK. Only 2 000 British troops remained under the arrangement, a mere five percent of the troops stationed during Confrontation. Australia would commit around 3 000 troops while New Zealand contributed around 1 000 forces.[261] Public discussions quickly observed the political intent rather than the military purpose of the arrangements[262], a perspective shared by officials like George Laking, who indicated in private that their own presence was "being kept alive primarily because the British feel they have a political commitment which must be honoured and which would be difficult for them to carry out if we and the Australians retreat".[263] Again, especially ground forces played a vital role in sustaining the belief in continued coopera-

---

257 ANZ AAFD W3738 811 Box 1316, CAB 222/3/1, Part 2, Notes of Meeting held with Lord Carrington, 3.8.1970.

258 Communique issued at the conclusion of the Five Power Ministerial Meeting on the External Defence of Malaysia and Singapore, London, 15./16. April 1971, quoted in: *Damon Bristow*, The Five Power Defence Arrangements. Southeast Asia's Unknown Regional Security Organization, in: Contemporary Southeast Asia 27/1, 2005, 1–20, 5.

259 Communique issued at the conclusion of the Five Power Ministerial Meeting on the External Defence of Malaysia and Singapore, London, 15./16. April 1971, quoted in: *Ralf Emmers*, The Role of the Five Power Defence Arrangements in Southeast Asian Security Architecture, in: William T. Tow/Brendan Taylor (Ed.), Bilateralism, Multilateralism and Asia-Pacific Security: Contending Cooperation, London/New York 2013, 87–99, 89.

260 *Ang Cheng Guan*, Malaysia, Singapore, and the Road to the Five Power Defence Arrangements (FPDA), July 1970–November 1971, in: War and Society 30/3, 2011, 207–225, 220.

261 *Millar*, Anglo-Australian Partnership, 84.

262 "A Gesture of Defence", Dominion, 20.4.1971.

263 NLNZ 92–258, 03/13, George Laking to Tim Francis, 14.5.1971.

tion, as Lord Carrington recalled in his memoirs: "It indicated that we had not completely abandoned our friends – pretty old friends – in that area."[264]

Despite remaining outside the Southeast Asian alliance framework, Canadians also assessed the impact of Five Power planning and Nixon's policy in 1969/1970. In June 1969, Canadian High Commissioner Hadwen judged that "the pattern of future five-power defence association by Britain, Australia and New Zealand with Malaysia and Singapore provides a satisfactory basis and an acceptable general atmosphere in which Canada can play its part in assisting these friendly countries to build security and defence forces".[265] While official Canadian policy adhered to the principle of non-commitment, Nixon's policy pushed further reviews to follow Hadwen's recommendation to engage more with local partners.[266] In a NATO brief, officials recommended discreetly encouraging regional associations: "In the context of increasing Western military disengagement"[267], it would be essential to sustain Asian members in their search for security, especially as regional alliances like ASPAC or ASEAN had not yet overcome hostilities between individual members. Canadian posts in the region also called for political action in times of uncertainty and local unease, and encouraged an active role. Both Canada's determination to recognise China and her retreat from the ICSC in Laos and Cambodia had suggested to local nations that Canada was turning its back on the region: "If we wish to be regarded as a Pacific nation we must now, decisively, begin to act as a Pacific nation."[268] Such calls allowed officials like Hadwen to urge for a larger military responsibility as "an essential part of our development assistance to the region".[269] His assessment was backed by security experts who criticised official departmental reviews on the region as too optimistic regarding strategic developments: "So much is at stake for Canada and the rest of the Western world in that part of the world (among others no doubt) that it is of vital interest to follow developments closely in order to adjust our policy to the changing realities of the situation."[270] In total, however, recommendations to appreciate the strategic links across the

[264] *Carrington*, Reflect on Things Past, 219.

[265] LAC RG25 A-3-c, Vol. 14594, 27-4-FPDA, CHC Kuala Lumpur (Hadwen) 472, 20.9.1969.

[266] LAC MG26 O7, Vol. 259, 313.45, Brief for Visit of Trudeau to Malaysia, 23.4.1970; see also *R. Stubbs*, Canada's Relations with Malaysia. Picking Partners in ASEAN, in: Pacific Affairs 63/3, 1990, 351–367.

[267] LAC RG25 A-3-c, Vol. 8600, 20-1-1-12, Part 7, NATO Far East Working Group, n. d. (October 1969).

[268] LAC RG25 A-3-c, Vol. 8615, 20-1-2-ASIA/PACIFIC, Part 1, CEmb. Bangkok (Cox), 15.1.1970.

[269] LAC RG25 A-3-c, Vol. 8615, 20-1-2-ASIA/PACIFIC, Part 1, CHC Kuala Lumpur, 2.1.1970.

[270] LAC RG25 A-3-c, Vol. 8615, 20-1-2-ASIA/PACIFIC, Part 1, Security and Intelligence Div. to Far Eastern Div., 14.1.1970.

Pacific remained marginal. Although the CDEA received outside reviews demanding a larger interest in the geopolitical developments in the region, few initiatives attempted to substantially reassess the country's regional policy, let alone give it a new direction by introducing new programs or decisions.

Meanwhile, following Trudeau's Pacific announcement in 1968, Australian officials also considered how to influence the Canadian geopolitical outlook. Already in the last weeks of the Pearson government, ADEA officials considered an appeal by Paul Hasluck to counterpart Paul Martin based on perceptions of greater regional interdependence: "It would be of immense satisfaction to us in this part of the world to be joining with Canada in a contribution towards political stability."[271] Keith Shann recommended a similar appeal to new CSEA Mitchell Sharp because of "a long-time worry we have had about Canadian apathy in the area (As opposed to her capacity, and very rapidly growing aid effort)".[272] This argument was further pushed over Australia's decision to retain forces in early 1969. In talks with the Canadian High Commission Canberra, Gordon Jockel indicated that the Australian government was convinced that both countries would enter "an age of 'systems of security', a fact which is significant for Australian-Canadian relations".[273]

At the same time, Australians were aware of the longstanding resistance in Canadian thinking to any military cooperation. When Trudeau visited Australia in May 1970, the *Sydney Morning Herald* praised the visit as coming at the right time concerning Britain's retreat, but harboured expectations: "But let us not pitch our hopes too high. It is fantasy to suppose that Canada can be persuaded to join in any form of regional defence arrangement or in a mutual security alliance on the lines of the ANZUS treaty."[274] New Zealanders seemed equally doubtful of a larger Canadian interest in the region. In a speech in late 1968, diplomat Hunter Wade commented that "Canada obviously has no sense of insecurity from Asia", meaning that it had "fairly consistently turned her face southwards and eastwards and historically has tried, not always successfully, to remain unengaged in Asia".[275]

Given the British decision, public discussions focused on Trudeau's profile as a new, unconventional and idealist Canadian that could introduce a shift in geopolitical priorities.[276] Trudeau's staff supported that image by preparing briefing papers for his visit that suggested a departure in foreign policy, laying "a greater emphasis on Canada's 'Pacific personality' – complementing (though

[271] NAA A1838 229/9/9/2, Part 2, Draft letter for AMEA Paul Hasluck to CSSEA Paul Martin, n. d. (February 1968).

[272] NAA A1838 229/9/9/2, Part 2, Keith Shann to ASEA, 11.9.1968.

[273] LAC RG25 A-3-c, Vol. 8842, 20-AUSTL-1-3, CHC Canberra 378, 25.2.1969.

[274] "Mr Trudeau", Sydney Morning Herald, 14.5.1970.

[275] *Hunter Wade*, Commonwealth Action in the Strategic Field; in: Commonwealth Journal Dec. 1968, found in: ANZ ABHS W4627 950, Box 4507, 434/8/1, Part 23.

[276] TNA FCO 7/1772, BHC Wellington (A. Galsworthy), 20.5.1970.

not of course replacing) our Atlantic, our North American and even our Arctic 'personality'".[277] The rhetoric of this could be easily translated into a fundamentally new policy based on Canada's identity as a Pacific nation that could resonate with the local enthusiasm for his visit. At the same time, however, it also indicated the limits of the Pacific outlook as just one field among Canada's international interests.

Therefore, Tasman doubts seemed ultimately confirmed in April 1972 when the New Zealand High Commission Ottawa reported after a lengthy discussion with Ivan Head, the political advisor to Trudeau, that the Canadian Pacific policy was largely related to approaches to China and Japan. According to Head, the review process of the previous years was designed to interlock Canadian national interests with international developments. Rather than aiming at a new role, Canada was more concerned over the attitude it would take on regional developments.[278]

Indeed, most of Canada's political emphasis on the Pacific was designed to enable an approach to China and Japan.[279] Moreover, the approach to Asian-Pacific nations under Trudeau was almost exclusively motivated by trade interests, a fact New Zealand representatives in Ottawa underlined in early 1971: "Australia and New Zealand still have a place in the Canadian sun but at the present that sun, for practical economic reasons, rises and sets on Japan and China. Canada's Pacific policy for the 1970s however is still a rather skinny animal – not much beyond bare bones."[280] The report continued that "the future relationship between Canada and New Zealand will be governed by tangible interests, rather than shared sentiment and tradition".[281] In retrospect, the limits of Canadian engagement with the region in contrast to Australia and New Zealand were highlighted in an interview with former diplomat Thomas Delworth. While Delworth presented himself as a strong advocate of Canada's relations with both Asia and Europe, he noticed that "it was Europe that gave us our sense of identity".[282] Given the predominance of the Atlantic community in Canadian outlooks, Asia continued to play a subordinate role in foreign policy considerations. Equally, aside from references to preferential cooperation and close relations in foreign policy, Australia and New Zealand judged larger Canadian commitment unlikely, and refrained from serious request for assistance in the following.

---

[277] LAC MG26 O7, Vol. 259, 313.45, Brief for Visit of Pierre Trudeau to Pacific area, n. d. (4.5.1970).

[278] ANZ ABHS W5761 6952, Box 123, SIN 337/1/1, NHC Ottawa, 25.4.1972.

[279] *Gérard Hervouet*, About Canada. Canada and the Pacific Basin, Ottawa 1988, 11 f.

[280] ANZ ABHS W4628 6950, Box 3, OTT 26/1/11, Part 2, NHC Ottawa, 29.1.1971.

[281] Ibid.

[282] Interview with Thomas Delworth, 26.10.1987, Summary in *Bothwell/Granatstein*, Trudeau's World, 316.

5.3 Groundworks for a New International Order

For Australia and New Zealand, the British decision to withdraw from East of Suez strongly challenged the concept of forward defence, but its deeper underpinnings proved resilient. Despite the multitude of events in 1968/69, combined with long-term developments such as early non-proliferation discussions establishing a Cold War détente, and the Sino-Soviet Split and the Cultural Revolution contributing to a demise of Chinese international interference, officials were slow in replacing their traditional strategy of containment. Particularly Australians and New Zealanders misjudged the fundamental changes taking place within the region from the mid-decade on.[283] Instead, a Cold War rhetoric of threat and uncertainty specifically linked to potential Chinese aggression was still applied to the region.

When Canadian policy, followed by American initiatives, considered engaging China, this step therefore appeared as a dramatic breakaway from Western principles of containment. The transformations starting in 1968/69 were not rapid in itself, but the lasting perceptions of the region as one dominated by instability made the developments appear unprecedented and fundamental. At the same time, continued governmental support for forward defence, despite the British and American reviews of their Southeast Asian policy, made the following amendments on regional strategy under Labo(u)r governments appear as equally swift and ground-breaking. Under Pierre Trudeau, Gough Whitlam and Norman Kirk, strategic principles were replaced by new concepts and norms. Most of all, Western governments reviewed their positions of non-recognition and containment in favour of engaging China, in turn resulting in reassessments of the communist threat and Cold War strategy.

Under the impression of a commencing international détente, Cold War bloc formation and confrontation was increasingly questioned. The Vietnam conflict had revealed how liberation movements could primarily be a result of domestic conflicts and only on a second tier would be sponsored by external communist powers. Trudeau, Whitlam and Kirk all criticised the binary approach to international affairs and sought out new fields of engagement. Instead of forward defence and traditional alliances, regionalism and policies of a 'Third Option'[284] became key concepts. This deemphasis of traditional frameworks was also shared among the great power alliances: Just as the 'Year of Europe' announced in American policies in 1973 correlated to Britain's entry into the EEC,

---

[283] *Edwards*, Nation at War, 186f.; *Rawdon Dalrymple*, Continental Drift. Australia's Search for a Regional Identity, Aldershot 2003, 27.

[284] The – ultimately unsuccessful – 'Third Option' was presented in 1972 in a Canadian policy paper as an option to divert trade interest on Europe and Japan following the Nixon Shock. *Head/Trudeau*, Canadian Way, 268–276; *Robert Bothwell*, Canada and the United States. The Politics of Partnership, Toronto 1992, 108–110.

the three Labour/Liberal governments pushed to tread new grounds in other parts of the world.[285]

All around the globe, the strong paradigm of Western containment as a security strategy began to fade. In this climate, concepts such as self-reliance and self-determination of regional frameworks were discussed as a fulfilment of national and regional sovereignty. With the advent of successful regional cooperation such as ASEAN, regional stability seemed to be in reach by other means than traditional alliances. This change of paradigm showed nowhere more than in the demise of alliances such as SEATO, and the continued opposition to foreign bases in the region.

The bilateral approaches between Australia and New Zealand, but also between them and Malaysia and Singapore, had served closer defence cooperation. This new character of defence cooperation was highlighted when Malaysia and Singapore established bilateral defence arrangements with the other partners of FPDA in May 1971.[286] Rather than relying on great power alliances at a time when tensions between East and West seemed to lessen, all three former dominions adopted a multilateralist policy on questions of supra-regional concern.[287] Aside from emphasising bilateral relations, they reviewed their options for a more self-reliant defence policy that resembled previous debates on an independent foreign policy.

The new emphasis on regional interaction and self-determination also lead to growing ideas of international responsibility among the former dominions. In and outside of these countries, demands for racial equality led to the abolition of policies previously established to secure a white and often British identity. Some could argue that the domestic change of norms went hand-in-hand with the international normative transformation resulting from decolonisation and liberalisation movements. Regarding the region, this change of norms contributed to a fuller body of ideas related to a Pacific role based on moral responsibility, partnership and integrity that was floated among all three former dominions.

5.3.1 The End of a Chinese Threat in Security Discussions

When John Hadwen met with Singapore's Lee Kuan Yew in early 1968, their discussions touched on topics that would amplify with the British announcement for a retreat in the following months. During the talk, Lee insisted Canada should contribute to Singapore's defence build-up, given that the small island nation was facing "an intensified power struggle in the Pacific" between

285 *Dobell*, Canada in World Affairs, 139 f.; *Curran*, Unholy Fury, 205.
286 *Bristow*, Five Power Defence Arrangements, 5.
287 *Smith/Cox/Burchill*, Australia in the World, 124.

the USA, Soviet Union and China, with the Chinese threat becoming "more sophisticated but remain[ing] equally dangerous and aggressive".[288] Lee's request came on the heels of a renewed anxiety over Chinese interference in the wake of Britain's policy changes. More importantly, his approach could result from shifting Canadian attitudes on Chinese recognition that would come to fruition under the premiership of Pierre Trudeau a few months later.

Although recognition had been under review for decades, even some Canadian officials were surprised when Pierre Trudeau announced that he would make the recognition of the PRC one of his first goals as Prime Minister. The surprise largely stemmed from a persistent adherence to American policy under Lester Pearson despite the unease over non-recognition among Canadian officials.[289] An important factor in Trudeau's announcement were the calls for new directions in foreign policy enthusiastically introduced with his premiership. Chinese recognition soon became the key issue to symbolise such a departure. For Trudeau himself, recognition embodied a personal goal after he had visited China in 1949 and 1960. His support for recognition was also rooted in his larger opposition to Cold War rhetoric and his anti-establishment attitudes.[290] Seeing the status of China as an "international anomaly"[291], Trudeau supported recognition as based on the reality of international affairs. In a speech held in May 1968, he also introduced his plans for recognition as one of increasing Canadian interest in Pacific affairs: "Because of past preoccupations with Atlantic and European affairs, we have tended to overlook the reality that Canada is a Pacific country too."[292]

By linking Chinese recognition to larger Pacific integration, Trudeau however seemed to fail to recognise other regional attitudes on the topic. Especially in Australia, his announcement had been received with some reservations. Although Canadian officials promised to consult with its partners, Australian officials feared a radical policy review following Trudeau's election.[293] When ADEA official Malcolm Booker met with Canadian High Commissioner Arthur Menzies, Booker charged the Canadian government for dismissing regional opposition to recognition: "Insofar as Canada had associated itself with European and Latin American Countries in attempting to bring about the admission of Peking to the United Nations, it had therefore diminished its standing as a Pacific power."[294] After Canada initiated its talks with China, AMEA Gordon Freeth re-

---

[288] LAC RG25 A-3-c, Vol. 8600, 20-1-1-12, Part 6, CHC Kuala Lumpur 40, 16.1.1968.

[289] *English*, Lester Pearson and China; see Martin's own recollection in *Bothwell/Granatstein*, Trudeau's World, 299 f.

[290] *Evans*, Engaging China, 23–27.

[291] *Head/Trudeau*, Canadian Way, 11.

[292] "Canada and the World", A Policy Statement by Prime Minister Pierre Elliott Trudeau issued on May 29, 1968, Statement and Speeches No. 68/17.

[293] NAA A1838 229/10/4/3, Part 2, AHC Ottawa Sav. 20, 7.5.1968.

[294] NAA A1838 229/10/4/3, Part 2, Note for File, 25.6.1968.

iterated this argument by pointing to the bad image Canada would create among Southeast Asian countries.[295]

Throughout Trudeau's initiative, Australians would go even beyond the American position in criticising the Canadian plans for causing repercussions on their position in Vietnam.[296] They also substantially differed from the New Zealand attitude. Here, officials were sceptical of the Canadian initiative given what they perceived as a continued Chinese threat, but appreciated the Canadian approach as "the best means of ascertaining whether in fact the Peking Government is disposed to seek wider and better relations with the world in general".[297] New Zealanders hoped that Canada would establish a channel for information and communication with the Communist regime.

Aside from the conduct of international affairs, it was the question of continued Chinese interference in Southeast Asia which influenced the different attitudes. While Australia upheld the idea of a Chinese threat and New Zealand mainly followed that position, Canada saw the need to overcome these perceptions by recognition, even in the eye of potential risks: "The evolution will not be smooth, and at times it may well be threatening, particularly to China's smaller neighbours, but it must come."[298] From a Canadian perspective, recognition would serve Cold War mediation as it would get China out of international isolation. However, threat discourses related to the region were still in transition among Canadian departments themselves, with some divisions still supporting traditional views of an alliance-based regional security order. When intelligence officials presented a paper on future instability in Southeast Asia in April 1970, diplomat Blair Seaborn felt compelled to write a strong response. Criticising the paper, he saw intelligence information presented in a misleading way to serve political allegations:

> "Underlying the paper is a fundamental assumption of a vast Sino-Soviet conspiracy […] to 'take over' Southeast Asia. […] The danger of this plot succeeding is enormously increased by the 'political' decision of the perfidious British to withdraw from East of Suez and by the Nixon Doctrine calling for a diminished US role in Southeast Asia."[299]

Seaborn clearly opposed what other parts of the Anglosphere still saw as the largest threat to Southeast Asia and global security, namely communist aggression. His comments indicate how some officials tried to resist the hegemonic

[295] NAA A1838 229/9/1, Part 4, Meeting of AMEA Gordon Freeth with CHC Arthur Menzies, 22.8.1969.

[296] LAC MG26 07, Vol. 487, Brief for Visit of Gorton, 24.3.1969; NAA A1838 229/9/1, Part 4, Notes for Prime Minister's Visit to Ottawa (2./3.4.1969), 21.3.1969.

[297] ANZ AAEG W3252 6956, Box 9, TKY 50/9/9, Part 6, "Situation in Treaty Area", SEATO Brief, 13.5.1969.

[298] LAC RG25, Vol. 10663, 23-3-1968, Brief for Commonwealth Prime Ministers' Meeting by Far Eastern Div. (Seaborn), 11.12.1968.

[299] LAC RG25 A-3-c, Vol. 8600, 20-1-1-12, Part 7, Far Eastern Div. (Seaborn) on Joint Intelligence Committee Paper "The Situation in Southeast Asia and the Far East", 23.4.1970.

polarised view of Cold War threat perceptions and instead aimed at unmasking some of the long-held convictions of Western containment. Nevertheless, not least because of internal doubts, Canadian officials had to be aware of the political consequences of their approach to China, particularly regarding Chinese claims of Taiwan. When bilateral relations were established in October 1970, Canadians agreed to a deliberately vague position. The joint communique read: "The Chinese Government reaffirms that Taiwan is an inalienable part of the territory of the People's Republic of China. The Canadian government takes note of this position of the Chinese government."[300] Although the formula of 'taking note' was considered a diplomatic success and was subsequently used by other countries[301], Canada soon changed directions and ultimately voted for the admission of China to the UN and the de-recognition of Taiwan.[302]

While Canadian considerations were still underway, Australian and New Zealand papers continued to insist on a Chinese threat. In late 1968, former New Zealand Ambassador to Bangkok Stephen Weir publicly warned not to underestimate Chinese interference and praised the presence of alliances such as SEATO.[303] During a visit to Ottawa in March 1969, John Gorton directly challenged the Canadian attitude with an insistence on local experience: "In other words, I, like most of the people who live in that area, as distinct from people who live in other areas, most of the people who live in that area don't dismiss the domino theory as being sheer nonsense. Neither do I."[304]

Both Australia and New Zealand adopted arguments of local first-hand knowledge to dismiss Canadian arguments. However, governments in both countries increasingly saw themselves put on the spot when domestic opposition made use of the Canadian initiative. In a speech in October 1968, New Zealand commentator Jack Hunn claimed that New Zealand should adopt a position of independent judgement on Chinese recognition similar to Canada.[305] Similarly, former Australian diplomat Gregory Clark used the Canadian position to delegitimise Australia's insistence on a continued threat: "If we compare Australia's attitude towards China with that of the United Kingdom, or, even better, with Canada, whose security dependence on the U. S. parallels that of Australia,

---

[300] Quoted in: *Michael B. Frolic*, The Trudeau Initiative, in: Paul M. Evans/Michael B. Frolic (Ed.), Reluctant Adversaries: Canada and the People's Republic of China 1949–1970, Toronto 1991, 189–216, 208.

[301] *Bothwell/Granatstein*, Trudeau's World, 306. In Australia, Gough Whitlam considered to adopt the Canadian formula in an Australian recognition, *Murphy*, Harvest of Fear, 271.

[302] *Arthur Andrew*, 'A Reasonable Period of Time'. Canada's De-Recognition of Nationalist China, in: Paul M. Evans/Michael B. Frolic (Ed.), Reluctant Adversaries: Canada and the People's Republic of China 1949–1970, Toronto 1991, 241–252.

[303] "New Zealand needs to give help to SEA", Opotiki News, 22.11.1968.

[304] NAA A1838 229/9/9/3, Part 1, Press Conference given by John Gorton in Ottawa, 3.4.1969.

[305] "Fresh Outlook Required on Strategy in Asia", New Zealand Herald, 18.10.1968.

its extremism becomes even more apparent."[306] These critiques fell in line with current academic questioning the 'Yellow Peril' as a hegemonic characterisation of Asia. Especially the conviction that Chinese intervention had dominated the Vietnam conflict crumbled under notions that North Vietnam was pursuing its own path.[307] In a speech in 1971, New Zealand lecturer Roy criticised the continued forward defence policy as obstructing good relations with its Asian neighbours. If officials would continue to follow

"the fatuous belief that Asians are quite happy to have their backyards turned into battlefield to prevent communism reaching New Zealand, then clearly New Zealanders have simply no idea how Asians feel about the prospect of seeing their respective countries turned into so many Vietnams."[308]

Roy criticised the continued strands of anti-communism and forward defence in the New Zealand government as inhibiting any real integration into the region. Some of this criticism had been anticipated within the NDEA where overseas posts in Asia had protested official policy as being too narrowly focused on New Zealand's Western allies and the defence character of most alliances with the region.[309]

Indeed, officials in most Western countries started to question the traditional set of anti-communist alliance in the wake of Cold War détente. The Australian Strategic Basis paper for 1971 highlighted the shift in power relations: "Globally the bipolar organisation of power is giving way to a more complicated strategic situation in which China, Japan and Western Europe have greater importance, and lesser states too are enabled to assert their independence and strengthen their economic and military capabilities."[310]

However, both Australia and New Zealand were slow to review long-established policies surrounding a Communist threat. Official government positions still saw great power alliance in combination with non-recognition as the best strategy, resulting in mounting pressure from outside circles when the official policy on China also started to shift with its most important ally on the issue, the USA. After claiming that the USA was also taking a new approach to its relations with China, Australian Leader of Opposition Whitlam used the following uncertainty about future Australian policy to visit the PRC with a Labor del-

---

306 *Clark*, Fear of China, 169.

307 *J. A. C. Mackie/Milton Osborne*, The Dominion Fallacy, in: Australian Neighbours, March/April 1968, 1–4, 1.

308 ANZ ABHS W5242 950, Box 33, 85/1/1, Part 12, "Dilemmas of New Zealand Defence in the Seventies", Speech given by Professor Roy at the ANZAAS Congress, 1.5.1971.

309 See the discussions on the New Zealand Foreign Policy Background Paper No. 170 in ANZ ABHS W5789 6945, Box 102, JKA 64/10/1 and ANZ ABHS W4628 6957, Box 21, SAI 63/1/1, Part 1.

310 NAA A5619 C470, Part 2, "The Strategic Basis of Australian Defence Policy – 1971", Cabinet Submission 107, 19.5.1971.

egation in July 1971.[311] Australia's Prime Minister William McMahon criticised this visit as approaching "the enemy" and damaging Australia's relations with the USA[312], but had to make an embarrassing retreat when US National Security Adviser Henry Kissinger's secret visit to China only days after Whitlam became public. Not only was Australia's China policy deemed outdated within days, but this episode also proved again the limited access Australia had to US policymaking despite its alliance status, leaving officials unable to predict this shift in US attitudes.

In contrast, Whitlam could present himself as aware of the trends in US foreign policy thinking. He endorsed the changed American policy towards China wholeheartedly and used the following trials and tribulations of the Conservative Party over the issue in his election campaign in 1972:

> "We cannot afford to limp along with men whose attitudes are rooted in the slogans of the 1950s – the slogans of fear and hate. If we made such a mistake, we would make Australia a backwater in our region and a back number in history. The Australian Labor Party – vindicated as we have been on all the great issues of the past – stands ready to take Australia forward to her rightful, proud, secure, and independent pace in the future of the region."[313]

In reality, engaging China had already become a bipartisan position indicated by tentative preparations for recognition under McMahon, yet opposition could present the government as out of touch with American politics.[314] More importantly, Whitlam could use the issue by underlining how attitudes of fear inhibited a larger integration into the region, thus creating an image of Australia as a backwards country.

Like Whitlam, New Zealand Leader of Opposition Norman Kirk supported Chinese recognition as he believed it would enable further stability in Southeast Asia.[315] At the same time, the issue was pursued with larger political bipartisanship within New Zealand. Although the NLP wanted the National Government to pursue recognition by entering negotiations, it still supported the two-China policy under Holyoake. Norman Kirk even went as far as to reject a delegation visit similar to Whitlam's trip in July 1971 and instead favoured an official cross-party mission.[316]

311 *Curran*, Unholy Fury, 118 f.

312 Quoted in: *James Curran*, 'The World Changes': Australia's China Policy in the Wake of Empire, in: James Reilly/Jing-dong Yuan (Ed.), Australia and China at 40, Chicago 2012, 22–43, 23.

313 Quoted in: *Burke*, Fear of Security, 133.

314 The potential bad outcome of a hurried change of Australian government policy on recognition was also noted in private by New Zealand officials, NLNZ 92–258, 03/13, Laking to Francis, 27.7.1971.

315 *David McCraw*, Norman Kirk, The Labour Party and New Zealand's Recognition of The People's Republic Of China, in: New Zealand Journal of Asian Studies 4/1, 2002, 46–61, 60.

316 Ibid., 54.

Still, recognition of China developed into the ultimate defeat of traditional threat discussions in both countries, where it was used as a symbolic issue of foreign policy departure similar to Canadian debates. Chinese recognition was among the first decisions Whitlam took even before forming a cabinet, when he led politics in a duumvirate with his Deputy Lance Barnard.[317] New Zealand followed the Australian course of swift recognition after Kirk's election. Although Kirk did not want to rush the issue, he nevertheless decided on simultaneous recognition of China with Australia on 22 December 1972.[318] The immediacy of the decision and the limited public protest against this decision indicates the demise of threat discourses in the perception of China. Notions of innovation and departure replaced old references to a foreign, alien and dangerous country within years. Bryce Harland, the first Ambassador to Peking, wrote in his valedictory dispatch in 1975: "We have begun to learn how to sleep, if not with an elephant, with a panda. And we have found that it is not so dangerous at all."[319] Harland's comments suggest the perceived need to establish a rapport with the communist regime, despite continued apprehension about its future politics. Ultimately, the Labo(u)r governments could present Chinese isolation as a risk on the way to regional security and international cooperation. Moreover, it was an intended departure from the uncertainty following the British decision for withdrawal: "In this view, China came to epitomise not only a new era of Asian belonging, but the means whereby Australia escaped the profound disorientation that attended its ambivalent exit from the British world."[320]

The recognition of China was a remarkable swift change from the attitudes of fear over the Chinese role in regional considerations held only a few years earlier. The change was also made possible by altered outlooks on international cooperation and commitment.

5.3.2 New Regimes of Equality and Responsibility under Whitlam, Kirk and Trudeau

Although Canada's lead towards Chinese recognition was internationally praised and was followed by Australia and New Zealand, other parts of its international influence waned under Trudeau. Particularly the concept of peacekeeping, previously hailed as a genuine Canadian trademark of international com-

[317] *Andrea Benvenuti/David M. Jones*, Engaging Southeast Asia? Labor's Regional Mythology and Australia's Military Withdrawal from Singapore and Malaysia 1972–1973, in: Journal of Cold War Studies 12/4, 2010, 32–62, 48.

[318] *McCraw*, Norman Kirk, 56–58.

[319] "Sleeping with the Panda", Valedictory Dispatch by Bryce Harland (NEmb. Peking), 24.11.1975, quoted in: *Chris Elder* (Ed.), New Zealand's China Experience. Its Genesis, Triumphs, and Occasional Moments of Less Than Complete Success, Wellington 2012, 188–194, 194.

[320] *Curran*, The World Changes, 24.

mitment, came under scrutiny in government circles. While one reason were ongoing general reviews of Canada's military commitments abroad, it was also the frustrating experience in Vietnam that led to the questioning of peacekeeping. By 1973, at the official end of the ICSC mission, most officials were disillusioned about their influence as mediators. The last Canadian Commissioner described the truce commission as "an ineffectual and rather pathetic body", "a sad monument to poorly conceived and poorly employed international machinery"[321] unable to improve or even solve the conflict.

Other events such as the sudden expulsion of Canadian UNEF forces from Gaza in late 1967 contributed to departmental doubts in the role of peacekeepers. The Canadian White Paper on defence resumed in 1970 that peacekeeping had "too often been frustrating and disillusioning", with many conflicts having "their roots in subversion and insurgency, and therefore […] not lend[ing] themselves easily to resolution through the use of internationally constituted peacekeeping bodies".[322] On a larger level, questioning peacekeeping was also caused by the marked decline in traditional Cold War views and ensuing hostilities. As the mediating role had drawn a lot of legitimisation from the specific bipolar front between two blocs, the emerging multipolar order following détente made such a role more complex and difficult to uphold. Lastly, Canadian officials started to doubt the concept of 'middlepowership', as the restoration of Western Europe led to the ascendancy of other countries that could claim such a role.[323]

Therefore, Trudeau's call for a foreign policy review was largely embedded in the realist perception that Canada's traditional position had vanished. He renounced the foreign policy of his predecessors that had given much credit to Canada's role as 'helpful fixer'.[324] Instead, his government considered the abolition of its peacekeeping role for one of being a reliable partner in bilateral relations. Such deemphasis of multilateralism was also expressed in Canada's recognition of China: It sought recognition first on a bilateral level rather than going through the UN.[325] Furthermore, correlating to the review of its defence role in alliances such as NATO, considerations for Canada's armed services focused on the concept of development assistance.

Ultimately however, despite all these objections, the idea of peacekeeping as an international role remained strong. While the government of Lester Pearson had established a certain tradition of peacekeeping that was now considered a Canadian legacy in public, it was also outside expectations that perpetuated the

---

[321] *Ross*, In the Interest of Peace, 24 f.

[322] *D. S. Macdonald*, Defence in the 70s: White Paper on Defence, Ottawa 1971, 39–40, quoted in: *Bothwell/Granatstein*, Trudeau's World, 128.

[323] *Tucker*, Canadian Foreign Policy, 10 f.

[324] *Thordarson*, Cutting Back, 174 f.

[325] *Andrew*, Middle Power, 90.

idea of Canada as a peacekeeper. Such expectations became clear at the end of Canada's first truce commission in Vietnam, when discussions for a new supervisory role resumed in 1973. While Trudeau opposed another Canadian intervention into the Vietnam conflict, Canadian officials were ultimately caught up by American pressure and public expectations to fulfil another supervisory role. Under the Paris Peace Treaty established for Vietnam in January 1973, they agreed to participate in the International Commission for Control and Supervision (ICCS).[326]

In parts, Canada experienced difficulties in implementing its own policy objectives in an existing framework of alliances and obligations similar to the struggles Australia and New Zealand tackled over their reviews of forward defence. All three countries aimed to introduce new normative regimes in relation to international conflicts, which were put under pressure by existing security alliances and structures. However, in contrast to Canada's shift away from internationalism, Australian and New Zealand reviews were still more driven by the loss of British support in a regional security framework. Political observers such as New Zealand lecturer Michael Stenson could criticise the continued emphasis of forward defence as the unquestioned rationale for engagement with the region. Stenson opposed what he saw as a "dead hand of tradition"[327], namely the continued support for a threat-based security narrative surrounding Southeast Asia:

> "The Malayan peninsula does not point in any meaningful sense 'like a finger in our direction'. Singapore is no longer a crucial sea communications centre for us. The Malay World is to our north but is not our nearest north. It is in fact only on the fringes of our immediate geographic and political region."[328]

As Stenson's criticism followed traditional detachment from the region, different overseas missions felt the need to respond with an endorsement of a military presence in Southeast Asia. Officials pointed out how much their presence had served both as a constructive force in building regional relationships as well as a stabilising influence in a destabilised region.[329] Two years later, also NDEA officials had become impatient amidst embryonic regional contacts. Speaking at the University of Otago, official Ralph Mullins addressed the slow pace of engaging with Southeast Asia. To him, remnants of colonial and imperial times still defined New Zealand's attitude:

> "The residue of the 'Little-Britain-of-the-South-Seas' attitude has been sympathetic to continuing links with the United Kingdom and the South Pacific, and even to the tran-

[326] *Ross*, In the Interest of Peace, 335–346; *Dobell*, Canada in World Affairs, 288–293.

[327] ANZ ABHS W5789 6945, Box 102, JKA 64/10/1, "New Zealand and the Malay World", Paper presented by Michael Stenson at the NIIA, May 1970.

[328] Ibid.

[329] ANZ ABHS W5789 6945, Box 102, JKA 64/10/1, NHC Kuala Lumpur, 21.10.1970 and NHC Singapore (Francis), 17.9.1970.

sition from a colony to a member of the Commonwealth, but to little else; a diffuse internationalism has been acceptable but not a bilateral relationship with other countries of the Pacific Area."[330]

Because of this attitude, New Zealand would not search for closer relations with other countries in the area. Clearly, officials like Mullins felt that despite achievements under the Five Power defence umbrella, New Zealand lacked a broader understanding and activism towards Southeast Asian cooperation. Regional arrangements were still defined by Anglocentric and not Southeast Asian markers of identity. As a result, the residues of Britishness proved inhibiting when it came to a true integration into regional affairs.

Meanwhile, the concept of forward defence posed similar dilemmas of reorientation, since it was undermined by the British decision and the global demise of its legitimising framework. Now, officials could less easily discharge allegations of colonialism and white supremacy related to the stationing of forces. Although they had underlined their own colonial upbringing and recent independence a few years earlier, officials became more aware of their connection to Britain that could be considered a "post-colonial hangover"[331] by locals. When discussing the future location of ANZAC headquarters in July 1969, the NDEA conveyed to Canberra its concerns that any military facility could be perceived as "white military enclaves in Southeast Asia".[332] Therefore, it recommended that any negotiation with local leaders should underline the regional role of New Zealand forces.

Australian and New Zealand officials also quarrelled with the British, European or simply white elements of their identity in other settings. The ADEA warned various posts in early 1970 that participation in regional arrangements such as ASEAN was not desirable, as "Australia would constitute a disparate element, a 'developed' 'European' country".[333] Commentator Ronald Munto noted that Australians would have difficulties being fully accepted in regional associations such as ASEAN if they would not shed off their British or White outlook: "If Australians still find it difficult to abandon the idea of being a far-flung outpost of European civilization, equally Asians find it extremely hard to regard the Australian as anything but a white European, vastly different in culture and outlook from the Asian."[334] From Singapore, New Zealand officials

---

330 "New Zealand's Defence Outlook", Paper presented by Ralph Mullins at the Seventh Residing School on New Zealand Foreign Policy, University of Otago, 13.5.1972, ANZ ABHS W5400 20358, Box 105, KL 104/3/1, Part 1.

331 ANZ ABHS W5400 20358, Box 156, KL 242/2/1, NHC Kuala Lumpur, 29.3.1967.

332 ANZ ABHS W4628 7148, Box 121, LONB 106/7 Part 7, Wellington to Canberra 1160, 28.7.1969.

333 NAA A1838 370/1/22, Part 3, ADEA to all Posts, 27.1.1970.

334 *Ronald Munto*, Pacific Signposts. 6) Australia's Regional Role in Asia – A Clear Necessity, in: Meanjin 4, 1969, 184–193, 185.

expressed similar concerns over a likely inclusion into ASPAC.[335] As a result, officials continued to struggle with how their national identity could be reconciled with their geographical setting. One obvious yet extremely contested field preventing better integration was the field of immigration. In the wake of the American announcement for Chinese recognition in summer 1971, diplomat Richard Woolcott summarised what was at stake for Australia:

"Australia is on the threshold of a bright future if it makes the right choices. We can stand still and allow ourselves to come to be regarded as a bucolic, inwards-looking, materialist, racist, self-satisfied, apathetic, pleasure-seeking member of the world community slumbering at the southern end of the globe – a sort of Anglo-American step-child which never really grew up; a second-hand, transplanted society which lost its momentum before it decided in which direction it wanted to move – or we can continue to become an accepted distinctive, tolerant and well-regarded nation in the Asia-Pacific region. The choice is ours."[336]

While officials like Woolcott recommended a change of policy as they pointed to the disadvantageous images their restrictive immigration laws created in Southeast Asia, both governments were still cautious about any step that could change the ethnic and cultural character of their societies. Nevertheless, tentative measures were taken to approach the region. On Australian immigration, Gorton followed early arrangements made under Holt.[337] Another measure was the growing emphasis on promoting languages and regional studies by establishing Asian studies centres.[338]

In the aftermath of the British decision, political commentators also urged to increase economic, cultural and touristic contacts with the region.[339] This line was generally advocated for international relations in all three countries, even more so as they felt increasingly challenged by the growing gap in relations to the 'Third World' and the questions of development. While Australian and New Zealand officials feared for their current policies to prevent further integration into the region, Canadian policymakers saw the struggles of the 'Global South' as a challenge to the international system of peace.[340] In a speech at the University of Alberta in March 1968, Trudeau told listeners that "the overwhelming threat to Canada will not come from foreign interests, or foreign ideologies or even – with good fortune – foreign nuclear weapons", instead it would come from the "two-thirds of the people of the world who are steadily falling farther

---

335 ANZ ABHS W4627 950, Box 770, 1/2/27, Part 5, Division Heads' Meeting, 27.7.1967.

336 Quoted in: *David Goldsworthy et al.*, Reorientation, in: David Goldsworthy/Peter Edwards (Ed.), Facing North: A Century of Australian Engagement with Asia, Melbourne 2001, 310–371, 311.

337 *Meaney*, End of 'White Australia', 179 f.

338 *Stephen FitzGerald*, Is Australia an Asian Country? Can Australia Survive in an East Asian Future?, St. Leonards 1997, 20 f.

339 *Munto*, Pacific Signposts, 187 f.

340 *Head/Trudeau*, Canadian Way, 9.

and farther behind in their search for a decent standard of living".[341] Military interaction was therefore rededicated to the idea of humanitarian relief, while military intervention was less considered as an option for international security.

The transnational character of these considerations was visible in Australia and New Zealand where similar concerns were linked to the question of stationed forces. In early 1968, New Zealand Chief of Naval Staff John Ross indicated a wish to follow Britain's retreat, as a continued presence could be charged as neo-imperialist: "it is just not fashionable in this day and age to embark on real estate and Base commitments in someone else's territory."[342] Despite such high-level doubts and calls for alternative policies, a conviction of the deterrence purpose remained strong. While officials were aware of the disadvantages of a continued forward defence position, at the same time political pressure and a continued belief in interventionist roles prevented a clear departure from this policy.[343]

A pronounced end of forward defence was only introduced by the governments of Gough Whitlam and Norman Kirk. Both had criticised the retention of forces after the British withdrawal. Whitlam saw it as "'a vestigial and nostalgic role in the affairs of the region'"[344], while Kirk called the decision "a review of history rather than a new plan or idea for the future".[345] Similar to Trudeau, both leaders would draw on notions of equality, justice and liberalisation that should be represented both in domestic and international politics.[346]

As Whitlam and Kirk were also influenced by the global questioning of Cold War principles, shifting outlooks under them were also applied to their defence alliances. Two frameworks that had been criticised for a while now drew to a close: SEATO and the Vietnam commitment. Over Britain's withdrawal and American isolationism, SEATO was increasingly considered as outdated. Like ASPAC, the anti-communist framework also lost its raison d'être with the US rapprochement to China.[347] Newspapers called the alliance an anachronism that would only point to the larger need to review forward defence and traditional alliance structures.[348] Under the Labo(u)r governments, opposition to SEATO became even more outspoken. Whitlam had publicly advocated against SEATO since the mid-1960s. Similarly, Kirk had declared in an interview that "as far

341 Quoted in: *English*, Just Watch Me, 59.

342 ANZ ABHS W5242 950, Box 33, 85/1/1, Part 12,"Future presence in SEA", Paper by New Zealand Chief of Naval Staff John Ross, 15.3.1968.

343 See e. g. NAA A1838 TS696/1/9, Part 3, James Plimsoll to Henry Bland, 23.7.1968.

344 Whitlam quoted in: NHC Canberra, ANZ ABHS W5400 20358, Box 97, KL 102/1/9, Part 6, NHC Canberra, 7.3.1969.

345 ANZ ABHS W5400 20358, Box 97, KL 102/1/9, Part 6, NDEA to NHC Canberra 355, 10.3.1969.

346 *Doig*, New Nationalism, 560 f.

347 *Halvorson*, Australia in Asia, 125 f.

348 The Australian, 13.11.1970.

as New Zealand is concerned, it [SEATO] is not part of […] our defences".[349] The charges resonated with the overall development within the organisation: While the 1972 SEATO Council Meeting still underlined the need for counter-insurgency operations[350], a year later, the organisation was stripped of its military framework. It would continue to exist in a state of ineffectiveness until its dissolution in 1977.

SEATO's demise coincided with the retreat from Vietnam. Similar to the alliance of SEATO, public support for the military commitment to Vietnam was in demise since the late 1960s, lending strong support to Whitlam's and Kirk's swift decisions to withdraw remaining troops from Vietnam in late 1972.[351] All three leaders of the former dominions also publicly denounced the American 'Christmas' bombing, leading to various levels of severed relations with the American administration.[352]

With a dissociation from their traditional alliances, officials hoped to frame their foreign policies as an independent departure from the past. This also included an outspoken distinction from the British connection. As New Zealand official Frank Corner recalled, Kirk's take on foreign policy should show that New Zealand was no longer "an appendage of Britain nor did he wish it to become an appendage of any other country".[353] In both countries, this departure was also induced by moral considerations transcending the binary outlook on global relations under the impression of the Cold War. Interestingly enough, on a global level, early considerations for a moral foreign policy stemmed from discussions in the Commonwealth. All three countries increased their commitment to the organisation after an era of doubts resulting largely from the violent disputes over Rhodesia and apartheid spanning the 1960s. Despite earlier hesitations, Trudeau and the Labo(u)r governments soon developed a more optimistic approach to the organisation, even more so as Britain seemed to withdraw as head of the organisation at the Commonwealth Prime Ministers' meeting in 1969.[354] Trudeau returned from the same meeting as a supporter of the Com-

---

349 ANZ ABHS W5789 6945, Box 102, JKA 64/10/1, Interview with Norman Kirk by The Round Table, 12.3.1973.

350 ANZ ABFK W5929 7291, Box 91, 95/3/1, Report by NCDS on his Visit to Australia, 21.7.1972.

351 *Allan Patience*, Australian Foreign Policy in Asia. Middle Power or Awkward Partner?, Cham 2018, 115; *Murphy*, Harvest of Fear, 206–211.

352 While Nixon put a "freeze" on relations with Australia and Canada, New Zealand could soon regain American access; *Curran*, Unholy Fury, 172; *Bothwell*, Politics of Partnership, 111; *David Malcolm Grant*, The Mighty Totara. The Life and Times of Norman Kirk, Auckland 2014, 265 f.

353 *Frank Corner*, Kirk Presents a New Zealand Face to the World, in: Margaret Clark (Ed.), Three Labour Leaders: Nordmeyer, Kirk, Rowling, North Palmerston 2001, 139–167, 144.

354 ANZ ABHS W5400 20358, Box 85, KL 90/3/2, Part 2, New Zealand Report on the Commonwealth Prime Ministers' Conference, 20.2.1969.

monwealth, describing it as "a meeting place where men are able to demonstrate the advantages of dissimilarity, the richness of diversity, the excitement of variety. Is that not what life is all about, to learn, to share, to benefit and to come to understand?"[355] In the following, the Trudeau administration endorsed the organisation as a bridge into the 'global South', and underlined the diversity within the group as an advantage point of international cooperation.[356] Trudeau further developed the idea of utilising the Commonwealth as a tool of development in the following years, for example, by incorporating discussions on governance into Commonwealth meetings to give practical advice to emerging nations.[357] The changing character of the organisation was indicated by the Singapore meeting in 1971 as it was the first true Commonwealth prime ministers' meeting outside of Britain, and was now called the Commonwealth Heads of Government Meeting (CHOGM). In Singapore, Trudeau again followed the path of his predecessors by supporting African calls for a Commonwealth Declaration of Principles, which underlined racial equality and the support for self-determination.[358]

Ironically, Trudeau did not avoid the role of a mediator within the Commonwealth, a role which he had refused to take on in other international circumstances. In parts, this acceptance sprang from his convictions as from domestic and international calls for such a role which drew on the images of traditional Canadian mediation.[359] At the same time, it illustrates the Commonwealth as a normative framework appreciated by all three former dominions, in spite of the transformations both of the British position and the former Empire. They still supported concepts rooting in British tradition, such as the principle of law and parliamentary democracy. At the same time, they departed from a British framework by emphasising 'Non-Alignment' or 'Third World' as new issues or characterisations of the organisation. All three saw an opportunity, but also a necessity of leading the organisation away from British dominance, especially as the Heath government advocated a series of controversial policies, for example, the arms sales with South Africa, which further contributed to the overall image of a world power in demise.[360]

Because of the British retreat from the organisation as from other parts of the former Empire, the pull of imperial norms or 'family values' within the organisation started to lessen. As a result, Trudeau, Whitlam and Kirk would move on to use the Commonwealth as a space to develop their own policies of inter-

355 Quoted in: *Boehm*, Canada and the Modern Commonwealth, 27.

356 LAC MG26 07, Vol. 487, Brief for Visit of John Gorton, 18.3.1969.

357 *Boehm*, Canada and the Modern Commonwealth, 31.

358 *Louis A. Delvoie*, The Commonwealth in Canadian Foreign Policy, in: The Round Table 310, 1989, 137–143, 138.

359 *Dobell*, Canada in World Affairs, 210 f.

360 *Murphy*, Britain and the Commonwealth, 272; *Lawrence J. Butler*, Britain and Empire. Adjusting to a Post-Imperial World, London 2002, 186 f.

national involvement. Instead of underlining Rhodesian and South African issues as domestic responsibilities, they were more willing to join African and Asian members in denouncing racism internationally. New Zealand, which had been previously cautious lest any criticism of the sister white settler colony Rhodesia now feared the association with white African segregation.[361] The question of racial equality resonated with other areas of foreign policy such as UN resolutions and sports contacts as well as with the question of domestic equality for indigenous people and immigrants of non-European descent.[362] Ironically, as the dominions were stripping off their immigration policies from discriminatory elements, Britain was severing its immigration policy. The introduction of the British Immigration Act in 1971, which removed the distinction between Commonwealth and foreign immigrants resulted in another crisis of Anglo-Dominion relations.[363] At the same time, it further nurtured perceptions that the former dominions were replacing Britain as (moral) stakeholders of the Commonwealth.

In all this, Trudeau's Canada again had been a role model for Whitlam and Kirk.[364] However, in embodying a certain fulfilment of a different, positive relationship under anti-racist norms, both leaders came to represent their own national governments of liberalisation and change. Over a decisive reference to regional responsibility, they were able to establish a policy different to the emphasis of Western supremacy under previous governments. In Australia, Gough Whitlam developed a policy of international responsibility and activism that could be related to ideas of middlepowership. His policies resembled some of the objectives advocated by Trudeau in his new foreign policy, namely the promotion of equality and self-reliance. However, while Trudeau's government was dismissing a "hollow multilateralism"[365] and the self-description as a middle power, Whitlam endorsed the concept as an opportunity to extend Australia's role in the Asian-Pacific region. He emphasised middlepowership as a Labor legacy of the 1940s internationalism[366], even though various strands of this concept had been circulated among officials before his term. Many commentators argued that Australia would be able to review its position not as a small power in comparison to the USA, but as a middle power among regional

[361] *Carlyon/Morrow*, Changing Times, 71 f.

[362] *Richard Thompson*, Race, Kinship and Policy: Africa and New Zealand, in: Malcolm McKinnon (Ed.), New Zealand in World Affairs: Vol. 2: 1957–1972, Wellington 1991, 95–121; *Curran*, The World Changes, 25 f.

[363] *Butler*, Britain and Empire, 188.

[364] Meeting Trudeau in summer 1970, Whitlam spoke with admiration of "the way in which the Canadian Government 'probed' into new areas of concern", LAC MG26 07, Vol. 487, Memorandum for File, 21.7.1970. During talks with Arnold Smith in 1973, Norman Kirk described Canada as the new leader of the Commonwealth, Records of talks between Norman Kirk and Arnold Smith, 3.4.1973, ANZ ABHS W5400 20358, Box 84, KL 90/1/1.

[365] CDEA official Alan Gotlieb quoted in: *Bothwell/Granatstein*, Trudeau's World, 94.

[366] *Dalrymple*, Continental Drift, 66.

equals such as Indonesia or Japan.[367] During a discussion at Australian National University, one commentator noted the change of Australian attitude towards the region:

"One is a quasi-imperial sentiment, a sense of rising power and influence based on increasing affluence and physical capacity. Another is of a moral nature, involving loyalty to people in the area with whom Australians have dealings, and a desire to honour commitments to them, for the sake not of the objectives which the commitments were entered but of the honour which one's given word demands."[368]

By linking the feeling to imperial times, officials could transfer the idea of moral obligation to new roles and relationships in the region. At the same time, a relationship based on trust was something unprecedented and new in relations with Southeast Asian countries, as the concept of trustworthy states was previously largely based on a shared background or alikeness. However, limits to such a transfer became visible when Whitlam tried to launch a Pacific Pact in 1973/74, hoping to propose a new regional scheme of security.[369] The ASEAN powers showed themselves uninterested, and were appalled when Whitlam suggested the inclusion of the PRC or North Vietnam into such a forum.[370] Moreover, some felt affronted by Whitlam's political style, indicating that overall some features were still inhibiting a new Australian role in the region.[371] Equally, Australia was ultimately unsuccessful in joining ASEAN, and officials accepted in 1972 that a membership seemed incompatible with the outlook of the organisation:

"Quite apart from the fact that the present members don't want us, or anybody else, as members, the central point is that the attractions and value of ASEAN stem from its smallness, the geographical proximity of member countries, their more or less community of interests and outlooks, and their 'Asian-ness'. Australia does not fit into this pattern, and I don't see that it ever will."[372]

In contrast, Norman Kirk was successful in harbouring friendly relations with smaller countries in Asia and the Pacific. With a strong stance on social justice and development aid, but also with the proposal for smaller nations to take the lead on issues such as nuclear disarmament, Kirk could establish a profile that attracted good relations with Southeast Asian countries.[373] Moreover, it was a clear attempt to shape an independent role for New Zealand. Kirk, who had already stated in 1971 that New Zealand's size should not be "an excuse or a rea-

---

367 *Munto*, Pacific Signposts, 190.

368 *Boyce*, Australian Attitudes to Security, 33.

369 *Thompson*, British Military Withdrawal, 149; *Dalrymple*, Continental Drift, 66.

370 *Halvorson*, Australia in Asia, 135 f.

371 *Corner*, New Zealand Face, 148.

372 'Australia and Asia', ADEA Memorandum, 27.4.1972, quoted in: *Halvorson*, Australia in Asia, 117.

373 *Grant*, Mighty Totara, 257–262.

son for failing to develop"[374] strong policies and arrangements with other countries, now insisted on a special role New Zealand could take since its size would not draw any suspicion: "New Zealand is quite well fitted for the job, for the simple reason that no one is afraid of us. With the exception of Laos and Singapore, we are the smallest country in the region. […] Indeed our very smallness as a country is an advantage in the field of forthright foreign policy."[375] Particularly within the Commonwealth, he could represent his premiership as advocacy of a less discriminatory organisation based on similar international outlooks. Despite Kirk's support for a continued close relationship with Britain for New Zealand, he welcomed the demise of British hegemony in the Commonwealth as paving the way to a community of equals.

Accordingly, in a speech at the New Zealand Institute for International Affairs (NIIA) in June 1971, he called for a different approach to Asia, to show

> "that we are not – as one Asian minister described us last year 'Some sort of European Noah's Ark adrift on a sea of Asian influence' – not a leaf to be blown about, not a country on the perimeter of Asia, but a country that sees its future in association with Asian countries, that measures its peace and security in the advancement of neighbouring countries, that has the will to do things that will demonstrate to Asia our sincerity and will capitalise on the extent of goodwill that we already enjoy."[376]

Here, both Whitlam and Kirk resembled each other in their approach. Whitlam had also used the platform of the Australian Institute for International Affairs (AIIA) to demand a closer identification with the region. In his view, this meant that Australia should become "A responsible household, who identifies the fire risks in his own neighbourhood and sees that they are removed before a conflagration starts".[377]

However, as historian Jack Doig has noted in the comparison of Whitlam's and Kirk's policies of moral foreign policy, they not only differed in the geographical area of activism, but also in the convictions their policies followed. While New Zealand hoped to set an example for international behaviour that resonated with its history as a 'social laboratory', Australia under Whitlam was convinced of the shaping moral influence it would have on international developments.[378] As a consequence, both leaders contrasted in their understandings of the right measures for regional interaction, which would also ultimately af-

[374] ANZ ABHS W4628 6957, Box 21, SAI 63/1/1, Part 1, Speech given by Norman Kirk at the Rotary Club Invercargill, 1.11.1971.

[375] "New Zealand and Southeast Asia. A Policy for the Seventies", Address by Norman Kirk to the Returned Services Association, June 1973, found in: TNA FCO 24/1845.

[376] ANZ ABHS W4628 6957, Box 21, SAI 63/1/1, Part 1, "New Zealand and its Neighbours", Paper given by Norman Kirk at the NIIA, June 1971.

[377] "Beyond Vietnam – Australia's Regional Responsibilities", Address by Gough Whitlam to North Queensland Branch of AIIA, quoted in: LAC RG25 A-3-c, Vol. 8842, 20-AUSTL-1–3, CHC Canberra 638, 19.6.1968.

[378] *Doig*, New Nationalism, 571, FN 69.

fect their respective forces stationed in Malaysia and Singapore. For Whitlam, the policy of responsibility was not one of military involvement. He had early on opposed the retention of forces and endorsed the decision of the Australian Labor Party (ALP) to make the abolition of Australia's ANZUK commitment a party policy in November 1971. Following his election, Whitlam proclaimed that the "idea of keeping a permanent garrison in Singapore [...] belongs to the past".[379] He understood the presence of Australian troops as inhibiting better relations with Asian neighbours and showed himself unavailing to British, New Zealand, and even local protests against a withdrawal. The decision largely coincided with a fundamental defence review that rejected any immediate threat to Australia. As Whitlam announced that a threat to Australia in the next ten to fifteen years was unlikely, defence interests now focused largely on the concept of self-reliance.[380]

On the other side of the Tasman, Kirk took a different position. Despite varying party voices, he remained firm in his support for a continued presence of New Zealand forces in the region. When asked about the ALP position on the issue, he underlined that New Zealand forces were committed to regional stability and confidence.[381] Despite a growing demise of military involvement in favour of other forms of regional interaction, his government considered this military presence as crucial, not only to prevent conflicts, but to also foster New Zealand's image among Southeast Asian nations: "They see our willingness to maintain forces in the area as evidence that we understand their problems, that we are serious in our desire to help them, and that we are willing to pay a price in terms of public criticism – that we are prepared to stand up and be counted."[382] Even when Australia ultimately decided to withdraw its ground forces and the logistic support crucial for the New Zealand presence in late 1974, Kirk and his successor Bill Rowling continued to support a military involvement as a form of regional cooperation.[383]

In the end, New Zealand would remain the most loyal of the former dominions, both to the military commitment it took as to Britain itself. Kirk urged him to reconsider when Whitlam announced Australia's intention to withdraw its elements from the ANZUK force. Parts of his argument was the concern for a continued British presence. Following the talks with Whitlam in January 1973, Kirk had told British Secretary of Defence Lord Carrington that he could "sleep better at night" if he knew a British presence was part of the security presence

379 NAA A7942, F59; quoted in: *Benvenuti/Jones*, Engaging Southeast Asia, 48.

380 *Arthur Tange/Peter Edwards*, Defence Policy-Making. A Close-Up View, 1950–1980: A Personal Memoir, St. Leonards 2008, 81.

381 ANZ ABHS W4628 6957, Box 21, SAI 63/1/1, Part 1, Television Interview "Point of View" with Norman Kirk, 7.11.1971.

382 "New Zealand and Southeast Asia. A Policy for the Seventies", Address by Norman Kirk to the Returned Services Association, June 1973, TNA FCO 24/1845.

383 See on the whole development of Labour position *McCraw*, Staying in Singapore.

in Southeast Asia.[384] Interestingly enough, Kirk had already shown himself regretful when the British decision on East of Suez had come in 1967/68, as noted by the British High Commission in Wellington: "when our High Commissioner first called on Mr. Kirk last November it was he who expressed more bitterly than any other Kiwi his regret at our then decision to withdraw from East of Suez by the end of 1971".[385]

5.4 Conclusion of Part 5

How much and how fast the security relationship between the former dominions and Britain had changed at the end of the 1960s was nowhere better expressed than by the Australian Prime Minister McMahon when he stated in 1971 that "Our line to Britain is no longer a lifeline [...] Britain's own security, while of concern to us, is no longer vital to Australia".[386] Although his statement caused a minor outcry, it soon became the accepted principle of an independent foreign policy. Now, security interests should no longer be defined by the British or American alliance. While Australia and New Zealand drew much of these realisations from failed allied cooperation in the wake of British and American retreat, Canada established this position more from a general pronouncement of independent thinking under Pierre Trudeau.

The emphasis on self-reliance and independence resulted from or coincided with a series of reviews dedicated to the British relationship. As the sources show, the close relations were now discarded for ideas of equal relations comparable to other foreign relations. This 'pragmatisation' of foreign affairs both in Britain as in the former dominions also meant that foreign affairs were organised along the lines of geopolitical and economic interests rather than along the lines of affiliation, tradition, and shared history. Both British and American shifts in policy were seen as an opportunity to appreciate alternative politics that made all three countries less vulnerable to changes in their alliance framework. While early reviews emphasised the pressure and urgency caused by these external factors and events, the discussions soon established narratives underlining the opportunity for independent policymaking, which was enhanced by the government change in all three countries.

Trudeau, Gorton and Whitlam, and Kirk all represented a departure from a foreign policy more or less adhered to since the end of the Second World War. They questioned old alliances and sought new angles to issues existing for many years. Their fresh approach was also rooted in a different generation-

[384] Wellington to FCO Telegram 11, 5.1.1973, quoted in: *Benvenuti/Jones*, Engaging Southeast Asia, 49.

[385] TNA FCO 24/950, BHC Wellington, 14.8.1970.

[386] The Australian, 22.2.1971.

al upbringing, since few of them and their staff embodied the colonial experience of their predecessors. An emotional appeal to the bonds of Empire would have been deemed less desirable and less convincing. The impact of generational change also affected long-held convictions about the Cold War: With little experience of the Second World War, analogies to Munich and totalitarianism, just as the reference to Singapore in 1942, could no longer draw these new policymakers into accepting the American rationalities for a military commitment to Southeast Asia.[387] Instead, they could campaign on a certain urgency that changes in foreign policy had been refused for too long, but which were necessary for the country's future course.[388] Policymakers were aware of the gravity of transformations around them, and officials like New Zealander Bruce Brown expressed the sentiment of a watershed moment: "The 1970s it seems clear, will see significant changes in the political and social pattern which was formed in the early 1950s. The era of alignment and non-alignment, of coherent groupings and categories shows many signs of breaking down."[389]

In all three countries, Chinese recognition would be the symbolic departure in foreign policy, by redefining a Chinese threat into a certain risk that had to be taken in order to allow better regional and international relations. In general, this change of framing allowed an activist policy of approach and engagement that enhanced regional and international cooperation.[390] At the same time, regional concepts launched the idea of trusting bilateral relationships to overcome the uncertainty created by fear of Asia. Ultimately, discussions on Southeast Asia resembled global discourses of Cold War détente and deescalation. While regional cooperation was substantially enhanced, it can also be argued that a new antagonist took China's place. With the rise of Soviet activity in the Indian Ocean in the late 1960s, Tasman threat discourses were diverted both to another potential aggressor and another theatre of potential conflict.

The retreat from an emotional discourse in foreign policy referring to imperial ties was both a response and a result of recent changes. As the new group of leaders witnessed the failure of communication during the East of Suez discussions as on other issues, a rational response seemed like a better strategy in negotiations with Britain. A regime of pragmatism and professionalism replaced conceptions of foreign policy determined by traditions and affiliations in an Anglo-Saxon or British community – prominently depicted in Trudeau's motto

[387] *Ninkovich*, Modernity and Power, 303.

[388] *Brookes*, Australia's Identity Anxiety, 144.

[389] *Bruce Brown*, "New Zealand's Approach to Asia and the Pacific" (Pacific Community 8/3 (1970), 549–563, 553), found in: ANZ ABHS W4628 6957, Box 21, SAI 63/1/1, Part 1.

[390] To follow Niklas Luhmann, the adoption of 'risk' as opposed to 'danger' implies a certain operability or management of future uncertainty or threat within known social parameters, thereby reducing contingency and allowing an active response to events laying in the future. *Michael King/C. J. Thornhill*, Niklas Luhmann's Theory of Politics and Law, Houndmills/New York 2005, 184–186.

'Reason before Passion'.[391] In consequence, expressions of affection or attachment were dismissed as nostalgia while notions of independence or nationalism grew in political status. Moreover, the rhetoric of middle power, 'Third Option', and regionalism symbolically reclaimed a scope of action that seemed lost during the defence negotiations with Britain, where officials gave the appearance of passivity and paralysis in response to alliance restraints. Even if their alternative politics largely remained symbolic and were remodified into a confirmation of previous alliances later on, the political space of action seemed broadened for the period of the early 1970s and allowed to overcome the feeling of crisis. Where uncertainty and anxieties had dominated discussions before, concepts applied to Southeast Asia focused now on the opportunities and alternatives provided by the retreat of Britain and the USA.

[391] *Kevin J. Christiano*, Pierre Elliott Trudeau. Reason before Passion, Toronto 1994.

Part 6

Conclusion – The End of the British Empire?

"The place was Queanbeyan. The hall was packed with a crowd of men and women of all ages, all occupations, all creeds, yes and all colours. That night tears came not only to my eyes and to many people around me when we stood and clapped, and stamped, and cheered when Gough Whitlam told us that when he became prime minister of Australia, the last vestiges of colonialism would disappear and our years of shame in Vietnam, and our behaviour to the Aborigines, and in our defence of the old, corrupt order of society could come to an end. It seemed then that the years of unleavened bread were over."[1]

In 1972, authors like Australian historian Manning Clark could impressively present the election of Gough Whitlam as one of unprecedented departure and relief. With Australia's commitment to Vietnam, but particularly with the colonial ties Clark mentioned, critics could cast Whitlam's predecessors into the role of those being hopelessly stuck in the past. In contrast, opposition to the Vietnam War meant "reflection, self-examination, and change"[2], and allowed supporters to present Whitlam's premiership as a "great national catharsis".[3] For many, the departure depicted in his policies established a first attempt to define Australia's identity without notions of imperial belonging.

Similar narratives were also dedicated to Norman Kirk in New Zealand, where his successor Bill Rowling remembered:

"Under the leadership of Norman Kirk, New Zealand's foreign policy was given new direction, new vitality, new immediacy. Not since the mid-1930s had New Zealand made such an impact upon the outside world. Never had New Zealand responded so promptly and imaginatively to the changes which were transforming the world in which we live."[4]

Similar to Trudeau's term in Canada, the governments of Whitlam and Kirk symbolised a period of self-affirmation and definition of national interest unprecedented in the post-war era. Even though many of their new policies would not stand the test of realist politics or the closer look at steps already taken before which allowed the rapid transformation the successive governments

[1] *Manning Clark*, The Years of Unleavened Bread, December 1949 to December 1972: Meanjin 32/3, September 1973, in: Manning Clark (Ed.), Occasional Writings and Speeches, Enfield 1981, 194–202, 202.

[2] *FitzGerald*, Australia an Asian Country, 20.

[3] Ibid., 23.

[4] Introduction by the Prime Minister, Annual Report of the Ministry of Foreign Affairs for the Year Ending 31 March, 1975, 1, quoted in: *Corner*, New Zealand Face, 166.

claimed for their administration[5], they could nevertheless establish a discourse that made their policies appear innovative, progressive and liberating. This discourse combined new agendas in domestic as well as international politics and thereby contributed to the all-encompassing feeling of change.

This perception of fundamental political change was related to the East of Suez debate. The British decision to retreat contributed to a considerable climate of uncertainty in the three former dominions, as it fell into a time of changing national, regional and global frameworks. At the same time, the decision was a motor for these changing frameworks, particularly forcing Australia and New Zealand to reconsider their foreign policy principles. For all three countries, Britain's decision to turn to Europe fundamentally challenged their self-perception as both British nations and as parts of the former Empire. The process of accepting Britain's retreat at a time of uncertainty caused conflicting emotions as policymakers felt forced to assess their British background and policies of close cooperation against growing geopolitical interests that increasingly differed from British directions. Despite mediatory efforts on both sides, the East of Suez debate created the perception that officials had to choose between continued close cooperation in the Anglosphere or a departure into foreign relations under principles of geopolitical interests.

The study of the East of Suez discussion shows how much the debate can be understood as both an indicator and as a catalyst for a change in Anglo-Dominion relations. For Australia and New Zealand, it also fundamentally affected their outlooks and identity. Both countries struggled with Britain's departure from a framework that relied on British resources of power and the principle of shared outlooks and practices. Moreover, the debate was enforced by a multipolarity of threats and crises, with further issues looming in the Commonwealth, the Southeast Asian region and, on a supra-regional level, in the theatres of a global Cold War. This multipolarity increased feelings of insecurity and danger, with time being an essential category with the urgency to act, the uncertainty of future developments and the historic impact of Britain's decision. Especially the latter was enforced by preceding or concurrent crises such as the Suez Crisis and the British EEC bids.

As a result, Australia and New Zealand felt forced to review their principles of foreign policy, which in turn generated a debate on their national outlook and identity. While diplomats and public servants felt uneasy with the embryonic state of regional relations compared to the sometimes suffocating demands of their great power alliances, governments in both countries and large parts of the public supported a traditional foreign and security policy within an Anglo-

[5] *Andrea Benvenuti/David Martin Jones*, Myth and Misrepresentation in Australian Foreign Policy. Menzies and Engagement with Asia, in: Journal of Cold War Studies 13/4, 2011, 57–78; *Halvorson*, Australia in Asia, 100 f.

centric framework. Up until the late 1960s, despite various points of friction in their relationship with Britain, officials were unwilling to substantially consider alternative routes in foreign policy. Such alternatives were also dismissed over a biased outlook in international affairs: Early international discussions on self-determination and anti-colonialism seemed to only reinforce ideas of a British world community and prevented a larger interaction with the Southeast Asian region up to the mid-1960s.

From the mid-1960s on, discussions on East of Suez revealed growing divergences as long-standing convictions of shared principles and interests in foreign policy eroded under the impression of a changing British position. It was not only the British rejection of regional security concerns that upset Tasman partners, but also the swift discard of traditional affiliations. The emotionally charged climate of talks moreover enforced perceptions of multiple other threats: With the deterioration in Vietnam, the uncertainty about China, and the ambivalence of US policy, Britain's plans for withdrawal were received with great anxiety. When the decision was finally taken, regret and sadness resulted from the idea that Britain was abandoning long-standing 'familiar' relationships in favour of 'foreign' countries in Europe.

The interesting point of the episode under review is how quickly some of the strategic concerns or issues were resolved or abandoned, while the fundamental issue of reorientation proved a lasting challenge. The swift resolution of the diplomatic conflict itself can be related to the change of policy-makers under the impression of altered normative frameworks. They not only introduced a new pragmatism in foreign affairs, but they also reacted to global discussions on self-determination with the rejection of interventionist military roles. All three new governments highlighted the cause of development and social justice as fundamental for international security and supported assistance and aid programs. These changed parameters in security considerations, such as a stronger emphasis of responsibility for smaller nations and developing countries, resulted in altered mental maps. In addition, it can be argued that the framework surrounding the British presence was replaced by self-sufficient defence roles and cooperation under FPDA. In a way, the demise of Britishness made the reevaluation of core values in fields such as foreign policy necessary to serve a new national cohesive identity. At the same time, this reevaluation was itself a product of the demise of Britishness as an identity marker.

The trajectories pointed out in the debates of the late 1960s continued in the next decade. Here, the three countries represent the struggles in coming to terms with alternative security frameworks experienced in other Western countries, where protests against the Vietnam War equally ended the political consensus on Cold War strategy. Instead of alliance security, internationalism and the moderation of conflicts by non-military means became more important, leading to policies such as defence diplomacy.[6] Moreover, the flawed idea of Western moral supremacy became visible over the failed American intervention in Vietnam, correlating to a more general demise of Western concepts of modernisation as a principle of progress. Similar to the decline of the British civilising mission, the experiences in Southeast Asia contributed to a renunciation of interventionist policies in favour of programs of soft governance such as development aid. At the same time, the Vietnam debate amplified foreign policy circles, with grassroots movements protesting issues such as nuclear proliferation and non-governmental organisations establishing themselves as global players in pursuit of international cooperation and humanitarian relief.[7] The changing discourse on self-determination, accompanied by new norms of anti-racism and equality, sustained efforts that would ultimately lead to a larger appreciation of international human rights. The end of the British and other empires saw the following period extensively focus on human rights, political, and socio-economic claims of the 'Third World'.[8]

Within each national diplomacy history, the period would introduce a certain management and trade orientation within the public service. Ultimately, the 'pragmatisation' in dealings with Britain, including its deemphasis of unwritten understandings and personal relationships, would mirror a more general trend of a bureaucratic reorganisation of foreign affairs in the three former dominions. In 1970, New Zealand renamed its Department of External Affairs into the Ministry of Foreign Affairs. In Australia and Canada, the Departments were renamed in the 1980s, in both cases following the merger of foreign and trade departments.[9] The large priority given to trade was obvious, and the introduction of new diplomacy regimes precipitated the period of free-market speech and neoliberalism that would define large parts of foreign policy in the late 1970s and early 1980s, when Robert Muldoon would announce: "Our foreign policy is trade. We are not interested in the normal foreign policy matters to any great extent, we are interested in trade."[10]

Diplomacy was now designed to serve the opportunity of business rather than the support of cooperation in a time of political instability. At the same time, the rise of a multipolar world order and the increased link between foreign

---

[6] *David Capie*, The Bilateral-Multilateral Nexus in Asia's Defence Diplomacy, in: William T. Tow/Brendan Taylor (Ed.), Bilateralism, Multilateralism and Asia-Pacific Security: Contending Cooperation, London/New York 2013, 115–131.

[7] *Eckel*, Utopie der Moral, 458–478.

[8] *Moyn*, Imperialism, Self-Determination, 172 f.

[9] The Canadian External Affairs and International Trade Canada was created in early 1982; the Australian Department of Foreign Affairs and Trade was introduced under Bob Hawke in 1987. *Andrew F. Cooper/Richard A. Higgott/Kim Richard Nossal*, Relocating Middle Powers. Australia and Canada in a Changing World Order, Vancouver 1993, 36–49.

[10] Interview with Prime Minister Robert Muldoon, New Zealand Review, Jan/Feb 1980, quoted in: *Corner*, New Zealand Face, 151.

and domestic issues in the early 1970s led foreign policy away from ideas of global security implementation by collective security.[11] Instead, regionalism and the multilateral approach over specific issues or interests replaced in parts the former alliance thinking. Nevertheless, the importance of the American alliance would continue, with most countries now pursuing this relationship on a bilateral basis.[12]

In summary, the British retreat to Europe proved both as a disintegrative force as much as it contributed to integrative transformations. While the three former dominions left a British-based framework, they entered new partnerships and arrangements that aligned more with geopolitical factors than with concepts of historical allegiance. Similarly, they had to face an international, globalising discourse on anti-colonialism and self-determination that enforced a reevaluation of their British belonging and questioned their identity and position as independent nations.

However, underlying questions of (post-)imperial identity evoked by the East of Suez debate lingered on. Although the new governments of the early 1970s succeeded in implementing new nationalism and independence as dominant narratives of identity, political reevaluation of Britishness regularly occurred afterwards and continues even today. Robert Muldoon is just one example in a list of policymakers who would readopt the British connection in the following decades. Recently, over the discussions on Britain's post-Brexit international relations, Australian High Commissioner to London, Alexander Downer Jnr., could revive the idea of "notions of trust" between both countries and concluded: "In this world, you need all the friends you can possibly find. For Australia, the UK is a very natural and a very easy friend, a very lovable friend in so many ways."[13]

Similarly, the question of regional integration proved a lasting challenge and a contested field in scholarly debates. On the one hand, Stephen FitzGerald's question '*Is Australia an Asian Country?*'[14] was still answered with an ambiguous 'no' in the 1990s; FitzGerald underlined the achievements for regional cooperation, but pointed to the considerable ignorance of Asian affairs. Only recently, Australian historian Dan Halvorson argued that Australia's most profound commitment to an Asian role dated to the years of the East of Suez debate (1966–1968), with a constant struggle to achieve similarly close relations

[11] *Cooper/Higgott/Nossal*, Changing World Order, 21 f.; *Thomas/Thompson*, Empire and Globalisation, 156 f.

[12] *Brendan Taylor*, Conceptualizing the Bilateral-Multilateral Security Nexus, in: William T. Tow/Brendan Taylor (Ed.), Bilateralism, Multilateralism and Asia-Pacific Security: Contending Cooperation, London/New York 2013, 8–17, 9 f.

[13] *Alexander Downer*, Australia and a Post-Brexit Britain, in: The Round Table 107/21–31, 2018, 26.

[14] *FitzGerald*, Australia an Asian Country.

in the following decades.[15] On the other hand, phenomena of continued military involvement such as New Zealand's commitment under FPDA up until 1989 would be increasingly considered an anachronism. However, the close ties established over defence would intensify links with the region, especially after Australia and New Zealand became dialogue members of ASEAN in 1974.[16] The greatest paradox would be the longevity of FPDA itself, given its initial half-hearted conception as a military framework, a transitional vehicle until Malaysia and Singapore could establish their own military capabilities. While it was almost non-existent in allied activities from the late 1970s on, it would gain new substance after the Cold War over refreshed regional concerns regarding China.[17] It would fall to Britain to also indicate how much the East of Suez debate was bound to a particular point in time: A British garrison would remain in Singapore until 1974, and Britain is still committed under FPDA. William D. James recently argued that while the base strategy surrounding substantial military posts in the area was abolished, the rationale for such a presence East of Suez was never abandoned and is still upheld by various British commitments to the region.[18]

Another limit to the debate is laid out in this study with the analysis of Canada. The unusual inclusion of Canadian foreign policy in this book brought some new insights, both to traditional writings on the country as a bystander or neutral actor in Southeast Asia as for the impact of Britain's retreat on Canada's outlook and self-perception. While the study confirms that the Canadian government generally played only a small role in Southeast Asian affairs, certain issues and connections nevertheless brought surprising moments of involvement. Clearly, the transnational level of discussions, stemming from the close relations among the dominions and Britain, served to include Canada in the debate on future Southeast Asian security at various points. The focus on discussions of military assistance and the Commonwealth showed that Canadian officials were indeed willing to review their non-committal position at times when it served their alliances or new partnerships. At the same time, the Canadian reception of the East of Suez debate reveals the limits of a British (post-)imperial community of defence. While Canadian officials sympathised with the Tasman struggles and shared some of their concerns, they had discarded the British framework for a predominant American defence alliance in the previous decade. Moreover, Southeast Asia remained less prioritised in their foreign policy considerations, given their strong Atlantic outlook.

Canadian concerns on the question of Anglocentric foreign policy would largely relate to domestic issues. At the same time, the review of the British

[15] *Halvorson*, Australia in Asia, 103.
[16] *McCraw*, Staying in Singapore, 16.
[17] *Emmers*, Role of the Five Power Defence Arrangements, 90 f.
[18] *James*, Global Britain's Strategic Problem.

connection started earlier than in the other former dominions. The Suez Crisis already showed how much the question of British support resonated with questions of national maturity, but also touched on issues of biculturalism and independent positions in the international sphere. At the same time, notions of concern and regret among some Canadian policymakers during the East of Suez discussions show that some still identified with British concepts and outlooks.

Furthermore, close relations stemming from imperial times still constituted a transnational community within which ideas and outlooks were shaped. Given their shared background, policymakers not only felt close to their counterparts, but they also used the dealings on security and foreign policy to assess their own position and definition. Close interactions and relationships also explain Canadian integration into issues outside its own security framework. As the study showed, the perception of being part of a community could shape responses to international issues along the line of shared principles and norms.[19] Since the Commonwealth connection served Canadians to review their non-committal position to the conflicts in Southeast Asia, it may be worth considering the depth of identification, with a further study on dealings of the former dominions with other so-called 'like-minded' states that were regularly drawn upon, such as Sweden or the Benelux states. Such a study could further contribute to the idea of a specific transnational community based on shared Commonwealth principles, or it might challenge the concept of a set of exclusive principles under a British umbrella in favour of more universal principles.

Finally, the study presents itself as an offer to include the three countries' experiences, their de-imperialisation, into the study of decolonisation. The presented argument for this inclusion is two-fold: One underlines elements of continuity, the other one elements of change.

For one, the East of Suez discussion reveals continued references of a shared British framework, expressed by emotions of regret and nostalgia and underlined by narratives of moral obligation and shared history. Therefore, the history of de-imperialisation of the dominions can contribute to an appreciation of these elements of continuity in other studies of decolonisation. On the other hand, the East of Suez debate shows societies under stress to adjust to changes, their demand for answers and adequate responses not only to outside challenges, but also to the lack of a distinct narrative in foreign policy that resonates with specific self-perceptions and national identities. In contrast to Fanon's 'cleansing force of violence', the transformative elements are related to an inner de-imperialisation, the change of national outlooks and perceptions of the former dominions' place in a world where the British allegiance was no longer the predominant factor. It is argued here that the challenges to change these mental

---

[19] *Halvorson*, Commonwealth Responsibility. For a similar approach, based on NATO's discussions on Out-of-Area issues, see *Veronica M. Kitchen*, The Globalization of NATO. Intervention, Security and Identity, Abingdon/New York 2010.

maps and the pressures to review elements of alliance such as shared principles and norms cut deep into the fabric of each nation's self-perception. Again, this does not suggest that the experiences of the three countries should be equated with experiences of colonial violence. Instead, the study advocates a closer look at the pressures of continuity and transformation that contribute to perceptions of uncertainty and stress. The amalgam of persistent and dynamic elements, of preserving and transformative forces is understood as being characteristic of decolonisation, and might also be applied to the specific experiences the former dominions shared.

In the debates in all three countries, identity markers of temporality were adopted through references to, e. g. 'national maturity' or 'adulthood', indicating the collective experience of transition that can be compared to other processes of decolonisation. At the first New Zealand Day in February 1974, Norman Kirk appealed to these perceptions when he spoke of a watershed moment: "As Britain joins her destiny with Europe's we must draw more upon the spiritual and cultural strength of the people who make our nation. We are ready. [...] All of us together are in our way making New Zealand."[20] Given the simultaneous draw on British traditions and the demarcation to a future British outlook, contemporaries such as Kirk could perceive themselves as crossing frontiers, as perceiving the growing gap between their own frame of experience and their horizon of expectations as threshold times.

Kirk's quote also underlines another important factor in considerations of decolonisation, namely the question of nationalism. As traversed in the beginning of this study, peoples from all three countries felt comfortable to refer to themselves simultaneously as British and Australian/Canadian/New Zealand. This analysis has highlighted how these notions were not perceived as incompatible, even at times when national interests seem to point in diverging directions. Therefore, Britain's retreat from this imagined community was first perceived as a void and only later endorsed as a precondition for a 'true' nation.

Curiously, the notions of 'new nationalism' would fall into an era of increasing contestation of the concept of the nation-state. While the manifold demands for national sovereignty had not only posed complex problems within international organisations such as the UN or the Commonwealth, the violent struggles conducted by national liberation movements also created doubts if the 'nation' was the righteous heir in a post-colonial state. At the same time, human rights movements[21] or global initiatives for nuclear-free zones contributed to the idea that certain issues had to be resolved outside the national framework.

[20] Speech of Norman Kirk at the New Zealand Day, 6.2.1974, quoted in: *Bill Jeffries*, Kirk's Prime-Ministership, 1972–1974, in: Margaret Clark (Ed.), Three Labour Leaders: Nordmeyer, Kirk, Rowling, North Palmerston 2001, 107–116, 115.

[21] *Roland Burke*, The Internationalism of Human Rights, in: Glenda Sluga/Patricia M. Clavin (Ed.), Internationalisms: A Twentieth-Century History, Cambridge 2017, 287–314.

However, in the former dominions, the references to a nation-state allowed policymakers to move from the close British ties of cooperation and sentiment to a concept of independent, self-reliant foreign policy and defence. While it would fall to following governments to come up with the content of this nation, the discursive shift from a 'British' nation to an 'Australian'/'Canadian'/'New Zealand' nation mitigated the challenges posed not only by Britain's turn to Europe, but also by correlating or concurring regional and global transformations. This prevalence of the nation-state as a transnational phenomenon also explains the confusion of distinguished historians such as Akira Iriye, who wonders about the continued manifestation of national historiography in the decades after the 1960s.[22] Rather than asking why historians would not pick up the trend of the increasing fragmentation of national activities and outlooks by looking outwards instead of inwards, the example of the former dominions instead shows how important the nation as a reference point for identification still was. The historiography of the following decades would play an essential role in the nation-building in all three countries.[23] Therefore, in the end, this study is also an argument not to perceive the nation as a monolithic, exclusive idea, but to understand it as a framework shaped by political and social demands in relation to a certain position in time and place.

22 *Iriye*, Global and Transnational History, 26 f.
23 *Curthoys*, Making National Histories.

Bibliography

Primary Sources

NAA: National Archives Australia

NAA (Sydney)

M157: Gough Whitlam Papers

M157, Box 38/27: Malaysia

NAA (Canberra)

A1209: Records of the Prime Minister's Department

A1209 1962/790: Greater Malaysia – British Long Term Defence Policy in South East Asia
A1209 1965/6124: British Defence Review – 1965
A1209 1965/6251: SEATO Council of Minister's Meeting 1966
A1209 1966/7335: British Defence Review

A1838: Records of the Department of External Affairs

A1838 67/1/3: United Kingdom – Foreign Policy – Relations with Australia – General
A1838 213/1: Singapore Defence Relations with United Kingdom – Withdrawal General
A1838 229/9/1: Canada – Relations with Australia – General
A1838 229/9/5: Canada – Relations with Australia – Representation in Australia (1954–1964)
A1838 229/9/9/2: Canada – Relations with Australia – Australia Visitors to Canada – Visit of Mr Casey and Mr Hasluck
A1838 229/9/9/3: Canada – Political – Relations with Australia – PM visit to Canada
A1838 229/10/4/3: Canada – Foreign Policy – Relations with China
A1838 370/1/1: New Zealand – External Relations – General
A1838 370/1/19: New Zealand – External Relations – Relations with Australia
A1838 370/1/19/1: New Zealand – Relations with Australia – Proposals for Federation
A1838 370/1/22: New Zealand – Relations with South East Asia
A1838 370/2/9: Australia's Relations with New Zealand – Reports on Visits to New Zealand
A1838 370/1/3: New Zealand – Relations with United Kingdom (1967–1975)

A1838 370/9/3: New Zealand-Australian Representation – Annual Review of Australian Relations
A1838 TS677/3: Strategic Basis of Australian Defence Policy
A1838 TS691/1/1: Britain – East of Suez
A1838 TS696/1: Australia – Strategic Interest and Defence Policies in Southeast Asia
A1838 696/1/9: British Withdrawal – Five Power Conference
A1838 TS696/1/9: British Withdrawal – Five Power Arrangements
A1838 TS682/4: AUS-UK-US-NZ Defence Discussions and Agreements other than SEATO
A1838 2461/13: SEATO Council of Ministers – 13th Meeting
A1838 3004/11/14: SEATO – General – Southeast Asia – General
A1838 TS3006/10/4/1: Quadripartite Discussions

A1945: Records of the Department of Defence

A1945 73/1/63: Letters from AJSS London – File 9
A1945 73/1/55: Letters from AJSS London

A2908/A3211/A9861: Records of the High Commission London

A2908 D25: United Kingdom Defence Policy
A3211 1969/1846: United Kingdom Defence Policy
A3211 1969/1847: Defence – Australia – Policy
A9861 3/12/77/8: Political and Economic United Kingdom Defence

A4940/A5619: Cabinet Files

A5619 C22: Withdrawal of British Defence Forces from Malaysia
A5619 C470: Strategic Basis of Australia's Defence Policy
A4940 C1473: Defence Aid to Malaysia and Singapore
A4940 C4626: Australian Defence Policy – Implications of United Kingdom withdrawal from Malaysia and Singapore
A4940 C4658: Discussion with Prime Minister of New Zealand, Oct. 1967

A9735: Records of the High Commission Kuala Lumpur

A9735 201/7/2: Malayan Defence – Strategic Reserve

M: Private Papers

M1003 (Alexander Downer Papers), DEFENCE EAST OF SUEZ
M1003 (Alexander Downer Papers), MALAYSIA-SINGAPORE
M3787 (John Gorton Papers), File 53: MAY-SGP – Australian Military Presence
M4295 (Harold Holt Papers), File 20: Press Conference and Briefings
M4324 (Keith Waller Papers), Box 2: John Keith Waller: Papers relating to [Department of External Affairs] Policy Review

LAC: Library and Archives Canada

MG26 N: Lester B. Pearson Fonds

MG26 N1, Vol. 2, Correspondence with Richard Casey
MG26 N3, Vol. 135, 313.45: London Jan 65 Conf.
MG26 N3, Vol. 319, 810 Secr.
MG26 N3, Vol. 319, 812.3-1964 Minutes Secret.

MG26 O: Pierre Elliott Trudeau Fonds

MG26 O7, Vol. 259, 313.45: Pacific Tour/Australia/New Zealand/Malaysia

MG: Further Private Papers held by the LAC

MG31 E47 (Arnold Cantwell Smith Fonds), Vol. 3: Diary
MG31 E83 (H. Basil Robinson Fonds), Box 13: Correspondence with Geoffrey Murray
MG32 B12 (Paul Martin Fonds), Vol. 23: Asian Tour

RG24: Records of the Department of National Defence

RG24-B-1, Vol. 21493, CSC 2137:12: Military Assistance to Malaya
RG24-B-2, Vol. 21577, 5-2-5040-12: Defence Measures and Plans – Military Assistance to Non-NATO countries

RG25: Records of the Department of External Affairs

RG25, Vol. 3072, File 10: "Canada's Asian Policy". Speech given by Paul Martin at the Fourth Annual Banff Conference on World Affairs, Banff, Alberta, August 26, 1966
RG25, Vol. 10663, 23-3-1968: Commonwealth – Heads of Government Meetings – 1968
RG25 A-3-b, Vol. 3338, 1894-40: Relations between United Kingdom and Australia
RG25 A-3-b, Vol. 3008, 3534-40: Australian Relations with Malaya and Singapore
RG25 A-3-b, Vol. 6379, 4457-B-40: Canada's Policy in the Far East (1950–1959)
RG25 A-3-b, Vol. 5074/6865, 4533-40: Australia-Canada Relations
RG25 A-3-b, Vol. 4245, 8250-C-40: Canada-Malaya Relations
RG25 A-3-b, Vol. 8205, 8250-H-40: Malaya-U. K. Relations
RG25 A-3-b, Vol. 3811, 8449-40: U. K.-New Zealand Relations – General File
RG25 A-3-b, Vol. 6613/6614, 11142-40: Canada-United Kingdom Relations
RG25 A-3-b, Vol. 7824, 12687-A-40: Prime Ministers Commonwealth Tour, 1958 – United Kingdom
RG25 A-3-b, Vol. 4728, 50058-40: Malayan Military Situation and Defence
RG25 A-3-b, Vol. 4731, 50062-40: Conditions in the Far East – Situation General
RG25 A-3-b, Vol. 4768, 50073-40: Far Eastern Regional Security Pact (ANZUS)
RG25 A-3-b, Vol. 4768, 50073-A-40: Far Eastern Regional Security Pact (ANZAM)
RG25 A-3-b, Vol. 6022/6023/6024, 50273-40: Defence of South East Asia – SEATO – General File
RG25 A-3-b, Vol. 6136, 50397-40: Malaya – Political Situation

RG25 A-3-c, Vol. 12617, 20-AUSTL-1-3-MLSIA: Political Affairs – Policy and Background – Foreign Policy Trends – Australia – Malaysia
RG25 A-3-c, Vol. 8842, 20-AUSTL-1-3: Political Affairs – Policy and Background – Foreign Policy Trends – Australia
RG25 A-3-c, Vol. 8402, 20-AUSTL-1-3-NZ: Foreign Affairs – Policy Trends – Australia and New Zealand
RG25 A-3-c, Vol. 8903, 20-BRIT-1-3-E. Suez: Policy and Background – British Disengagement East of Suez
RG25 A-3-c, Vol. 10092, 20-CDA-9-FE: PA – Visits – Far Eastern
RG25 A-3-c, Vol. 8917, 20-INDON-1-3-MLSIA: Policy and Background – Foreign Policy Trends – Indonesia – Malaysia
RG25 A-3-c, Vol. 8871, 20-NZ-1-3: Political Affairs – New Zealand – Policy and Background – Foreign Policy Trends
RG25 A-3-c, Vol. 10041, 20-1-2-AUSTL: Policy and Background – Canada's Foreign Policy Trends and Relations – Australia
RG25 A-3-c, Vol. 8599/8600, 20-1-1-12: Political Affairs – Global Trends – Far East South East Asia and Oceania
RG25 A-3-c, Vol. 8615/8616, 20-1-2-ASIA/PACIFIC: Policy and Background – Canadian External Policy and Relations Asia – Pacific – Foreign Policy Review
RG25 A-3-c, Vol.10055, 20-1-2-NZ: Political affairs – Policy and Background – Canada's foreign policy Trends and Relations – New Zealand
RG25 A-3-c, Vol. 10042, 20-1-2-BRIT: Policy and Background – Canadian external relations – Britain
RG25 A-3-c, Vol. 10054, 20-1-2-MLSIA: Political affairs – Policy and Background – Canada's foreign policy trends and relations – Malaysia (1967–1978)
RG25 A-3-c, Vol. 10660, 23-1-AUSTL: Commonwealth – Policy – Development – Australia – – Commonwealth – Policy, Development – Australia
RG25 A-3-c, Vol. 10282, 27-1-2-AUSTL: Defence – Policy and Plans – Countries other than Canada – Australia
RG25 A-3-c, Vol. 10282, 27-1-2-BRIT: Defence – Policy and Plans – Great Britain
RG25 A-3-c, Vol. 10285, 27-1-2-MLSIA: Policy and Plans – Countries other than Canada – Malaysia
RG25 A-3-c, Vol. 11393, 27-4-CWLTH: Defence – Organizations and Conferences – Commonwealth Conference
RG25 A-3-c, Vol. 14594, 27-4-FPDA: Defence – Organizations and Conferences – Five Power Defence Arrangements
RG25 A-3-c, Vol. 10317, 27-8-AUSTL: Defence – Bilateral Relations with Canada – Australia
RG25-A-4, Vol. 3171, 36-1968/3: Special Task Force on European Country Studies – Western Europe – Britain
RG25-B-12, 36-For.P.-Cda+Pac: Canada and the Pacific

ANZ: Archives New Zealand

AAFD: Record of the Cabinet Office

AAFD W3738 811, Box 1312, CAB 222/1/1: Commonwealth Defence General
AAFD W3738 811, Box 1316, CAB 222/3/1: Defence – Southeast Asia – General

AAFD W3738 811, Box 1321, CAB 223/13/1: Defence of Pacific – Australia – General
AAFD W3738 811, Box 1321, CAB 224/1/1: Defence of New Zealand – General

ABFK: Records of the Joint Service Organisation (New Zealand Department of Defence)

ABFK W5767 19754, Box 10, 1/4/4: New Zealand Defence Machinery – Chief of Staff Committee – Papers
ABFK W5767 19754, Box 93, 43/3/1: Commonwealth Defence – Defence Discussions
ABFK W5767 19754, Box 95, 45/1/1: Collective Defence Arrangements – General
ABFK W5767 19764, Box 95, 46/2/1: Commonwealth Regional Defence – Far East – General
ABFK W5929 7291, Box 91, 95/3/1: Report on Visits Overseas by Chief of General Staff/Chief of Defence Staff/MoD/P
ABFK W5767 19754, Box 119, 156/1/1: Malaysia – General
ABFK W5767 19754, Box 123, 156/2/9: Malaysia – Defence – New Zealand Military Assistance (Use of NZ Forces)
ABFK W5807 7281, Box 166, 226/7/3: New Zealand Government – CWLTH Defence – AUS/NZ/UK Strategic Reserve
ABFK W5807 7281, Box 174, 226/7/24: New Zealand Government – CWLTH Defence – British Withdrawal Far East

AAEG/ACIE/ABHS: Records of the Department of External Affairs

AAEG W3252 6956, Box 9, TKY 50/9/9, Part 6: Security – SEATO – Council Meetings
ACIE 8798, Box 227, 59/2/176/1: Visits – Right Honourable W Nash to Southeast Asia
ACIE 8798, EA1 234, 59/2/209: Visits – PM to AUS for ANZUS and SEATO, 1966
ACIE 8798, EA1 103, 156/10/2: Imperial Defence – AUS/NZ Cooperation
ACIE 8798, W2619, Box 218, 440/7/5, Part 1: Individual Countries – Asia – External Relations – Australia
ACIE 8798, W2619, 434/8/1, Part 6: Individual Countries – Southeast Asia – Defence – General
ABHS W4627 950, Box 770, 1/2/27: Office Administration – Constitution and Administration – Meetings of Division Heads
ABHS W4627 950, Box 1409, 56/2/3: NZ Affairs – Foreign Policy – Foreign Affairs Committee – Minutes Meetings EA Committee
ABHS W5242 950, Box 33/34, 85/1/1: War Affairs: Defence of NZ – General – General
ABHS 5242 950, Box 68, 87/32/1: War Affairs – NZ Forces- Defence Commitments – General
ABHS W5422 950, Box 3, 111/1/3/1: International Affairs: Security – General – Representations from Public General
ABHS W5422 950, Box 34, 111/3/3/15: International Affairs – ANZUS – Council Meetings
ABHS W4627 950, Box 3762, 201/2/3/1: United Kingdom: External Relations – USA
ABHS W4627 950, Box 3812, 203/3/6: Australia – Foreign Affairs – Australia's Representatives Overseas
ABHS W4627 950, Box 4022, 253/3/5/1: Malaysia – Defence – Anglo/Malayan Defence Agreement (AMDA)

ABHS W4627 950, Box 4028, 253/3/6/2: Malaysia – Defence – Use of Commonwealth Forces after Independence/Defence – Presence of AUS and NZ Troops (Post British Withdrawal)
ABHS W4627 950, Box 4508, 434/8/8: Southeast Asia: Defence – BDCC – General
ABHS W4627 950, Box 4505–4507, 434/8/1: Southeast Asia: Defence – General
ABHS W4627 950, Box 4667, 455/7/3: Singapore – Defence Aid
ABHS W5533 22128, Box 12, CBA 22/2/1: Reporting – Annual Reports – General
ABHS W5533 22128, Box 92, CBA 50/8/2: International Security Affairs – Pacific and Asian – ANZUS
ABHS W5533 22128, Box 154, CBA 89/1/1: AUS/NZ Relations – General
ABHS W5402 18069, Box 119, BRU 64/1/6: New Zealand – Foreign Relations – Australia
ABHS W5789 6945, Box 102, JKA 64/10/1: New Zealand Affairs: ER – New Zealand Relations with Southeast Asia – Political (1969–1974)
ABHS W5400 20358, Box 84, KL 90/1/1: Commonwealth Affairs – General
ABHS W5400 20358, Box 85, KL 90/3/2: Commonwealth Affairs – Conference and Meetings – PM Conferences
ABHS W5400 20358, Box 85, KL 101/1/2: Pacific and Asian Security – General – AUS/NZ/US (ANZUS)
ABHS W5400 20358, Box 88, KL 101/5/1: Pacific and Asian Security – Canberra Information Conference – Four Power Information Conference
ABHS W5400 20358, Box 91, KL 102/1/4: British/CWLTH Presence in Far East//Pacific – General – Commander in Chief, Far East, Meetings
ABHS W5400 20358, Box 96/97, KL 102/1/9: British/CWLTH Presence in Far East/Pacific – General – AUS/NZ Policy in Southeast Asia
ABHS W5400 20358, Box 108, KL 103/6/3: Defence – South Vietnam – New Zealand Military Assistance
ABHS W5400 20358, Box 105, KL 104/3/1: New Zealand Defence Papers – General
ABHS W5400 20358, Box 156, KL 242/2/1: Australia – External Relations – General
ABHS W4628 7148, Box 36, LONB 62/1: New Zealand Foreign Affairs – General
ABHS W5503 7148 142, LONB 65/1: Commonwealth Affairs – General
ABHS W5503 7148, Box 250, LONB 69/8: International Affairs – Australia
ABHS W4628 7148, Box 115/116, LONB 106/2/7: Defence – General – CWLTH – Malaysia
ABHS W4628 7148, Box 117, LONB 106/3: Defence – General – New Zealand
ABHS W4628 7148, Box 118, LONB 106/4/2: Defence General Pacific ANZUS Meetings
ABHS W4628 7148, Box 119, LONB 106/5: Defence – General – Southeast Asia – General
ABHS W4628 7148, Box 119, LONB 106/5A: Defence – Southeast Asia – General: Four Power Planning
ABHS W4628 7148, Box 120/121, LONB 106/7: Defence – General – United Kingdom: General
ABHS W4628 7148, Box 123, LONB 106/7/1: Defence – General: United Kingdom – Policy in Southeast Asia
ABHS W4628 6958, Box 51, NYP 3/22/4: Political Affairs – Southeast Asia – Singapore
ABHS W5579 6958, Box 184, NYP 3/40/3: Political Affairs – Canada/Chinese Communist Relations

ABHS W5579 6958, Box 184, NYP 3/40/4: Political Affairs – Canada – Canada/New Zealand Relations (1969–1970)
ABHS W4628 6950, Box 9, OTT 88/1/1: Canada – Defence – General
ABHS W5631 22310, Box 193, PAR 222/1/1: Political Reporting – Southeast Asia and Indochina – General
ABHS W4628 6952, Box 9, SIN 251/1/7: Regional Affairs – General – ASEAN
ABHS W5761 6952, Box 123, SIN 337/1/1: Canada – General
ABHS W4628 6957, Box 21, SAI 63/1/1: NZ Affairs: Foreign Affairs – General
ABHS W4628 6957, Box 23, SAI 68/1/1: NZ Affairs – Defence – General

TNA: The National Archives, Kew (UK)

DEFE: Records of the Ministry of Defence

DEFE 11/637: Far East – Chief of Staff Committee

DO: Records of the Dominion Office

DO 164/39: Australian Defence Policy
DO 169/198: Attitude of Australian Representative to SEATO in Respect of Laos Situation
DO 169/439: British Defence Policy in Southeast Asia and Implications of Singapore's Recession
DO 169/444: Defence Arrangements for South East Asia (1966)
DO 35/5008: Canadian Attitude Towards the Commonwealth

FO: Records of the Foreign Office

FO 1091/89: Defence Policy in Southeast Asia
FO 371/129758: Views on United Kingdom held by Minister of Australia in Saigon

FCO: Records of the Foreign and Commonwealth Relations Office

FCO 7/1772: Policy of Canada in Asia and the Pacific (Trudeau's Pacific Tour)
FCO 7/1773: Foreign Policy Review (Canada)
FCO 24/91: Far East Defence: Singapore and Malaysia – Visit Thomson
FCO 24/92: Visit of George Thomson, Secretary of State for Commonwealth Affairs, to Singapore, Malaysia, New Zealand and Australia in relation to further defence cuts, January 1968
FCO 24/188: AUS-UK Relations (1967)
FCO 24/189: AUS-UK Relations (1967)
FCO 24/284: Visit by J. Marshall (NZ) to UK (May 1967)
FCO 24/950: Visit of Norman Kirk as Leader of the Opposition to SEA, 1970
FCO 24/1845: New Zealand's Attitude towards SEA (1973)
FCO 46/54: United Kingdom Multilateral Policy and Planning – Far East Quadripartite Consultations
FCO 63/28: Canada – United Kingdom Relations

FCO 68/38: Canada – Relations with Britain, other Commonwealth Countries and the Commonwealth (Constitutional)

PREM: Records of the Prime Minister's Office

PREM 13/889: Far East Defence Planning
PREM 13/890: Far East Defence Planning Part 2
PREM 13/1454: Far East Defence Planning Part 3
PREM 13/1455: Far East Part 4

NLA: National Library of Australia

MS10135: Garry Woodard Papers

MS10135, Box 5, File 23: Correspondence, 1954–2013

MS4622: Sir Kenneth Bailey Papers

MS4622, Box 5, File 36: Australia and Asia

TRC: Oral History Section

TRC 1023: Interview with Arthur Tange by J. D. B. Miller, April 1981
TRC 4903: Interview with William Pritchett by Garry Woodard, 28.10.2002/4.2.2003

NLNZ: National Library of New Zealand, Alexander Turnbull Library Collections

92-258: George Laking Papers

92-258, 03/25: Personal Correspondence with Macdonald (London)
92-258, 03/13: Personal Correspondence with Francis (Singapore)
92-258, 04/16: Miscellaneous Papers on Foreign Policy

MS-Papers-6759: Alister McIntosh Papers

MS-Papers-6759-362: Personal Correspondence with Hunter Wade (3)
MS-Papers-6759-135: Reports of Discussions between Holyoake and Overseas Officials (C4)
MS-Papers-6759-224: Personal Correspondence with Charles Bennett (59/1)
MS-Papers-6759-356: Personal Correspondence with Malcolm Templeton

Trinity College, Toronto

F2307: John Hadwen Papers

F2307, Series 2, Box 2: Personal Files

Newspapers Articles

Australian Newspaper Articles

"UK Asian Defence Cuts", Canberra Times, 19.1.1966.
Burns, A. L., Letter to Editor: Mature and flexible policies, Canberra Times, 27.1.1966.
"Still East of Suez", The Bulletin, 11.6.1966.
"The SEATO Rites", The Bulletin, 9.7.1966.
"Forward into Asia", Age, 21.4.1967.
"A (distant) study of the Chinese puzzle. Our Gordon Jockel visits a 'Think Tank'", Sydney Morning Herald, 6.6.1967.
"We must do more for ourselves", The Australian, 20.7.1967.
"The Great Retreat", Age, 20.7.1967.
"New look in political arrogance", The Australian Financial Review, 28.7.1967.
"A Case for Dr Freud?", The Australian Financial Review, 23.10.1967.
Grant, Bruce, "Holt and Asia", Age, 22.12.1967.
Millar, T. B., "Where do We stand?", Canberra Times, 19.1.1968.
Tipping, E. W., "The Kiwi who wants to be alone", Melbourne Herald, 22.1.1968.
"Our man in London: be hard-headed" (Comment by 'Observer'), The Bulletin, 27.1. 1968.
"Backing away from Britain?", The Bulletin, 2.3.1968.
Brass, Douglas, "A chance for Mr Gorton to get down to specifics", The Australian, 27.3.1968.
"As we were", Sydney Morning Herald, 13.6.1968.
"NZ's Omega Affair", Canberra Times, 20.7.1968.
Stockwin, Harvey: "Retreat from Malaysia", The Bulletin, 18.1.1969.
"Mr Trudeau", Sydney Morning Herald, 14.5.1970.
Juddery, Bruce: "Regional five-power 'posse' takes shape", The Canberra Times, 6.8. 1970.

Canadian Newspaper Articles

"Help for our Malaysian partner", Toronto Daily Star, 25.6.1964.
Gallagher, James H. (Toronto, Ontario), "If Malaysia Falls", Letter to Editor, Toronto Star, 16.1.1965.
"The Battleground is Asia", Toronto Daily Star, 19.1.1965.
Feldspar, Bernard (Trenton, Ontario), "Help Malaysia", Letter to Editor, Toronto Daily Star, 21.1.1965.
"Keep hands off Canada, PM warns", Globe and Mail, 28.11.1967.
Lynch, Charles, "Advantages in Being Equal", Ottawa Citizen, 3.12.1968.
Robertson, Fraser: "Looking into Business. Pepin's Tradewinds blow Westward Ho", Globe and Mail, 1.5.1969.

New Zealand Newspaper Articles

"NZ Diplomatic Services Abroad", Auckland Star, 2.1.1963.
"Ribs for an Umbrella", Auckland Star, 5.6.1963.
"NZ Must Expand her Defences Along with Australia", Evening Post, 15.6.1963.

"Are Some More Equal than Others?", Northland Times, 13.1.1966.
Entwisle, Arnold, "SEATO Council Meeting", Lookout Broadcast, 2.7.1966.
Templeton, Ian, "Revised Defence Priorities Don't Please Services", Auckland Star, 13.6.1967.
"British Abdication East of Suez", New Zealand Herald, 20.7.1967.
"Good Move Says Kirk", New Zealand Herald, 20.7.1967.
"British no more, Australia seeks an image", New Zealand Herald, 21.7.1967.
"East of Suez", Sunday Times, 23.7.1967.
"Doesn't Anyone like Britain any more?", Christchurch Star, 24.7.1967.
"Britain assesses future of Asia", New Zealand Evening Post, 26.7.1967.
"Can Australia be a Mother to Us?", Evening Post, 27.7.1967.
"Who Do We Think We Are?", New Zealand Listener, 11.8.1967.
Jennings, George, Letter to Editor on Editorial "Who Do We Think We Are?", New Zealand Listener, 1.9.1967.
"A Surfeit of Self", New Zealand Listener, 17.11.1967.
"The Anzacs – again", Auckland Star, 10.1.1968.
"Anzac Battalion", The Press, 12.1.1968.
"The Day Britain let us down", Dominion, 18.1.1968.
"Twilight of an Empire", Evening Post, 18.1.1968.
"Urgent Look at Defence", Dominion, 23.1.1968.
"Folding the Flag", New Zealand Listener, 2.2.1968.
"After Britain, Who?", New Zealand Listener, 9.2.1968.
Gager, Owen, Letter to Editor, New Zealand Listener, 23.2.1968.
"Nobody willing to step in", Auckland Star, 26.2.1968.
"Prime Minister's Job", Christchurch Star, 2.3.1968.
"SEATO has very Limited Uses", Auckland Star, 1.4.1968.
"Is SEATO Just a Paper Tiger?", Evening Post, 6.4.1968.
Hunn, J. K., "Constructive Defence", New Zealand Listener, 31.5.1968.
"Battle of wits in SE Asia", Dominion, 10.6.1968.
"Ill-Prepared for Vital Defence Decisions", Auckland Star, 10.6.1968.
Youren, H. W. to Editor, New Zealand Listener, 21.6.1968.
Reader M. Weatherall, Letter to the Editor, New Zealand Listener, 21.6.1968.
Templeton, Ian, "Forward Strategy for NZ in Asia", Christchurch Star, 24.6.1968.
McKinnon to Editor, New Zealand Listener, 25.6.1968.
"Fresh Outlook Required on Strategy in Asia", New Zealand Herald, 18.10.1968.
"New Zealand needs to give help to SEA", Opotiki News, 22.11.1968.
"New Zealand Defence Role in SEA", Evening Star, 23.12.1968.
"Flexible Defence Role in Malaysia", Auckland Star, 26.2.1969.
"Maturity in Foreign Policy", New Zealand Herald, 7.3.1969.
"A Gesture of Defence", Dominion, 20.4.1971.

Cartoons

Tanner, Les, "Please Adjust Your Dress Before Leaving", The Bulletin, 6.5.1967.
Petty, Bruce, "Once more into the breech, dear friends ...", The Australian, 20.7.1967.
Collette, Aubrey, "What d'ya mean take over", The Australian, 20.7.1967.
Minhinnick, Gordon, "Stepping Stones", New Zealand Herald, March 1969.

Published Statements and Speeches

Statement by the Right. Hon. Arthur Calwell in the Australian House of Representatives (AHoR), 2.8.1945, CPD, Vol. 31, 4911.

The Sinews of Peace ('Iron Curtain Speech'), Speech given by Right. Hon. Winston Churchill at Westminster College Fulton, Missouri, 5.3.1946. URL: https://winstonchurchill.org/resources/speeches/1946-1963-elder-statesman/the-sinews-of-peace/. Accessed August 22, 2019.

Agreement Establishing the South Pacific Commission, Canberra, 6.2.1947, URL: https://www.dfat.gov.au/about-us/publications/historical-documents/Pages/volume-12/551-agreement-establishing-the-south-pacific-commission. Accessed December 6, 2020.

Address by the Right. Hon. Prime Minister Louis St. Laurent, 26.11.1956, Canadian Parliamentary Debates, 22nd Parliament, Fourth Session, 19–26.

Ministerial Statement by the Right. Hon. Robert Menzies in AHoR, Commonwealth Parliamentary Debates (CPD) 39/1963, 25.9.1963, 1338 f.

Ministerial Statement by the Right. Hon. Keith Holyoake, New Zealand Parliamentary Debates (NZPD), Vol. 336, 20.9.1963, 2015.

New Zealand Department of External Affairs: Annual Report of the New Zealand Department of External Affairs (1965).

Statement by Harold Holt following the visit of Denis Healey, 3.2.1966, in: Current Notes on International Affairs (CNIA) 37/2 (February 1966), 77–80.

Speech by the Right. Hon. Paul Hasluck in the AHoR, in: CNIA 37/4 (April 1966), 190–198.

Statement by Right. Hon. Michael Stewart at the National Press Club Australia, 26.6.1966, in: CNIA 37/6 (June 1966), 390–392.

Address by the Right. Hon. Harold Holt to the National Press Club 30.6.1966, in: CNIA 37/6 (Juni 1966), 321–325.

Holt, Harold, "All the way with LBJ". Speech at a state reception, White House, Washington D. C., 30.6.1966, in: Sally Warhaft (Ed.), Well May We Say …: The Speeches that Made Australia, Melbourne 2004, 123–124.

Statement by the Member of Parliament John McLeay in the AHoR, CPD 9/1967, 2.3.1967, 321–324.

Speech by the Right Hon. Harold Holt in the AHoR, 12.4.1967, in: CNIA 38/4 (April 1967), 140–145.

Address by the Right. Hon. Paul Hasluck at the First Conference of the Veterans of Asian-Pacific Wars, 12.4.1967, in: CNIA 38/4 (April 1967), 163–164.

Address by the Right. Hon. Harold Holt in the AHoR, 4.5.1967, in: CNIA 38/5 (May 1967), 191–193.

Statement by the Right. Hon. Harold Holt on 19.7.1967, in: CNIA, 38/7 (July 1967), 295–296.

"New Dimensions in Canadian Foreign Policy", 16.5.1967, Speech given by Paul Martin at the University of New Brunswick in: Canadian External Affairs (1967), 194–199.

Speech given by Gough Whitlam in the AHoR, CPD 33/1967, 17.8.1967, 218–227.

Statement by the Member of Parliament Peter Nixon in AHoR, CPD 33/1967, 17.8.1967, 247–250.

Statement by the Liberal Member of Parliament William Haworth in the AHoR, CPD 35/1967, 31.8.1967, 664–670.

Statement by the Right Hon. Paul Hasluck, 13.10.1967, in: CNIA 38/10 (October 1967), 419–426.

"Canada and the World", A Policy Statement by Prime Minister Pierre Elliott Trudeau issued on May 29, 1968, Statement and Speeches No. 68/17.

Downer, Alexander, Australia and a Post-Brexit Britain. In: The Round Table 107, 2018, 21–31.

Published Sources

Ashton, S. R./Bridge, Carl/Ward, Stuart (Ed.), Documents on Australian Foreign Policy. Australia and the United Kingdom 1960–1975, Barton 2010.

Ashton, S. R./Louis, W. R. (Ed.), British Documents on the End of Empire. Series A, Vol 5: East of Suez and the Commonwealth 1964–1971. Vol. 1: East of Suez, London 2004.

Bailey, Kenneth, Australia, Asia and World Security: Address given at CIIA and Dalhousie University, 12.5.1966, in: Dalhousie Review 46/3, 1966, 295–304.

Blanchette, Arthur E. (Ed.), Canadian Peacekeepers in Indochina, 1954–1973. Recollections, Ottawa 2002.

Bothwell, Robert/Granatstein, Jack L., Trudeau's World. Insiders Reflect on Foreign Policy, Trade, and Defence, 1968–84, Vancouver 2017.

Brebner, John B., North Atlantic Triangle. The Interplay of Canada, the United States and Great Britain, New Haven 1945.

Boyce, Peter J., Australian Attitudes to Security, in: Thomas B. Millar (Ed.), Australian-New Zealand Defence Co-operation, Canberra 1968, 16–34.

–, The Bonds of Culture and Commonwealth in Southeast Asia, in: Journal of Southeast Asian Studies 2/1, 1971, 71–77.

Boyce, Peter J./ Davis, R. K., Malaysia tests the Commonwealth, in: Australian Quarterly 37/3, 1965, 59–68.

Carrington, Peter Alexander Rupert, Reflect on Things Past. The Memoirs of Lord Carrington. 2. publ., London 1988.

Clark, Gregory, In Fear of China, Melbourne 1967.

Clark, Manning, The Years of Unleavened Bread, December 1949 to December 1972, in: Meanjin 32/2, 1973, in: Manning Clark (Ed.), Occasional Writings and Speeches, Enfield 1981, 194–202.

Crocker, Walter R., Australian Ambassador. International Relations at First Hand, Carlton 1971.

–, Travelling Back. The Memoirs of Sir Walter Crocker, South Melbourne 1981.

Dee, Moreen (Ed.), Australia and the Formation of Malaysia, 1961–1966, Barton 2005.

Downer, Alexander, Six Prime Ministers, Melbourne 1982.

Eayrs, James (Ed.), The Commonwealth and Suez. A Documentary Survey, London 1964.

Grant, Bruce, Australian Defence: Two Views, 1968: I. Regional Role, in: Australia's Neighbours 4/52–53, 1968, 1–4.

–, Pacific Signposts: 3) Shattered Images, in: Meanjin 27/3, 1968, 261–272.

–, Australia's Defence Policy, in: Quadrant, Jan–Feb 1969, 37–41.

Grattan, M., Armed Neutrality – A Foreign Policy for Australia, in: Australian Quarterly 40/4, Dec. 1968, 44–56.

Heeney, Brian D., The Things that Are Caesar's. The Memoirs of a Canadian Public Servant, Toronto 1972.
Holmes, John W., A Canadian's Commonwealth: Realism Out of Rhetoric, in: The Round Table 11, 1966, 335–347.
–, The Commonwealth and the United Nations, in: William Baskerville Hamilton (Ed.), A Decade of the Commonwealth: 1955–1964, Durham 1966, 349–365.
–, Canada and the Pax Americana, in: Harvey L. Dyck/Hans P. Krosby (Ed.), Empire and Nations: Essays in Honour of Frederic H. Soward, Toronto 1969, 73–90.
Horne, Donald, The Lucky Country. The Classic Study of Australia in the Sixties, Ringwood 1964.
Ignatieff, George, The Making of a Peacemonger. The Memoirs of George Ignatieff, Toronto 1985.
Menzies, Sheila/Menzies, Arthur R., Australia & the South Pacific. Letters Home, 1965–1972, Manotick 2009.
Mahajani, Usha, Is Australia Part of Asia?, in: Australian Quarterly 36/2, 1964, 25–34.
Munto, Ronald, Pacific Signposts: 6) Australia's Regional Role in Asia – A Clear Necessity, in: Meanjin 4, 1969, 184–193.
Nash, Walter, A New Zealand View, in: The English-Speaking World XLII/4, July 1960, 23–25.
New Zealand Ministry of Foreign Affairs (Ed.), Statements and Documents, 1943–1957, Wellington 1972.
Public Expenditure in 1968–69 and 1969–1970, Cmnd. 3515, London H. M. S. O., January 1968.
Reid, Escott, Radical Mandarin. The Memoirs of Escott Reid, Toronto 1989.
Renouf, Alan, The Champagne Trail. Experiences of a Diplomat, Melbourne 1980.
Ritchie, Charles, Diplomatic Passport. More Undiplomatic Diaries 1946–1962, Toronto 1981.
–, Storm Signals. More Undiplomatic Diaries, 1962–1971, Toronto 1987.
Supplementary Statement on Defence Policy, Cmnd 3357, 18.7.1967, London H.M. S. O., July 1967.
Teichmann, Max, Australian Defence: Two Views, 1968: II. Disengagement, in: Australia's Neighbours 4/52–53, 1968, 4–8.
Waller, Keith, A Diplomatic Life. Some Memories, Nathan 1990.
Watt, Alan, The Evolution of Australian Foreign Policy 1938–1965, Cambridge 1967.
–, Australian Diplomat, Sydney 1972.
Westbrook, George, Foreign Policy Review: January–June 1968, in: Australian Quarterly 40/3, 1968, 92–103.
Wilczynski, J., The Economics and Politics of Wheat Exports to China, in: The Australian Quarterly 37/2, 1965, 44–55.

Literature

Anderson, Benedict, Imagined Communities. Reflections on the Origin and Spread of Nationalism. Revised ed., London 2006.

Andreatta, Filippo, Collective Security: Theory and Practice of an Institution for Peace in the XXth Century, London 1996. PhD Thesis.

Andrew, Arthur, 'A Reasonable Period of Time'. Canada's De-Recognition of Nationalist China, in: Paul M. Evans/Michael B. Frolic (Ed.), Reluctant Adversaries: Canada and the People's Republic of China 1949–1970, Toronto 1991, 241–252.

–, The Rise and Fall of a Middle Power. Canadian Diplomacy from King to Mulroney, Toronto 1993.

Andrews, Eric, The Australian Centenary of Defence. Volume 5: The Department of Defence, Melbourne 2001.

Anthony, Mely C. (Ed.), An Introduction to Non-Traditional Security Studies. A Transnational Approach, Los Angeles 2016.

Ashton, S. R./Wm R. Louis, Introduction, in: S. R. Ashton/W. R. Louis (Ed.), British Documents on the End of Empire. Series A, Vol 5: East of Suez and the Commonwealth 1964–1971: Vol. 1: East of Suez, London 2004, XXIX–CXXXV.

Atkinson, Joel, Australian Support for an Independent Taiwan Prior to the Recognition of the People's Republic of China, in: Australian Journal of Politics & History 57/1, 2011, 68–85.

Ayson, Robert, When Cooperation Trumps Convergence: Emerging Trends in Australia-New Zealand Defence Relations, in: Security Challenges 2/3, 2006, 25–39.

Baker, Richard W. (Ed.), Australia, New Zealand, and the United States. Internal Change and Alliance Relations in the ANZUS States, New York 1991.

Ball, Simon J., Harold Macmillan and the Politics of Defence: The Market for Strategic Ideas during the 'Sandys Era' Revisited, in: Twentieth Century British History 6, 1995, 78–100.

Ballantyne, Tony, The Changing Shape of the Modern British Empire and its Historiography, in: The Historical Journal 53/2, 2010, 429–452.

Bayly, Christopher Alan/Harper, Timothy N., Forgotten Wars. The End of Britain's Asian Empire, London 2007.

Beecroft, Stephen, Canadian Policy towards China, 1949–1957: The Recognition Problem, in: Paul M. Evans/Michael B. Frolic (Ed.), Reluctant Adversaries: Canada and the People's Republic of China 1949–1970, Toronto 1991, 43–72.

Belich, James, Making Peoples. A History of the New Zealanders from Polynesian Settlement to the End of the Nineteenth Century, Auckland 2001.

–, Paradise Reforged. A History of the New Zealanders from the 1880s to the Year 2000, Honolulu 2001.

–, Replenishing the Earth. The Settler Revolution and the Rise of the Anglo-World 1783–1939, Oxford 2009.

Belich, James/Darwin, John/Frenz, Margret et al. (Ed.), The Prospect of Global History, Oxford/New York 2016.

Bell, Coral, Dependent Ally. A Study in Australian Foreign Policy, St. Leonards 1984.

Benvenuti, Andrea, Shifting Priorities: Australia's Defence Ties to Britain in the Aftermath of Empire, in: History Compass 2, 2004, 1–11.

–, A Parting of the Ways: The British Military Withdrawal from Southeast Asia and its Critical Impact on Anglo-Australian Relations, 1965–68, in: Contemporary British History 20, 2006, 575–605.
–, Australian Reactions to Britain's Declining Presence in Southeast Asia, 1955–63, in: The Journal of Imperial and Commonwealth History 34/3, 2006, 407–429.
–, The British Military Withdrawal from Southeast Asia and its Impact on Australia's Cold War Strategic Interests, in: Cold War History 5/2, 2006, 189–210.
–, Anglo-Australian Relations and the 'Turn to Europe', 1961–1972, London 2008.
–, The British are "Taking to the Boat": Australian Attempts to Forestall Britain's Military Disengagement from Southeast Asia, 1965–1966, in: Diplomacy & Statecraft 20/1, 2009, 86–106.
–, The Heath Government and British Defence Policy in Southeast Asia at the End of Empire (1970–71), in: Twentieth Century British History 20/1, 2009, 53–73.
–, Australia, the 'Marshall Experiment' and the Decolonisation of Singapore, 1955–56, in: Journal of Southeast Asian Studies 43/2, 2012, 257–279.
–, Cold War and Decolonisation. Australia's Policy towards Britain's End of Empire in Southeast Asia, Singapore 2017.
Benvenuti, Andrea/Moreen Dee, The Five Power Defence Arrangements and the Reappraisal of the British and Australian Policy Interests in Southeast Asia, 1970–75, in: Journal of Southeast Asian Studies 41/1, 2010, 101–123.
Benvenuti, Andrea/David M. Jones, Myth and Misrepresentation in Australian Foreign Policy: Menzies and Engagement with Asia, in: Journal of Cold War Studies 13/4, 2011, 57–78.
–, With Friends Like These: Australia, the United States, and Southeast Asian Détente, in: Journal of Cold War Studies 21/2, 2019, 27–57.
–, Engaging Southeast Asia? Labor's Regional Mythology and Australia's Military Withdrawal from Singapore and Malaysia 1972–1973, in: Journal of Cold War Studies 12/4, 2010, 32–62.
Benvenuti, Andrea/Stuart Ward, Britain, Europe, and the 'Other Quiet Revolution' in Canada, in: Phillip Buckner (Ed.), Canada and the End of Empire, Vancouver 2005, 165–182.
Blainey, Geoffrey, The Tyranny of Distance. How Distance Shaped Australia's History, Melbourne 1966.
Blaxland, John C., Strategic Cousins. Australian and Canadian Expeditionary Forces and the British and American Empires, Montreal 2006.
Boehm, Peter, Canada and the Modern Commonwealth: The Approaches of Lester Pearson and Pierre Trudeau, in: Bulletin of Canadian Studies 3/1, 1979, 23–39.
Bongiorno, Frank, The Price of Nostalgia: Menzies, the "Liberal" Tradition and Australian Foreign Policy, in: Australian Journal of Politics & History 51/3, 2005, 400–417.
–, Comment: Australia, Nationalism and Transnationalism, in: History Australia 10/3, 2013, 77–84.
Booth, Ken/Wheeler, Nicholas J., The Security Dilemma. Fear, Cooperation and Trust in World Politics, Basingstoke 2008.
Bormann, Patrick/Freiberger, Thomas/Michel, Judith (Ed.), Angst in den Internationalen Beziehungen, Göttingen 2010.
Bothwell, Robert, Canada and the United States. The Politics of Partnership, Toronto 1992.

–, Eyes West: Canada and the Cold War in Asia, in: Greg Donaghy (Ed.), Canada and the Early Cold War, 1943–1957: Canada au Début de la Guerre Froide, 1943–1957, Ottawa 1998, 59–70.

–, Canada's Moment: Lester Pearson, Canada and the World, in: Norman Hillmer (Ed.), Pearson, the Unlikely Gladiator, Montreal 1999, 19–29.

–, The Further Shore. Canada and Vietnam, in: International Journal of Canadian Studies 51/1, 2001, 89–114.

– *(Ed.)*, Canada Among Nations, 2008. 100 Years of Canadian Foreign Policy, Montreal 2014.

Bourke, Joanna, Fear and Anxiety: Writing about Emotion in Modern History, in: History Workshop Journal 55, 2003, 111–133.

Boyce, Peter J./Angel, J. R. (Ed.), Independence and Alliance. Australia in World Affairs 1976–80, Sydney 1983.

Brawley, Sean/Mathew Radcliffe, Losing the Blanket, Building a Fence: Australian Anxiety and the End of Military Colonialism in Malaysia, in: The Journal of Imperial and Commonwealth History 45/6, 2017, 1026–1048.

Brett, Judith, The Menzies Era, 1950–1966, in: Alison Bashford/Stuart McIntyre (Ed.), The Cambridge History of Australia: Vol. 2: The Commonwealth of Australia, Cambridge 2003, 112–134.

Bretts, Raymond F., Decolonisation: A Brief History of a Word, in: Remco Raben/Els Bogaerts (Ed.), Beyond Empire and Nation: The Decolonization of African and Asian Societies, 1930s–1960s, Leiden 2012, 23–38.

Bridge, Carl/Bongiorno, Frank/Lee, David (Ed.), The High Commissioners. Australia's Representatives in the United Kingdom, 1910–2010, Barton 2010.

Bridge, Carl/Kent Fedorowich, Mapping the British World, in: Carl Bridge/Kent Fedorowich (Ed.), The British World: Diaspora, Culture, and Identity, London/Portland 2003, 1–15.

– *(Ed.)*, Munich to Vietnam. Australia's Relations with Britain and the United States since the 1930's, Carlton 1991.

– *(Ed.)*, The British World. Diaspora, Culture, and Identity, London/Portland 2003.

Bristow, Damon, The Five Power Defence Arrangements: Southeast Asia's Unknown Regional Security Organization, in: Contemporary Southeast Asia 27/1, 2005, 1–20.

Brookes, Stephanie, Politics, Media and Campaign Language. Australia's Identity Anxiety, London/New York 2017.

Brubaker, Rogers/Frederick Cooper, Beyond "Identity" in: Theory and Society 29/1, 2000, 1–47.

Buchanan, Keith, Banned by Tides: New Zealand in the Asian Century, in: Chris Elder (Ed.), New Zealand's China Experience: Its Genesis, Triumphs, and Occasional Moments of Less Than Complete Success, Wellington 2012, 176–179.

Buckner, Phillip (Ed.), Canada and the End of Empire, Vancouver 2005.

–, The Long Goodbye. English Canadians and the British World, in: Phillip Buckner/R. D. Francis (Ed.), Rediscovering the British World, Calgary 2005, 181–208.

– *(Ed.)*, Canada and the British Empire, Oxford 2010.

–, Canada and the End of Empire, 1939–1982, in: Phillip Buckner (Ed.), Canada and the British Empire, Oxford 2010, 107–126.

–, Introduction: Canada and the British Empire, in: Phillip Buckner (Ed.), Canada and the British Empire, Oxford 2010, 1–21.

Buckner, Phillip/Francis, R. D. (Ed.), Rediscovering the British World, Calgary 2005.

Budde, Gunilla/Conrad, Sebastian/Janz, Oliver (Ed.), Transnationale Geschichte. Themen, Tendenzen und Theorien, Goettingen 2010.
Burbank, Jane/Cooper, Frederick, Empires in World History. Power and the Politics of Difference, Princeton 2010.
Burke, Anthony, Fear of Security. Australia's Invasion Anxiety, Cambridge 2008.
Burke, Roland, Decolonization and the Evolution of International Human Rights, Philadelphia 2010.
–, The Internationalism of Human Rights, in: Glenda Sluga/Patricia M. Clavin (Ed.), Internationalisms: A Twentieth-Century History, Cambridge 2017, 287–314.
Burnett, Alan, New Zealand Policies Towards Australia 1960–1972, in: The Australian Quarterly 45/1, 1973, 78–91.
Burton, Antoinette M. (Ed.), After the Imperial Turn. Thinking With and Through the Nation, Durham 2003.
–, The Trouble with Empire. Challenges to Modern British Imperialism, Oxford et al. 2015.
Butler, Lawrence J., Britain and Empire. Adjusting to a Post-Imperial World, London 2002.
Butler, Lawrence J./Sarah Stockwell, Introduction, in: L. J. Butler/Sarah Stockwell (Ed.), The Wind of Change: Harold Macmillan and British Decolonization, Houndmills/Basingstoke 2013, 1–19.
Cain, Frank (Ed.), Menzies in War and Peace, St. Leonards 1997.
Capie, David, The Bilateral-Multilateral Nexus in Asia's Defence Diplomacy, in: William T. Tow/Brendan Taylor (Ed.), Bilateralism, Multilateralism and Asia-Pacific Security: Contending Cooperation, London/New York 2013, 115–131.
Capie, David/Gerald McGhie, Representing New Zealand: Identity, Diplomacy and the Making of Foreign Policy, in: James H. Liu (Ed.), New Zealand Identities: Departures and Destinations, Wellington 2005, 230–241.
Carlyon, Jenny/Morrow, Diana, Changing Times. New Zealand since 1945, Auckland 2013.
Cavell, Richard (Ed.), Love, Hate, and Fear in Canada's Cold War, Toronto/Buffalo 2004.
Chakrabarty, Dipesh, Provincializing Europe. Postcolonial Thought and Historical Difference. Reissue, Princeton 2008.
Champion, C. P., The Strange Demise of British Canada. The Liberals and Canadian Nationalism 1964–1968, Montreal/Ithaca 2010.
Chapnick, Adam, The Canadian Middle Power Myth, in: International Journal 55, 2000, 188–206.
–, Canada's Voice. The Public Life of John Wendell Holmes, Vancouver 2009.
Chatterjee, Partha, A Brief History of Subaltern Studies, in: Gunilla Budde/Sebastian Conrad/Oliver Janz (Ed.), Transnationale Geschichte: Themen, Tendenzen und Theorien. 2. publ., Goettingen 2010, 94–104.
Chesterman, John, Natural-Born Subjects? Race and British Subjecthood in Australia, in: Australian Journal of Politics & History 51/1, 2005, 30–39.
Christiano, Kevin J., Pierre Elliott Trudeau. Reason before Passion, Toronto 1994.
Clark, Margaret (Ed.), Three Labour Leaders. Nordmeyer, Kirk, Rowling, North Palmerston 2001.
Clausen, Mads, 'Falsified by History': Menzies, Asia and Post-Imperial Australia, in: History Compass 6/4, 2008, 1010–1023.

Clément, Maéva/Sangar, Eric (Ed.), Researching Emotions in International Relations. Methodological Perspectives on the Emotional Turn, Cham 2018.

Cole, Douglas, The Problem of 'Nationalism' and 'Imperialism' in British Settlement Colonies, in: The Journal of British Studies 10/2, 1971, 160–182.

Collins, Rebecca, Concealing the Poverty of Traditional Historiography: Myth as Mystification in Historical Discourse, in: Rethinking History 7/3, 2003, 341–365.

Conrad, Sebastian, What Is Global History?, Princeton 2016.

Cooper, Andrew F., Keeping in Touch: Patterns of Networking in the Canadian-Australian Diplomatic Relationship, in: Margaret MacMillan/Francine McKenzie (Ed.), Parties Long Estranged: Canada and Australia in the Twentieth Century, Vancouver 2003, 249–266.

Cooper, Andrew F./Higgott, Richard A./Nossal, Kim R., Relocating Middle Powers. Australia and Canada in a Changing World Order, Vancouver 1993.

Corner, Frank, Kirk Presents a New Zealand Face to the World, in: Margaret Clark (Ed.), Three Labour Leaders: Nordmeyer, Kirk, Rowling, North Palmerston 2001, 139–167.

Cotton, James, The Australian School of International Relations, New York 2013.

Cullen, Poppy, Kenya and Britain After Independence. Beyond Neo-Colonialism, Cham 2017.

Curran, James, The "Thin Dividing Line": Prime Ministers and the Problem of Australian Nationalism, 1972–1996, in: Australian Journal of Politics & History 48/4, 2002, 469–486.

–, The Power of Speech. Australian Prime Ministers Defining the National Image, Carlton 2006.

–, 'The World Changes': Australia's China Policy in the Wake of Empire, in: James Reilly/Jing-dong Yuan (Ed.), Australia and China at 40, Chicago 2012, 22–43.

–, Unholy Fury. Whitlam and Nixon at War, Carlton 2015.

Curran, James/Ward, Stuart, The Unknown Nation. Australia After Empire, Melbourne 2010.

Curthoys, Ann, We've Just Started Making National Histories, and You Want us to Stop Already?, in: Antoinette M. Burton (Ed.), After the Imperial Turn: Thinking With and Through the Nation, Durham 2003, 70–90.

Dalrymple, Rawdon, Continental Drift. Australia's Search for a Regional Identity, Aldershot 2003.

Darby, Phillip, British Defence Policy East of Suez, 1947–1968, London 1973.

Darwin, John, British Decolonization Since 1945: A Pattern or a Puzzle?, in: The Journal of Imperial and Commonwealth History 12/2, 1984, 187–209.

–, Britain and Decolonisation. The Retreat from Empire in the Post-War World, Basingstoke 1988.

–, Britain's Withdrawal East of Suez, in: Carl Bridge (Ed.), Munich to Vietnam. Australia's Relations with Britain and the United States since the 1930's, Carlton 1991, 140–158.

–, A Third British Empire? The Dominion Idea in Imperial Politics, in: Judith Brown/Wm R. Louis (Ed.), The Oxford History of the British Empire, Volume IV, Oxford 1999, 64–87.

–, After Tamerlane. The Rise and Fall of Global Empires, 1400–2000, New York 2008.

–, The Empire Project. The Rise and Fall of the British World-System 1830–1970, Cambridge 2009.

Davidson, Jim, The De-Dominionisation of Australia, in: Meanjin 38/2, 1979, 139–153.

–, De-Dominionisation Revisited, in: Australian Journal of Politics & History 51/1, 2005, 108–113.

Day, David, The Great Betrayal. Britain Australia & the Onset of the Pacific War 1939–42, North Ryde 1988.

–, 27 December 1941: Prime Minister Curtin's New Year Message: Australia's Look to America, in: Martin Crotty/David A. Roberts (Ed.), Turning Points in Australian History, Sydney 2008, 129–142.

Dee, Moreen, The Regional Significance of the Indonesian-Malaysian Confrontation 1963–1966, And The Lessons Australia, New Zealand And Great Britain Drew From It, in: Melbourne Historical Journal 27/27, 1999, 84–99.

Delvoie, Louis A., The Commonwealth in Canadian Foreign Policy, in: The Round Table 310, 1989, 137–143.

Dennis, Peter, The Oxford Companion to Australian Military History. 2. ed., Oxford 2008.

Dennis, Peter/Grey, Jeffrey/Edwards, Peter G., Emergency and Confrontation. Australian Military Operations in Malaya & Borneo, 1950–1966, St. Leonards 1996.

Dibb, Paul, The Self-Reliant Defence of Australia: The History of an Idea, in: Ronald Huisken/Meredith Thatcher (Ed.), History as Policy: Framing the Debate on the Future of Australia's Defence Policy, Canberra 2007, 11–26.

Dobell, P., Canada in World Affairs, 1971–1973, Toronto 1985.

Dockrill, Michael L., British Defence Since 1945, Oxford/New York 1989.

Dockrill, Saki, Britain's Retreat from East of Suez. The Choice Between Europe and the World?, Houndmills/New York 2002.

Doig, Jack, New Nationalism in Australia and New Zealand: The Construction of National Identities by Two Labo(u)r Governments in the Early 1970s, in: Australian Journal of Politics & History 59/4, 2013, 559–575.

–, The Australian and New Zealand Governments' Responses to Britain's Decline in the 1960s: Identity, Geopolitics and the End of Empire, in: Journal of New Zealand & Pacific Studies 1/1, 2013, 41–54.

Donaghy, Greg, Coming Off the Gold Standard: Re-Assessing the "Golden Age" of Canadian Diplomacy: Paper presented to the symposium A Very Modern Ministry: Foreign Affairs and International Trade Canada, University of Saskatchewan, 28 September 2009. URL: http://www.suezcrisis.ca/pdfs/Coming%20off%20the%20Gold%20Standard.pdf. Accessed May 25, 2021.

–, Parallel Paths. Canadian-Australian Relations Since the 1890s, Ottawa 1995.

–, The Rise and Fall of Canadian Military Assistance in the Developing World, 1952–1971, in: Canadian Military History 4/1, 1995, 75–84.

– *(Ed.)*, Canada and the Early Cold War, 1943–1957. Canada au Début de la Guerre Froide, 1943–1957, Ottawa 1998.

–, Introduction, in: Greg Donaghy (Ed.), Canada and the Early Cold War, 1943–1957: Canada au Début de la Guerre Froide, 1943–1957, Ottawa 1998, 14–29.

–, Minding the Minister: Pearson, Martin, and the American Policy in Asia, 1963–1967, in: Norman Hillmer (Ed.), Pearson, the Unlikely Gladiator, Montreal 1999, 131–149.

–, Tolerant Allies. Canada and the United States, 1963–1968, Montreal 2002.

–, "A Sad, General Decline?": The Canadian Diplomat in the 20th Century, in: Robert Bothwell (Ed.), Canada Among Nations, 2008: 100 Years of Canadian Foreign Policy, Montreal 2014, 41–60.

Donaghy, Greg/Carroll, Michael K. (Ed.), In the National Interest. Canadian Foreign Policy and the Department of Foreign Affairs and International Trade, 1909–2009, Calgary 2011.

–, Introduction, in: Greg Donaghy/Michael K. Carroll (Ed.), In the National Interest: Canadian Foreign Policy and the Department of Foreign Affairs and International Trade, 1909–2009, Calgary 2011, 1–9.

Doxey, Margaret, Canada and the Modern Commonwealth, in: Behind the Headlines 40/2, 1982, 1–17.

Duara, Prasenjit, Introduction: The Decolonization of Asia and Africa in the Twentieth Century, in: Prasenjit Duara (Ed.), Decolonization: Perspectives From Now and Then, London 2008, 1–18.

Easter, David, Britain and the Confrontation with Indonesia, 1960–1966, London 2004.

Eaton, H. B., Something Extra. 28 Commonwealth Brigade 1951 to 1974, Edinburgh 1993.

Eayrs, James, In Defence of Canada. Vol. 5: Indochina – Roots of Complicity, Toronto 1983.

Eckel, Jan, Utopie der Moral, Kalkül der Macht. Menschenrechte in der globalen Politik nach 1945, in: Archiv für Sozialgeschichte 49, 2009, 437–484.

Edelman, Murray J., The Symbolic Uses of Politics, Urbana 1964.

Edwards, Peter, Prime Ministers and Diplomats. The Making of Australian Foreign Policy; 1901–1949, Melbourne 1983.

–, The Origins of the Cold War, in: Carl Bridge (Ed.), Munich to Vietnam. Australia's Relations with Britain and the United States since the 1930's, Carlton 1991, 70–86.

–, Some Reflections on the Australian Government's Commitment to the Vietnam War, in: Jeffrey Grey/Jeff Doyle (Ed.), Vietnam: War, Myth and Memory: Comparative Perspectives on Australia's War in Vietnam, Crows Nest 1992, 1–13.

–, A Nation at War. Australian Politics, Society and Diplomacy During the Vietnam War, 1965–1975, St. Leonards 1997.

–, Sir Arthur Tange. Last of the Mandarins, St. Leonards 2006.

Edwards, Peter/Pemberton, Gregory, Crises and Commitments. The Politics and Diplomacy of Australia's Involvement in Southeast Asian Conflicts, 1948–1965, Sydney 1992.

Elder, Chris (Ed.), New Zealand's China Experience. Its Genesis, Triumphs, and Occasional Moments of Less Than Complete Success, Wellington 2012.

Elkins, Caroline/Susan Pedersen, Introduction: Settler Colonialism: A Concept and Its Uses, in: Caroline Elkins/Susan Pedersen (Ed.), Settler Colonialism in the Twentieth Century: Projects, Practices, Legacies, New York 2005, 1–20.

Emmers, Ralf, The Role of the Five Power Defence Arrangements in Southeast Asian Security Architecture, in: William T. Tow/Brendan Taylor (Ed.), Bilateralism, Multilateralism and Asia-Pacific Security: Contending Cooperation, London/New York 2013, 87–99.

English, John, Lester Pearson and China, in: Paul M. Evans/Michael B. Frolic (Ed.), Reluctant Adversaries: Canada and the People's Republic of China 1949–1970, Toronto 1991, 133–147.

–, Speaking Out on Vietnam, 1965, in: Don Munton/John J. Kirton (Ed.), Canadian Foreign Policy: Selected Cases, Scarborough 1992, 135–152.

–, Just Watch Me: The Life of Pierre Elliott Trudeau. 2. Ed., Toronto 2009.

–, Two Heads Are Better Than One: Ivan Head, Pierre Trudeau and Canadian Foreign Policy, in: Greg Donaghy/Kim R. Nossal (Ed.), Architects and Innovators: Building the Department of Foreign and International Trade, 1909–2009, Montreal 2009, 239–252.

Eustace, Nicole, Emotion and Political Change, in: Susan Matt/Peter N. Stearns (Ed.), Doing Emotions History, Urbana 2014, 163–183.

Evans, Gareth J./Grant, Bruce, Australia's Foreign Relations in the World of the 1990s. 2. Ed., Carlton 1995.

Evans, Paul M., Engaging China. Myth, Aspiration, and Strategy in Canadian Policy from Trudeau to Harper 2014.

Evans, Paul M./Frolic, Michael B. (Ed.), Reluctant Adversaries. Canada and the People's Republic of China 1949–1970, Toronto 1991.

Fanon, Frantz, The Wretched of the Earth, New York 1968.

Fenton, Damien, To Cage the Red Dragon. SEATO and the Defence of Southeast Asia, 1955–1965, Singapore 2012.

Fernando, Joseph M., The Cold War, Malayan Decolonization and the Making of the Federation of Malaysia, in: Albert Lau (Ed.), Southeast Asia and the Cold War, London 2012, 67–85.

FitzGerald, Stephen, Is Australia an Asian Country? Can Australia Survive in an East Asian Future?, St. Leonards 1997.

Flanagan, Jason, The Vietnam War at Home and Abroad, in: Shirleene Robinson/Julie Ustinoff (Ed.), The 1960s in Australia: People, Power and Politics, Newcastle 2012, 199–216.

Frolic, Michael B., The Trudeau Initiative, in: Paul M. Evans/Michael B. Frolic (Ed.), Reluctant Adversaries: Canada and the People's Republic of China 1949–1970, Toronto 1991, 189–216.

Gare, Deborah, Britishness in Recent Australian Historiography, in: The Historical Journal 43/4, 2000, 1145–1155.

Garner, Joe, The Commonwealth Office, 1925–1968, London 1978.

Gifford, Peter, The Cold War across Asia, in: David Goldsworthy/Peter Edwards (Ed.), Facing North: A Century of Australian Engagement with Asia, Melbourne 2001, 171–219.

Goldsworthy, David, Losing the Blanket. Australia and the End of Britain's Empire, Carlton South 2002.

Goldsworthy, David, David Dutton/Peter Gifford et al., Reorientation, in: David Goldsworthy/Peter Edwards (Ed.), Facing North: A Century of Australian Engagement with Asia, Melbourne 2001, 310–371.

Goldsworthy, David/Edwards, Peter (Ed.), Facing North. A Century of Australian Engagement with Asia, Melbourne 2001.

Granatstein, Jack L., A Man of Influence. Norman A. Robertson and Canadian Statecraft, 1929–1968, Ottawa 1981.

–, Canada 1957–1967. The Years of Uncertainty and Innovation, Toronto 1986.

–, How Britain's Weakness Forced Canada Into the Arms of the United States, Toronto 1989.

–, The Ottawa Men. The Civil Service Mandarins 1935–1957, Toronto 1998.

–, From Mother Country to Far Away Relative: The Canadian-British Military Relationship From 1945, in: Canadian Military History 18/1, 2009, 55–60.

–, When the Department of External Affairs Mattered: An When It Shouldn't Have, in: Greg Donaghy/Michael K. Carroll (Ed.), In the National Interest: Canadian Foreign Policy and the Department of Foreign Affairs and International Trade, 1909–2009, Calgary 2011, 69–79.

Granatstein, Jack L./Bothwell, Robert, Pirouette. Pierre Trudeau and Canadian Foreign Policy, Toronto 1990.

Grant, David M., The Mighty Totara. The Life and Times of Norman Kirk, Auckland 2014.

Greenwood, Gordon/Harper, Norman (Ed.), Australia in World Affairs. 1961–1965, London 1968.

Greiner, Bernd/Weber, Claudia/Walter, Dierk et al. (Ed.), Angst im Kalten Krieg, Hamburg 2009.

Grey, Jeffrey, War in the British World in the Twentieth Century, in: Phillip Buckner/R. D. Francis (Ed.), Rediscovering the British World, Calgary 2005, 233–250.

–, Coming of Age: Australian Defence and Strategic Policy in the Cold War, in: Ian McGibbon/John Crawford (Ed.), Seeing Red: New Zealand, the Commonwealth and the Cold War 1945–91, Wellington 2012, 127–134.

Grey, Jeffrey/Doyle, Jeff (Ed.), Vietnam: War, Myth and Memory. Comparative Perspectives on Australia's War in Vietnam, Crows Nest 1992.

Guan, Ang C., Malaysia, Singapore, and the Road to the Five Power Defence Arrangements (FPDA), July 1970–November 1971, in: War and Society 30/3, 2011, 207–225.

Gurry, Meg, Identifying Australia's 'Region': From Evatt to Evans, in: Australian Journal of International Affairs 49/1, 1995, 17–31.

Gustafson, Barry, Kiwi Keith. A Biography of Keith Holyoake, Chicago 2008.

Gyngell, Allan, Fear of Abandonment. Australia in the World Since 1942, Carlton 2017.

Gyngell, Allan/Wesley, Michael, Making Australian Foreign Policy, New York 2003.

Hack, Karl, Defence and Decolonisation in Southeast Asia. Britain, Malaya and Singapore 1941–1968, Richmond 2001.

Haglund, David G., The North Atlantic Triangle Revisited: (Geo)Political Metaphor and the Logic of Canadian Foreign Policy, in: American Review of Canadian Studies 29/2, 2009, 211–235.

Halloran, Mary, John Hilliker/Greg Donaghy, The White Paper Impulse: Reviewing Foreign Policy Under Trudeau and Clark, in: International Journal: Canada's Journal of Global Policy Analysis 70/2, 2015, 309–321.

Halvorson, Dan, From Commonwealth Responsibility to the National Interest: Australia and Post-War Decolonisation in South-East Asia, in: The International History Review 40/4, 2018, 870–892.

–, Commonwealth Responsibility and Cold War Solidarity. Australia in Asia, 1944–1974, Acton 2019.

Hanning, Hugh, East of Suez – Facts and Figures, in: International Affairs 42/2, 1966, 253–260.

Hansen, Lene, Security as Practice. Discourse Analysis and the Bosnian War, London 2006.

Harland, Bryce, On Our Own. New Zealand Emerging in a Tripolar World, Wellington 1992.

Harper, Norman, A Changing Commonwealth in A Chaotic World, in: Australian Outlook April, 1965, 20–34.

Hatzivassiliou, Evanthis, Out-Of-Area: NATO Perceptions of the Third World, 1957–1967, in: Cold War History 13/1, 2012, 67–88.

Head, Ivan L./Trudeau, Pierre E., The Canadian Way. Shaping Canada's Foreign Policy 1968–1984, Toronto 1995.

Henrikson, Alan K., Mental Maps, in: Michael J. Hogan/Thomas G. Paterson (Ed.), Explaining the History of American Foreign Relations, Cambridge 1991, 177–193.

Hervouet, Gérard, About Canada. Canada and the Pacific Basin, Ottawa 1988.

Hilliker, John/Greg Donaghy, Canadian Relations with the United Kingdom at the End of Empire, 1956–1973, in: Phillip Buckner (Ed.), Canada and the End of Empire, Vancouver 2005, 25–46.

Hilliker, John F./Barry, Donald, Canada's Department of External Affairs. Vol. 2: Coming of Age, 1946–1968, Montreal 1995.

Hillmer, Norman (Ed.), Pearson, the Unlikely Gladiator, Montreal 1999.

Hillmer, Norman/Granatstein, Jack L., Empire to Umpire. Canada and the World to the 1990s, Toronto 1994.

Hirschhausen, Ulrike von, A New Imperial History? Programm, Potenzial, Perspektiven, in: Geschichte und Gesellschaft 41, 2015, 718–757.

Hirschhausen, Ulrike von/Jörn Leonhard, Zwischen Historisierung und Globalisierung: Titel, Themen und Trends der neueren Empire-Forschung, in: Neue Politische Literatur 56, 2011, 389–404.

Hobsbawm, Eric, Introduction: Inventing Traditions, in: Eric Hobsbawm/Terence Ranger (Ed.), The Invention of Tradition, Cambridge 1993, 1–14.

Holland, R. F., The Imperial Factor in British Strategies From Attlee to Macmillan, 1945–63, in: The Journal of Imperial and Commonwealth History 12/2, 1984, 165–186.

–, The Pursuit of Greatness. Britain and the World Role, 1900–1970, London 1991.

Holmes, John W., The Shaping of Peace: Canada and the Search for World Order, 1943–1957. Vol. 1, Toronto 1979.

–, The Shaping of Peace: Canada and the Search for World Order, 1943–1957. Vol. 2, Toronto 1982.

–, Canada and the Vietnam War, in: Jack L. Granatstein (Ed.), Canadian Foreign Policy: Historical Readings, Toronto 1986, 198–208.

Hopkins, A. G., Rethinking Decolonization, in: Past & Present 200/1, 2008, 211–247.

Horner, David M., Strategic Command. General Sir John Wilton and Australia's Asian Wars, South Melbourne 2005.

Howe, Stephen, Empire and Ideology, in: Sarah Stockwell (Ed.), The British Empire: Themes and Perspectives. 2. publ., Malden 2010.

– *(Ed.)*, The New Imperial Histories Reader, London 2010.

Howson, Peter/Aitkin, Don (Ed.), The Howson Diaries. The Life of Politics, Ringwood 1984.

Hudson, W. J., The Suez Crisis of 1956, in: Carl Bridge (Ed.), Munich to Vietnam. Australia's Relations with Britain and the United States since the 1930's, Carlton 1991, 114–129.

Hudson, Wayne/Geoffrey Stokes, Australia and Asia: Place, Determinism and National Identities, in: Geoffrey Stokes (Ed.), The Politics of Identity in Australia, Cambridge 1997, 145–157.

Huggan, Graham, The Oxford Handbook of Postcolonial Studies, Oxford 2013.

Hughes, Philip, Division and Discord: British Policy, Indochina, and the Origins of the Vietnam War, 1954–1956, in: Kent Fedorowich/Martin Thomas (Ed.), International Diplomacy and Colonial Retreat, London 2001, 94–112.

Hyam, Ronald, Britain's Declining Empire. The Road to Decolonisation 1918–1968, Cambridge 2008.

Igartua, José E., 'Ready, Aye, Ready' No More? Canada, Britain and the Suez Crisis in the Canadian Press, in: Phillip Buckner (Ed.), Canada and the End of Empire, Vancouver 2005, 47–65.

–, The Other Quiet Revolution. National Identities in English Canada, 1945–71, Vancouver 2006.

Ingleson, John/David Walker, The Impact of Asia, in: Neville Meaney (Ed.), Under New Heavens: Cultural Transmission and the Making of Australia, Port Melbourne 1989, 287–324.

Iriye, Akira, Global and Transnational History. The Past, Present, and Future, Basingstoke 2013.

Iriye, Akira/Saunier, Pierre-Yves (Ed.), The Palgrave Dictionary of Transnational History, Basingstoke 2009.

James, William D., Global Britain's Strategic Problem East of Suez, in: European Journal of International Security 6/2, 2021, 171–189.

Jansen, Jan C./Osterhammel, Jürgen, Decolonization. A Short History, Princeton/Oxford 2017.

Jeffries, Bill, Kirk's Prime-Ministership, 1972–1974, in: Margaret Clark (Ed.), Three Labour Leaders: Nordmeyer, Kirk, Rowling, North Palmerston 2001, 107–116.

Jenkins, John P., White Supremacy. URL: https://www.britannica.com/topic/white-supremacy. Accessed September 5, 2019.

Jones, Matthew, A Decision Delayed: Britain's Withdrawal from South East Asia Reconsidered, 1961–68, in: The English Historical Review 117/472, 2002, 569–595.

–, Conflict and Confrontation in South East Asia, 1961–1965. Britain the United States and the Creation of Malaysia, Cambridge 2002.

–, The Radford Bombshell: Anglo-Australia-US Relations, Nuclear Weapons and the Defence of South East Asia, 1954–1957, in: Journal of Strategic Studies 27/4, 2004, 636–662.

Kandiah, Michael/Gillian Staerck, 'At the Top Table': British Elites' Perceptions of the UK's International Position, 1950–91, in: J. Young/E. Pedaliu/M. Kandiah (Ed.), Britain in Global Politics Volume 2: From Churchill to Blair. 2. publ., London 2014, 179–197.

Kavic, Lorne, Canada and the Commonwealth: Sentiment, Symbolism and Self-Interest, in: Commonwealth Journal 65/257, 1975, 27–49.

Keating, Thomas F., Canada and World Order. The Multilateralist Tradition in Canadian Foreign Policy. 2. publ., Toronto 2002.

Kember, James, New Zealand Diplomatic Representation in Southeast Asia: The 1950s and 1960s, in: New Zealand Journal of Asian Studies 11/1, 2009, 385–401.

Kennedy, Dane, Australian Policy Towards China, in: Gordon Greenwood/Norman Harper (Ed.), Australia in World Affairs. 1961–1965, London 1968, 397–415.

King, Michael/Thornhill, C. J., Niklas Luhmann's Theory of Politics and Law, Houndmills/New York 2005.

Kitchen, Veronica M., The Globalization of NATO. Intervention, Security and Identity, Abingdon/New York 2010.

Koch, Sebastian, Identitätskrisen nach dem Ende des Britischen Empire. Zur kulturellen Neu-Verortung in Kanada, Australien und Aotearoa Neuseeland, Forthcoming [2022].

Kristensen, Jeppe, "In Essence Still a British Country": Britain's Withdrawal From East of Suez, in: Australian Journal of Politics & History 51/1, 2005, 40–52.

Lake, Marilyn/Reynolds, Henry, Drawing the Global Colour Line. White Men's Countries and the International Challenge of Racial Equality, Cambridge 2008.

Lau, Albert, Decolonization and the Cold War in Singapore, 1955–9, in: Albert Lau (Ed.), Southeast Asia and the Cold War, London 2012, 43–66.

–, Introduction: Southeast Asia and the Cold War, in: Albert Lau (Ed.), Southeast Asia and the Cold War, London 2012, 1–12.

– *(Ed.)*, Southeast Asia and the Cold War, London 2012.

Lee, David, 'Shaw, Sir Patrick (1913–1975)'. URL: http://adb.anu.edu.au/biography/shaw-sir-patrick-11667/text20845. Accessed August 18, 2019.

–, Australia and Allied Strategy in the Far East, 1952–1957, in: Journal of Strategic Studies 16/4, 1993, 511–538.

–, Search for Security. Political Economy of Australia's Postwar Foreign and Defence Policy, St. Leonards 1995.

–, The Curtin and Chifley Governments, Liberal Internationalism and World Organisation, in: David Lee/Christopher Waters (Ed.), Evatt to Evans: The Labor Tradition in Australian Foreign Policy, St. Leonards/Canberra 1997, 48–61.

–, The Origins of the Menzies Government's Policy on Indonesia's Confrontation of Malaysia, in: Frank Cain (Ed.), Menzies in War and Peace, St. Leonards 1997, 72–98.

Lee, David/Moreen Dee, Southeast Asian Conflicts, in: David Goldsworthy/Peter Edwards (Ed.), Facing North: A Century of Australian Engagement with Asia, Melbourne 2001, 262–309.

Leffler, Melvyn P./Westad, Odd A. (Ed.), The Cambridge History of the Cold War. Volume I: Beginnings, Cambridge 2010.

Lehmkuhl, Ursula, Pax Anglo-Americana. Machtstrukturelle Grundlagen anglo-amerikanischer Asien- und Fernostpolitik in den 1950er Jahren, München 1999.

Leonhard, Jörn, Introduction: The "Longue Durée of Empire": Toward a Comparative Semantics of a Key Concept in Modern European History, in: Contributions to the History of Concepts 8/1, 2013, 1–25.

Liland, Frode, Explaining NATO's Non-Policy on Out-of-Area Issues During the Cold War, in: Gustav Schmidt (Ed.), A History of NATO: The First Fifty Years, Houndmills 2001, 173–189.

Litt, Paul, Trudeaumania, Vancouver/Toronto 2016.

Lloyd, Lorna, Britain and the Transformation from Empire to Commonwealth: The Significance of the Immediate Post-War Years, in: The Round Table 86/343, 1997, 333–360.

–, Us and Them? The Changing Nature of the Commonwealth Diplomacy, in: Journal of Commonwealth & Comparative Politics 39/3, 2001, 9–30.

–, Diplomacy With a Difference. The Commonwealth Office of High Commissioner 1880–2006, Leiden/Boston 2010.

Longinotti, Edward, Britain's Withdrawal from East of Suez: From Economic Determinism to Political Choice, in: Contemporary British History 29/3, 2014, 318–340.

López, Alfred J., Introduction: Whiteness after Empire, in: Alfred J. López (Ed.), Postcolonial Whiteness: A Critical Reader on Race and Empire, Albany 2005, 1–30.

Louis, W. R., Withdrawal from the Gulf, in: W. R. Louis (Ed.), Ends of British Imperialism: The Scramble for Empire, Suez, and Decolonization, London et al. 2006, 877–906.

Louis, William R./Owen, Roger (Ed.), Suez 1956. The Crisis and Its Consequences, Oxford/New York 1989.

Louis, Wm R., The Dissolution of the British Empire and the Era of Vietnam, in: American Historical Review 107/1, 2002, 1–25.

Lowe, David, Menzies and the 'Great World Struggle'. Australia's Cold War, 1948–1954, Sydney 1999.

–, Percy Spender's Quest, in: Australian Journal of International Affairs 55/2, 2001, 194–197.

–, Australia's Cold War: Britishness and English-Speaking Worlds Challenged Anew, in: Phillip Buckner/R. D. Francis (Ed.), Rediscovering the British World, Calgary 2005, 361–80.

–, Australia, New Zealand and Cultural Diplomacy in the Cold War: An Unanticipated Consequence of the Colombo Plan for Aid to South and South-East Asia, in: Ian McGibbon/John Crawford (Ed.), Seeing Red: New Zealand, the Commonwealth and the Cold War 1945–91, Wellington 2012, 167–182.

Lowe, Peter, Contending with Nationalism and Communism. British Policy Towards Southeast Asia, 1945–65, Basingstoke 2009.

Luhmann, Niklas, Trust, in: Christian Morgner/Michael King (Ed.), Trust and Power, Cambridge/Medford 2017, 1–114.

Lynch, Brian J. (Ed.), Celebrating New Zealand's Emergence. A Tribute to Sir George Laking and Frank Corner, Wellington 2005.

Lyon, Peter, The Commonwealth and the Suez Crisis, in: William R. Louis/Roger Owen (Ed.), Suez 1956: The Crisis and Its Consequences, Oxford/New York 1989, 257–273.

Mackenzie, Hector, Delineating the North Atlantic Triangle: The Second World War and Its Aftermath, in: The Round Table 95/383, 2006, 101–112.

Mackie, J. A. C./Milton Osborne, The Dominion Fallacy, in: Australian Neighbours March/April 1968, 1–4.

MacLaren, Roy, Commissions High. Canada in London 1870–1971, Montreal 2010.

Mann, Jatinder, "Leavening British Traditions": Integration Policy in Australia, 1962–1972, in: Australian Journal of Politics & History 59/1, 2013, 47–62.

– *(Ed.)*, Citizenship in Transnational Perspective. Australia, Canada, and New Zealand, Cham 2017.

–, Redefining Citizenship in Australia, Canada, and Aotearoa New Zealand, New York 2019.

Mann, Michael, Globalization, Macro-Regions and Nation-States, in: Gunilla Budde/Sebastian Conrad/Oliver Janz (Ed.), Transnationale Geschichte: Themen, Tendenzen und Theorien. 2. publ., Goettingen 2010, 21–31.

Martin, Paul, New Dimensions in Canadian Foreign Policy: Speech given at the University of New Brunswick, 16.5.1967, in: External Affairs 19/5, 1967, 194–199.

Matthews, Trevor/John Ravenhill, Adrift in an Alien Sea? Australian Perspectives on the World, in: Richard W. Baker (Ed.), Australia, New Zealand, and the United States. Internal Change and Alliance Relations in the ANZUS States, New York 1991, 159–182.

May, Alex (Ed.), Britain, the Commonwealth and Europe. The Commonwealth and Britain's Applications to Join the European Communities, Basingstoke 2001.
–, Commonwealth or Europe? Macmillan's Dilemma, 1961–63, in: Alex May (Ed.), Britain, the Commonwealth and Europe: The Commonwealth and Britain's Applications to Join the European Communities, Basingstoke 2001, 82–110.
McCourt, David M., What Was Britain's "East of Suez Role"? Reassessing the Withdrawal, 1964–1968, in: Diplomacy & Statecraft 20/3, 2009, 453–472.
McCraw, David, The Demanding Alliance: New Zealand and the Escalation of the Vietnam War, in: Australian Journal of Politics & History 34/3, 1988, 307–319.
–, Norman Kirk, The Labour Party and New Zealand's Recognition of The People's Republic Of China, in: New Zealand Journal of Asian Studies 4/1, 2002, 46–61.
–, Change and Continuity in Strategic Culture: The Cases of Australia and New Zealand, in: Australian Journal of International Affairs 65/2, 2011, 167–184.
–, Staying in Singapore? New Zealand's Third Labour Government and the Retention of Military Forces in Southeast Asia, in: New Zealand Journal of Asian Studies 14/1, 2012, 1–17.
McCulloch, Tony, The North Atlantic Triangle: A Canadian Myth?, in: International Journal 66/1, 2010/11, 197–207.
McDougall, Derek, The Wilson Government and the British Defence Commitment in Malaysia-Singapore, in: Journal of Southeast Asian Studies 4/2, 1973, 229–240.
–, The Malayan Emergency and Confrontation, in: Carl Bridge (Ed.), Munich to Vietnam. Australia's Relations with Britain and the United States since the 1930's, Carlton 1991, 130–139.
–, Australia and the British Military Withdrawal From East of Suez., in: Australian Journal of International Affairs 51/2, 1997, 183–194.
McGibbon, Ian, The Defence of New Zealand 1945–1957, in: Alister McIntosh (Ed.), New Zealand in World Affairs: Vol. 1: 1945–1957, Wellington 1977, 143–176.
–, Forward Defence: The Southeast Asian Commitment, in: Malcolm McKinnon (Ed.), New Zealand in World Affairs: Vol. 2: 1957–1972, Wellington 1991, 9–39.
–, New Zealand and the Korean War. Vol. 1: Politics and Diplomacy. Reprint, Auckland 1996.
– *(Ed.)*, Unofficial Channels. Letters Between Alister McIntosh and Foss Shanahan, George Laking and Frank Corner; 1946–1966, Wellington 1999.
– *(Ed.)*, The Oxford Companion to New Zealand Military History, Auckland 2000.
–, The Defence Dimension, in: Anthony L. Smith (Ed.), Southeast Asia and New Zealand. A History of Regional and Bilateral Relations, Singapore/Wellington 2005, 7–31.
–, New Zealand's Vietnam War. A History of Combat, Commitment and Controversy, Wollombi 2010.
–, Introduction, in: Ian McGibbon/John Crawford (Ed.), Seeing Red: New Zealand, the Commonwealth and the Cold War 1945–91, Wellington 2012, 13–21.
–, Australian-New Zealand Relations and Commitments to Asian Conflicts 1950–1972, in: Journal of Military History 81/4, 2017, 1059–1074.
McGibbon, Ian/Crawford, John (Ed.), Seeing Red. New Zealand, the Commonwealth and the Cold War 1945–91, Wellington 2012.
McIntosh, Alister (Ed.), New Zealand in World Affairs. Vol. 1: 1945–1957, Wellington 1977.

–, The Origins of the Department of External Affairs and the Formulation of an Independent Foreign Policy, in: Alister McIntosh (Ed.), New Zealand in World Affairs: Vol. 1: 1945–1957, Wellington 1977, 9–36.

McIntyre, David, Canada and the Creation of the Commonwealth Secretariat, 1965, in: International Journal 53/4, 1998, 753–777.

McIntyre, Laurence, Reflections on Australian Diplomacy, in: Peter J. Boyce/J. R. Angel (Ed.), Independence and Alliance: Australia in World Affairs 1976–80, Sydney 1983, 311–319.

McIntyre, W. David, The Significance of the Commonwealth, 1965–90, Basingstoke 1991.

–, Imperialism and Nationalism, in: Geoffrey W. Rice/William Hosking Oliver (Ed.), The Oxford History of New Zealand. 2. publ., Auckland 1992, 337–47.

–, Background to the Anzus Pact. Policy-Making Strategy and Diplomacy 1945–55, Basingstoke 1995.

–, British Decolonization, 1946–1997: When, Why and How Did the British Empire Fall?, Basingstoke/New York 1998.

McKenna, Mark, The Captive Republic. A History of Republicanism in Australia, 1788–1996, Cambridge 1996.

McKenzie, Francine, In the National Interest: Dominions' Support for Britain and the Commonwealth After the Second World War, in: The Journal of Imperial and Commonwealth History 34/4, 2006, 553–576.

McKercher, Asa, Sound and Fury: Diefenbaker, Human Rights, and Canadian Foreign Policy, in: Canadian Historical Review 97/2, 2016, 165–194.

McKinnon, Malcolm (Ed.), New Zealand in World Affairs. Vol. 2: 1957–1972, Wellington 1991.

–, Independence and Foreign Policy. New Zealand in the World Since 1935, Auckland 1993.

Mclean, Craig, R. G. Casey and Australian Foreign Policy: Engaging with China and Southeast Asia, 1951–1960. PhD Thesis, Victoria University Melbourne, October 8, 2008.

McLean, David, From British Colony to American Satellite? Australia and the USA During the Cold War, in: Australian Journal of Politics & History 52/1, 2006, 64–79.

Meaney, Neville, The End of 'White Australia' and Australia's Changing Perceptions of Asia, 1945–1990, in: Australian Journal of International Affairs 49/2, 1995, 171–189.

–, Australia and the World, in: Neville Meaney (Ed.), Under New Heavens: Cultural Transmission and the Making of Australia, Port Melbourne 1989, 379–450.

– *(Ed.)*, Under New Heavens. Cultural Transmission and the Making of Australia, Port Melbourne 1989.

–, Britishness and Australian Identity: The Problem of Nationalism in Australian History and Historiography, in: Australian Historical Studies 32/116, 2001, 76–90.

–, Britishness and Australia: Some Reflections, in: Carl Bridge/Kent Fedorowich (Ed.), The British World: Diaspora, Culture, and Identity, London/Portland 2003, 121–135.

–, Look Back in Fear: Percy Spender, the Japanese Peace Treaty and the ANZUS Pact, in: Japan Forum 15/3, 2003, 399–410.

Middlemiss, Danford W./Sokolsky, Joel J., Canadian Defence. Decisions and Determinants, Toronto 1989.

Millar, Thomas B., Australian Defence, 1945–1965, in: Gordon Greenwood/Norman Harper (Ed.), Australia in World Affairs. 1961–1965, London 1968, 251–312.

–, Anglo-Australian Partnership in Defence of the Malaysian Area, in: A. F. Madden/W. H. Morris-Jones/Kenneth Wheare (Ed.), Australia and Britain: Studies in a Changing Relationship, Sydney 1980, 71–89.

–, Australia in Peace and War. External Relations Since 1788, Canberra 1991.

Millar, Thomas B./Casey, Richard G. (Ed.), Australian Foreign Minister. The Diaries of R. G. Casey, 1951–60, London 1972.

Miller, J. D. B., Australia and the Crisis, in: William R. Louis/Roger Owen (Ed.), Suez 1956: The Crisis and Its Consequences, Oxford/New York 1989, 275–283.

Moyn, Samuel, Imperialism, Self-Determination, and the Rise of Human Rights, in: Akira Iriye/Petra Goede/William I. Hitchcock (Ed.), The Human Rights Revolution: An International History, Oxford 2012, 159–178.

Munton, Don/Kirton, John J. (Ed.), Canadian Foreign Policy. Selected Cases, Scarborough 1992.

Murphy, John, Harvest of Fear. A History of Australia's Vietnam War, Boulder 1993.

Murphy, Philip, Book Review: The Queen's Other Realms: The Crown and Its Legacy in Australia, Canada and New Zealand, in: The Journal of Imperial and Commonwealth History 37/4, 2009, 629–636.

–, Britain and the Commonwealth: Confronting the Past – Imagining the Future, in: The Round Table 100/414, 2001, 267–283.

Ninkovich, Frank A., Modernity and Power. A History of the Domino Theory in the Twentieth Century, Chicago 1994.

Nossal, Kim R., A European Nation? The Life and Times of Atlanticism in Canada, in: John English/Norman Hillmer (Ed.), Making a Difference? Canada's Foreign Policy in a Changing World Order, Toronto 1992, 79–102.

O'Reilly, Marc J., Following Ike? Explaining Canadian-Us Co-Operation During the 1956 Suez Crisis, in: Journal of Commonwealth & Comparative Politics 35/3, 1997, 75–107.

Oakman, Daniel, The Seed of Freedom: Regional Security and the Colombo Plan, in: Australian Journal of Politics & History 46/1, 2000, 67–85.

Onslow, Sue, The Commonwealth and the Cold War, Neutralism, and Non-Alignment, in: The International History Review 37/5, 2015, 1059–1082.

Ovendale, Ritchie, The English-Speaking Alliance. Britain, the United States, the Dominions and the Cold War 1945–1951, London 1985.

Page, Don, The Representation of China in the United Nations: Canadian Perspectives and Initiatives, 1949–1971, in: Paul M. Evans/Michael B. Frolic (Ed.), Reluctant Adversaries: Canada and the People's Republic of China 1949–1970, Toronto 1991, 73–105.

Parr, Helen, Britain, America, East of Suez and the EEC: Finding a Role in British Foreign Policy, 1964–67, in: Contemporary British History 20/3, 2006, 403–421.

Parsons, Timothy H., The Rule of Empires. Those Who Built Them, Those Who Endured Them, and Why They Always Fall, Oxford/New York 2010.

Patience, Allan, Australian Foreign Policy in Asia. Middle Power or Awkward Partner?, Cham 2018.

Peden, George C., Suez and Britain's Decline as a World Power, in: The Historical Journal 55/4, 2012, 1073–1096.

–, Recognising and Responding to Relative Decline: The Case of Post-War Britain, in: Diplomacy & Statecraft 24/1, 2013, 59–76.

Pemberton, Gregory, An Imperial Imagination: Explaining the Post-1945 Foreign Policy of Robert Gordon Menzies, in: Frank Cain (Ed.), Menzies in War and Peace, St. Leonards 1997, 154–175.

Penrose, Sandra K., Recognising the People's Republic of China: A Reappraisal of Australian Foreign Policy During the First Menzies Ministry 1950–51, in: Australian Journal of Politics & History 44/2, 1998, 209–224.

Pettman, Ralph, The Radical Critique and Australian Foreign Policy, in: Peter J. Boyce/J. R. Angel (Ed.), Independence and Alliance: Australia in World Affairs 1976–80, Sydney 1983.

Pham, Phuong L., Ending "East of Suez" The British Decision to Withdraw From Malaysia and Singapore, 1964–1968, Oxford 2010.

Pickering, Jeffrey, Britain's Withdrawal from East of Suez. The Politics of Retrenchment, Houndmills 1998.

–, Politics and 'Black Friday': Shifting Power in the Cabinet and the Decision to Withdraw From East of Suez, November 1967–January 1968, in: Twentieth Century British History 12/2, 2002, 144–170.

Pierce, Peter, 'Never Glad Confident Morning Again': Australia, the Sixties and the Vietnam War, in: Jeffrey Grey/Jeff Doyle (Ed.), Vietnam: War, Myth and Memory: Comparative Perspectives on Australia's War in Vietnam, Crows Nest 1992, 69–80.

Pijovic, Nikola, The Commonwealth: Australia's Traditional 'Window' Into Africa, in: The Round Table 103/4, 2014, 383–397.

Preston, Andrew, Balancing War and Peace: Canadian Foreign Policy and the Vietnam War, 1961–1965, in: Diplomatic History 27/1, 2003, 73–111.

Preston, Richard A./Ian Wards, Military and Defence Developments in Canada, Australia and New Zealand: A Three Way Comparison, in: War & Society 5/1, 1987, 1–21.

Prince, Robert, The Limits of Constraint: Canadian-American Relations and the Korean War, 1950–51, in: Journal of Canadian Studies 27, 1992, 129–152.

Pugsley, Christopher, From Emergency to Confrontation. The New Zealand Armed Forces in Malaya and Borneo 1949–1966, Melbourne 2003.

Rabel, Robert, The World Turned Upside Down? New Zealand Politics Until 1984, in: Richard W. Baker (Ed.), Australia, New Zealand, and the United States. Internal Change and Alliance Relations in the ANZUS States, New York 1991, 89–108.

–, Vietnam and the Collapse of the Foreign Policy Consensus, in: Malcolm McKinnon (Ed.), New Zealand in World Affairs: Vol. 2: 1957–1972, Wellington 1991, 40–63.

–, The Vietnam Antiwar Movement in New Zealand, in: Peace & Change 17/1, 1992, 3–33.

–, New Zealand and the Vietnam War. Politics and Diplomacy, Auckland 2005.

Raben, Remco/Bogaerts, Els (Ed.), Beyond Empire and Nation; The Decolonization of African and Asian Societies, 1930s–1960s, Leiden 2012.

Radcliffe, Mathew, Malaya Bound: Australia's Colonial Perceptions of Asia, 1955–1965, in: History Australia 12/3, 2015, 76–96.

Reddy, William M., The Navigation of Feeling. A Framework for the History of Emotions, Cambridge 2006.

Reford, Robert W., Peacekeeping at Suez, 1956, in: Don Munton/John J. Kirton (Ed.), Canadian Foreign Policy: Selected Cases, Scarborough 1992, 58–77.

Reinold, Theresa, Sovereignty and the Responsibility to Protect. The Power of Norms and the Norms of the Powerful, London/New York 2013.

Reynolds, David, Empire, Region, World: The International Context of Australian Foreign Policy since 1939, in: Australian Journal of Politics & History 51/3, 2005, 346–358.

Reynolds, John, Recognition by Trade: The Controversial Wheat Sales to China, in: Australian Outlook 18/2, 1964, 117–126.

Roberts, George, My War, 1965, in: Arthur E. Blanchette (Ed.), Canadian Peacekeepers in Indochina, 1954–1973: Recollections, Ottawa 2002, 112–116.

Roberts, Priscilla, Tweaking the Lion's Tail: Edgar J. Tarr, the Canadian Institute of International Affairs, and the British Empire, 1931–1950, in: Diplomacy & Statecraft 23, 2012, 636–659.

Robinson, Alan, Trends in Australian-New Zealand Relations, in: Australian Quarterly 41/1, 1969, 43–51.

Robinson, Henry B., Diefenbaker's World. A Populist in World Affairs, Toronto 1989.

Robinson, Shirleene/Ustinoff, Julie (Ed.), The 1960s in Australia. People, Power and Politics, Newcastle 2012.

Rolfe, Jim, New Zealand Defence Policy during the Cold War, in: Alexander Trapeznik/Aaron Fox (Ed.), Lenin's Legacy Down Under, Dunedin 2004, 35–56.

Rolls, Mark G., Growing Apart: New Zealand and Malaysia, in: Anthony L. Smith (Ed.), Southeast Asia and New Zealand. A History of Regional and Bilateral Relations, Singapore/Wellington 2005, 209–262.

Rosenwein, Barbara, Worrying about Emotions in History, in: American Historical Review 2002, 821–845.

–, Problems and Methods in the History of Emotions, in: Passions in Context 1, 1–32.

Ross, Douglas A., In the Interest of Peace. Canada and Vietnam 1954–1973, Toronto 1984.

Sachsenmaier, Dominic, Global Perspectives on Global History. Theories and Approaches in a Connected World, Cambridge 2011.

Said, Edward W., Orientalism, London 1978.

Sarty, Roger, The Interplay of Defence and Foreign Policy, in: Robert Bothwell (Ed.), Canada Among Nations, 2008: 100 Years of Canadian Foreign Policy, Montreal 2014, 111–141.

Schreuder, Deryck M./Ward, Stuart (Ed.), Australia's Empire, Oxford 2008.

Seaborn, Blair, Mission to Hanoi: The Canadian Channel, May 1964–November 1965, in: Arthur E. Blanchette (Ed.), Canadian Peacekeepers in Indochina, 1954–1973: Recollections, Ottawa 2002, 85–111.

Seah, Joshua-John T. S., Imperial Outposts and the War Beyond: Singapore, Hong Kong and the British Empire's Land Force Contribution to the Korean War, in: The Journal of Imperial and Commonwealth History 45/4, 2017, 672–696.

Seltmann, Clara, Butter, Wut und Tränen. Australien, Kanada und Neuseeland während Großbritanniens Verhandlungen mit der Europäischen Wirtschaftsgemeinschaft, 1958–1973, Tübingen 2020.

Shipway, Martin, Decolonization and its Impact. A Comparative Approach to the End of the Colonial Empires, Malden 2008.

Simpson, Brad, Self-Determination and Decolonization, in: Martin Thomas/Andrew S. Thompson (Ed.), The Oxford Handbook of the Ends of Empire, Oxford 2018, 452–435.

Sluga, Glenda/Clavin, Patricia M. (Ed.), Internationalisms. A Twentieth-Century History, Cambridge 2017.

–, Rethinking the History of Internationalism, in: Glenda Sluga/Patricia M. Clavin (Ed.), Internationalisms: A Twentieth-Century History, Cambridge 2017, 3–14.

Smith, Anthony L. (Ed.), Southeast Asia and New Zealand. A History of Regional and Bilateral Relations, Singapore/Wellington 2005.

Smith, Gary/Cox, Dave/Burchill, Scott, Australia in the World. An Introduction to Australian Foreign Policy, Oxford 2005.

Smith, Simon, General Templer and Counter-Insurgency in Malaya: Hearts and Minds, Intelligence, and Propaganda, in: Intelligence and National Security 16/3, 2001, 60–78.

Solarz, Marcin W., 'Third World': The 60th Anniversary of a Concept That Changed History, in: Third World Quarterly 33/9, 2012, 1561–1573.

Spickard, Paul R., Race and Nation, Identity and Power: Thinking Comparatively about Ethnic Systems, in: Paul R. Spickard (Ed.), Race and Nation: Ethnic Systems in the Modern World, New York 2004, 1–29.

Stairs, Denis, The Diplomacy of Constraint. Canada the Korean War and the United States, Toronto 1974.

–, Reviewing Foreign Policy, 1968–70, in: Don Munton/John J. Kirton (Ed.), Canadian Foreign Policy: Selected Cases, Scarborough 1992, 189–204.

–, Realists at Work: Canadian Policy Makers and the Politics of Transition from Hot War to Cold War, in: Greg Donaghy (Ed.), Canada and the Early Cold War, 1943–1957: Canada au Début de la Guerre Froide, 1943–1957, Ottawa 1998, 91–116.

Stearns, Peter N./Carol Z. Stearns, Emotionology: Clarifying the History of Emotions and Emotional Standards, in: The American Historical Review 90/4, 1985, 813–836.

Stenson, Michael, The Origins and Significance of 'Forward Defence' in Asia, in: Alister McIntosh (Ed.), New Zealand in World Affairs: Vol. 1: 1945–1957, Wellington 1977, 177–198.

Stewart, Gordon T., An Objective of US Foreign Policy since the Founding of the Republic: The United States and the End of Empire in Canada, in: Phillip Buckner (Ed.), Canada and the End of Empire, Vancouver 2005, 94–116.

Stockwell, A. J., British Imperial Policy and Decolonisation in Malaya, 1942–1952, in: The Journal of Imperial and Commonwealth History 13/1, 1984, 68–87.

–, Malaysia: The Making of a Grand Design, in: Asian Affairs 34/3, 2003, 227–242.

–, Suez 1956 and the Moral Disarmament of the British Empire, in: Simon C. Smith (Ed.), Reassessing Suez 1956: New Perspectives on the Crisis and its Aftermath, Aldershot 2008, 227–238.

Stockwell, Sarah, Ends of Empire, in: Sarah Stockwell (Ed.), The British Empire: Themes and Perspectives. 2. publ., Malden 2010, 269–293.

– *(Ed.)*, The British Empire. Themes and Perspectives, Malden 2010.

–, Britain and Decolonization in an Era of Global Change, in: Martin Thomas/Andrew S. Thompson (Ed.), The Oxford Handbook of the Ends of Empire, Oxford 2018, 65–101.

Stokes, Geoffrey, Introduction, in: Geoffrey Stokes (Ed.), The Politics of Identity in Australia, Cambridge 1997, 1–20.

– *(Ed.)*, The Politics of Identity in Australia, Cambridge 1997.

Strahan, Lachlan, Australia's China. Changing Perceptions from the 1930s to the 1990s, Cambridge 1996.

Stubbs, R., Canada's Relations with Malaysia: Picking Partners in ASEAN, in: Pacific Affairs 63/3, 1990, 351–367.

Stursberg, Peter, Lester Pearson and the American Dilemma, Toronto, Ontario 1980.

Subritzky, John, Britain, Konfrontasi and the End of Empire in Southeast Asia, 1961–1965, in: The Journal of Imperial and Commonwealth History 28, 2000, 209–227.

–, Confronting Sukarno. British, American, Australian and New Zealand Diplomacy in the Malaysian-Indonesian Confrontation, 1961–5, New York 2000.

Suri, Jeremi, The Cold War, Decolonization, and Global Social Awakenings. Historical Intersections, in: Cold War History 6/3, 2006, 353–363.

Tange, Arthur/Edwards, Peter, Defence Policy-Making. A Close-Up View, 1950–1980: A Personal Memoir, St. Leonards 2008.

Tarling, Nicholas, Britain, Southeast Asia and the Onset of the Cold War, 1945–1950, Cambridge 1998.

–, Britain, Malaysia and Southeast Asia: Past, Present and Future, in: International Journal of Asia Pacific Studies 6/1, 2010, 77–93.

–, The British and the Vietnam War. Their Way with LBJ, Singapore 2017.

Taylor, Brendan, Conceptualizing the Bilateral-Multilateral Security Nexus, in: William T. Tow/Brendan Taylor (Ed.), Bilateralism, Multilateralism and Asia-Pacific Security: Contending Cooperation, London/New York 2013, 8–17.

Templeton, Malcolm (Ed.), An Eye, an Ear and a Voice. 50 Years in New Zealand's External Relations 1943–1993, Wellington 1993.

–, Ties of Blood and Empire. New Zealand's Involvement in Middle East Defence and the Suez Crisis, 1947–57, Auckland 1994.

Thakur, Ramesh, Defence Reviews in Australia, Canada, and New Zealand, in: International Journal: Canada's Journal of Global Policy Analysis 42/4, 1987, 890–897.

Thomas, Martin/Andrew Thompson, Empire and Globalisation: From 'High Imperialism' to Decolonisation, in: The International History Review 36/1, 2013, 142–170.

Thomas, Martin/Thompson, Andrew S. (Ed.), The Oxford Handbook of the Ends of Empire, Oxford 2018.

Thompson, Richard, Race, Kinship and Policy: Africa and New Zealand, in: Malcolm McKinnon (Ed.), New Zealand in World Affairs: Vol. 2: 1957–1972, Wellington 1991, 95–121.

Thompson, Sue, British Military Withdrawal and the Rise of Regional Cooperation in South-East Asia, 1964–73, Basingstoke 2014.

Thordarson, Bruce, Cutting Back on NATO, 1969, in: Don Munton/John J. Kirton (Ed.), Canadian Foreign Policy: Selected Cases, Scarborough 1992, 174–188.

Tomlinson, Tom, What was the Third World?, in: Journal of Contemporary History 38, 2003, 307–321.

Tow, William T./Taylor, Brendan (Ed.), Bilateralism, Multilateralism and Asia-Pacific Security. Contending Cooperation, London/New York 2013.

Trood, Russell B., Australian Diplomatic Practice: Methods and Theory, in: Journal of Asian and African Studies 25/1, 1990, 88–113.

Tsokhas, Kosmas, Dedominionization: The Anglo-Australian Experience, 1939–1945, in: The Historical Journal 37/4, 1994, 861–883.

Tucker, Michael, Canadian Foreign Policy. Contemporary Issues and Themes, Toronto 1980.

Ucko, David H., The Malayan Emergency: The Legacy and Relevance of a Counter-Insurgency Success Story, in: Defence Studies 10/1–2, 2010, 13–39.

Vucetic, Srdjan, The Anglosphere. A Genealogy of a Racialized Identity in International Relations, Stanford 2011.

Walker, David, Survivalist Anxieties? Australian Responses to Asia, 1890s to the Present, in: Australian Historical Studies 120, 2002, 319–330.

Ward, Stuart, A Matter of Preference: The EEC and the Erosion of the Old Commonwealth Relationship, in: Alex May (Ed.), Britain, the Commonwealth and Europe: The Commonwealth and Britain's Applications to Join the European Communities, Basingstoke 2001, 156–180.

–, Australia and the British Embrace. The Demise of the Imperial Ideal, Carlton South 2001.

–, Transcending the Nation: A Global Imperial History?, in: Antoinette M. Burton (Ed.), After the Imperial Turn: Thinking With and Through the Nation, Durham 2003, 44–56.

–, "Post-Imperial" Australia: Introduction, in: Australian Journal of Politics & History 51/1, 2005, 1–5.

–, Worlds Apart: Three "British" Prime Ministers at Empire's End, in: Phillip Buckner/R. D. Francis (Ed.), Rediscovering the British World, Calgary 2005, 399–420.

–, Security: Defending Australia's Empire, in: Deryck M. Schreuder/Stuart Ward (Ed.), Australia's Empire, Oxford 2008, 232–258.

–, Sir Alexander Downer and the Embers of British Australia, in: Carl Bridge/Frank Bongiorno/David Lee (Ed.), The High Commissioners: Australia's Representatives in the United Kingdom, 1910–2010, Barton 2010, 145–163.

–, The New Nationalism in Australia, Canada and New Zealand: Civic Culture in the Wake of the British World, in: Joan Beaumont/Neville Meaney (Ed.), Australia and the World. A Festschrift for Neville Meaney, Sydney 2013, 191–214.

Waters, Christopher, After Decolonization: Australia and the Emergence of the Non-aligned Movement in Asia, 1954–55, in: Diplomacy & Statecraft 12/2, 2001, 153–174.

–, Conflicts with Britain in the 1940s, in: David Lowe (Ed.), Australia and the End of Empires: The Impact of Decolonisation in Australia's Near North, 1945–65, Geelong 1996, 69–86.

–, The Menzies Government and de Gaulle's Proposal for the Neutralisation of Southeast Asia: 1963–1965, in: Frank Cain (Ed.), Menzies in War and Peace, St. Leonards 1997, 138–153.

–, A Failure of Imagination: R. G. Casey and Australian Plans for Counter-Subversion in Asia, 1954–1956, in: Australian Journal of Politics & History 45/3, 1999, 347–363.

Webster, David, Canadian-Indonesian Relations 1945–1963: International Relations and Public Diplomacy. PhD Thesis, April 2005.

–, Fire and the Full Moon. Canada and Indonesia in a Decolonizing World, Vancouver 2009.

Westad, Odd A., The Global Cold War. Third World Interventions and the Making of Our Times. 3. Ed., Cambridge 2018.

Woodard, Garry, Ministers and Mandarins: The Relationship between Ministers and Secretaries of External Affairs 1935–1970, in: Australian Journal of International Affairs 54/1, 2000, 79–95.

Wright, Robert, Trudeaumania. The Rise to Power of Pierre Elliott Trudeau, Toronto 2016.

Young, John W., Twentieth-Century Diplomacy. A Case Study of British Practice 1963–1976, Cambridge 2008.

Index

28th Brigade, *see* CSR

Abdul Rahman, Tunku 65, 87–89, 99 f., 108, 121, 139, 192, 241
Anglo-American relations 62, 68, 120, 126, 142, 175 f., 179 f.
Anglo-Australian relations 129 f., 182 f., 191, 206 f., 209–211, 214
– and defence cooperation 34 f., 76–78, 90–93, 95–97, 124, 127 f., 135 f., 230–232, 245–247
– and World War II 30–33, 76
Anglo-Canadian relations 133–135, 146–148, 196, 212–214, 222
– and foreign policy 46 f., 80, 109, 133–135
Anglo-Dominion relations 4 f., 21, 62 f., 126, 131, 195–197, 265, 274–277
– and Britain's turn to Europe 83–85
– and consultation 69–71, 125 f., 135 f., 139 f., 144, 194
– and defence 57
– and foreign policy 45 f., 49–59
– and joint war efforts 76, 124 f., 127, 130–132, 158, 181–183, *see also* moral obligation
– and security 23
– and Suez Crisis 68–74
Anglo-Malayan Defence Agreement (AMDA) 66, 87, 89 FN, 121, 123, 156, 229, 231
Anglo-New Zealand relations 206
– and defence cooperation 34 f., 76–78, 91 f., 124, 230 f., 237–241, 245–247
– and World War II 30–33, 76
Anglosphere 9, 35, 53, 56, 178 f., 182, 187, 221, 279
ANZAC Pact 31 f., 35, 49, 78
ANZAM 41, 43, 76, 91 f., 95, 228
ANZUS 34 f., 43, 89 f., 95–97, 177 f., 180, 217–219

ASEAN 188, 247, 260, 266, 278
ASPAC 188, 247, 261, 263
Australia
– and attitudes towards Asia 37–41, 92 f., 107 f., 112, 114 f., 155 f., 159 f., 167–169, 187–193, 232, 260, 265 f., 277 f.
– and British withdrawal from Southeast Asia 90 f., 94–96, 122, 125–132, 136–140, 143–146, 149–163, 179, 191, 197 f.
– and commitments to Southeast Asia 93, 97, 100 f., 107 f., 110 f., 187–192, 215–217, 227–233, 235–242, 260 f., 262 f., 265 f.
– and Commonwealth 34, 81, 184, 263–265
– and decolonisation 18 f., 110
– and defence review 76–78, 143, 150, 214–217
– and diplomatic representation 32
– and foreign policy review 92, 115, 191, 206 f., 209–211
– and forward defence 93, 95, 101, 131, 151 f., 154, 168, 181 f., 186, 215–217, 230, 255, 259 f., 262 f.
– and immigration 38 f., 184, 202 f., 261
– and Malaysia 93, 107 f.
– and new nationalism 211
– and People's Republic of China 104–106, 170–174, 192 f., 254–257, 266
– and public debate on foreign policy 193, 219 f., 254 f.
– and reactions to Britain's turn to Europe 82–85, 141 f., 183 f., 191, 206, 223
– and SEATO 89 f., 262 f.
– and self-reliance 210
– and Suez Crisis 68
– and US alliance 32–34, 95, 96 f., 108 f., 132, 180, 216 f., 244 f.

– and Vietnam 101, 107 f., 174 f., 178 f., 181 f., 263
Australian identity 13, 39, 114 f., 124, 187, 189–192, 198, 210 f., 260 f., 265 f.
Australian–Canadian relations 48 f., 53 f., 103 f., 163 f., 171 f., 248 f.
Australian–Malaysian relations 155, 227–229, 238–241
Australian–New Zealand relations 31, 49, 78 f., 223–226
– and defence 78 f., 96, 224

Bailey, Kenneth 103, 168, 171, 198
Bailey, Peter 187
Barwick, Garfield 90, 96, 105, 114
Bennett, Charles 125 FN, 114
Bentley, W. 162
Berendsen, Carl 70, 195 FN
Blakeney, F. J. 75
Booker, Malcolm 90, 252
Britain
– and bases in Southeast Asia 88, 111, 184–186
– and bases outside of Southeast Asia 94, 123, 150, 153, 156, 158, 161
– and Commonwealth 61 f., 69 f., 82, 85 f., 130 f., 184 f., 213 f., 345, 264
– and defence review 74, 119–123, 149–154
– and EEC entry 82–86, 123, 140–142, 144, 214, 245, 250
– and Europe 61, 83 f., 123, 141–143, 147, 184 f., 198, 214, 245
– and forward defence 131, 151 f., 154
– and Konfrontasi 67, 86, 109–112, 120, 153 f., 179
– and relations in Southeast Asia 88
– and SEATO 89 f., 156
– and Suez Crisis 68–74
– and Vietnam 162, 173 f., 175 f.
– and world role 61 f., 69 f., 120, 123, 180, 184–186, 197, 214
British Empire 6 f., 14, 18 f., 120
– and decolonisation 5 f., 16–19, 62, 82, 85, 110, 213, 263–265
– and dominions 2 f., 7, 62 f.
– and immigration 8
British exceptionalism 6 f., 62, 109, 157 f.
British Pound devaluation 122, 143
British withdrawal East of Suez 10, 76, 88, 119–123, 128 f.
– and public reactions 139, 145, 160, 162, 202, 206 f., 209 f.
British world community 8 f., 15, 76, 82 f.
Britishness 6–8, 18 f., 53–57, 83, 147, 196, 275, 277
Brown, George 122, 136, 138, 141, 154, 179–181, 186, 189 f., 192, 196
Buchanan, Keith 116
Bunting, John 94, 129, 151, 207
Butterworth 64 FN, 237, 240

Calwell, Arthur 39 FN, 170, 223
Cambridge 44, 55 f.
Canada
– and British withdrawal from Southeast Asia 88, 127, 132 f., 163–167, 183, 233–235
– and commitment to Southeast Asia 39 f., 80 f., 97 f., 100, 106 f., 127, 163–67, 183, 222, 233–235, 247–249, 278 f.
– and Commonwealth 80–82, 98–100, 110 f., 147, 164 f., 179, 184, 263–265
– and decolonisation 18 f., 109
– and diplomatic representation 32, 47, 80, 89
– and foreign policy review 220–222, 233–235, 247–249, 258
– and military assistance 99 f., 164–167, 234
– and Pacific 13, 40, 164–166, 222, 233, 247–249, 252
– and peacekeeping 42, 54, 69, 98 f., 164, 171, 184, 234, 257–259
– and People's Repulic of China 104, 171 f., 252–254
– and public debate on foreign policy 219 f.
– and reactions to Britain's turn to Europe 83, 142, 214
– and Suez Crisis 68 f., 70–72, 134
– and US alliance 32–34, 77, 176
– and Vietnam 41 f., 47, 49, 89, 98, 106 f., 176 f.

Canada-Malaysia relations 89, 97–100, 106 f., 113
Canada-New Zealand relations 47 f., 53, 164 f., 222 f., 248 f.
Canadian identity 13, 71 f., 112 f., 147, 198, 247–249
Canberra 1, 32, 76, 89, 94, 127, 130, 132, 136 f., 144, 181, 194, 225, 237, 240, 248
Canberra Agreement, *see* ANZAC Pact
Canberra Pact, *see* ANZAC Pact
Carrington, Lord 61 FN, 245–247
Casey, Richard 38, 48 f., 55 f., 58 f., 73 f., 77, 97 FN
CENTO 43, 97 FN
CLARET 100, 109–111
Clark, Gregory 193, 220, 254 f.
Clark, Manning 220, 273
Cold War 14–16, 35 f., 59, 102 f., 107 f., 112, 167–169, 250, 255, 258, 270, 274 f.
Commonwealth 8 f., 14 f., 25–27, 50–53, 62 f., 81, 75 f., 112–114, 169, 184 f., 213 f., 279
– and defence 39 f., 65, 93–95, 97, 155, 157, 164 f.
– and discourses of equality 184, 263–265
– and EEC debate 83–86
– and foreign policy 50–54
– and identity 52 f., 110 f., 184
– and Malaysia 93–95, 97, 107–109, 111 f., 155, 239
– and Vietnam 111
Commonwealth meetings 22, 50–53, 73, 263 f.
Commonwealth Office (CO) 82
Commonwealth Relations Office (CRO) 82
Commonwealth relations, and Suez Crisis 68–73
Commonwealth Strategic Reserve Far East (CSR) 64 FN, 65, 94, 157, 178
Confrontation, *see* Konfrontasi
Critchley, Thomas 137, 153, 185, 231 f.
Crowe, Colin 212 f.
Crown 50, 52, 55, 75, 210, 214
Day, D. O. 104
de Gaulle, Charles 85, 105, 144, 148
decolonisation 3, 14–19, 36, 38, 64–66, 102, 169, 279 f.
Delworth, Thomas 249
Diefenbaker, John 25 FN, 50–53, 72, 77, 80, 83, 97
Doidge, Frederick 39 FN
domino theory 40, 168, 179, 254
Downer, Alexander 126, 129 f., 136–138, 145 f., 195 f., 206, 210 f., 214
Downing Street No. 10, 50 f.
Drew, George 50 FN, 82, 83 FN

East of Suez policy 1 f., 5, 64, 120–123, 196 f., 244, 278
Eastman, Allan 238 f.
emotions 2, 20 f., 23, 71, 131 f., 140, 145, 195–197, 206 f., 274, 279
End of Empire 4 f., 10 f., 19, 21
English-speaking alliance *see* Anglosphere
Europe 30, 36 f., 43, 107, 115, 122 f., 159, 164, 171, 175, 182–186, 201 f., 220 f., 249 f., 258, 260
Evatt, Herbert 71

Fairhall, Alan 237 f., 244
Fanon, Frantz 18, 279
FitzGerald, Stephen 193, 277
Five Power Defence Arrangements (FDPA) 204, 246 f., 251, 275, 278
foreign policy, study of 22–26
Fortress Australia 215, 218 f., 243, *see also* Australia and forward defence
forward defence 41, 101 f., 105, 186, 169, 250, 259 f.
Freeth, Gordon 252 f.

global history, study of 12
Gordon, Walter 99
Gore-Booth, Paul 212 f.
Gorton, John 210–212, 215 f., 239–242, 254, 261, 269
Grant, Bruce 199, 215, 232
Greater Malaysia 66, 90, *see also* Malaysia, Federation of

Guam Doctrine 180, 203 f., 226, 244 f., 253

Hadwen, John 52 f., 165–167, 183, 222, 233 f., 247, 251
Harland, Bryce 257
Hartnell, Geoffrey 149 f.
Hasluck, Paul 53, 97, 106 f., 129, 131, 136 f., 150, 152, 163, 175, 181 f., 185 f., 196, 237, 248
Hassett, Frank 135 f., 143, 173 f.
Haworth, William 182
Head, Ivan 202 FN, 249
Healey, Denis 126 f., 145, 151 f., 154, 170, 185, 190–192, 196
Heath, Edward 204, 245 f., 264
high commissioners 26, 50
Holland, Sidney 41, 51 FN, 52
Holt, Harold 1, 128–132, 136, 138–140, 143, 156, 162, 164, 175, 179, 186 f., 189, 190, 192, 196, 198 f., 207, 211, 261
Holyoake, Keith 25 FN, 78, 82, 111, 125, 128, 136, 139, 144, 151, 153 f., 156, 159–162, 164 f., 174, 178, 189, 201, 207, 224, 233, 237 f., 241, 243, 256
Horne, Donald 115, 211
Howson, Peter 125 f., 154, 216 f.
Hulme, Alan 144
Hunn, D. H. 162
Hunn, Jack 218 f., 243, 254

identity 6, 13, 18–22, 55, 280 f.
Imperial Defence College 56, 175
imperial imagination 4, 14, 84, 195, 231
India 40 f., 61, 63 f., 73, 80, 110, 163, 184
Indochina 41 f., 47, 94 f., 115, *see also* Vietnam
Indonesia 37 FN, 66 f., 80, 86, 92, 95, 102, 107–111, 121, 125, 185, 188, 191, 236 f., 266
International Commission for Control and Supervision (ICCS) 259
International Commission for Supervision and Control (ICSC) 41 f., 49, 80, 98, 164 f., 171 f., 176, 234, 247, 258, *see also* Canada, and Vietnam
Irwin, Arthur 58 f.

Jockel, Gordon 174 f., 180, 192 f., 197, 240, 244, 248
Johnson, Lyndon B. 176, 178, 203, 216
Johnston, Charles 1, 126, 130, 136, 152, 170, 190, 194, 210

Kipling, Rudyard 64, 146, 185, 192
Kirk, Norman 203, 207, 224 f., 250, 256 f., 262–269, 273, 280
Konfrontasi 66 f., 94, 110 f., 117, 120 f., 149, 153
Korean War 33 f., 39 f., 65, 98, 104
Kuala Lumpur 80, 97, 160, 190, 236

Laking, George 140, 144, 160, 173, 177, 208 f., 218, 225, 246
Landrum, Brian 87
Laurent, Louis St. 42, 70, 72, 80
Lee Kuan Yew 88 f., 121, 123, 139, 159, 192, 241, 251 f.
like-mindedness 42, 46, 52 f., 279
London 32, 46 f., 50 f., 55 f., 61, 71 f., 89, 97, 1200, 122, 124, 126, 135–138, 140 f., 145–150, 153, 155, 156 f., 159, 172 f., 175, 180 f., 186, 195 f., 209, 211, 231, 277

Macmillan, Harold 50, 74, 78, 82, 90 f., 105
Malaya 41, 47, 65 f., 80 f., 87–89, 97, 240
Malaya, and Emergency 36 FN, 65, 87, 179
Malaysia 66 f., 86 f., 94 f., 97–113, 137, 153, 155, 157–161, 165–167, 174 f., 178–180, 184, 188–191, 206 f., 217, 223, 227–231, 233 f., 236–241, 251, 278
– and Federation of 66, 88 f., 90–93, 121
Malaysian-Singapore relations 88, 121, 149, 152, 233, 236 f.
Maori population 113 f.
Marshall, John 25 FN, 138, 155, 157
Martin, Paul 99, 106, 112, 133 f., 147, 171, 176, 248
McBride, Philip 40 f., 75
McDonald, Thomas 140
McEwen, John 101, 127, 152, 182 f., 223
McIntosh, Alister 38, 49, 54 FN, 114 FN, 127 f., 153

McLeay, John 182
McMahon, William 214, 256, 269
McNicol, David 223 f.
mental map 14 f., 43, 47, 59, 160, 198, 275, 279 f.
Menzies, Arthur 81, 163, 172, 234, 252
Menzies, Robert 25 FN, 41, 48, 51–53, 68, 77, 81, 85, 90 f., 93, 151–153, 182, 187, 187
middle power 53, 112 f., 265 f., 271
Miller, J. D. B. 192
moral obligation 21, 23, 27, 75 f., 93 f., 124 f., 130–132, 138, 140, 146, 158, 181–183, 194 f., 243, 266, 279
Mullins, Ralph 161, 259 f.
Murray, Geoffrey 120, 134 f., 196 f.

national symbols 4 f., 8, 13, 16, 52
nationalism 8, 39, 55, 102, 167, 208 f., 211, 240, 243, 271, 277, 280 f.
neutralisation 102 f., 105 f., 173
New Zealand
– and attitudes towards Asia 37–41, 113–115, 160, 167–169, 189 f., 259 f., 266–268
– and British withdrawal from Southeast Asia 86 f., 94–96, 122, 136–140, 145, 149, 151, 153 f., 156 f., 159 f., 268 f.
– and commitments in Southeast Asia 87, 189 f., 228–231, 235–247, 259 f., 262 f., 266–268, 278
– and Commonwealth 34, 81 f., 86, 111, 184, 263–265, 267
– and decolonisation 18 f.
– and defence review 76–78, 217–219
– and diplomatic representation 32
– and foreign policy review 207–209
– and forward defence 95, 131, 151, 154, 168, 172 f., 186, 218 f., 230, 255, 259 f., 262 f.
– identity 13, 39, 113 f., 116, 189, 198, 208, 224 f., 243, 259 f., 267 f., 280
– and immigration 38 f., 184, 202 f.
– and People's Republic of China 104–106, 172 f.
– and public debate on foreign policy 218 f., 221, 243, 254
– and reactions to Britain's turn to Europe 84–86, 141, 180
– and SEATO 90, 207, 262 f.
– and self-reliance 208 f., 243
– and Suez Crisis 68–70
– and US alliance 32–34, 90, 95–97, 178 f., 180, 217 f.
– and Vietnam 101, 107 f., 174, 263
New Zealand-Malaysia relations 228–231
Nixon Doctrine *see* Guam Doctrine
Nixon, Richard 180, 203 f., 216, 226, 244 f., 247, 250 FN, 263 FN
North American Air Defence Agreement (NORAD) 77
North Atlantic Treaty Organisation (NATO) 15, 16 FN, 22 FN, 33 f., 42 f., 57, 90, 97 FN, 120, 133, 142, 171, 174, 221, 247, 258, 279 FN
North Atlantic Triangle 24, 33

Oliver, W. P. 124
Osborn, Rowen 191
Ottawa 32, 47 f., 103, 127, 147, 164 f., 172, 222, 249, 254
Oxford 44, 55 f.

Pacific Pact 40, 266
Pacific War 30–32, 36, 41, 64, 181, 219
Pearson, Lester B. 42, 48 f., 52, 55, 58 f., 69, 73, 110, 127, 142, 146–148, 176 f., 212, 252, 258
Penang 64 FN, 237
People's Republic of China (PCR) 37, 67 FN, 104–106, 168–177, 192 f., 204, 249, 257, 266, 270, 278
Pepin, Jean-Luc 222
Plimsoll, James 152, 158, 171, 183, 207, 216, 228 f., 238
policymakers 24–26, 54–59
postcolonial studies 8 FN, 16–18
Powell, Enoch 85 f. FN
prime ministers 25, 50–54
Prince Philip 146
Pritchett, William 45, 197 f.

race, discourses of 7–9, 37–39, 74, 102, 109–111, 113 f., 184–186, 189, 191 f., 238, 265

racism, *see* race, discourses of
Razak, Tun Abdul 112
recolonisation 36, 63
Rhodesia 184, 225, 263, 265
Ritchie, Charles 71 f., 147, 214
Robertson, Norman 70 f., 72 FN
Robinson, Basil 196
Robinson, Ray 48
Ronning, Chester 98, 172
Rusk, Dean 56, 141, 176, 185

Sandys, Duncan 74–77
Seaborn, Blair 98, 253
SEATO, and Malaysia 87–90
self-determination 54, 81, 102, 109, 115, 169, 185, 191, 234, 251, 275–277
self-reliance 2, 5, 204, 223, 234, 244, 251, 265, 268 f.
sentiment 78, 84, 136–139, 155, 161 f., 194–196, 206
Shann, Keith 92 f., 107 f., 151, 232, 248
Sharp, Mitchell 212 f., 248
Shaw, Patrick 78 f.
Singapore 26, 30 f., 46, 57, 64–66, 119, 150–152, 155–157, 160, 165 f., 170, 174, 184, 188, 190 f., 204, 227–233, 236–241, 244, 246, 251 f., 259 f., 264, 267 f.
– and secession 121, 125 f., 149, 264
– fall of 30, 75, 126, 210, 270
Smith, Arnold 56, 184
South Africa 3, 81 f., 225, 264 f.
South Pacific Commission 31
Southeast Asia Treaty Organisation (SEATO) 15 f., 22 FN, 42 f., 47, 57, 65, 87–90, 92, 94 f., 97 FN, 105, 115, 120, 154, 156 f., 174, 179, 207, 218 f., 230, 254, 262 f.
Spender, Percy 34
Statute of Westminster 3, 6, 21
Stenson, Michael 259
Stewart, Michael 130–132, 134, 175, 178, 194
Suez Crisis 68–74, 87, 279
Sukarno 66 f., 92, 100

Taiwan 37, 171, 173, 254
Tange, Arthur 46, 49, 103 f., 109, 115
Teichmann, Max 215
Templeton, Malcolm 186, 218
Terendak 64 FN, 226 FN, 237 f., 240
Tet Offensive 203, 216, 230
Third Option 250, 271
Third World 14, 16, 110, 261 f., 264, 276
Thomson, George 1, 97, 144 f., 159–161, 182, 185
Thornton, Leonard 160, 231
Tipping, E. W. 224
transnational history 12
Trudeau, Pierre E. 51, 148, 203 f., 211 f., 220–222, 233, 248 f., 250, 252 f., 257–259, 261–265, 269–271, 273
trust 21, 46, 52, 71, 91, 96, 126, 128, 138 f., 143, 145, 156, 161, 177, 196 f., 213, 230–232, 266, 277

United Nations (UN) 14 f., 22 FN, 40, 69, 104, 169, 191, 219
United Nations Emergency Force (UNEF) 69, 258

Vietnam War 90, 98, 101–103, 106–112, 151, 153 f., 162, 164, 168 f., 171–186, 201–203, 223 f., 230, 232, 242–244, 263, 266, 275 f.
Vietnam War, and protest 178, 182, 185, 202 f., 220 f., 262 f., 273, 275

Wade, Hunter 112, 248
Waller, Keith 93, 244
Watt, Alan 38, 49, 80, 242
Wellington 32, 48, 56, 59, 89, 96, 144, 218, 223, 225, 230, 269
West New Guinea 92
white settler colonies 3, 7, 18, 184
Whitehead, George 222
whiteness 8, *see also* race, discourses of
Whitlam, Gough 5 FN, 51, 170, 203, 207, 220 FN, 250, 255–257, 262 f., 264–269, 273
Wilson, Harold 101, 119–121, 127–129, 132, 136–138, 147, 149, 151–154, 156, 165 f., 180, 185–187, 192, 211
Woodard, Garry 82 f., 85, 177
Woolcott, Richard 261

Zohrab, Doug 236 f., 239